ECONOMICS AND LIBERALISM IN THE RISORGIMENTO

A Study of Nationalism in Lombardy, 1814–1848

ECONOMICS
AND LIBERALISM
IN THE RISORGIMENTO

A Study of Nationalism in Lombardy, 1814–1848

BY

KENT ROBERTS GREENFIELD

INTRODUCTORY ESSAY BY
ROSARIO ROMEO

Revised Edition

THE JOHNS HOPKINS PRESS
BALTIMORE
1965

To

JOHN MARTIN VINCENT

MASTER AND FRIEND

INTRODUCTORY ESSAY

THIS book, first published in the United States in 1934, is the work by which the author is best known in Italy. At that time a current of sympathy for Italy and things Italian, awakened among English and American admirers and supporters of the Risorgimento, was still very much alive. It had been carried forward and diffused among the cultivated classes of the English-speaking world by the histories of Bolton King and Trevelyan in England and by such writers as Thayer, the historian of Cavour and of the dawn of Italian independence, in the United States. Thayer called the Risorgimento "the most marvelous and difficult struggle for freedom recorded in modern times."[1] Even after the first World War this vision of the Risorgimento as one of the great realizations of modern liberty continued to inspire English historians, from Hancock to Berkeley and Griffith.

Then fascism began to cast a shadow on the Italian scene. But even for those least disposed to indulgence for a totalitarian Italy another Italy remained, that of the liberal tradition now personified by Benedetto Croce and such exiles as Salvèmini, to justify the survival of the old admiration and sympathy. "While Croce lives," wrote a historian of the stature of Charles A. Beard in 1934, in his review of the English translation of Croce's *Storia d'Europa*, "Italy lives, the old Italy of the Renaissance and Mazzini. At more than three-score-and-five Croce wears the crown of eternal morning on his brow."[2] Even fascism benefited to some extent by that ancient sympathy and friendship. One of the most cultivated and sincere friends of Italy to be found in modern England observed in the difficult years following World War II: "It is the fashion among Italians to accuse the English of having admired and encouraged their fascism—but in many cases what they meant to admire was not the superficial black shirt, but the enduring intellectual vigor and the rich temperament of the nation, which had, if you will, for reasons of domestic necessity put on such a vesture, soiling their nation's

---

[1] W. R. Thayer, *The Life and Times of Cavour* (Boston and New York: Houghton Mifflin Co., 1911), II, 507.
[2] *Journal of Modern History*, 1934, VI, 85.

authentic glories with false appearances, so that if one wished to praise the former, it was often necessary at least to tolerate the latter."[3]

Such was the atmosphere in which the work of Greenfield on Lombardy originated. Originally inspired by an interest in Mazzini, "whose fascination it is difficult to resist," it was chiefly directed toward illustrating "the training and education of the *élite* who rallied about Cavour and led the nation to statehood," and tracing those steps in the movement of Italian life that were bound to establish "a cultural alliance with England and France . . . and nourish in the Italian mind a new kind of self-respect and independence of spirit."[4] This inspiration underlies the understanding and sympathy for the intellectual and idealistic atmosphere of Lombardy in the Risorgimento which is one of the best qualities of this book, and gives it a power of re-evocation and of profoundly human history that remains its dominant note, above and beyond specific researches and findings.

In the years in which Greenfield wrote, fascism was inspiring ultra-nationalistic tendencies in the historiography of the Risorgimento, a search for self-sufficiency at any price, a denial of any bearing or influence of the French Revolution. Greenfield did not fail to condemn, in no uncertain terms, such political interpositions, conspicuously personified in that field of studies by De Vecchi. He also declared, in regard to historical method, his distrust of the positions of Gentile and of the assumption that he perceived in "actualism," namely, that only the historian permeated with philosophy can write history, that, indeed the philosopher is the only true historian.[5] But liberal Italy and the intellectual tradition of the Risorgimento preserved for him, as we have seen, all of its old fascination.

In short, if one is thinking of the dominant tone of most of the investigations and writings that Anglo-American historians have dedicated to the history of Italy in recent years, this is a work born in an atmosphere and with an inspiration that would have to be described as belonging to other times and another age. George Macaulay Trevelyan could observe, at the fiftieth anniversary of the unification of Italy, that "nothing is more remarkable—though to believers in nationality and ordered liberty nothing is more natural—than the stability of the Italian Kingdom."[6] Even in 1932 G. F.-H. Berkeley could say of Italy

[3] Cecil J. S. Sprigge, "Storia politica dell'Italia moderna," tr. it., Bologna, 1963, p. 22.

[4] K. R. Greenfield, *Economia e Liberalismo nel Risorgimento* (Bari: Laterza, 1964), pp. 4–5; below, p. 287.

[5] K. R. Greenfield, "The Historiography of the Risorgimento since 1920," *Journal of Modern History,* 1935, VII, 49ff.

[6] Quoted in A. Passerin d'Entrèves, *Reflections on the Kingdom of Italy* (Oxford, 1947).

that "no other [nation] in Europe has made so much progress during the last seventy years."[7] But the best known of Trevelyan's postwar disciples, Denis Mack Smith, has built a good part of his reputation on an effort to show that, on the contrary, the Kingdom of Italy "was to prove highly unstable" and that this was due to flaws in its original creation, thus consciously opposing himself to "the particular historical tradition in which I had been educated."[8]

In the United States these positions have found an echo in scornful appraisals of the labor movement by historians like Neufeld; in the thesis of "amoral familialism" as the basis of Italian moral life advanced by the sociologist Banfield; in contemptuous representations of the Italian national character by the political scientist Kogan. This radical change of attitudes and judgments obviously has its roots in the war and the disastrous collective insufficiency of the Italian nation as measured against the imperial ambitions proclaimed by fascism. One finds an obvious parallel in the recent Anglo-American historiography dedicated to the history of Germany, where Stein and Fichte, Bismarck and Hegel are at will called on to answer for the crimes of Hitler and Rosenberg. It would be easy to observe with respect to all this that the historiography of the victors, so violent in its polemic against German political realism, furnishes a valid confirmation of one of the fundamental doctrines of the adversary, namely: that the original impulse to cultural life and the directon it takes lies in the success of force. But it is far from certain that the way out of such intellectually sterile positions can be found in nationalistic reproaches and resentments, apt only to foment and feed further misunderstandings; and to these, be it said, Italian writers on England and above all on the United States have in the past made a most ample contribution. The right path is the one indicated by a group of students of things Italian in the United States who are working in concrete terms on the history of our country. To them is due, among other things, the founding of the American Section of the Istituto per la Storia del Risorgimento (1955), which has since become the Society for Italian Historical Studies. This brings together such scholars as H. Stuart Hughes, William Salomone, Shepard B. Clough, and Greenfield himself, who was its first President and who continues to give dedicated attention to the history of our country, witnessed by the diligent bibliography that he recently compiled of the studies of Italian history that have appeared in the United States in recent years.[9]

[7] *Italy in the Making, 1815 to 1846* (Cambridge, 1932), p. ix.

[8] *Cavour and Garibaldi, 1860* (Cambridge University Press, 1954), p. 6.

[9] "La storiografia americana e l'Italia," *Rassegna storica del Risorgimento,* 1962, XLIX, 237–260.

Obviously one cannot say, in comparing the present with the prewar period, that nothing has changed even for these scholars, though they do not share in the misunderstanding and postwar rancors mentioned above. In their eyes, too, "the Italophilia of our cultivated classes" of the pre-fascist period appears "for the most part the result of tourist trips and poetic memories," and is to be judged as the product of a "quite ingenuous affection," of which Trevelyan in England and Thayer in the United States must be pointed out as the chief exponents. The teaching of Salvèmini, even under fascism, helped to remove traditional ideas and points of view, "arming us against too easy explanations and warning us that we must always give heed to the problems and sufferings of the poor and not forget the importance of the South in the history of Italy." Thus writes H. Stuart Hughes,[10] author, among other writings, of a little volume, *The United States and Italy*, which is recommended for the unprejudiced courage and fairness of its evaluations.[11]

Revision of the traditional appraisal of the recent history of Italy had taken place in Italian historiography and culture before it appeared in Anglo-American historiography, and it certainly cannot be said to have been less radical among ourselves than abroad. On the contrary, the great historical failure of the second World War generated a "defeatist historiography," as it has justly been called. The disasters and miseries of the present nurtured a kind of political abdication and radical skepticism regarding the national potentialities and aptitudes of the Italian people, which still largely characterizes wide intellectual circles in our country. But if all this has brought, and still brings, with it errors and rash devaluations, there is no doubt that the experience of recent years and the effective break with the past, signalized by the end of the old Risorgimento state, has helped in a large way to throw light on weaknesses and problems of Italy which the successes, and still more the unitary mysticism of the past, tended to keep in the shadow. They have again brought under discussion basic questions which seemed to have been solved decades ago; have helped to draw attention to sectors of investigation previously neglected; and have therefore helped to give us a more realistic and more critically profound vision of the history and reality of our country.

It is to be noted, however, that the need for some of these deeper soundings had already been maturing in the culture of the prewar period. How profound and widespread they were as regards a better

---

[10] "Gli studi di storia italiana in America," *Rassegna storica del Risorgimento,* 1958, XLV, 273–274. See also Donald McKay, "Storici americani sul Risorgimento," *ibid.,* 1954, XLI, 404–409.

[11] (Cambridge, Mass.: Harvard University Press, 1953), revised ed., 1965.

knowledge of the economic and social history of our country is witnessed by the appearance of Greenfield's work and the weighing of the historiographical situation that it produced regarding those problems. Greenfield, releasing his volume in 1934, declared that his chief purpose was "to give an impulse to non-political studies of the Risorgimento. Such studies, extended gradually throughout the peninsula and over the whole period of the movement, should in time give more substance and color to our ideas of nationalism in Italy and of the foundation on which Cavour and his colleagues based their success." He did not conceal his dissatisfaction with the fact that, regarding apparently unforeseen events like the Five Days of Milan, "histories of the Risorgimento offer no explanation except in terms of exasperated idealism and no background except in a previous series of insurrectionary episodes."[12]

This was by no means a matter of isolated cases. Greenfield furnished ampler justification of his view in an article on studies of the Risorgimento published since 1920.[13] In that he showed not only the breadth and certainty of his knowledge of Italian studies but posed some precise needs derived from observing the cultural situation. The economic-juridical school, he observed, had exhausted its forces "too soon (or so an outsider may feel) for the study of the Italian revolution to have derived from it the fullest possible benefit." Not indeed that he regarded as desirable a deterministic interpretation of the Risorgimento on socio-economic grounds: on the contrary, he underscored the fact that "when applied to the Risorgimento, the ideas of the leaders [of that school] were modified. The school was at no time avowedly deterministic, and the principles of economic determinism broke down completely on the *phenomena* of that movement." It therefore appeared to the economic-juridical school as directed "by an *élite* who could not possibly be construed as an economic class, and who sought out and used as means to an ulterior end the forces by which they were supposed to be dominated." This was the view to which Greenfield had declared his adherence in his book dedicated to Lombardy. It shows, furthermore, how far he was from the initial determinism which Omodeo, even in 1940, thought he could attribute to him.[14] What was actually being presented in Greenfield's book was a vision that embraced a full evaluation of the reality of the country, not in the light of classical Marxism or other causal schemes of interpretation, but as a formative process developing new forces or groups of interests. The effect of these was

[12] *Economics and Liberalism in the Risorgimento* (Baltimore: The Johns Hopkins Press, 1934), pp. viii and xi.
[13] See above, note 5.
[14] Review in *La Critica*, 1940, XXXVIII, 306–308.

not so much a push along the road to unification as to quicken among the bolder and more thoughtful spirits of the intellectual class the image of a new and more up-to-date Italy, capable of putting itself in step with the more advanced European West. The embryo of a capitalistic bourgeoisie which was forming before unification in the more advanced parts of Italy, and in Lombardy above all, is the generative nucleus of a society of modern type in Italy. Even if the liberal and unitary thrust did not come from it, no history of the Risorgimento would seem satisfying that did not take into account the decisive part it played in the process of resurgence, by arraying itself under the flags and ideas agitated by the *avant-garde* groups of intellectuals. "By 1848 . . . an Italian public opinion had been formed that could never again be governed successfully by the principles and methods of the *ancien régime,* less because the material interests of the Italian community had been revolutionized than because the public had been indoctrinated with a new conception of those interests."[15]

This was the type of economic and social history, technically rigorous and documented, yet free from deterministic prejudices, that could have succeeded best in an environment as strongly dominated by idealism as the Italian was in those years. And, in fact, on the appearance of the English edition and, still more, of the Italian, hope that the work might serve as a model and incitement to students of the Risorgimento was almost unanimously expressed by its reviewers. Halperin in the United States had already noted that Greenfield had been "among the first in this country to call attention to the wholly inadequate appraisal of earlier writers, and in the present study he has performed a service of the highest value by indicating the rich possibilities of the non-political approach."[16] Italian reviewers remarked that the same observation applied to studies in our own country, where it had a graver bearing. Greenfield's work, Borlandi observed, suggests "a conclusion that has a bitter taste: that of seeing how, with all our misapplied ideal-spirituality, we have ended by abandoning to the hands of foreign cultivators studies like those of the American Greenfield, or the Frenchman Pingaud, or the Russian Tarlé."[17] But we stopped with laments, without deriving from them that stimulus to new studies that Greenfield himself had hoped that his work would serve to impart. With the appearance of the Italian translation in 1940, Angelo Marchi expressed the hope that the easier accessibility of the volume might now stimulate in Italian historians "the desire to take under examination an order of

[15] *Economics and Liberalism,* 1934, pp. 134, 238.
[16] *Journal of Modern History,* 1934, VI, 467–468.
[17] *Rassegna storica del Risorgimento,* 1935, XXII, fasc. 1, 625.

facts pertaining to our national Risorgimento that has until now been all but entirely neglected." At that date he could still list only the minor precedent of Prato for eighteenth-century Piedmont, and for Lombardy only the contributions of Barbagallo, Ciasca, Sandonà, and the studies contained in the volume commemorating the centenary of the Cassa di Risparmio per le Provincie Lombarde.[18]

On the other hand, Omodeo, greatest and most authoritative representative of the idealistic school of historians, failed to take any position on this aspect of the book, being preoccupied, as we have seen, with tilting at that shadow of initial determinism which he thought that he perceived in Greenfield's exposition—mistakenly, as we have noted and as was at once brought out by other reviewers. Greenfield had put on the carpet the question of the history of an economy and of a society in terms that were certainly most acceptable to idealism as a basis of discussion, that is to say, outside of every determinism and "class"-ism. He placed at the center of historical life, within an empirically constructed cultural framework, that free creativity of consciousness and activity to which idealism was trying to restore all reality. But the reaction of idealistic historiography was frankly inadequate to cope with the importance of the problem that a work such as Greenfield's posed.

Must one, therefore, speak of an opportunity thrown away? Perhaps; but the fact is that at that date, under the pressure of the war and the moral and cultural upheaval that it produced, it was in any case too late, in this sector of studies, for that to happen which had not happened in the previous years. That inadequate reaction nevertheless remains—an indication of the general insufficiency that much Crocean historiography manifested after the war, when those problems presented themselves with a much more massive rush under the pressures of a renewed Marxism, and then of empiricism and Anglo-American sociologism. That insufficiency played no secondary role in producing the relative decline of the positions that idealism had until then held in Italian historiography.

It is not surprising, then, that the greatest fortune and broadest efficacy of Greenfield's work must be ascribed to the years since the war. Dedicated to the region of Italy furthest advanced economically and in civilized living, and to the connection between its economic development and the political movement of the Risorgimento, it deals directly with some of the most debated issues of contemporary Italian historiography. The richness of the documentation, the precision of the analysis, and above all the liveliness and concreteness of the narration, giving a

[18] *Nuova Rivista Storica,* 1941, XXV, 131.

human content and substance to events, and thereby achieving fully an object so rarely attained by our economic historians, have assured its lasting and ever-renewed success among scholars. Furthermore, subsequent investigations, succeeding each other with much greater intensity than after the first World War—those of Romani, of Caizza, of De Maddalena, of Sapori—have all confirmed the soundness and coherence of the constructive lines of the work.

What, one may ask, is its bearing on the most recent debates about the problem of Italy's contemporary economic development which scholars are still pursuing? Undoubtedly, in their more up-to-date formulations, they apply methodologies which have been elaborated since Greenfield wrote. In this sense an attempt to draw conclusions regarding specific points now under discussion would not be helpful. But it is to be observed, in the first place, that this detracts nothing from the actuality of the book as a historical work, which is realized on a plane higher than the technical level on which discussions of development are now being expounded. And, again, a close consideration of the results that Greenfield attained reveals implications which assist in answering even specific questions raised by the debate over the development of Italy.

Take, for example, the problem of the accumulation of investment capital in the first period after unification, and of its function in activating the mechanism of development. Lombardy on the eve of 1848 (and the situation was not different in 1860, no great structural progress having been achieved in that decade, which was one of grave difficulties for the Lombard economy) was already characterized by a rather high degree of commercialization in agrarian activities, even though the sector of peasant self-sufficiency remained large. A rather extensive foreign trade in agricultural products and raw materials, together with an internal demand that continued to be of greater dimensions, but did not have the same strategic function as foreign demand in producing the economic revival of the region, permitted Lombard agriculture to realize monetary profits which, along with extensive reinvestment in agricultural production, activated the formation of "capital reserves," that is to say, of savings, which appear to have been "considerable."[19] Undoubtedly, one must not exaggerate the total of such capital reserves. They did, indeed, insure enterprisers of disposable money at low cost during the greater part of the year. But they were still insufficient during the seasonal harvest of silk cocoons and spinning operations, from May to the end of June, to meet even the normal demands for

[19] Below p. 139.

short-term credit on the part of traders and spinners. On those occasions these had to pay very high rates for capital and resort to the credit of foreign traders.[20] The inadequacy and defects of the credit organization certainly contributed to such difficulties. Even when these are taken into account there is no doubt that phenomena such as those just recorded reveal a structural situation which in certain respects strongly hampered the capacity of the Lombard economy for development. Prosperous agricultural activities and related commercial activities allowed large segments of the regional economy to assume the rhythm of a moderately sustained accumulation. But restriction of the opportunities for investment produced a true and proper "strangulation" which, by limiting the possibilities for productive employment of profits and accumulated yields, brought about, in turn, a slowing down of the potential rhythm of the country's economy. This was kept in a stage, not indeed of "stagnation," but certainly of very slow development as a result of being caught in a vicious circle. The breakout and the impulse to a more sustained process of development was to come when "alluring temptations of business" attracted disposable funds, putting at the service of more enterprising elements mobile resources that had accumulated in the hands of the landed interest, still resistant and distrustful. In turn the more or less inactive means that were accumulating through the business activities of rather substantial ranks of small and medium manufacturers, artisans, merchants, and agricultural renters were conducted by the banking system to points where they were required by the active elements. Thus the temporary surpluses of some were used to make up for the scarcity of ready money in the hands of those who had initiative and who, within the scope of the work to be done, offered prospects of employing them profitably.[21]

All this produced, as Sapori makes clear in the passage quoted, a notable development of banking institutions adapted to mobilize the country's savings, which were supported by a real agricultural and commercial activity that was in a phase of progress. But the point of departure of the new phase lay in the "alluring temptations of business" just mentioned, that is to say, in the ampler market that presented itself after unification. This in turn depended on the breakout produced, in the first place, by the construction of railroads. This weightily affected the contacts of the Milanese and Lombard economy with that of the rest of the country.

[20] *Ibid.*, pp. 140–41; A. Sapori, *L'economia milanese dal 1860 al 1915,* in *Storia di Milano,* XV (Milan, 1962), 899.
[21] Sapori, *L'economia milanese,* p. 863.

The events of 1858–60 found already completed the connection of Bologna with Pavia (not directly with Milan), the trunk line from Milan to the Ticino (Milan-Magenta-Ticino), the Milan-Venice trunk. With the Pontrebbia-Stradella line constructed in 1860 Milan was connected with Genoa by way of Piacenza (1861). [But] the true direct conjunction with the great Tyrrhenian port took place only in 1867 with the construction of the Pavia-Voghera link, following five years after that between Milan and Pavia. In 1860 the trunk line between Rho and Gallarate was built as a branch of that between Milan and Magenta, and over it Milan could be linked, in 1865, with Varese and Sesto Calende.

The construction of the railway net had favorable repercussions on markets, as, for example, that for the dairy products of the Lower Milanese, which began to extend toward the regions of Central Italy. Profits derived from expansion of the market were in turn translated into savings which encouraged the formation of banks of deposit and discount.[22]

Hence the critical function of state expenditures for these fundamental infrastructures to which, as has been said, was due the breakout from the preceding circle of semi-stagnation; and the importance, as a result, that this state intervention assumes in economic life. It had a determining influence (logically prior, even if chronologically inseparable) on the vaster process of capital accumulation, which now, taking off in a certain fashion from this state intervention, got under way.

The new State was a necessary mechanism, which had its costs; and it was to form a complex of indispensable works favoring the advance of civilized life through economic progress. . . . For the totality of the nation's industries to be able to meet foreign competition it was necessary that individual firms be able to avail themselves of lower costs of transportation, of ample and rapid communications, of facilities for payment in money, of standardized measures affecting commerce and industry, of public protection for the safe and orderly development of the activity of entrepreneurs. The main weight of these costs, which weighed indeed on the whole population, fell on the classes that were least well off. Inevitably, however, taxation transferred them, to a quite considerable extent, to the economic system itself, to business and property. On the other hand, such commitments, which were necessary, were met by recourse to the capital market to an extent and in ways that could not fail to compete unfavorably with economic activities.[23]

All this advanced those transformations, qualitative even more than quantitative, which were already observable in the Milanese economy

---

[22] *Ibid.*, pp. 860–861.   [23] *Ibid.*, p. 903.

in the first twenty years after unification,[24] and are the indispensable premise for understanding historically the new road the Italian economy began to take at the beginning of the twentieth century.

It may seem—and with some justification—that such considerations have led us rather far afield from Greenfield's work. But let it be remembered, first of all, that conclusions drawn from this, as from every historical work of broad scope, have to be evaluated in the general picture of the historical process; and, in the second place, that the situation of semi-stagnation which was to be overcome with unification is precisely that which Greenfield analyzes in the first part of his book. It was embodied in a singular concomitance of factors of immobility and progress, which the author has sought to distinguish, in its dual aspect, in his chapter-headings ("Lombard Agriculture"—"Agricultural Progress"; "Lombard Manufacturing Industry"—"Industrial Progress"). "One can say," he observes, "that the complexion of agrarian life in Lombardy underwent a revolution between 1814 and the middle of the century. Indeed even today it is broadly the same as it then became."[25] But this did not provide the conditions for industrialization. "The manufacturers of Lombardy lived in a Europe cut up by the high tariffs of the Restoration and were encircled by the prohibitive system of Austria." The domestic market, supplied in part by the products of rural and household industry, "did actually suffice to float a factory production of cotton and a large-scale, if still somewhat primitive, manufacture of cheap textiles, but it was too narrow to support an extensive structure of mechanized industry." Agriculture continued to dominate the economic life of the region, and its conservative atmosphere gave the tone to the whole rhythm of production and trade; above all was lacking "in the class possessing capital the daring spirit of enterprise," typical of the English entrepreneurial class; "the capital remained in the hands of the conservative proprietary class who gave the tone to Lombard society. When it began to accumulate in other hands, it tended to seek safe and solid investment in land, which conferred on its owner the universally desired respectability of proprietorship."[26]

It is just this resistance of the economic bourgeoisie to great revolutionary ventures that induces Greenfield to deny an economic interpretation to the Risorgimento. From the economic progress in Lombardy and elsewhere, especially in the North,

it would be natural, he observes, to infer that Italian liberalism reflected a movement of the middle class to gain control of society. The defect of this thesis is that the liberal program was initiated, expounded, and propagated, not by an aspiring and self-conscious

[24] *Ibid.,* p. 906.   [25] Below p. 53.   [26] Below pp. 125–126.

bourgeoisie, with strong economic interests to serve, but by landed proprietors and a group of intellectuals many of whose leaders were of the aristocracy. . . . There is no evidence to color the view that the liberal publicists were being pushed by a rising capitalistic class or were prompted to act as its mouthpiece. In fact they were exerting themselves to rouse a timid and lethargic bourgeoisie to a consciousness of its interests.[27]

Precisely for this reason Greenfield was led to direct his attention largely to the development of the propaganda and ideas of moderate liberalism, basing himself on a vast and unsurpassed knowledge of the periodical press and publicists of the time, studied with profound intelligence and sensitivity to the motives that inspired it. His treatment of this subject still remains the best to be read.

In evaluating the political efficacy of the work of the moderates, Greenfield reverts to a distinction which, as Omodeo observed, had been made by De Sanctis between Mazzinian idealism and the practical and realistic spirit of moderatism. "The moderates [Greenfield writes] believed it to be important that they should survive and continue in action. Their immediate objective was to incite their countrymen to go as far as they legally could in developing an Italy united by vital economic and cultural interests, an Italy which, instead of lamenting its fate or kicking against the pricks, should live vigorously the life that it was permitted to live."[28] And in this they undoubtedly scored real successes, diffusing a state of mind that penetrated the most influential circles of the peninsula and deprived Austria of support even among the elements of society traditionally most hostile to revolutionary action as the members of the nobility were. Even for them nothing remained "but the armed power of Austria to prevent them from seeking the political as well as the economic emancipation of their country."[29]

There is no doubt, however, that this distinction between the role of the moderates and of the Mazzinian democrats deserves to be discussed further and deepened. Omodeo observed that excessive fidelity to the formula of De Sanctis had led Greenfield into positions difficult to defend, such as his inclusion of Cattaneo in a framework much closer to the moderate than to the democratic program, excluding this from any part in those concrete discussions of economic and civil progress of which the democratic Cattaneo was actually the greatest exponent.[30] Marchi, on the other hand, replied that Cattaneo's position before 1848, directed toward the transformation of the Habsburg Empire into a confederation of free states of different nationality under the same dynasty,

[27] Below p. 263.
[28] Below pp. 264–265.
[29] Below p. 53.
[30] Omodeo, *La Critica,* 1940, XXXVIII, 306–308.

was basically no nearer to the "democratic" than to the moderate thesis.[31] Still we have left, in all its amplitude, the problem of the revolutionary function of democratism and Mazzinianism as a force exciting that will to act and that spirit of sacrifice which is a very different thing from interest in the material progress of the modern world, and which was indispensable in effecting the transition from the moral isolation of Austria in Italy to open revolt against her. In this sense the position of Greenfield must lead back to one of the currents of prewar Anglo-American historiography to which reference was made at the beginning of this essay, and which was characterized by an insistent devaluation of Mazzinianism as a force endowed with genuine political efficacy, while for Italian students this thesis entered a phase of crisis with the analysis that Omodeo, twenty years ago, devoted to the relations between Mazzinianism and Cavourian policy. But even these positions which still lend themselves to discussion, together with the results that can be regarded as having been definitively established, are further evidence of the vitality and current value of the work that is now offered anew both to Italian- and English-speaking readers.

ROSARIO ROMEO

Institute of Modern History
University of Studies, Rome

[31] *Nuova Rivista Storica,* 1941, XXV, 140–143.

PREFACE TO THE REVISED EDITION

THIS study might not have been undertaken but for the help and encouragement of H. Nelson Gay, who was a friend to every American student of Italy. I shall also always remember gratefully Salvatore Pugliese, whose friendliness and hospitality deepened my love of the Italian people and whose studies were one of my chief inspirations. The reader of the first chapter will be aware of how close Count Stefano Jacini brought me to the traditions and living realities of my subject, and I wish he were living to know how much his interest and assistance contributed to keeping alive public interest in this book. I acknowledge also with cordial appreciation the many courtesies of the late Ettore Verga, Director of the Museo Civico of Milan, and his assistants; of Professor Antonio Monti, Director of the Museo del Risorgimento of Milan; of kindly Signor Picozza, of the Brera Library, and of Signor Giussani, ever helpful custodian of the hall of study in the Archivio di Stato of Milan; of Professor Menghini, then Director of the Museo del Risorgimento of Rome; and of those who made easy and pleasant my use of the Harvard and Yale University libraries and that of my own university, the Johns Hopkins. My researches in Italy were made possible by a fellowship awarded me in 1929 by the Trustees of the Sterling Fellowship Fund of Yale University and by a grant-in-aid of the Social Science Research Council, whose assistance I acknowledge gratefully. My debt to The Johns Hopkins University is hard to express —a debt not only to particular colleagues and students, but to the stimulating and friendly atmosphere of an institution that justifies its reputation of making every possible sacrifice for the encouragement of its scholars.

Whatever value my chapters on economics have had or may have for students of economic history is due to the vigorous criticism of my colleague, Professor Frederic C. Lane. The manuscript was also read by Professor Frederick B. Artz, of Oberlin College, and received a searching attention and criticism from my friend and former colleague at Yale, Townsend Scudder, III. But the best in anyone's thought and work is so largely attributable to his friends and colleagues that I should have to name them all to do justice to my sense of indebtedness.

The book was written with the non-Italian student of the Risorgimento, represented by the author's own interests and needs as a historian, chiefly in mind. But, although denied a native historian's inborn feeling for his material, I hoped, of course, that it might contribute something of a stimulus or new data to the Italian colleagues who had generously aided me. Its chief purpose was to give an impulse to non-political studies of the Risorgimento which, if extended throughout the peninsula and over the whole movement, might impart more substance and color to our knowledge of nationalism in Italy. Professor Romeo's *Introduction* to the present edition gives a generous indication of the extent to which these hopes have been realized.

The reception of the original English edition by Italian reviewers was gratifying beyond my expectations. But the most gratifying and consequential response from Italy came in 1938 in a letter from Gino Luzzatto, then known to me only as one of the leading economic historians of our time and as editor of the *Nuova Rivista Storica*, in which he had recently reviewed the book. He now wrote me, on October 8, 1938: "Removed from teaching for reasons of which you are aware, and foreseeing that it will be very difficult, if not impossible, for me to continue to write for Italian reviews and to publish, in Italy, under my own name, I have thought of employing a little of the time that remains at my disposal in translating . . . *Economics and Liberalism in the Risorgimento*, and Laterza of Bari, perhaps the best and most serious of our publishers, has at once fallen in with the idea." Such was the origin of the first Italian edition, published in 1940.

A more gratifying honor would be hard for a scholar, particularly one with liberal inclinations, to imagine. Given the circumstances, I could be permitted to feel, and to suspect that Gino Luzzatto felt, that the book, telling how Italians of the nineteenth century had, in spite of despotism, laid the basis for liberation from that despotism, was being enlisted in another Italian struggle for freedom. It was a matter of deep regret to me that Gino Luzzatto's name could not appear in that edition. Fortunately it could, and did, appear before his death in the second Italian edition, published by Laterza in 1964.

The present text in English is based on that edition. It therefore includes Professor Rosario Romeo's "Introductory Essay" and an additional chapter on "Capital and Credit"—a chapter that owes much to expert improvements that Professor Luzzatto introduced in translating it; and it embodies other amendments suggested by critics of earlier editions.

KENT ROBERTS GREENFIELD

Baltimore, Maryland

TABLE OF CONTENTS

INTRODUCTION

MASSIMO d'Azeglio's phrase, "a conspiracy in open daylight," might have been used as the title of this book. Leaving aside as sufficiently well known the conspiracies and risings of the so-called "parties of action" during the formative period of the Risorgimento, I have sought to describe the open effort of the liberal patriots of a part of Italy directly under alien rule to give life to ideas and institutions on which the independence of their country could be built.

At the Restoration Lombardy was not only the most important part of Italy under foreign domination but was the richest and most "progressive" of the Italian communities. Furthermore, its capital, Milan, led the peninsula in the making of books and in the publication of journals addressed to the whole of Italy. Another reason for the choice of Lombardy as the subject of such a study as the present was the fact that it is precisely in the case of Lombardy that the usual historical approach to the problems of the Risorgimento leaves most to be desired. In Lombardy, with the Five Days of Milan (March 18-23, 1848), there was an abrupt and sudden leap from apparent inertia and political immaturity to heroic and self-directed action, and for this the histories of the Risorgimento offer no explanation except in terms of exasperated idealism and no background except in a previous series of insurrectionary episodes. The present volume is the result of a search for a more satisfying interpretation.

Actually the beginnings of this interpretation came to me through the medium of an interest in Joseph Mazzini. Mazzini is a figure whose fascination, especialy for youth, it is difficult to resist. But as a historian I found myself at an *impasse* when I faced the question of determining his influence. Mazzini's ideals were a light in the sky; it can safely be said that to many a young Italian they were a presage of dawn, and excited a hope which must be reckoned among the forces that united Italy. But because Mazzini consistently willed *Italia una* and the outcome of the Risorgimento was unity, it does not therefore follow that Mazzini was chiefly or even largely responsible for that outcome. The great revolutionary dreamer himself said bitterly that he had wished ten and the sum of his work was only two. And yet in histories of the

1

Risorgimento Mazzini and his apostolate of unity continue to be ranked among the three or four primary factors in the making of Italy. Perhaps they were, but the historian cannot know. The assumption that they were is an example of the tendency, not confined to students of the Risorgimento, to emphasize as important that which obviously and consciously tended towards the actual outcome and to neglect or under-emphasize forces that were blind and action that was motivated by aims and sentiments not even consciously patriotic. "We willed ten and produced two," Mazzini exclaimed, and, as has justly been said, "to produce that 'two,' other forces, foreign to his thought and action, contributed powerfully."[1] What were these other forces?

The present study was undertaken with the belief that, although a satisfying answer to that question could not be given without a series of investigations far beyond the powers of a single author, a profitable step toward an answer would be to study the changes in the life of one important region of Italy, with the question in mind to what extent this environment and the changes in it affected the ideas and proposals of the elements that finally rallied around Cavour, and to explore more fully sources of their faith that his program was the right one.

As early as 1916 Professor Raffaele Ciasca, at the suggestion of Gaetano Salvèmini, had made an invaluable pioneer survey of the literature in which the economic changes preceding the Revolution of 1848 were reflected and in which their significance for Italy was discussed.[2] This was followed in 1921 by the late Professor Giuseppe Prato's masterly study of thought and public life in Piedmont on the eve of 1848—a model of what can be achieved in reconstructing the process by which Italian society and its outlook were being altered during the first half of the nineteenth century.[3] Other Italian scholars had made contributions to the type of history represented by these studies.[4] Professor Romeo has indicated in his *Introductory Essay* the

---

[1] Gaetano Salvèmini, *Mazzini* (Catania, Battiato, 1915), p. 151.

[2] *L'origine del "Programma per l'opinione nazionale Italiana" del 1847-'48,* in *Biblioteca storica del Risorgimento italiano,* serie VIII, No. 3 (Milan-Rome-Naples, 1916).

[3] *Fatti e dottrine alla vigilia del 1848: l'associazione agraria subalpina e Camillo Cavour,* in *Biblioteca di storia italiana recente, 1800–1870,* X, 133–484 (Turin: Bocca, 1921).

[4] For example, Arnaldo Agnelli, "Il fattore economico nella formazione dell'unità italiana," in *Il Risorgimento italiano,* March–April, May–June, 1913, Anno VI, 253-278; 471-488; the essays of R. Broglio d'Ajano on "La politica doganale degli Stati Italiani dal 1815 al 1860," in the *Giornale degli Economisti,* 1911, XLIII, 438-457; 517-530; 619-663; 1912, XLIV, 440-477, covering the Pontifical State (1815-1860) and the Kingdom of Sardinia (1815-1834) but never completed; Salvatore Pugliese, *Due secoli di vita agricola nel Vercellese nei secoli XVIII e XIX* (Milano, 1908); and the studies in *La Cassa di Risparmio delle*

extent to which studies with this orientation have multiplied in recent years.[5]

In the present work, two of its sections, Part I, "Economics," and the chapters describing the journalism of the period are monographic, and necessarily so, because of the lack of spadework by previous historians—except in the case of Piedmont. Part I is not only an economic description, but attempts to reconstruct the civil life of Lombardy and follow its internal evolution from the Restoration of 1814 to the eve of the revolt of 1848. Part II reflects a movement of ideas that exercised an influence throughout Italy. It therefore has a broader general interest. But it is, in my view, inseparably connected with Part I. If it describes a current of thought that was becoming national it originated in the thinking of a particular community, and in order to understand what that community thought, it seemed to me important to know how it lived. Indeed, one of my guiding purposes was to seek out the relation between changes in economic and social institutions and habits on the one hand, and the evolution of ideas on the other.

One critic of the first edition of the book, M. Georges Bourgin, concluded that I had failed to consider the historical theories of Marx. Another authoritative reviewer, Adolfo Omodeo, came to the opposite conclusion, and criticized the book as based on an assumption of economic determinism.

I could hardly have avoided facing the questions raised by the widespread debate in our time of Marx's historical theories, even had I not read, in M. Bourgin's own neat and competent summary of the Risorgimento, his conclusion that the Risorgimento must be regarded as the work of a bourgeoisie rising to a consciousness of its class interests.[6] In fact, one of my primary interests was to test this theory in a region of Italy where it seemed most likely to be confirmed. On pp. 263–264 will be found my conclusion that, in the case of Lombardy between 1814 and the Revolution of 1848, the theory is inadequate to account for the facts.

---

provincie Lombarde nella evoluzione economica della regione, 1823-1923 (Milano, Cassa di Risparmio, 1924). Agnelli strongly urged the need of this approach to the Risorgimento in his article "Il materialismo storico e il Risorgimento italiano. Posizione del problema," in *Rendiconti del R. Istituto Lombardo di scienze e lettere,* 1913, XLVI, 183 ff.

[5] Above, p. xviii. Inhibited perhaps by modesty he does not mention his own fine study, *Il Risorgimento in Sicilia* (Bari: Laterza, 1950), or refer to his valuable collection of essays, *Dal Piemonte sabaudo all'Italia liberale* (Turin: Einaudi, 1963).

[6] Georges Bourgin, *La formation de l'unité italienne* (Paris, 1929), p. 2.

In a generous review of the 1964 Italian edition of this book Professor Aurelio Macchioro recognizes that the facts which it presents do not support the doctrine of economic determinism. But he believes that they rule out only economic determinism and not a Marxist interpretation. He thinks that the facts that I have presented in the book show me to be "a distant cousin . . . of [my] imagined adversary."[7] Barring Marx's deterministic assumptions and predictions, that is true, if what is meant is that I am one of many non-communist historians who have been influenced by Marx's interpretation of historical processes. Certainly we have come to perceive more sharply the extent to which both the institutional structures and intellectual "superstructures" of post-Renaissance Europe were reshaped by changes in the material conditions of European society—changes that were taking place more and more rapidly in the seventeenth, eighteenth, and nineteenth centuries; and to see that economic interests, and therefore the "bourgeoisie," were playing an increasingly influential role in those structural changes. Except for Marx's sharpening and systematization of the relationship between materialistic interests and intellectual systems, such perceptions were hardly original with him. But his historical analysis was certainly influential in opening our eyes to the value of such conceptions in the interpretation of history.

As for the situation in North Italy in the period 1814–1848, the "philosophy" of the Lombard patriots had evidently come to turn on their belief that the progress of their region and the future of Italy were dependent on the force that free capitalistic enterprise could exert in bringing their country abreast of the more advanced nations of the West, and they did their best to encourage it and to incite the possessors of wealth to engage in it. It can furthermore hardly be doubted that the growing strength of that class became an important factor in permitting Italy to free itself from Austrian domination with the support of France and England. But this is not to say that even in Lombardy, economically the most "modern" part of Italy, the Risorgimento was the work of a class-conscious bourgeoisie. A movement toward an economic and intellectual Risorgimento is discernible in Lombardy during the period from 1814 to the Revolution of 1848 but no evidence found to date permits one to believe that the bourgeoisie in the Marxian sense of that term was the driving force in it.

Though Part I and the chapters on journalism are limited to a single region, they have an interest, I believe, not only in relation to the history of the Risorgimento, but also for the economic historian, as a historical

---

[7] *Studi storici,* anno V, no. 3, July-September 1964, 568.

description of a rather important community in an economically conservative, or, as one would now say, "underdeveloped" part of Europe under the initial impact of the Industrial Revolution. I have been encouraged by the reception of previous editions to believe that the several parts of the book, taken in their connection of thought, offer some additional light on the main problem faced by the historian of the nineteenth century in evaluating the forces that produced the triumphs of national liberalism.

PART I

ECONOMICS

CHAPTER I

LOMBARD AGRICULTURE

THE underlying and all-embracing framework of the social life of the Lombard community in the first half of the nineteenth century was its agricultural system. Agriculture was still its fundamental and dominant industry. Stefano Jacini estimated that in 1855 agriculture occupied three-fifths of the population, and that one-half of the population were peasant tillers of the soil.[1]

The agriculture of Lombardy presented then as now a great variety of products, types of cultivation, and forms of tenure, because of the extraordinary diversities of the region, which embraced on the north the snow-clad peaks and the long winters of the Alpine yokes of Sondrio and the Valtellina, and on the south the interminable Plain, the long summers, and the moist and sluggish atmosphere of the Po Valley. The variety of climate and terrain is further increased by the presence of the Alpine lakes, in their deep sun-warmed basins, capable of producing sub-tropical fruits, and by the spurs which the mountains send out into the Plain, forming the distinct region of the *collini*, the Hills.

The types of agriculture corresponding to these diversities may be described for convenience of reference in a summary characterization as falling into three zones: the Mountains, the Hills and the Plain.

Utilization of the soil began in the mountains at the point where the retreat of the snowline permitted the pasturing of flocks and herds on all but the highest Alpine yokes.[2] At an elevation of 800 to 1800 metres a band of resinous woods was still to be found. Even on these heights one saw "the courageous struggle with nature begin": tiny step-like terraces appeared on the flanks of the mountains and a mosaic of tiny farms in the valleys.[3]

The products of the Mountain zone were sheep and cattle, chestnuts and chestnut wood, honey, wine and cereals. The flocks and herds were

---

[1] Stefano Jacini, *La proprietà fondiaria e le popolazioni agricole in Lombardia* (2d. ed., Milano and Verona, Civelli G. e C., 1856), p. 47.

[2] That is, from 1800 to 2000 metres. C. Correnti, "Indicazioni storiche e statistiche della Provincia di Bergamo," *Annali universali di statistica,* 1844, LXXXII, 160. For the *Annali,* see below, pp. 160–171.

[3] *Ibid.;* Jacini, p. 163.

9

pastured on the mountains in summer on lands that were still reserved as commons. The shepherds and cattlemen were a patriarchal and semi-nomadic population who in winter drove their property to the Plain. In the Hills and the Plain the shepherds were regarded as little better than thieves, and their flocks were inferior and on the decline. The drovers were a more substantial class who had a considerable capital in their herds,[4] and who entered into regular contracts for winter pasturage with the proprietors of the Plain. But their livelihood was threatened by a movement among these proprietors to emancipate themselves from the need of using mountain cattle to supplement their own herds in winter, for the cattle of the mountains were not only inferior but brought diseases with them.[5]

The resident farmers who were the permanent inhabitants of the Mountain zone were for the most part small proprietors, numerous in proportion to the cultivable area. Tenacious and hardy, they turned to account the work of large families and the natural fertilizers provided by the abundance of leaves and the presence of great numbers of cattle. Beginning in little valleys close under the timber zone where some rye could be grown, they put every foothold of soil into potatoes, vegetables, wheat and rye, and raised Indian corn where the valleys lay sufficiently open to the sun.[6] At a time when roads were poor and transportation costs excessive they had pushed to the limit the cultivation of cereals in order to free themselves from dependence on the grain of the Plain. They raised little hay and kept few cattle. With the improvement of roads they were threatened by the competition of grains from below.[7] This population of little proprietors lived in squalid houses of brick and stone and cultivated their land in tiny plots. Not only were the farms small, but each holding was likely to be parcelled into scattered strips—often merely a terrace—owing to the practice of dividing estates among the heirs and allotting to each son a little of each kind of soil.[8] At best they lived close to the margin of subsistence and in times of misfortune easily fell victim to money-lenders.

---

[4] Sometimes as much as 100,000 lire. Jacini, p. 152.

[5] Jacini, pp. 152-157.

[6] Correnti, "Indicazioni storiche," p. 161.

[7] Jacini, p. 156.

[8] Jacini, pp. 127; 161–163. "It is considered a shame not to possess something; according to the local phraseology, 'di non aver una crosta al sole." John Bowring, *Report on the Statistics of . . . the Lombardo-Venetian States,* Great Britain, House of Commons, Sessional Papers, 1839, XVI, Commissioners, etc. (3), p. 96.

Below this zone of forest, mountain pastures, vineyards and precariously cultivated valleys lay the Hills. Along the upper edge of this zone stretched a narrow band of piedmont whose agriculture differed little from that of the Mountains except in the elevation at which it was carried on and in the greater number of open valleys in which grain could be raised. In the first half of the nineteenth century viticulture predominated on the hillside terraces still familiar to the traveller.[9] This strip of piedmont included the basins of the lakes, on whose slopes appeared orchards of olives, oranges and lemons. But most of the second zone consisted of the Hill country and the long slopes toward the Plain— that is to say, most of the Province of Brescia, the Bergamasque as far south as the point where the Bremba enters the Adda, and the greater part of the famous and lovely Brianza north of Milan.

The chief products of the Hill zone were mulberries, grapes, wheat and Indian corn.[10] Some beans, lentils and carrots were also raised. The soil was not rich and the rotation of cereal crops practiced west of the Adda tended to exhaust its fertility. To restore it the tares were plowed under or clover was planted with the wheat and plowed under with the stubble, or manure was applied. Irrigated meadows for forage were created where there was a trickle of water that could be utilized, but forage was scarce, animals were few, and the land suffered from the scarcity of manure. The spade was the characteristic instrument of cultivation: "the mulberry and the spade," wrote Stefano Jacini, "are the two mines of wealth of the region." The region yielded good returns in spite of unscientific cultivation, a result which Jacini attributed to spade-culture and close attention.[11]

In the Hill zone the peasant-proprietor of the mountain valleys disappeared and his place as cultivator was taken by a dense population of peasant-tenants known generically as *coloni*.[12] The estates of the

---

[9] Of the 320,000 pertiche italiane in this piedmont strip, in the Province of Bergamo, 120,000 were in vineyards. Correnti, "Indicazioni storiche," p. 162. The pertica italiana equalled 1,000 square metres. 10 pertiche italiane or "nuove" make 1 ettare.

[10] The data for the description that follows were chiefly drawn from Cesare Correnti, "Indicazioni storiche e statistiche della Provincia de Bergamo," *Annali*, 1844, LXXXI, 48–69; 168–216; LXXXII, 138–173; 265–278; 1845, LXXXIII 46–56; Francesco Spreafico, "Alcune notizie intorno all' agricoltura e allo stato degli agricoltori nella Brianza," *Politecnico*, 1844, VII, 139–175; and Jacini, *La proprietà fondiaria*. For the *Politecnico* see below, pp. 181 ff.

[11] Jacini, p. 177.

[12] Jacini estimated the proportion of proprietors as from 1-5 to 1-7. *Ibid.*, pp. 173-174.

proprietors were relatively small.[13] The land was cultivated in little
farms, in general by families of share-tenants.[14]

Under the form of share-farming, known in Italy as *mezzadria*,
which was prevalent in the Hill zone, the proprietor supplied the land
and such plantings as the mulberries and vines, and looked after the
breaking up of uncultivated land and the construction of vineyard
terraces. In short, he was responsible for such equipment and operations
as were likely to result in the permanent improvement of the property.[15]
In some cases the proprietor advanced the cows, the oxen, the more
costly implements, such as the wagon and the plow, and the principal
seeds. These "aids" or *scorte*, as they were called, were restored or
replaced by the tenant at the expiration of the lease. The peasant, as a
return for his labor and that of his family, received one-half of the
product, except in the case of the mulberries and generally of the vineyards. The proprietor took the whole of the silk and the grapes and
credited the tenant with a stipulated share.[16] Taxes and the expense of
manures, water rents for irrigation, and vine-props were divided by
halves. The peasant got a house, for which he was sometimes obliged
to pay a rental, and an allowance of straw for his cattle and of wood
for his fire. He had, besides, the vegetables that he raised in his garden,
his chickens, and his milk and calves. Of these the proprietor might take
a portion known as "tithes" or "appendices," which, according to contemporary observers, were sometimes burdensome; and he might also
require of the tenant a certain number of days' labor on his own land
at a stipulated wage.[17] The proprietor kept the woods for himself; and
"some proprietors reserve the meadows or a portion of them which they
have worked by day laborers; others reserve the hillside vineyards and

[13] Spreafico said of the Brianza that in spite of the fact that the rich Milanesi
had bought up the land around their villas, "the farms of the most well-to-do
citizens rarely exceed 1000 *pertiche nuove*," that is, 100 hectares, *Politecnico*, 1844,
VII, 139-140.

[14] The engineer Possenti comparing conditions on a possible railway line through
Bergamo in the upper part of this zone and another lower down through Treviglio estimated that the average area of a farm on the upper line was 45.21
pertiche (italiane), on the lower, 95.66 *pertiche*—roughly 4½ and 9½ hectares,
Annali, 1841, LXIX, 86. In the Brianza there were many little farms of less
than 10 *pertiche* (or 2½ acres). Spreafico, p. 140. Correnti estimated that a crop-
sharing family of five or six robust individuals could work a farm of about 50
pertiche (roughly, 12½ acres) with hoe culture; one of about 100 *pertiche*
(roughly, 25 acres), if provided with a pair of oxen. *Annali*, 1844, LXXXII,
268-269.

[15] Spreafico, p. 146.

[16] He took the silk in the Bergamasque, and both in the Brianza. Correnti,
Annali, 1844, LXXXII, 268; Spreafico, p. 149.

[17] Correnti, *op. cit.*, p. 268; Spreafico, pp. 148-149.

the grassy banks, while certain portions of inferior meadow are yielded to the peasant for the nourishment of his animals."[18]

Such a contract called for some money payments on the part of the tenant, and his debt in cash was usually increased by grants of aid which the proprietor made to him during the year, often including the eggs of the silkworm, which were regularly charged to the tenant. But the account was settled on a credit basis. It was customary, at least in the Brianza, for the proprietor, taking the whole of the crop of grapes and silk, which he marketed, to charge the tenant's debts to his share of the proceeds of their sale.[19] Besides, the tenant, obliged to furnish his labor to the proprietor at a stipulated wage, might work off his debt. The account was balanced each year at St. Martin's, but was allowed to run on from year to year and seldom closed.[20]

Leases were renewed annually, generally by verbal agreement and without written instruments, and might be terminated by either party on six months' notice. But usually they ran on indefinitely, sometimes for generations and even for centuries.[21] At a change of tenants the equipment remained on the land and the debts of the peasant, whether personal or resulting from a deterioration of the farm or its equipment, he paid with his animals or his implements.[22]

The extent to which the proprietor intervened to supervise the *colono* varied greatly with the region and the personality of the landlord. In the Bergamasque the numerous smaller proprietors were noted for the close attention that they devoted to their farms.[23] But in general the landlord seems to have exercised his personal supervision only when important decisions were to be made, and then "rather as an associate than an arbiter."[24] Secured against ruinous losses and left largely to their own devices, the families of share-croppers came "to love the soil as their own." This attachment of the cultivator to the soil impressed contemporary Lombard writers as one of the strong recommendations of the system of share tenure.[25]

The contract just described was a transition form of tenure. The share-cropping families of five or six individuals who lived under it had been preceded on this soil by a larger patriarchal type of families known as *massari*, some of which still survived towards the middle of the century; and the share contract was "itself giving way, especially in the Brianza, to a modification of it known as the "grain-rent."

The older share-tenure families known as *massari* had consisted of

---

[18] Correnti, *op. cit.*, p. 268.
[19] Spreafico, p. 149.
[20] *Ibid.*; Correnti, *op. cit.*, p. 269.
[21] Spreafico, p. 148.

[22] Correnti, *op. cit.*, p. 269.
[23] *Ibid.*, pp. 266-267.
[24] Spreafico, p. 147.
[25] Spreafico, p. 143; Jacini, pp. 181-182.

three or four related couples who rented a large farm on a crop-sharing lease and who owned a plow and oxen. The operations of the little colony were governed by the common male ancestor if he was living, assisted by the *massara* or farm mother who directed the household and the *bifolco* who tended the livestock. A contemporary Lombard writer describes such a *massaria,* "composed of thirty persons. The old head had been dead for some time, and the good and numerous family still remained united, though at a sacrifice, for love of the old grandmother . . . who spun and spun sitting beside the smoky fireplace." There was a regular division of house and field labor directed by the oldest brother, who was custodian of the common fund of money, distributed the food and clothing, and maintained order in the family. In the intervals of field labor its members wove hats and hampers, made and mended shoes, spun and wove cloth, cut wood and carpentered.[26] But even such families of *massari* as survived were less patriarchal than formerly, owing to the new roads which were breaking down such self-contained units, and also to the policy of the proprietors who were finding a division of their land among smaller family groups more profitable even though it required a larger outlay of capital.[27]

On the other hand, this more recent form of crop-sharing lease was rapidly being supplanted in the grain-bearing district of the Brianza by the grain-rent. This form of contract imposed the same obligations as the normal crop-sharing lease except that all the immediate products of the soil, barring the grapes and the cocoons of the silkworm, remained in the hands of the peasant, and he paid the landlord with a given quantity of grain. This was fixed at such a point as to compel the tenant to plant at least two-thirds of the land in cereals.[28] Such a contract relieved the proprietor of the necessity of close supervision and it extracted a larger yield from rich farms where one-half of the crops more than sufficed to maintain the family of the peasant and might tempt him to be lazy. It hung a sword of Damocles over the peasant's head, for the quota of grain exacted from him might be varied at will, though in general the proprietors seem to have appreciated their interest in maintaining their tenants in a reasonable state of well-being.[29] The peasant did not oppose the spread of the grain-rent, presumably because it gave him a sense of freedom and appealed to his hope of greater gains.[30] For the fortunate and enterprising peasant it was indeed a further step towards personal liberty, for under its terms he and the

[26] Carlo Ravizza, *Un curato di campagna* (Milano, Pirola, 1841), p. 238. See below, pp. 249–250.

[27] Spreafico, p. 142.

[28] Spreafico, p. 151.

[29] Jacini, pp. 198-202.

[30] Spreafico, p. 151.

landlord were "two free parties who enter into a free social contract on equal conditions, so that the peasant is raised almost to the level of the proprietor."[31] The effect on the land was injurious for the contract led to a pressure cropping of wheat and maize in alternation which tended to exhaust the soil and at the same time to increase the scarcity of meadows and herds.

Money leases were rare in the Hill zone. Some ambitious peasants rented small farms outright but experience showed that they generally involved themselves in obligations beyond their strength and the relationship ended in loss to themselves and damage to the interests of the proprietor.[32] In general money leases were restricted to the estates owned by pious foundations and those of the few great proprietors of the region, such as the noble house of Giovanelli in the Bergamasque.[33] They were regarded with disfavor as alienating from the soil the fruitful affection both of landlord and tenant. "Rented farms," wrote Correnti of the Bergamasque in 1844, "can easily be recognized by a certain neglect which characterizes them, in contrast with neighboring property cultivated and caressed under the eye of the master."[34] The leaseholds on the estates of the pious foundations seem to have been of considerable extent, with "the strange result that the peasant who works precisely those lands intended for the relief of public misery is reduced to the most wretched condition."[35]

The proprietors of the Hills did not reside in the countryside. They had their residential headquarters in the cities or the more active commercial towns and visited their farms only to rusticate or to superintend and settle accounts.[36] The region of the Hills, with its clear, cool air and beautiful landscapes, was then as now the scene of the *villeggiature* that played such an important part in the social life of the Lombard cities, and villa sites were much in demand. The proprietors bought up the land around their villas, a circumstance that tended to increase the average size of the estates and force up the price of the land in the Brianza, the playground of the Milanese landlords, and in the hills around Bergamo. Some landlords employed stewards (*fattori*) to supervise their farms, and thus created a class of men whose moral and social authority in the

---

[31] Ravizza, p. 239, note 1. Jacini took the opposite view and named as one of the vicious effects of the *fitto a grano* its tendency to reduce the peasant to a serf. Jacini, pp. 203-205.

[32] Spreafico, pp. 144-146.

[33] The Giovanelli owned 20,000 *pertiche* (about 5000 acres). The Luoghi Pii included the works department (*fabbricerie*) of cathedrals, but not the ecclesiastical benefices. Correnti, *op. cit.*, p. 266.

[34] *Ibid.*, p. 267.

[35] Spreafico, p. 144.

[36] Spreafico, p. 142.

communes was considerable.[37] The proprietors of Bergamo were noted for an "immoderate love of acquiring land and extracting the greatest possible profit from it by improvements," and superintended their tenants in person, dispensing with the *fattore*. Under the system of share-farming the landlords not only had a direct interest in keeping an eye on their estates but were responsible for marketing successfully the surplus product. With the increase in value of silk as a market crop this function was to become of great importance in its bearing on the progress of Lombard agriculture and indeed on the whole economic life of the community.

The yield of the soil in the Hill zone was regarded by contemporaries as remarkable and was reported by them to be steadily increasing between 1815 and the middle of the century. They attributed this prosperity to the virtues of share-farming and to the personal interest which many of the proprietors took in the improvement of their farms. In the Bergamasque this interest seemed to Correnti to border on avarice. But if these proprietors were tenacious they were conservative and would adopt innovations only when their success had been thoroughly tested.[38] Spreafico found many of the proprietors of the Brianza indifferent to the care of their farms, "as if not yet convinced of the advantages of agrarian science and almost not even aware of its existence," and further blamed the avarice of the landlords in squeezing high rents from their tenants for the fact that the soil remained "far from giving that abundance of products which among the lights of today one might expect of it." On the other hand the interest of the proprietors in pushing the culture of the silkworm was making a difference in their attitude both to their methods of farming and to their tenants.[39] As for the stewards, they, like the proprietors, "in the lack of appropriate agricultural instruction," rarely possessed a scientific knowledge of their business, though they were credited with a considerable equipment of empirical knowledge.[40] The agriculture of the Hills, in short, was showing progress, without being progressive in the sense in which the contemporary liberal publicist would have desired it to be.

Descending from the Hills to the Plain, one encountered an entirely different agriculture, a system peculiar to Lombardy, which both fascinated and filled with pride the minds of some of Lombardy's most brilliant publicists.[41] The Plain comprised the part of the Provinces of

---

[37] Spreafico, pp. 161-162.   [39] See below, pp. 45-47, 51-52.

[38] Correnti, *op. cit.*, pp. 265-266.   [40] Spreafico, p. 161.

[41] Notably Giandomenico Romagnosi and Carlo Cattaneo in our period. The data for the description that follows in the text are largely drawn from Cattaneo's MS notes on the agriculture of the Plain, preserved in the Museo del Risorgimento of Milan, and from his published writings.

Milan, Bergamo, Brescia and Mantua lying south of a line "which, passing a little above Milan and then changing direction to pass some miles
below Brescia, reaches the Mincio at the foot of the Mantuan Hills."[42]
The tract thus defined embraced more than one-third of the area of
Lombardy.

To understand the economic geography of the Lombard Plain it is
necessary to have well in mind the geographic and climatic peculiarities
of the region. The observer descending from the Hills, with their clear
atmosphere and their infinite variety of contour, finds himself in a new
world. On the clearest days he can see the crests of the Alps and the
Apennines low on the skyline; but such days are rare and he must
usually be satisfied with the unvarying horizon of a vast level. Through
it wander the tributaries of the Po, full and swift in spring, reduced in
summer to a thin trickle and exposing wide white beds of gravel to the
continuous blaze of the sun, in striking contrast to the lush vegetation
on every side. Monotonous as it is this region has always had an
extraordinary fascination for the understanding eye.

> That uniform horizon over an immense plain, broken by long and sym-
> metrical rows of willows and poplars which leave no human habitation
> to be seen anywhere about; the extended meadows populated by grazing
> herds; the great silence broken only by the subdued murmur of the
> waters gurgling against the banks or spurting from the locks [of
> the irrigatory canals] or dripping through the cracks of an aqueduct;
> the wide, straight roads bordered by tall trees and flanked by three or
> four irrigation ditches, which run alongside at different heights and
> often one above the other; the ditches which carry prosperity to limit-
> less stretches of territory, but which often mean poverty to those who
> build them; the great Plain, on which our ancestors left the traces of
> bloody local hatreds in frequent castles and in the ill-starred name of
> some village; and now on the great Plain that vast solitude, in a
> region where the land is a machine which has for its principal agents
> the sun, the water and the herds—a solitude disturbed now and then by
> the tenants travelling by carriage or by peasants taking their crops to
> town in carts drawn by four horses: all this forms a whole which
> inspires a mingled sense of greatness and of sadness.[43]

The Plain of Lombardy owes its exuberant fertility to a system of
irrigation for which a basis is laid in its singular geography and
climate.[44] The waters that fertilize it are not supplied by the Po, which

---

[42] Carlo Cattaneo, "L'agricoltura delle Basse," MS essay in M.R.M., Fondo
Cattaneo, plico 21, cartella 127.10.
[43] Ravizza, pp. 256-258.
[44] The data for the description that follows are drawn chiefly from *D'alcune
istituzioni agrarie dell'Alta Italia applicabili a sollievo dell'Irlanda: lettere del
Dottor Cattaneo a Robert Campbell* (Milano, Bernadoni, 1847).

serves it only as a drainage outlet, but by rivers that descend from the Apennines and from the glaciers of the Alps. The Alpine lakes play the part of great natural storage tanks located high above its floor. The close proximity of the Alps assures a steady supply of water. The sea-winds, robbed of their moisture in crossing the higher Alpine spurs, deposit ice on them even in summer, and this produces a continuous flow of water into the lakes and the rivers. Side by side are the cold air of the hills and mountains and the hot air of the Plain, and the hotter the air rising from the Plain the more snow and ice there is on the mountains. From the sky the Lombard Plain receives but little moisture. The rainfall is confined to thirty or forty days in spring, winter and autumn, chiefly in the autumn. The summer is uniformly serene; and because the air is dried by the mountain winds, which act like a sponge on the exhaltations of the Plain, the region has an even temperature day and night.[45] As Carlo Cattaneo remarked, it "may be said to have a European climate, with a summer almost Egyptian"; hence the possibility of rice-culture.

The region west of the Adda, comprising the lower Milanese and Pavia, is that most favored by these conditions, as its rivers flow from mountains always capped with ice. Here by the middle of the nineteenth century the irrigated area was eight-tenths of the surface. East of the Adda only five-tenths was then irrigated, because the Bremba and the Oglio rivers flow from hills that do not hold their snow in summer. South of the Po irrigation was scarce because the rivers descending from the Apennines are not snow-fed.

The advantages which the climate and physical configuration of the region offer for a system of irrigation are crowned by a gentle but continuous tilt of the land. From Somma Lombardo, at the foot of Lake Maggiore, with a height of 266 metres above sea-level, it slopes away towards the southeast to an elevation of only seven metres at the point where the Po enters the Veneto beyond Mantua—a fall of 260 metres in 200 miles, or of one and one-third metres per mile. This inclination provides for a continuous flow of the water from the lakes, which act as natural reservoirs, and the region had therefore no need of a pumping system. In the territory of Milan and Mantua a part of the water was supplied by natural springs or *fontanili*, especially precious because the water rising from them is warmer than the air in winter and could be used to create the so-called winter meadows, which remain green in the midst of snow and ice, and from which two or more cuttings of forage could be taken between October and March. But the

[45] Seldom rising above 33° centigrade during the day or falling below 25° at night.

principal source of water was the lakes, which supplied in our period three-fourths of the 30,000,000 cubic metres of water discharged daily into the Plain.

The basic and distinctive element of agriculture in the Lombard Plain was its system of irrigation. The great arterial canals, which supplemented the lake-fed rivers in carrying men and goods and driving mills as well as in irrigating the countryside, had been built up through centuries by public and private enterprise. Some of the largest had been built in the later Middle Ages and the Renaissance when such creations of engineering skill were still unknown to the rest of Europe. From the master-canals and the Alpine rivers a continuously moving veil of water was spread over the vast slope of the Plain by a web of minor canals, ditches and sluices—the work of generations of patient tillers of the soil. The web has grown to such complication that at points in the Pavese one may see trenches of flowing water at as many as five levels, crossing each other in stone aqueducts of different and apparently widely separated dates. The area irrigated by this system measured 4230 square kilometers, or one-fifth of the surface of Lombardy.[46]

Fully to appreciate the agriculture of the Lombard Plain it is necessary to bear in mind the fact that the soil itself is not a gift of nature. Originally the surface of the Plain consisted largely of swamp, clay, gravel and sand. Over strata of sand and gravel mixed with clay a film of cultivable soil has been developed, so thin, in the district of Lodi and Crema, that, according to Cattaneo, a deep plowing would ruin a farm for years.[47] By a long process of leveling, by patient removals and transfers of earth, this precious surface has been built up and graded by generations of cultivators until every field is sloped at just the angle necessary to keep the water moving and yet not allow it enough force to carry the soil away; to avoid stagnation and yet to catch the benefit of the precious moisture.

On the great irrigated levels of this region small farms and sharecroppers almost entirely disappeared and their place was taken by large estates and by a class of renters who directed the highly specialized labor of communities of peasants and farm hands engaged in the cultivation and the other activities of widely spaced estates. The characteristic products were forage crops and rice. The Plain also produced flax and mulberries and large quantities of grain.

[46] "Prospetto della navigazione interna delle provincie lombarde con alcune notizie sulla loro irrigazione," *Politecnico,* 1841, IV, 414.

[47] "Notizia economica sulla Provincia di Lodi e Crema, estratta in gran parte dalle memorie postume del colonnello Brunetti," per cura del dott. C. Cattaneo, *Politecnico,* 1839, I. 141.

Carlo Cattaneo made a division of the Plain into three agricultural areas based on the proportion of land subjected to irrigation. The first was the region between the Ticino, Po and Adda Rivers, that is, the Lower Milanese, which was almost entirely irriguous and given over to the production of forage. Cattaneo called this "the cheese-making Plain." The second area embraced the Cremonese, the Province of Lodi and Crema, and lower Brescia. Here the irrigated surface fell away to a proportion of from eight- to five-tenths of the total. This Cattaneo called "the linen-bearing Plain." Finally there was the Province of Mantua, only one-tenth of which was irrigated, and which he named "the wine-bearing Plain."[48] Cereals were produced in all three areas— to such an extent in the Mantuan district that Jacini called that region "the granary of Lombardy."[49] The mulberry was grown in the Cremonese and the Mantuan Plain and its culture was being extended in the Lower Milanese, as it was in the Hill zone; but if the mulberry was dominant in the Hills, the irrigated meadow, cultivated intensively for forage, remained, with the rice-field, distinctive of the Plain.

Thus the agricultural industry to which irrigation chiefly contributed was the manufacture of cheese. Every traveller from Milan to Pavia is familiar with the fresh green of the artificial meadows, cut up into little squares by a silvery network of gently flowing water. This type of culture is brought to its highest pitch in the so-called *marcite* over which a film of water is kept moving all the year round, so that the meadows remain lush and yield cuttings of forage even in the dead of winter.[50] This type of meadow, requiring a nice calculation of temperature, quantity and movement in the control of water, could be produced only with the help of the warm springs or *fontanili* mentioned above; and such meadows occupied only one-tenth of the irrigated surface. The other type of meadow, the *prato stabile*, was not irrigated in winter and consisted of fields on which grain crops were alternated with forage. Where there was enough subsoil clay to give the surface the requisite tenacity of moisture, the water was used to create plantations of rice, the other characteristic product of the Plain.[51] With forage crops and rice,

[48] MS notes. M.R.M., Fondo Cattaneo, cartella 127.10.

[49] Jacini, p. 243.

[50] The *marcita* is so called, not by derivation from *marcire*, to rot or putrefy, but from "*a Marzita,* because hay is taken from it in the month of March." A. S. M., Presidenza, Atti segreti, cartella 88, busta 516, plico 1, note entitled: "*1805. Prati detti a marcita.*"

[51] In 1843 it was estimated that the cultivation of rice in Lombardy employed more than 400,000 persons. Note by Giuseppe Sacchi on P. Racchetti, "Delle risaie nel territorio cremasco in relazione allo stato della popolazione milanese," *Annali*, 1843, LXXV, 17.

in elaborate rotations, the Plain was made to grow flax and cereals, chiefly wheat, rye, millet and maize.

The fertility of the soil was preserved by these rotations and by the use of the abundant manure supplied by the dairy cattle of the region,[52] and in the meadows just to the south of Milan by the sewage of the metropolis.[53] In the rotation with rice, which occupied a nine-year cycle, the land was manured six times; in the rotation without rice, on a six-year cycle, four times.[54] In this elaborate system of field-grass agriculture everything was turned to account. The meadows fed the cattle, and these produced manure for the plowed fields, which in turn supplied straw for the herds.[55] Even the rows of trees between the fields were made to do double service, assisting irrigation by tempering the influence of wind and sun, and furnishing wood which otherwise would have had to be sought at a great distance. The consequence was that, the city of Milan alone excepted, "our Plain has no need to resort to the mountains for any sort of fuel except charcoal."[56]

The visible peculiarity of the agriculture of the Lombard Plain is the division of its level surface into comparatively small fields marked off by rows of willows and poplars which are almost always double along the roads and ditches. The fields are small but the farms, unlike those of the Hill zone, are of considerable extent. A farm of 325 acres[57] was

---

[52] Cattaneo estimated that the stables "between Milan, Lodi and Pavia contain 100,000 head of cattle, 100,000 hogs and 25,000 horses." Cattaneo, *Instituzioni agrarie*, p. 34.

[53] Giuseppe Devincenzi, "Relazione sull'agricoltura dell'alto e basso Milanese; letta il 26 settembre 1844 alla Sezione di Agronomia del VI Congresso scientifico italiano in Milano," *Annali*, 1844, LXXXI, 331. The quantity of sewage thus utilized was not great, most of it being carried off by the drainage canals and rivers. Cattaneo, *op. cit.*, p. 33.

[54] The rotation with rice was as follows:

First year: grain, with meadow clover, which yielded a crop after the harvest.
Second year: clover, with manure.
Third and fourth years: meadow clover followed by a spontaneous crop of *trifoglio repens* (commonly called *ladino*), and other grasses, with manure each year.
Fifth year: part flax, part *granturco,* and after the flax. sometimes millet, sometimes *maiz quarantino.*
Sixth year: Indian corn with manure.
Seventh, eighth and ninth years: rice, with manure in the last two years.
The rotation without rice was the same except for the last three years.
Devincenzi, p. 334. The different "models" of rotation are described by Bowring, *Statistics*, p. 102.

[55] Cattaneo, *Istituzioni agrarie*, p. 34.

[56] Cattaneo, MS notes in M. R. M., Fondo Cattaneo, cartella 127.

[57] 1300 *pertiche nuove* or *decari;* 1950 *pertiche Milanesi.* The extent of the estates of the Jacini family of Milan in the Cremonese in 1929 were as follows in *pertiche Cremonesi:* Canova, 1,182; Barletta, 372; San Gervasio, 2,931; Gallarano,

regarded by Cattaneo as "fair-sized" and also as the most economical unit of exploitation. The proprietors were absentees, who lived in the cities and did not visit their estates on the Plain even in the vacations, which they spent in their villas on the lakes or in the Hills.[58] The agriculture of the Plain was left in the hands of a class of renters.[59] They rented on a lease which was renewable each year, but which commonly ran for nine to twelve years and often for much longer periods.[60] Cattaneo knew a renter of the Plain in whose family a lease had descended since 1663,[61] and the son of the present renter of San Gervasio, an estate of the Jacini family in the Cremonese, told me with quiet pride that his family had directed that estate since the eighteenth century. The renter of the irrigated region of Lombardy was indeed no ordinary peasant farmer. To work an estate he had to possess not less than a hundred head of cattle, a good number of horses, and a stock of grain, straw, hay, manure, agricultural implements and vehicles, and he was generally required to give a security for his lease, or to pay a year's rent in advance.[62] He paid an annual rent of from 120 to 180 lire per hectare. The amount of circulating capital which he invested in the land was estimated in 1844 to be approximately 40,000 lire per 100 hectares, a sum equal to the net income for three years.[63] In short, the renter had to be a man who could command a considerable capital.

The renter's intest in the estate was secured by an institution that was prevalent throughout Lombardy and which was highly praised by patriotic observers. This was the *consegna*, or consignment, an inventory that accompanied the lease and that recorded the exact condition in which the leasehold was turned over to the tenant. In the Plain the inventory was drawn up by one or more engineers who acted as arbiters in case of dispute. The *consegna* was a true statistical description of the farm that covered everything—the state of the canals and waters, the value of the manure left on the land and its degree of maturity, the trees and shrubs and their precise condition, the buildings and their appurtenances down to the very locks on the doors. When the farm was surrendered the renter was credited with every improvement and, after due allowance had been made for the depreciation of permanent

1,600; Convento, 1,200. From notes courteously supplied to the author by Count Stefano Jacini. 12 *pertiche cremonesi* equal about 10 *pertiche italiane* or 1 hectare.

[58] Cattaneo, *Istituzioni agrarie*, p. 74.
[59] *Fittaiuoli.*
[60] Devincenzi, p. 333.
[61] MS notes, M. R. M., Fondo Cattaneo, cartella 127, plico 21.
[62] Cattaneo, *Istituzioni agrarie*, p. 74.
[63] Devincenzi, *Annali*, 1844, LXXXI, 335.

structures, was charged with every damage to the property, including even that sustained by the soil as a result of the type of rotation that he had practiced. The effect of the *consegna* with its annual balancing of the account between lord and tenant, was to stimulate improvements. "Encouraged by this far-sighted custom, the renter considers the land as his own, and employs his care and his money even in those improvements whose duration exceeds the term of the lease," at expiration of which "he receives his capital back, after having enjoyed the interest on it derived from the increased annual revenue of his fields."[64]

The operation of these estates of the Plain was focused in great farmsteads which were (and are) in part the dwelling-place of a community of men and animals and in part a factory. They centered in the home of the renter which was often a structure of considerable dignity, surmounted by a cupola and a bell. Its great kitchen, with an open hearth, was a scene of the liveliest activity, bearing witness, to use the words of a contemporary observer, "to a great daily business and to the abundance of all the products of it. Eight or ten fowling pieces on a rack attached to the wall, and five or six dogs, setters or sleuth-hounds, squatting by the fireplace or moving about the kitchen, announced the diversions and the habits of the family. There was a continual coming and going of stewards, overseers of the fields, plowmen, cheese-makers, herdsmen; and standing in front of the fire the old renter received the reports of the day, consulted, gave orders."[65] In a typical farmstead of the Plain the house of the renter, isolated from the other buildings, was surrounded by several courtyards, each destined to a particular service.[66] One was almost entirely occupied by the great paved threshing floor, and was flanked on one side by the tenements of the farmhands (*case coloniche*), and on another, perhaps, by a spacious portico which was the storehouse of the farm implements. By this court ran the stream that turned the mill and the rice-thresher—machines long known to Lombard agriculture and regarded as two of its most ingenious inventions.[67] Other courts, surrounded by stables and hay-barns and the hovels of plowmen and herdsmen, were assigned to the horses and cattle, which sometimes stood in the middle of the court under a long roof open on both sides. On the more progressive farms, as at San Gervasio, the cattle were housed in closed stables, which might be veritable bovine cathedrals.[68]

[64] Cattaneo, *Istituzioni agrarie,* p. 59.   [65] Ravizza, pp. 259 ff.

[66] The description that follows in the text was compiled in part from contemporary sources, in part from the author's observations of the estate of San Gervasio at Casalbuttano, which he was courteously permitted to visit by the present Count Stefano Jacini under that gentleman's guidance.

[67] Ravizza, p. 263.

[68] I have specifically in mind those which Count Stefano Jacini built at San Gervasio towards the middle of the last century.

Along the sides of one of the great courts, "cluttered with plows, carts, and piles of wood and scattered with chickens that scratched and clucked about"—and with the numerous small children of the peasantry —would be found the buildings where the milk was handled; the *casone* where the butter and cheese were manipulated—with an enormous kettle seething over a great fire, and "the half-naked cheese-makers waiting till the milk is ready for them to reach in and collect the *cacio*"—and the storage shed for the cheeses (*formaggeria*), "where the precious product arranged on great shelves in order of maturity awaits the cheese-broker, who with a tap of his sagacious hammer passes on its merits and puts it in commerce"—a true "library of cheeses."[69] Off one of the courts would be seen the vegetable garden of the renter himself and a group of little garden plots cultivated by each family of peasants, and "on an artificial mound four great elms which shaded the ice-house." From the road one of these farmsteads seems a rectangular walled village, its buildings tile-roofed, and the walls of the barns formed of a kind of lattice of bricks. A veritable village it is, often enclosing the almost self-contained lives of three hundred or more persons. Sometimes a *campanile*, rising above the roofs beside the farm-belfry, shows that the community has even an altar of its own.

Within these communities and subject to the orders of the renter there was a hierarchy of peasant specialists which reflects the extent to which the division of labor was carried on these heavily capitalized estates. "Let us enter one of those great irrigated farms," wrote the economist Gioia in 1825, ". . . and we shall find, (1) a man who *all year round* attends to the making of cheese without being occupied with any other business; (2) a man who *all year round* oversees the cows whether in the stalls or in the pastures; (3) a man who *all year round* drives the horses and goes to and from the markets; (4) a man who takes care of the oxen, plows the fields, transports the manure; (5) a man who attends to the distribution of the waters, etc."[70] The cheese-maker (*casaro*), the cowherd (*famiglio*), the field-master (*camparo*), who also looked after the irrigation system, the stable-man (*cavalcante*) and the herdsman (*bifolco*) who tended and drove, respectively, the horses and cattle, were the most important of the specialists and were the best paid. There might also be a peasant who attended to the threshing of rice (*pilatore*). Also there was a *bazzalone* who cooked for the whole establishment.[71] At noon and towards evening, when the

[69] Ravizza, pp. 264-265.
[70] *Annali*, 1825, III, 110.
[71] Cattaneo, MS notes, "Salari," in M. R. M., Fondo Cattaneo, cartella 127, plico 21.

farm bell was rung, the *bazzalone* stood in a portico near the renter's house and dished out the minestra and distributed bread to each family, whose women, old men and children came with crocks and pails to fetch their ration.[72] The specialized peasants received their housing free, in two rooms, one on the ground-floor with a fireplace and one above; a kitchen-garden; allotments of salt, oil, butter, milk, meat and wood; exemption from certain personal taxes which were paid by the landlord; a portion of the produce from the fields which their families cultivated; and, finally, a wage.[73] Each of these specialists had under his orders a number of peasants (*coloni*) who performed the manual labor of the stables, the dairies and the fields. The unskilled peasants were day-laborers (*giornalieri*), and although their families had, besides free shelter and their daily ration of food, the fruits and vegetables from the small gardens which they cultivated and a hog which they killed once a year, they had no stake of their own in the land. Shifted as they were from one operation to another with the seasons, they formed a rural proletariat. At certain seasons their number was increased by drifting day-laborers, mountaineers who descended to the Plain at harvest-time and in winter, and woodcutters, also from the mountains, who slept in the hay-barns on sacks which they carried with them in their migrations.[74]

The crop-sharing family of the Hills was better off than the farm hands of the Plain whose manner of living has just been indicated, but its standard of living was low. Its members were satisfied if they did not lack "morning and evening a good piece of bread, made with corn meal mixed with rye or a *polenta*, at noon a minestra of rice or of flour paste mixed with cabbage, rapeseed or green vegetables. The side dishes are garden fruits and some dairy products, and the condiments are oil, bacon and sometimes butter." The peasant bought salt, rice and bacon.[75] His simple, ill-ventilated cottage had a dirt floor and unplastered walls.[76]

The return on an investment in land varied with the different zones of agriculture. The price of land in the Mountains rivalled that of the rich soil of the Plain.[77] Jacini estimated that the profit on an investment

---

[72] Ravizza, p. 265.
[73] Cattaneo, *loc. cit.* There is an elaborate description of these specialized laborers, their functions and wages, in Bowring, *Statistics,* pp. 103–104.
[74] *Ibid.*
[75] Spreafico, p. 166.
[76] Ravizza, p. 78.
[77] It "not rarely sold for 1 Austrian lira per square metre." Correnti, *Annali,* 1844, LXXXII, 161. Jacini gives 1000 Austrian lire per *pertica milanese,* or 15,000 lire per *hectare* (p. 164). 15 *pertiche milanesi* were equivalent to 1 hectare. 1 Austrian lira was worth 1.145 Italian or French lira. A. Sandonà, *Il Regno Lombardo Veneto,* 1814–1859 (Milano, 1912), p. 268.

in Mountain land was only from one to one and one-half per cent.[78]
Inasmuch as this land was on the margin, in the Ricardian sense of the
word, its high market value is surprising, and was accounted for in
contemporary writings by the love of the small peasant proprietors for
their independence and security.[79] The market value of the land in the
Hill zone was lower than that of the Mountain farms but was comparatively high.[80] It was enhanced by the demand of the lords for villa sites
in this picturesque region, also by its eligibility for middle class investments and "the excessive desire of country traders to mount to the
honors of possession, which according to their restricted notions seems
more important than wealth."[81] In some parts of the Hill zone, notably
in the Bergamasque, a strong attachment to the soil which bore fruit in
agricultural improvements went hand in hand with this social ambition,
and helps to explain the fact that the price of small holdings was well
above their economic value.[82] The average return on investment in the
land of the Hills was three per cent or less. That from the much richer
soil of the Plain was estimated at four per cent.[83] In general, the income
from investment in land in the period from 1815 to 1848 seems to have
ranged from two to five per cent, with an average between three and
four per cent.[84] It was lower than that of capital invested in trade or
industry, which in 1837 averaged five or six per cent. The premium on
investment in land reflects the social habits of the community, and the
much coveted prestige of being a *"possidente."*

With its roots deep in the soil and its habits steeped in tradition the
agricultural community which was the backbone of Lombard society
was naturally conservative. At the same time it contained certain elements, and was showing certain tendencies, that were favorable to
progress and the introduction of improvements.

[78] Jacini, *ibid.*
[79] *Ibid.*
[80] 40 to 60 Italian centesimi per square metre in the Brianza. Spreafico, p. 141.
Correnti gives 60 centesimi to 1 Austrian lira for the lower Hill zone in the
Province of Bergamo. *Op. cit.,* p. 164. Around the city of Bergamo, where land
was in demand for villa sites, the price went as high as 80 centesimi to 1 Austrian
lira. Engineer G. Possenti, "Il voto e le illustrazioni della Commissione d'esame
per la scelta della linea da Milano a Brescia," *Annali,* 1841, LXIX. 86. Some
vineyards in the picturesque country on the upper edge of the Hill zone, where
villa sites were at the greatest premium, brought as much as 2 Austrian lire per
square meter. Correnti, *op. cit.,* p. 161.
[81] Spreafico, p. 141; also Correnti, *Annali,* 1844, LXXXII, 267.
[82] Correnti, *ibid..* p. 267.
[83] Spreafico, p. 141; Jacini, pp. 248-249.
[84] These estimates are confirmed by Engineer G. Possenti, *Annali,* 1841, LXIX,
85, and [Filippo De Boni] "Difesa contro un'accusa ufficiale." Extract from the
Cronaca (Lausanne, Bonamici, August 30, 1847), Nos. 10-12, p. 11.

Its proprietary class was composed of the small farmers of the Mountains and the city-dwelling landlords of the Hills and the Plain. The little proprietors of the Mountains were isolated from the main body of the community and were too much absorbed in wringing a livelihood from their precarious farms to be open to the current suggestions of progress. Some of the landlords of the Hill zone took a personal interest in their estates and were constantly introducing improvements, though displaying great cautiousness regarding "modern" or "scientific" innovations. The rich proprietors of the Plain lived at their ease in the cities and paid little or no attention to the cultivation of their estates which they treated simply as an investment.[85] An exception must be made of a class of these proprietors who were not of the nobility, yet were true country gentlemen, residing in the provinces and supervising their own farms. The type is represented by Stefano Jacini, author of the treatise on *La proprietà fondiaria in Lombardia,* and subsequently a collaborator with Cavour, as Minister of Public Works in the first cabinet of the Kingdom of Italy, and director of the great Agrarian Inquest of the Kingdom made in 1877-1885.[86] The palazzo of the Jacini at Casalbuttano is typical of the position such a family occupied in the community—not a villa but a house made to live in the year round and to form a working part of a great agricultural establishment directed by the proprietor in person. Landlords of the type of Jacini formed a true agrarian middle class which seems not to have existed in any other part of Italy during the Risorgimento. Conservative, it was nevertheless in direct contact with the practice of agriculture and at the same time free from the rigidity which handicapped the hereditary nobility in adjusting themselves to the requirements of modern life. It was prepared therefore to lend substance and backing to the small group of nobles who were liberal and progressive and ready to break with the tradition of their caste.

But the class was probably not numerous. In the district of Codogno "the masters of only seven of the thirty-six 'houses'—large and small—that existed in the district in 1835 lived in the district; the majority of

---

[85] Jacini, p. 374; G. Sacchi, *Annali,* 1847, XCIII, 189. Lady Morgan observed that "the nobility go regularly at St. Martin's to settle with their tenants and frequently stay until Christmas. Their other visits to the country are few and distant, and their *villeggiaturas* last but a few days." Lady Sydney Morgan, *Italy* (London, Colburn, 1821), I, 214.

[86] For his background and life see Stefano Jacini, *Un conservatore rurale della nuova Italia* (Bari, 1926, 2 v.), an example of the invaluable type of biography that serves the student of history by illuminating the position and outlook of a whole social class.

the remainder enjoyed the delights of Milan."[87] The provincial proprietors were gravitating towards the capital—drawn by the increasing
economic and social attraction which the capital was exercising on the
whole of Lombard society. About 1840 it was observed that almost
all of the wealthier families of Lodi and Como had for a long while had
houses in Milan. "The same tendency prevails openly in Cremona and
Crema; Pavia, Mantua and Bergamo are not exempt from it, only
Brescia remaining refractory."[88] Jacini in 1855 noted this concentration
on Milan.[89] Its effect had just been strikingly illustrated in the history
of his own family. His father, though deeply attached by sentiment to
his estates in the provinces, found it impossible to resist the strong pull
which the metropolis was exerting on the proprietary class and first
rented apartments in Milan, then in 1855 purchased the town house in
the Via Lauro in which the family has resided ever since.[90]

As for the actual tillers of the soil in the zones where tenant farming
prevailed, the share-croppers were part of a system in which customary
procedures were still the rule, while in the families of *massari* fossils of
a more patriarchal structure were still to be found. The crop-sharing
families lived out their lives in a web of largely personal relationships
in which money and contact with the market played an insignificant part.
Sharefarming had its virtues, which were praised by liberal contemporaries, chief among them the protection it gave the peasant against
having to shoulder the whole loss in case of crop failures, and the
interest it gave him in faithful and industrious tillage. But whatever
its virtues it was not adapted to those forms of cultivation which
modern commerce and industry seemed to require[91] If any progress
was to take place under this system, it had to come from the energy and
intelligence of the proprietor. At least his relationship with the tenant
under this tenure gave the landlord an interest in passing on to the
cultivator his knowledge of improvements, and in the case of silk-culture
this interest was of considerable effect.

In the Plain, where agricultural operations were directed largely by
the class of renters, the complexion of society was determined by the
capitalistic character of the prevalent form of exploitation. The pro-

---

[87] "G. D.," "Notizie statistiche sulle fabbriche di formaggio nel distretto di
Codogno in Lombardia," *Annali*, 1839, LIX, 99-105.
[88] MS on "La popolazione della Lombardia," Vol. II, ch. ix, M. R. M., Fondo
Cattaneo, cartella 127.11, plico 21. The MS is not dated but was probably composed about 1842.
[89] Jacini, p. 48.
[90] Jacini, *Un conservatore rurale*, I, 10.
[91] Luigi Serristori, 'Dell'attuale condizione dell'industria in Italia," *Annali*,
1845, LXXXV, 9-17.

prietors were the absentee capitalists of this system, and the renters, themselves provided with considerable sums of capital, were its entrepreneurs. The renter-tenants of the Plain seem to have been a vigorous, ambitious and responsible class of men. Some of them had passed their early years in school and were sending their sons to the universities.[92] Jacini gave them high praise for their social qualities. "Within their households, if luxury is unknown, one finds simple abundance and meets with a frankness of character, a good humor and a cordiality which conciliate the sympathy of all who visit them." He cited as witnesses the young engineers who practiced their profession in the region : "every one of them will remember fine autumn evenings when the hours passed with a swiftness hardly known in the gilded parlors of the capital."[93] In the city the renters' wives were known by a certain pretentiousness of dress "carried into the minutest details, which distinguished the women-folk of rich renters."[94] An ostentatious prosperity was probably limited to a few families, but its existence indicates the possibilities of the renter's vocation.

Ravizza found among their sons some of "the handsomest and strongest" youth of Lombardy, "tall and slender, but strong in bone and muscle, with faces breathing energy and impatience . . . persuaded that wine, a cigar and joy are the best antidotes for malaria, but at the same time honorable and sincere, generous and cordial. . . . Confident in their practical knowledge of agriculture, which indeed seems sometimes to accomplish miracles, they are not ignorant of theory nor do they refuse fine and useful innovations. Boastful of their strength, seekers of adventures and perils, they roam the vast fields with a gun slung across their shoulders and a pack of dogs at their heels."[95] To Ravizza also we owe a picture of an old renter, vigorous and dominating at seventy, idealized in all probability, but a figure easily possible under the conditions which we know to have existed.

His forbears were among the oldest renters of that neighborhood and had enriched themselves at the beginning of the last century [the eighteenth] when the luxurious and thriftless landlord . . . had rented his fifteen possessions in the Plain to the head of the family for a great sum paid in advance. . . . The wealth of the family had increased at the beginning of the present century with the rise in price of all provisions, and Signor Carlo Siro would have been able to increase it still more, if he had had the courage to present himself with

[92] Cattaneo, *Istituzioni agrarie*, p. 74; Devincenzi, in *Annali*, 1844, LXXXI, 336; Jacini, p. 251; Ravizza, pp. 260-261.
[93] Jacini, pp. 260-261.
[94] Ravizza, pp. 260-261.
[95] Ravizza, p. 267.

many of his colleagues to buy the lands of the Church. . . . Nevertheless he was a wealthy gentleman and while he kept his eldest son with him, two other sons superintended other vast farms.

Ravizza represents this old renter as having no greater delight than in showing off the improvements he had made—

> waste places changed into green and extensive meadows, watery marshes converted into perennial runnels, costly edifices of stone supporting the irrigation canals, . . . granaries full to bursting, the immense hay-barns, the stables of great horses and vigorous oxen, the *barchi,* where among the hundred Swiss cows our own make a good showing. . . . However, in spite of the urban luxury brought even to these great families of the Plain, Signor Carlo Siro had remained faithful to the old ways, except that he had substituted a fine carriage for the dusty one-horse shay in which his father had visited the markets, and had taken care to have all his sons instructed in the colleges and at the University.[96]

From this contemporary description and others one gets the impression of a type that was self-reliant and enterprising but hard-headed and cautious in the face of improvements.

Besides the resident proprietors and the renters the society of the Plain contained other middle class elements in the public physicians supported by the communes, and the considerable body of engineers and hydraulic police (*compari d'acqua*) required by the irrigatory system. These engineers were men of high character and technical skill, "whose continuous relations with the renters," Cattaneo remarked, "must have contributed much to the progress of agriculture." "This and other middle class elements," he continued, "are statistically much more numerous in our country than in Belgium or in France itself."[97]

Over against this directing class must be set the great mass of wage-workers on the estates of the region—the proletariat of this highly capitalized agriculture. Some of these, such as the cheese-makers, were highly skilled, and, as has already appeared, enjoyed a degree of comfort and security, but the majority seem to have lived in a bovine stupor. As long as they remained at work, their lot was not too unhappy. They received free housing. They would live well, Cattaneo thought, but for the malaria which cursed the region at the end of summer.[98] Still they remained proletarians, with no attachment to the soil. They had no prospect of securing a portion of it for their own use. A lover of the Hills coming among them found them "pale and flabby."[99]

[96] Ravizza, pp. 260-261, 265. The quotation has been somewhat re-arranged.
[97] *Istituzioni agrarie,* p. 74.
[98] *Ibid.,* p. 75.
[99] Ravizza, p. 267.

Wandering from one dairy-farm to another in search of a new master, destined to live amid a great network of indivisible latifundia which little by little absorb the small neighboring properties . . . they have neither that respectful joviality, nor that ingenuity and love of the land, nor those patriarchal family traditions which often adorn the *massari* of the upper Milanese. While the animals are housed in magnificent stables, it is often the case that the poor cultivators are lodged in filthy and unhealthful huts. . . . Wrapped in the miasma of the vast summer fermentation they resignedly await the fever every year and bear it without grumbling, if only a graver malady does not send them to populate the hospitals of the nearby cities. In a country of abundant living, in the midst of fat and numerous cattle, they do not have meat to eat, because the needs of agriculture and the frequent epidemics of cattle-plague render it too dear.[100]

The problem of the agricultural laborer of the Plain was inherent in the system and in spite of all the improvements in education and sanitary conditions it still persists. It was a problem that was beginning to trouble the public-spirited observers of the first half of the nineteenth century for it created a submerged mass that was potentially restless[101] but what was worse from the point of view of progress and patriotism, normally inert. "Slaves of the glebe," Luigi Torelli called them and declared that to awaken their patriotism the first step necessary would be to change the social and economic order so as to give them at least some share in the life of the community. "On this population there is no hope to be founded, since it lacks any motive of excitement; and although one such motive, namely education, is not excluded for the future, it is of the present that we speak."[102]

The directive and professional elements of the society of the Plain were bound together by an extraordinarily close web of relationships that were imposed by the irrigatory system. The users of any given irrigatory canal were bound together in an association (*consorzio*). When they were few, the association was informal and the principal user assumed the responsibilities of administration. When they were more numerous the *consorzio* became a legal body whose executive officers were an engineer and a *comparo d'acqua* (officer of the hydraulic police). This police officer, to quote Cattaneo, "may truly be called the executive arm of our irrigative agriculture." His office required

---

[100] Ravizza, p. 266. Cattaneo also pointed out the moral difference between the *coloni* of the Plain and those of the Hills. The rudest of those on the Plain were the shepherds and the drifting day-laborers. *Istituzioni agrarie*, p. 67.

[101] Stefano Jacini described their relations with the renters as marked by neither affection nor hatred. Where the day laborers were numerous "a ferment of hatred and anarchic passions arises, especially in bad years." Jacini, p. 283.

[102] *Pensieri di un anonimo Lombardo* (Paris, L. R. Delay, 1846), pp. 37–39.

diligence, a character that would inspire confidence, and an eye trained to detect changes and thefts of the water.[103] Over the whole surface of the irrigated country was spread a vast closely articulated time-table, in accordance with which each member of the *consorzii* was entitled to receive in turn his quota of water through the sluices of the main canal under the eye of the *camparo d'acqua*.[104] Thus every owner of this soil and his agents were dependent on the punctual daily coöperation of all the rest.

The division of labor and the field-grass agriculture of the Lombard Plain represent an advanced stage of agronomy. But in estimating its progressiveness one must bear in mind the fact that it was not the result of the foresight and directive genius of a group of enterprising individuals as was the capitalistic agriculture of contemporary England. Rather it was the work of many generations of men and represented the gradual adaptation of a society to the singular geography and climate of its place of habitation. The distribution of labor through the year, and the continuous employment of animals, persons and implements on an estate of the Plain was due, as Cattaneo remarked, not to individual planning but to the requirements of an artificial distribution of water.[105] The result reflected patience and tenacity of effort and qualities of foresight, civic wisdom and rational fair play in such institutions as the laws and customs governing the use of water,[106] and the yearly inventory and balance protecting improvements made by the tenant, which well might inspire a patriot like Cattaneo with pride and faith in Italian competence,

---

[103] Carlo Cattaneo, *Notizie naturali e civili su la Lombardia* (Milano, 1844), I, 236–237.

[104] An example of these time-tables is to be found in Cattaneo, *Istituzioni agrarie*, p. 37.

[105] *Ibid.*, p. 35.

[106] One of the most admirable was a practice which involved the extension of the principle of eminent domain to cover the peculiar needs of an expanding system of irrigation. In brief, it required that a proprietor must allow water to pass through his land to that of a proprietor with holdings lower down, if the latter desired its use for agricultural or industrial purposes; and the proprietor still farther on, at a lower level, could not refuse to admit the discharge of water so used from the fields next above his. He would of course seldom have an interest in refusing to do so. The proprietor seeking the use of the water was required by law to build an acqueduct through the property of his neighbor on higher ground and pay him an indemnity for the land that it occupied. This practice which seemed to indicate so well the intelligent adaptability of the population to its environment crystalized in the ancient Municipal Statutes of Milan (*De acquis conducendis*) and passed into the common law of the region at the beginning of the sixteenth century. Cattaneo, *Notizie*, I, 198-199. The history and significance of the system were elaborated by G. D. Romagnosi in his treatise *Della condotta delle acque secondo le dottrine del Pecchio e la intermedia e recente legislazione tanto della monarchia austriaca quanto di tutti gli altri regni, principati e ducati d'Italia* (Milano, tipografia di Commercio, 1822-1825, 6 v.).

and justify him in reading useful lessons to English landlords regarding their relations with the peasants of Ireland. The system was regarded as a triumph of the fundamental virtues of a race,[107] but its history did not justify expectations of progress in the sense of flexibility or the rapid introduction of new methods of culture.

The presence of two other groups conditioned the agricultural life of Lombardy in all of its parts. These were the doctors and the priests. Every commune either supported, or joined adjacent communes in supporting, a physician who furnished medical services free of charge to the poor. The practice had begun in private philanthropy with the doctors whom rich proprietors took to the country to attend their families while in *villeggiatura*. By 1844 it could be affirmed that "there is not a corner of the country so lost in the Alps that one cannot find there at a practicable distance a physician paid a stipend to assist poor families." The writer of this observation remarked with patriotic satisfaction that the number of doctors in Lombardy per unit of territory was greater than in Belgium, "which is regarded as the most flourishing country on the continent."[108] This feeling of pride in the public medical service of Lombardy was frequently expressed. The body of professional men whose presence in the rural districts it insured was credited with the promptness with which Lombardy accepted vaccination and with the diminution of superstition and crimes of violence.

The position and influence of the village priest is less easy to define, but his ubiquitous presence is a fact that must be taken into account. Cattaneo said of him in 1841 that he was "the keystone in which all the lines of life [in the countryside] center."[109] He entered directly into the economic life of the peasants with the first claim on a share in the fruit of their toil which every peasant family paid him and on the collection of which he seems to have kept a jealous eye.[110] He was the inspector of the local school and often its only teacher; he acted as an informal magistrate; and he had the souls of a people faithfully Catholic in his sole custody. There is a classic portrait of a "good curate of the Brianza" in Carlo Ravizza's *Un curato di campagna*. This priest was the incarnation of evangelical piety, intelligent, tolerant and strong, who besides the cure of souls exercised himself to lead his people gently into the paths of a more intelligent economic and social life. The portrait is no doubt an idealization. But there is good reason to believe that among

[107] "It was a question of life or death but energy conquered, and this is now one of the richest lands in the world." Devincenzi, in *Annali*, 1844, LXXXI, 332.
[108] Dr. C. Canziani, "Sull'ordinamento sanitario nelle IX Provincie della Lombardia," *Politecnico*, 1844, VII, 223–241.
[109] *Politecnico*, 1841, IV, 454.
[110] Salvatore Anau, in *Annali*, 1847, XCIV, 84.

the parochial clergy of the region were to be found many liberal and enlightened men, devoted to the interests of their country as well as of their parishes. Certainly they were leaders, under Don Ferrante Aporti, in the patriotic movement for the *asili d'infanzia,* which swept the country, in the face of Papal disapprobation.[111] It is a notable fact that the parish priests of Lombardy figured frequently in the liberal patriotic writings of the period in a most favorable light while these remained entirely silent regarding the higher clergy and the Church. Cattaneo represented the outlook of this literature and at the same time hinted at the reason for the line drawn in favor of the parish priests when he wrote: "Since the inexorable necessity of the times caused the monastic congregations to disappear from this fair country, subject as they were to uncertain and distant influences, this institution [the parish priesthood] entirely local in character, reigns supreme in the hearts of our people. The parochial organization, child of the country, nurtured in the country, foreign to all commotions that occur beyond the limits of each separate part of the country, incapable of opposition and turbulence, almost inaccessible to fanaticism, may be the most powerful and certain minister of the common prosperity."[112]

[111] See C. J. A. Mittermaier (Geheimrath und Professor in Heidelberg), *Delle condizioni d'Italia* (Leipzig, G. B. Hirschfield; Milan and Vienna, Tendler e Schäfer, 1845, tr. from the German of *Italienische Zustände,* Heidelberg, 1844), p. 190. For the *asili,* see below, pp. 215–219.

[112] Review by Cattaneo of Ravizza's *Un curato di campagna, Politecnico,* 1841, IV, 454-455.

CHAPTER II

AGRICULTURAL DEVELOPMENT

G IVEN the constitution of the Lombard agricultural community, it would be vain to expect an agricultural revolution in Lombardy comparable with that which took place in England during the eighteenth century under the leadership of such proprietors as Lord Townsend, Coke of Holkham or Bakewell. With these gentlemen farmers of England the spring to action had been indirectly commercial. It lay in the interest of a class who saw their position and power threatened by the rich merchants and who, having been retired to the country by a political revolution, found in their estates, scientifically directed, a means of recouping their fortunes.[1] Moreover the commerce of England had created the market that insured the success of their expensive experiments. Neither the commercial nor the educational conditions of Lombardy were ripe for such a movement. Scientific farming goes hand in hand with the commercial spirit, with its sharp emulation, its balancing of profit and loss, its knowledge of markets, and its long views ahead. This was as yet undeveloped in Lombardy, where the farmer was easily satisfied with a small profit and the respectability of proprietorship. The progress of agriculture in Lombardy was further conditioned by the ignorance of the cultivator. The Austrian Government set up a remarkable system of universal and compulsory primary education. But the attendance of peasant children was hard to secure. The system made great progress,[2] but chiefly in the cities and towns, especially in the Hill zone where agriculture was linked with industry and the peasants could find some practical account in reading, writing and arithmetic. In the rural districts the schools were deserted as soon as field work began and the children quickly forgot what they had learned, finding no regular use for it.[3] The failure of the system was particularly striking in the Plain. In 1846 in the Provinces of Milan and Cremona, one-fourth of the boys of school age were unschooled, in Lodi and Crema one-third, in Mantua and Pavia almost one-half.[4] Luigi Serristori, sum-

---

[1] Paul Mantoux, *The Industrial Revolution in England in the Eighteenth Century* (translation by Dorothy Page, London. 1928), pp. 163–164.
[2] See below, pp. 211–214.
[3] Spreafico, pp. 169-170, Jacini, p. 77.
[4] *Annali*, 1847, XCIII, 190.

ming up the reasons for the backwardness of Italian agriculture, declared that the fundamental one was "the ignorance of the cultivators and of many of the proprietors."[5]

But in spite of restricted literacy and scientific knowledge, a limited commercial stimulus and social conservatism, the agriculture of Lombardy progressed in the period 1814-1848. The most conspicuous change was an increase in the quantity of its product, which accompanied the expansion of the home market for foodstuffs and the foreign market for silk.

Lombardy had a dense population to feed. In 1836, if the Mountain zone was excluded, its population was the densest in Europe, denser by twenty per cent than that of Belgium. Even if the Mountain zone was included the population of Lombardy per square unit of surface was greater than that of any other country of Europe but Belgium.[6] Its great consumers' market for the products of the soil was in its numerous cities and towns. In 1836 Lombardy had nine cities of more than 10,000 inhabitants, with a population of 400,000 out of a total population of 2,474,674.[7] Towns of from 2,000 to 17,000 inhabitants accounted for 700,000 more persons; so that it could be said in 1836 that "almost one-half of the population of Lombardy lives in a state of urban or near-urban aggregation."[8] The most important urban market was Milan, which in 1836 had 185,000 inhabitants.[9]

The population of Lombardy was increasing steadily between 1814 and 1848, in spite of its great density and the effect of the crisis of 1817 and the ravages of the cholera epidemic which swept the country in 1836-1837. From 1814 to about 1840 it increased by 395,403.[10] The rate of increase was slow, a result that was natural in view of the extent of the mountain wastes, the crowded soil and the advanced state of agricul-

---

[5] *Annali*, 1845, LXXXV, 14.

[6] 114.611 per square kilometer. Belgium 125; British Isles 76.5; Ireland 94; France 60.25. Cattaneo, "Sulla densità della popolazione in Lombardia e su la sua relazione alle opere pubbliche," *Politecnico*, 1839, I, 32-33.

[7] This total is that given by the *Annali*, 1837, LIV, 238.

[8] Cattaneo, article cited above, note 6.

[9] *Ibid.*, p. 42. The figure for 1825 was 161,100 according to the *Annali*, 1825, IV, 170, but there is room for uncertainty as to the identity of the basis of the two totals and also as to the reliability of the statistics used by the *Annali*. Cattaneo states that his figures were drawn from "various good unpublished sources." *Politecnico*, 1839, I, 46, note 1. All of these figures seem to have included the soldiers stationed in the city, for, according to the *Tafeln zur Statistik der öster-reichischen Monarchie* (zusammengestellt von der K. K. Direktion der Administrativen Statistik) 1831, Tafel 2, the population of Milano in 1831 (exclusive of soldiers) was 130,383; in 1846, 156,326.

[10] MS chapter on "La popolazione della Lombardia," Vol. II, ch. IX, M. R. M., Fondo Cattaneo, cartella 127.11, plico 21.

tural exploitation. The total population in 1818 was 2,167,782,[11] in 1831 2,380,697, in 1846 2,670,833.[12] From 1818 to 1830 the annual rate of increase was .7 per cent; from 1818 to 1837, .6 per cent.[13] In the thirty-six years following 1818 the average annual increase was .8 per cent.[14] This fell below the rate of increase of the Austrian Monarchy as a whole, which was 1.06 per cent (from 1841 to 1846), and that of England, Prussia and Russia, but considerably exceeded that of France, whose population was growing by only .6 per cent a year during the first half of the nineteenth century.[15]

Among the cities Milan was especially important as an expanding market. From 1834 to 1847, the period for which regular statistics are available, the growth of its population steadily led that of the other parts of Lombardy.[16] The Province of Milan in which the metropolis was located accounted for one-third of the total increase in the population of all Lombardy between 1814 and 1840, although it occupied only one-eleventh of the total area and at the Restoration contained only one-fifth of the population.[17] There are intimations that the consumers' market created by the metropolis was growing not only in size but in capacity, thanks to an increasing circulation of wealth. The rough estimates of the amount of capital employed in Milan returned each year by the president of the Chamber of Commerce show an increase of twenty-five per cent between 1836 and 1838, a gain that was maintained except for a slight reduction of the level, attributed to disturbances in

---

[11] Jacini, p. 38.

[12] *Annali,* 1832, XXXI, 85; 1847, XCII, 92. The figure for 1846 does not include the military. See Sandonà, pp. 88–89. The number of soldiers in Lombardy in 1831 was 40,917, in 1846 32,216, according to the *Tafeln zur Statistik der österreichischen Monarchie,* 1831, Tafel 2; 1846, Pt. I, Tafel 2. In this source the civilian population for 1831 is given as 2,380,526.

[13] These ratios and the reasons stated above for the slow growth are taken from a review of Johann Springer, *Statistik des österreichischen Kaiserstaates* (Vienna, 1840), by "Dr. D. . . . ," *Annali,* 1840, LXIV, 48-63.

[14] Jacini, p. 38.

[15] Prussia, 1.46 per cent from 1816 to 1849 (according to the tables of Hoffmann and Dietrich), Russia, more than 1 per cent (according to Tegoborsky), England, 1.11 per cent. Jacini, p. 39.

[16] This statement is based on the statistics of population published annually in the *Annali.* Exception must be made of 1837 when all of Lombardy except Mantua and Pavia lost in population owing to the cholera epidemic.

[17] The gain was distributed as follows:

Milan and Pavia	20	per cent
Cremona and Mantua	13	" "
Valtellina	11.9	" "
Como and Bergamo	11.5	" "
Lodi and Crema	7.7	" "
Brescia	5.5	" "

"La popolazione della Lombarda," MS in M. R. M., Fondo Cattaneo.

the silk trade, between 1842 and 1846, to be followed by a sharp drop
in the crisis of 1847-1848.[18] In 1840 the Chamber referred to "the ever-
increasing luxury" as accounting for an extraordinary activity in the
carriage industry in that year.[19] A higher standard of consumption
was reflected also in the building trades of the city. In 1841 the Chamber
reported a considerable increase in the number of more pretentious
buildings under construction. "The number of such buildings put up in
1840 and the decorations in 'live stone' which are being extended also
to the smaller buildings explains the number of such artisans noted."[20]
A year later Cattaneo wrote: "It is hard to find a single street in Milan
where half or more than half of the houses have not been redecorated
within the last few years."[21]

The demands of the home market were increasing with the growth
of population, especially that of the cities, but the market to whose
expansion Lombard agriculture responded most sharply was the foreign
market for silk. This market had exerted its influence on Lombardy
before the French Revolution and in the Napoleonic era silk was regarded by the Lombards "as the palladium of our riches."[22] But in the
generation following 1814 the demand for silk in England and America
and throughout the European continent increased by leaps and bounds.
At first the chief market for Lombard silk was London. Indeed, immediately after 1814, when commercial relations between Italy and
England were resumed after the collapse of the Continental System,
the London market enjoyed a virtual monopoly of the Italian supply, at
a moment when the mechanization of the industry was reducing the price
of the manufactured product and leading to a rapid increase in its consumption. Through the London market the Italian proprietor was
brought under the influence of the fluctuations and changes due to the
growth of the factory, the unrest of factory labor, the tariff policy of
Great Britain, the expansion of its overseas trade and the competition
of continental as well as Asiatic producers.

In meeting this particular appetite of the new industrial world that
was forming beyond the Alps the Lombard proprietors at first enjoyed
a privileged position. Their silk was not equal in quality to that of

[18] Reports of the President of the Chamber of Commerce on the condition of
private industry in the city, M. C. M., Ragioneria municipale, cartella 4 (1833 ff.).

[19] "Elenco dei principali stabilimenti industriali colla indicazione del personale
impiegato . . .," October 19, 1840, *ibid.*

[20] *Ibid.*, cartella 34, no. 3804, November 7, 1841.

[21] *Politecnico*, 1842, V, 595. For a description of the virtual rebuilding of
Milano in the period, see R. Ciasca, "L'evoluzione economica della Lombardia," in
Cassa di Risparmio della Lombardia, pp. 389-392.

[22] Eugène Tarlé, *Le blocus continental et le royaume d'Italie* (new edition, Paris,
Alcan, 1931), p. 228.

Fossombrone (in the Papal State) or to the best produced in Piedmont; but the exportation of crude silk from Piedmont was forbidden by law,[23] and all that the other states of the peninsula produced could not satisfy the growing hunger of the North for the silks of Italy, which even without improvement, were at first of a finer quality than could be procured elsewhere. In the years immediately after the reëstablishment of peace the Lombard proprietors had merely to set their sails to a fair wind and to concern themselves only with increasing the quantity of their output. But they had embarked on a course on which they were presently to feel the sharp competitions of a Europe far more progressive than they were quite aware. The French producers were increasing their output.[24] Even more serious for Lombardy were the effects of British enterprise. During the Continental Blockade, which threatened the supply of silk from Italy, the English introduced the mulberry and the Italian method of extracting silk into Bengal. The experiment did not bear fruit at once on the London market, and for some years after 1815 the Italians contemplated with complacency their virtual monopoly of the supply of the finer qualities of crude silk. But the Indian supply, brought to London and marketed under preferential conditions by the East India Company, increased and improved steadily, the British manufacturers began to adjust themselves to the use of the cheaper Indian silks, and the Lombards found their snug position endangered.

A sensational incident that occurred at Milan in 1826 shows how the truth was being broken in to them. The firm of Marietti, a Milanese exporting house, published a circular in which it proclaimed the homely truth that the trade in Italian silks was suffering because the Lombard proprietors were holding out for a price which could not be maintained in London against the competition of the silks of Asia. The Governor of Lombardy, probably stirred up by the outraged proprietors, ordered the Milan Chamber of Commerce to investigate the affair. In defence of their action, the Marietti firm declared that: "The competition of Indian silks with ours has now reached such a point that in the past

---

[23] The prohibition was gradually lifted by royal decrees of April 7, 1835, April 9, 1836, and August 12, 1841, after a prolonged agitation, in which the liberal journals of Lombardy assisted. *Annali,* 1836, XLVIII, 89-91; Prato, pp. 264-279; also see below, pp. 168–170.

[24] In 1830 the Chamber of Commerce of Milan reported a momentary suspension of the demand from Lyons—then a market of increasing importance to the prosperity of Lombardy They attributed this in part to political events, in part to the fact that the cocoons produced in France were now more abundant than the Italian. M. C. M. Camera di Commercio, cartella 564, September 17, 1830. The French harvest of cocoons more than doubled between 1823 and 1830. Frederick B. Artz, *France under the Bourbon Restoration* (Cambridge, 1931), p. 206.

year the Marietti firm itself found a considerable profit in drawing from London Bengal silks, which, worked up here, are being sold to Italian consumers in spite of being overloaded with so many transportation charges." In their report to the Governor, the merchants of the Chamber, while censuring the Marietti firm for indiscretion, admitted the facts and referred to the "fatal competition of Indian silks in the London market."[25] By 1827 the quantity of Indian silks sold at London was double that of the Italian product; moreover they were selling at prices as low as those of the Italian silks and rivaling them even in the finer qualities.[26] The increase of Bengal silk sold in London was accompanied by that of an even more formidable rival, the white silk of China. It was this rival which gave the *coup de grâce* to the Italian trade in England when China was finally opened to British merchants after the Opium War of 1842, and by 1848 silks from the Orient had almost closed the London market to all but the finest grades of silk from Italy.[27]

But if the London market had narrowed and lost its leading position in the commercial economy of Lombardy, the loss had been more than compensated by the growing demand from other quarters, particularly France and Germany, and in 1855 the foreign trade of Lombardy in crude silk and silk yarns shipped to all parts of Europe had increased to about five million pounds a year.[28]

The quantitative increase of the agricultural output of Lombardy in response to these demands is reflected in the reclamation of uncultivated land that was taking place, in the considerable augmentation of the gross yield of the soil, and in the phenomenal extension of silk culture.

Reclamation was encouraged by the official award of medals. The editors of the *Annali* remarked on the occasion of such an award in 1830 that "the progressive breaking up of uncultivated lands in Lombardy is a luminous fact which will have to be pondered by anyone investigating the beneficial effects of the recent economic reorganization of this our country." According to their views agriculture could not progress, while the land was in large part held by privileged bodies.

[25] M. C. M., Camera di Commercia, cartella 564, November, 1826.

[26] *Annali*, 1827, XIII, 87-98. Tables which show the increase of Oriental silks brought to the London market between 1825 and 1847 are to be found in *Annali*, 1833, Bulletino, p. 158; *Politecnico*, 1839, I, 98; *Annali*, 1846, LXXXVIII, 62; M. C. M. Report on export duty on crude silk, Camera di Commercio, cartella 173, 1847. For a full report, supplied by Czoernig, on the competition of oriental with Italian silks on the London market, see Bowring, *Statistics*, p. 106.

[27] See below, p. 60.

[28] G. Frattini, *Storia e statistica delle industrie manifatturiere in Lombardia* (Milano, 1856), p. 55. For the development of the market for Lombard silk, see below, pp. 59-60.

Private property and free competition, they affirmed with a somewhat doctrinaire note of assurance, will make all the "squalid" wastes disappear.[29] Contemporary writers also saw in the progress of rural manufactures, increasing the means of the peasant who turned to it a part of his own and his family's time, an impulse that was extending cultivation. Cattaneo, describing the cottage-industry in the cotton-manufacturing district of Milan in 1839, said: "The riches produced by a manufacture which provides clothing for almost all of the agricultural population of Lombardy-Venetia have in a few years brought under cultivation some thousands of waste fields and will end with conquering the thankless nature of the soil."[30] Spreafico remarked in regard to agriculture in the Brianza that the sale of monastic and communal lands had increased the number of proprietors. This "still goes on increasing through the influence of commerce and industry, which are raising from poverty an ever-increasing number of persons."[31]

As to the distribution of the process of reclamation among the three zones of agriculture, it is safe to assume that in the Mountains it had been carried as far as the assiduity of the peasant-proprietor could push it. Of the strip of territory along the lower edge of the Hill zone, that now traversed by the railway from Milan to Venice, Cattaneo said that in 1836 it was "not easy to measure a hundred paces of woods or waste" on it.[32] With regard to the Plain, we owe to Cattaneo again the calculation that towards the middle of the century in the rich dairy-province of Lodi and Crema 27.9 per cent of the land lay uncultivated or uncultivable.[33] According to the figures used by Jacini the irrigated area in the Plain was pushed from 420,000 to 427,200 hectares between 1844 and 1855.[34] Part of the land turned to cultivation consisted of land that had formerly belonged to the communes and was gradually

---

[29] The occasion for this observation was the award of gold medals to the Duke Carlo Visconti Modrone for reclaiming a territory of 500 *pertiche* on the Ticino river in the district of Soma, and to Luigi Arrigoni for redeeming a tract at Busnate, and of silver medals to Dr. Domenico Fumagalli and Pompeo Acerbi. *Annali,* 1830, XXVI, 93. In 1833 the *Annali* highly praised the proprietors of Valcuvia (Como), near Lake Maggiore, who had formed an association to put into effect a scheme of irrigation, draining the marsh of Careggio by means of a canal and irrigating an area of 2170.8 *pertiche,* besides reclaiming 300.86 *pertiche* from submersion. *Annali,* 1833, Bulletino, pp. 193-196. For the progress of reclamation on the initiative of individual farmers, see also Jacini, p. 220.

[30] Cattaneo, "Sulla densità della popolazione in Lombardia e sulla sua relazione alle opere pubbliche," *Politecnico,* 1839, I, 38.

[31] Spreafico, p. 141.

[32] *Annali,* 1836, XLVIII, 291.

[33] Ms notes in the hand of Cattaneo, M. R. M., Fondo Cattaneo, plico XIII, cartella 118, No. 14.

[34] The figure for 1844 is taken from Lombardini. Jacini, pp. 230-231.

being alienated, part of unreclaimed marsh or wilderness which was being redeemed by private enterprise. In 1849 Cesare Correnti estimated the area of waste land, exclusive of the commons, that had been plowed or planted with forest since the middle of the eighteenth century at 42,000 *pertiche censuarie* (roughly 16,000 acres),[35] and the area of swampy land reduced to rice fields at 46,000 *pertiche*—in round numbers 17,500 acres. In the same interval 95,000 *pertiche* or 35,854 acres of plowed land had been turned into meadows, but Correnti calculated that an equal extent of sterile land had been plowed under, so that the area of plowed land remained constant for a century. If the area of unreclaimed land plowed under or turned into rice fields was indeed 183,000 *pertiche* or 72,966 acres (Correnti's estimate), it would amount to about .01 per cent of the total area "subjected to ordinary cultivation," which was 17,300,000 *pertiche milanesi* in 1855.[36]

There can be no doubt that measured in terms of product Lombard agriculture made very considerable progress between the Restoration and 1848. Liberal publicists complained of inertia, ignorance, and deficient enterprise, but it was the comparison with more progressive countries than Italy that made them sharp in criticism, and their impatience was that of the optimist. None of them speaks of stagnation or a retreat. Spreafico complained in 1841 that the soil of Lombardy "remains far from giving the abundance of products that among the lights of today one might expect of it," and blamed this backwardness on the avarice of the proprietors, but only after having recorded the relative prosperity that silk-culture had brought to peasant and proprietor alike in the Brianza.[37] In 1844 Correnti remarked a general improvement of agriculture in the Province of Bergamo. In 1814 the province had imported large quantities of wheat; in 1844 the importation had very much diminished and instead the importation of maize, rice, and wine was increasing, "sign of greater prosperity among the humble folk who had abandoned the use of millet and black grain."[38] In general, contemporary observers assumed without argument an increasing prosperity, "with the diffusion of instruction, with the opening or roads and markets," in short, with "the changed conditions of the century, which had so greatly increased the revenue of the land."[39] As for the gross yield, we have the

[35] That is, of the *pertica* used in the cadastral survey of the eighteenth century, probably the *pertica milanese*. 18 *pertiche milanesi* equalled 10 *pertiche italiane*.

[36] Jacini, p. 54. Correnti's estimates are in *Pronipote del Vesta-Verde*, 1849, pp. 99 ff.

[37] Spreafico, p. 157.

[38] Correnti, in *Annali,* 1844, LXXXII, 147.

[39] Ravizza, pp. 81, 165.

weighty testimony of Jacini that it had increased much faster than the population and might be held to have been considerably more than doubled in the first half of the nineteenth century.[40]

Forage crops and the mulberry were the two kinds of planting that were being extended most rapidly, and the output of cheese and silk increased at a rate which, in the case of silk, impressed contemporaries as little short of phenomenal.

The growing demand for dairy products is reflected in the tendency that manifested itself to convert irrigated plow-land into meadows.[41] In 1834 it was estimated that in the past eighty years the quantity of Parmesan cheese produced in Lombardy had more than tripled.[42] In 1844 the production of Parmesan amounted to 14,000 tons, "one-half of which was marketed in Lombardy-Venetia, and the other half exported."[43] The animals that produced it yielded also five thousand tons of butter, part of which was shipped as far as Venice and Genoa—an output valued at 900,000 francs.[44] In the same year, 1844, Cattaneo noted that *stracchino,* the soft cheese made at Gorgonzola, north of Milan, was beginning to be shipped out of the country. The clotted milk was brought from Lodi and Pavia over distances up to twenty-five miles. Cattaneo pointed out that the development of this manufacture gave the farmers of the Plain a direct interest in the promotion of railroads inasmuch as rapid transit would double the value of the industry.[45]

But the primary product of Lombardy that showed the most impressive increase in quantity was silk. In the absence of reliable statistics no exact measure of this can be given but the evidence available leaves no doubt of the fact that it was considerable. As early as 1826 a group of Milanese merchants asserted that "the supply [of silk] among us has been doubled in the last twenty years."[46] Ten years later Cattaneo estimated that production was increasing at the rate of eight per cent a year, while the value of silk had increased within a short time more than a hundred per cent, "so that we ourselves are astonished at it, and almost

---

[40] Jacini, p. 42.
[41] Correnti estimated that since the middle of the eighteenth century 95,000 *pertiche* had thus been converted. *Pronipote del Vesta-Verde,* 1849, p. 99.
[42] Increasing from 16,000 to more than 50,000 "forms." *Annali,* 1834, XXXIX, 86. None of the so-called *cacio parmigiano* of commerce was made in Parma.
[43] Note in the hand of Cattaneo, M. R. M., Fondo Cattaneo, cartella 127.8. In 1836 Cattaneo valued the export of cheese from the district centering in Lodi and the Adda at from 18,000,000 to 20,000,000 francs "Ricerche sul progetto di una strada di ferro da Milano a Venezia," *Annali,* 1836, XLVIII, 297.
[44] M. R. M., Fondo Cattaneo, cartella 127.8.
[45] MS notes in M R. M., Fondo Cattaneo, plico 21, cartella 127, 1844.
[46] Report on the circular of Marietti and Company by a committee of the Milan Chamber of Commerce, M. C. M., Camera di Commercio, cartella 564.

frightened."[47] According to one estimate the total output of Lombardy and Venetia increased from 1,860,000 pounds (Milanese pounds of about 12 ounces) in 1800 to 2,900,000 pounds in 1815, and then mounted steadily to 4,710,000 pounds in 1841.[48] In 1848 the Chamber of Commerce of Milan, in a report to the Government, referred to "the marvelous increase of the silk crop, which from 1827 to 1848 has almost tripled the output of crude silk and promises still further increases."[49] The promise was fulfilled. In 1853 the total product of Lombardy-Venetia consumed at home and abroad was estimated at 5,789,485 pounds; that of Lombardy alone at 4,000,000, worth in round numbers, 91,500,000 Austrian lire.[50] In 1855 Frattini affirmed that owing to the improvement of the European market, especially of that for silk, "the value of farms was almost immediately doubled and the territorial wealth [of Lombardy] increased by almost one hundred per cent."[51] In 1859, according to Professor Ciasca, Lombardy-Venetia was producing more crude silk than all France.[52]

The part of Lombardy that produced most of the silk was the Hill zone. Cattaneo said in 1836 that if one wished to trace on a map the region of Lombardy most given to sericulture "it would be necessary to draw a line from Brescia through Bergamo, the Brianza, and Como, towards Lake Maggiore."[53] This was the belt in which the culture of the silkworm had been concentrated in the Napoleonic era.[54] But from 1814 to 1848 it was not only intensified in this zone but was extended into the Plain.[55] For example, the weight of silk cocoons produced in the Milanese more than doubled between 1814 and 1841.[56] That of the cocoons produced in the Province of Cremona more than tripled between 1815 and 1835 while its market value increased more than six-

---

[47] "Ricerche sul progetto," *op. cit.*, p. 296.

[48] Statistics from the *Gazzetta di Venezia* reproduced in the *Annali*, 1842, LXXIV, 278-280. Note that the figures include Venetia, but the silk production of Venetia was only about one-third that of Lombardy. The same table gives 3,350,000 pounds for Lombardy and 1,360,000 pounds for Venetia in 1841. The same figures, with the additional estimate of 3,840,000 lbs. as the output of Lombardy in 1820, are given by Mittermaier, p. 61.

[49] M. C. M, Camera di Commercio, cartella 564.

[50] Frattini, pp. 54-56.

[51] *Ibid.*, p. 48.

[52] Ciasca, *Programma*, p. 370.

[53] *Annali*, 1836, XLVIII, 296.

[54] Tarlé, p. 71.

[55] "The cultivation of the mulberry is being extended even in the region of Lodi and in some parts of Pavia and Lower Milan where the *marcite* and rice fields do not prevent it." Jacini, p. 239.

[56] Adriano Balbi, *L'Austria e le primarie potenze: saggi di statistica comparativa, raccolti e ordinati da Eugenio Balbi* (Milan, 1846), p. lix.

fold.[57] Such facts lay behind the local proverb: "The shadow of the mulberry is the shadow of gold." A native economist declared in 1855 that, as a consequence of the extension of this golden shadow, Lombardy "with the exception of the high mountain summits has almost totally changed in aspect."[58]

The social as well as the economic effects of the rapid development of this great money crop were to be felt throughout the Lombard community. Even in the Plain when mulberry plantations were extended into that region, it was the landlords who took the initiative in extending the culture and improving the product, and who sold the crop,[59] and one effect of the expansion and flourishing prosperity of the trade in silk was to stimulate the interest of the proprietary class in their estates. The proprietors of the Brianza were described in 1844 as having "succeeded with words and example and with assiduous diligence in conquering the prejudices and correcting the rude habits of the peasant, and the art [of silk culture] has been renovated in a few years on the best principles."[60] The proprietors of Lombardy became noted for the personal attention they gave to the culture of the silkworm. The *Gazzetta di Venezia* declared in 1836 that the Venetian silk-growers of Treviso had much to learn from the example of their Lombard confrères. "In Lombardy in the months of May and June the well-to-do repair to their fields and there, if not continuously, at least by frequent visits, oversee the peasants in the rearing of the silkworms and stand at the side of the silkworm tenders to observe the most minute details, in order to find a remedy if some part of the worms does not prosper, being informed of all the good published methods and of the practices recognized as the best"; and they made it an object of ambition to be able to boast of economies and good returns.[61] The proprietors set up on their estates those reeling mills (*filande*), whose smokestacks may still be seen, rivaling each other in height like slim feudal towers, above the low tile roofs of the provincial towns. In disposing of the reeled silk to merchant exporters of Milan or Bergamo, the proprietor was brought into indirect touch with the foreign market. When he erected a reeling mill he became to some extent an industrialist.

Carlo Ravizza supplies a contemporary picture of a resident proprietor of the Brianza who had become a silk producer and set up a silk mill on his estate:

[57] *Annali*, 1836, XLVIII, 74.
[58] Frattini, p. 58.
[59] For the application of the crop-sharing contract to the mulberry plantations of the Plain, see Jacini, p. 262.
[60] Spreafico, pp. 149–150.
[61] Quoted in *Annali*, 1836, XLVIII, 74.

I often went to that house, where one found two gazettes, some commercial journals and the few books which came out from time to time on the enterprises and products of our industry. One saw at once that this was a rural family tied to the great movement of society. It pleased me to see in the halls, in the courtyard, under the porticoes, that activity which results from the happy interweaving of agriculture with the industry which in a few years has doubled the value of our land. The head of the house, a handsome man of forty years, tall, strong, bronzed by the sun of the Brianza, administered his estate which was rented in small portions to as many crop-sharing families, and at the same time directed a great silk-winding mill, and kept the accounts and carried on the correspondence. He was eager for all the political and commercial news, and one could always tell from the expression of his face whether the news was good or bad. . . . I liked to stop in one of those halls on the ground floor where they put the silk in order to send it to Milan. Some experimented to determine the grade or fineness of the floss, wrapping it a hundred times on the testing instrument which is called the *provino*, and making a skein of it, put it on the bobbin (*cavigliatoio*) to double it, twist it, and by means of a little metal tube, make an elegant skein of it; others make a fine compact mass of all these tightly packed skeins, neatly arranging them one upon the other in a little basket and then tying them in the middle; still others baled up the packages and fitted them into boxes to be loaded and shipped: a varied business, vast but tranquil, in those happy chambers, whence the glance wandered through the open windows to a little village on the back of the mountain opposite, in the midst of a great silence broken only by the not distant mill, which made itself heard with a roar not unlike that of a great waterfall.[62]

The expansion of the trade in silk affected directly or indirectly the interests of the whole economic community, whether proprietors, merchants, industrialists, bankers, peasants or publicists; and the proprietors, who had drifted so easily into the profitable current of the silk-trade began to be hammered by the merchants and publicists alike to bestir themselves and take a more intelligent interest in their business. The merchants, thoroughly alarmed, demanded lower prices to enable them to meet competition from abroad. The firm of Marietti in the circular just cited declared that the proprietors would either have to accept lower prices or face the prospect of limiting or abandoning the industry.

Individual calculation may sometimes suggest drawing gain from the elevation of prices whether of raw materials or of manufactures; but national and public calculation counsels multiplying the gain in

[62] Ravizza, pp. 245–246.

proportion to the quantity of the output marketed instead of seeking it from an excessive price. The first is easier, but can be acquired only at the cost of a future loss of all profit. The other is perennial, and besides, communicating itself at large, gives an electric impulse to the whole active population and preserves the industrial and commercial character of the nation. . . . One often sees among the most sensible people that obstinacy that children manifest.[63]

The liberal publicists of Lombardy adopted the point of view and expanded the argument of the merchants. The journals, notably the *Annali universali di statistica* in a persistent campaign directed by Giandomenico Romagnosi and later by Carlo Cattaneo, sought on the one hand reforms in the local commercial and banking organization which would liberate the Italians from the London monopoly[63a] and place their trade on the basis of wider markets, and on the other hand called on the proprietors to seek their profit in lower prices and the improvement of their output. The warning which the *Annali* sounded in 1826, the year in which the Marietti circular was fluttering the Lombard dovecotes, will serve as an example. The silks of Bengal, the editors admitted, might not be as brilliant as the Italian; "but not for this should the Italians remain with their hands in their pockets, persuaded that they possess the preference forever and everywhere; therefore we pray them with warmth to employ every study to be making the quality always better."[64] Carlo Cattaneo above all the rest, although he was optimistic about the commercial prospects of the Lombard silk industry, never wearied of using his vigorous pen to urge improvements in the technique of sericulture and the silk industry. The Agronomical and Technological Section of the Congresses of Italian Scientists took up the cause, and its Commission on Sericulture reported to the ninth annual session at Venice in 1847 the urgent need of improvement, especially in the quality of the cocoons, "this being the defect for which in general our silks are not held in esteem nor stand the competition of French silks. I have the honor to report that it is held that Italy is the most advanced of all the nations in all that concerns the art of winding silk; and that she only has need to extend, or better say to render more popular and common, the improvements that have been introduced, which are still confined to a very few."[65]

With the propaganda for a more expert sericulture went a continuous demand of the journals for a more scientific technique in all branches

---

[63] M. C. M., Camera di Commercio, cartella 564, November, 1826.
[63a] See below, pp. 168-170.
[64] "The Editors," *Annali*, 1826, VII, 240, note 1.
[65] *Annali*, 1847, XCIV, 257.

of agriculture, for agricultural schools, for improved implements, finally for an agrarian association. It is an interesting commentary on the state of mind of the Lombard proprietors that they formed no such institutions as the Georgofili of Florence or the fruitful Agrarian Association founded by Balbo, Cavour and their associates in Piedmont.[66] But if the results of the agitation for improvements fell short of its mark, it is still a fact of the greatest importance that the proprietary class of Lombardy were drawn by their interest in silk into a position that put them at the very center of its economic life, and that in that position they were exposed to a constant fire both from the merchants and the enlightened journalists striving to wake them up to the conditions and exigencies of a changing world.

A change of spirit in the agricultural system of Lombardy during the first half of the nineteenth century is reflected in certain changes that took place in the forms of tenure and exploitation and in the social life of the community.

There was a steady increase in the number of proprietors, which was accompanied by an increase in the number of small holdings, at least in certain regions. Jacini estimated that between 1838 and 1850 the number of proprietors increased by 11.54 per cent, while the population was increasing by only 10.20 per cent.[67] On the other hand he noted a tendency to the concentration of landed property in the Provinces of Milan, Lodi and Crema, and Pavia, all in the Plain, the region of highly capitalized farming.[68] "We believe," he wrote, "that we can assert that in the Cremasco the system of vast cultivation tends constantly to extend itself, to the advantage of good agriculture."[69] In the Hill zone he found an equilibrium in the number of proprietors in the Provinces of Bergamo and Mantua and an increase in Brescia and Como. In Sondrio, in the Mountain zone, there was an extreme increase.[70]

An impulse had been given to the multiplication of proprietors by the final suppression of feudal rights and the sale of the lands of the

---

[66] In 1844 the Commission on Agriculture in the Upper and Lower Milanese, reporting to the Agronomical and Technological Section of the Milan Congress of Scientists, expressed itself strongly in favor of an Agrarian Institute for Lombardy. *Annali*, 1844, LXXXI, 329-338. There was a movement for such an association in the Society for the Encouragement of the Arts and Crafts in Milan. Salvatore Pugliese, "Iniziative per promuovere l'attività economica in Lombardia nella prima metà del Secolo XIX," in *La Cassa di Risparmio delle Provincie Lombarde nella evoluzione economica della regione* (Milano, 1923), p. 434.

[67] Jacini, p. 96. According to his calculation there was one landed proprietor to every eight inhabitants.

[68] *Ibid.*, p. 98.

[69] *Ibid.*, p. 281.

[70] *Ibid.*, p. 98.

monastic corporations, the Church and the communes which had taken place during the French occupation of Lombardy.[71] In the Brianza, between 1760 and 1837, the number of proprietors increased by more than twenty per cent.[72] The number went on increasing—a tendency which a contemporary observer attributed to "the influence of commerce and industry, which are raising from poverty an ever increasing number of persons."[73] In the journals and the other economic literature of the period the process of division was a generally accepted fact. Ravizza's statement of it is representative: "the middle classes grow richer every day and on the other hand the law and time work continually to divide and diminish the ancient privileged patrimonies."[74] The following quotation reflects the outlook of the liberal patriot and idealist on the changes that followed the completion of the cadastral survey, the redemption of the *regalie*, and the liberation of feudal and communal lands —in short, the legal changes affecting tenure that took place in Lombardy in the second half of the eighteenth century:

> Unexpected events, giving land and capital to the most daring and adventurous, created a middle class which rose full of activities and hopes. Feudal oppressions disappeared, together with many of the powerful families reduced to a single heir. . . . In place of the unlimited estates of a few great lords, for whom profusion and idleness was a domestic tradition and surrounding themselves with the idle and keeping a retinue of dogs and servants a daily pomp, appeared many smiling farms watched over and enriched by modest and intelligent proprietors who had the habit of industry and thrift. Within the hateful precinct of the nobleman's parks, on the latifundia cultivated by servants who had never seen their master and to whom, however assiduous their work, was never given the hope of possession, in wilderness swamps, on wooded tracts laid waste by improvident communes, settled a thousand families who draw subsistence and comfort from the

[71] The process had been arrested under Napoleon. In 1803 Melzi, as Vice-President of the Italian Republic, decreed "the restoration to ex-feudal proprietors of allodial property occupied by the State where still in its possession; as also that occupied by the municipalities." *Bolletino delle leggi della Repubblica Italiana*, 1803, No. 67, quoted by Antonio Coppi, "Discorso sulle servitù e sulla libera proprietà dei fondi in Italia," *Annali*, 1841, LXVII, 306-307. But this property remained subject to common law. At the Restoration in 1814 there were only two surviving impediments to the negotiability of land. One was the *contratto a livello*, which imposed the payment of a quitrent in perpetuity; the other a group of seventy fiefs, conferring feudal privileges over a few estates and a number of hydraulic and fishing rights. These were protected by a special Feudal Court. They still survived in 1855 but were of little importance. Jacini, pp. 99–100.

[72] From 5,833 to 7,480.

[73] Spreafico, p. 141.

[74] Ravizza, p. 89.

surrounding land, care for every forgotten scrap of it and study its every hidden prerogative; who every year increase their small incomes and thereby the national revenue, who love the countryside in which they were born and in which they enjoy the dignity of proprietorship. . . . Well-to-do merchants, tired of risky enterprises and desirous of repose in the possession of property, entered the uninhabited and ruinous palaces, restored the villas to brilliancy and elegance, where, having put aside the surly seriousness of the counting house, they appear well-bred and courteous; they multiplied precious plantings on the sterile slopes and infrequent level spaces; they stimulated the hidden energy of the soil with huge expenditures; they substituted houses that are comfortable and sometimes elegant for the unhealthful huts of the tenants; they erected great edifices for the culture of silkworms and for drawing the silk; collected the dispersed or stagnant waters to set going factories or improve irrigation; distributed the land more equitably among the families of cultivators, and gave them new animation by more careful and evident management.

On this soil [of ours] was thus established an agriculture which was marvelously allied with manufacturing industry, and the one was the root of the other, and this a cause of increment to that, and the silk-merchants risen in every village increased exceedingly the number of small local proprietors, and the capitalistic manufacturers and merchants loved more and adorned this country, which was for them the fount of such unexpected riches. . . .

When roads were opened even to the smallest communes, whoever had a little wealth wished to have a house in the country. . . . The patrician landlords seeing that the ancestral fortune was progressively diminishing among the sons, and finding themselves face to face with classes newly arisen but rich and instructed, not only pay greater heed to their own education and that of their sons, but during their prolonged sojourns in the country, watching over their extensive farms, and studying their better production, procure for themselves, along with an increase of wealth, the noblest and dearest occupation.[75]

A moment's reflection will suggest that in this happy picture the changes that we know to have taken place are heightened and idealized, but it serves to indicate what hopes of a beneficent revolution those changes could inspire in the mind of a patriotic observer.

It is interesting to note in passing that land of the communes was being partitioned in Lombardy at about the same time that the commons were being enclosed in England, but with very different consequences. In Lombardy the process resulted in increasing the number of

---

[75] Ravizza, pp. 275–278. The author represents the peasants themselves as buying up and reclaiming waste land.

small estates instead of large ones; and as it was not being promoted by any such fierce pressure from a profit-seeking agriculture, it was not being pushed with anything like the same ruthlessness. Some of the common lands still existed towards the middle of the century. The commune in the Brianza in which Ravizza's good curate resided

> possessed wastes and woods, but could not draw income from them. They had never been able to obey the law which orders the communes to sell or rent their lands because the prejudice was too strong that the heather on the wastes is the dowry of agriculture and that the poor cannot live without going to get wood on the common. The efforts of the good curate triumphed. An intelligent proprietor took these lands on a lease: agriculture thus acquired a vast territory on which several families were lodged; the commune saw its revenue unexpectedly increase.[76]

Jacini thought that the question of communal land was the most important of all in a description of Lombard agriculture. Strongly in favor of its alienation to private owners, he affirmed that while the process was still lagging in 1855, progress by that time was notable.[77]

In the Hill zone the rent of land was increasing—a tendency generally attributed to the prosperity of the silk industry, in which the peasant seemed to be sharing.[78] With it went the disintegration of the patriarchal *massarie* and the extension of the grain-rent described above. Both of these were changes that signified at once a further liberation of the share tenant as a contractual agent and a sharper emphasis on the purely economic relation between landlord and tenant. In short, the system in the Hill zone was showing signs of an infiltration of commercial influence and of the idea of farming for the market. Furthermore, the peasant of the Hills sometimes found his hut being rebuilt, enlarged, and ventilated, thanks not to the interest of the landlord in the welfare of the tenant but to his solicitude in surrounding the silkworm

---

[76] Ravizza, p. 122. The law referred to was the Sovereign Resolution of April 16, 1839. The alienation of uncultivated commons was mandatory; that of cultivated land optional according to the needs of the respective communes. Jacini, pp. 137–138.

[77] *Ibid.*, pp. 137–141.

[78] Spreafico, pp. 156–157. "Many causes," according to this author, "conspired to better the fate of the peasant, but among them are especially to be mentioned the numerous and costly plantations of mulberries and the improvement introduced in the nurture of silkworms, which besides increasing the revenue with their precious product, had an indirect influence on every branch of agricultural industry." A. Sega wrote to the same effect in the *Rivista europea*, 1840, III, Pt. 1, 252. For the *Rivista europea*, see below, pp. 160ff.

with conditions favorable to its well-being.[79] To the great outflowing stream of silk, a stream of gold, can be traced the economic source of most of the changes that were taking place in Lombard agriculture.

It must be added that with the change in the economic atmosphere in which the Lombard proprietor lived went a change in the spirit of a section of the younger Milanese nobility which in a sense anticipated it. The change was noticed immediately after the Restoration. The Napoleonic régime launched the younger nobles into a more active life and under the Restoration they suffered from a sense of suffocation. Lady Morgan found them interesting themselves in their country places after the English fashion. "They are now agriculturists, manufacturers, speculators, and spread their vast capital (formerly hoarded in chests) over the whole country. . . . We have it on the testimony of the noblest of them, that they have considerably increased their revenues by this abjuration of aristocratic prejudices."[80] All students of the Risorgimento are familiar with this group which centered in the Counts Porro-Lambertenghi and Federico Confalonieri. They travelled in France and England, where they made it a business to familiarize themselves with "the progress of the century." This they saw in terms of practical enterprises for the public good. They sought to introduce into their country illumination by gas, the use of Tyne coal, steam navigation on the Po, an Athenaeum for Milan, schools for the poor.[81] They also experimented with improvements in agriculture, particularly in the production of silk. Count Porro set up a plant for the extraction of silk by the Gensoul method of heating the cocoons with steam. Count Dandolo, another of these liberal and enlightened proprietors, already known for his successful experiment with the introduction of merino sheep from Spain,[82] published tracts on the improvement of vines and the culture of the silkworm and introduced the use of steam in unwinding the cocoons—an innovation that qualified him in the eyes of a later observer as "a man destined by Providence to put Italian silk in competition with those of Asia in the market of Europe and America."[83]

---

[79] Spreafico, p. 167. Frattini wrote in 1855 that, thanks to the high price of raw silk on the European market, and the extension of silk culture, "the tumble-down houses of the peasants had been changed in large part into comfortable and well-ventilated habitations because of the culture of the silkworm"; indeed, that excepting the Mountains and the Plain, the aspect of Lombardy had been almost entirely changed in the past thirty years. Frattini, p. 59. See also Jacini, p. 223.

[80] Lady Sydney Morgan, *Italy*, I, 190–191.

[81] See below, pp. 199–202.

[82] Tarlé, p. 292.

[83] Francesco Lencisa, "Sopra l'industria della seta," *Annali*, 1831, XXIX, 135. Dandolo's writings on viticulture and sericulture were praised by "G. P[ecchio]" in the *Conciliatore*, November 22, 1819, No. 24, p. 96.

In view of all these circumstances it cannot be said that the complexion of agrarian life in Lombardy underwent a revolution between 1814 and the middle of the century. Indeed even today it is broadly the same as it had then become. Today, however, it moves with a far livelier rhythm, in harmony with a new commercial and industrial order. In the first half of the nineteenth century a movement in that direction had begun and was in process of acceleration. The statistics on which one must depend do not permit an exactly measured description of it but the evidence leaves no doubt that it took place. It was sufficiently impressive to inspire observant contemporaries with the hope of a new order of things for the country and for Italy. Taken in connection with the progress of trade and manufactures and the economic movement in the rest of Europe, the changes for the better in Lombard agricultural industry seemed to the liberals to have opened a bright panorama of prosperity and better living. The changes that impressed them most were the multiplication of estates, the progress of reclamation, the increasing production of cheese and silk for the export trade, the increasing interest of the proprietors in the business of farming—all attended by a steadily increasing prosperity of agriculture. The key to this progress was silk. It not only multiplied riches but it made the proprietors businessmen. It multiplied their relations with the outside world, particularly with England and France, and gave them a direct and personal interest in the changes that were affecting those countries as markets for their product—an interest which the liberals vigorously plied to excite them to a participation in scientific knowledge and public life.

A considerable section of the wealthier aristocracy preserved a Castilian aloofness. They were the group among whom the *Austriacanti* —the lovers of Austria—were to be found. But an equally important section of the nobles, especially those of the generation that came of age about 1830, threw themselves into the liberal thought of their time, and supported the leaders of the business and professional community in an agitation for changes that would give Lombardy, and Italy, its proper place in the new civilization that was developing elsewhere in Europe. Their commercial affiliations conspired with their cultural traditions to swing them into the orbit of the progressive West. With the disappearance of their fear of innovations there remained nothing but the armed power of Austria to prevent them from seeking the political as well as the economic emancipation of their country.

CHAPTER III

COMMERCE

AGRICULTURE overshadowed all other forms of economic activity in Lombardy during the first half of the nineteenth century. It created the conservative atmosphere which the whole economic community breathed; it was the chief source of wealth; and it employed most of the available resources of capital. Stefano Jacini estimated that the total sum invested in agriculture was more than six times that invested in commerce and industry combined.[1] Commerce was subordinate to agriculture, but it was through the interests of Lombardy as a trading community, particularly its interest in the transit trade and in marketing silk, that it was directly affected by the economic revolution that was taking place outside of Italy—a revolution as much commercial as industrial, which seemed to offer the peoples on its periphery a fatal choice between Reaction and Progress. Canals and hard roads, the steamship and the railroad, were re-shaping the whole framework of markets, both domestic and foreign, and steam was ushering in a new epoch in the commercial relations of Europe with the Orient and with North and South America. What was the position and outlook of the class in Lombardy immediately and practically concerned with these changes?

Unfortunately, some of the most elementary characteristics of the local trading organization are wrapped in the obscurity in which the historian is often left groping by the contemporary assumption that what is familiar needs no description. But some inferences can be made as to the rôle which commerce played in the economic life of the community, and it is at least possible to state the problems that were agitating the Lombard merchants and the patriotic publicists who championed their interests, and from the contemporary discussion of these problems by the merchants themselves to learn something of their outlook on the revolution that was taking place in European commerce.

The primary task of Lombard commerce was to move the products of local agriculture. This produced certain crops not entirely consumed on the spot—grain and cattle in the Mountains; citrous fruits, wine, the cocoons of the silkworm, and some grain in the Hills; dairy products, grain, and some silk on the Plain.

[1] Agriculture, including mortgages: 2,424,000,000 Austrian lire; commerce and industry (less wages): 381,069,880 Austrian lire. Jacini, table opposite p. 115.

As a consumers' market the agricultural population of Lombardy was not constituted to produce active trading. Its masses were peasants whose standard of living was low and who provided themselves with almost all of their own requirements. The commodities that the peasant of the Hill country bought were salt, rice, flour-paste and bacon; all the rest were the fruit of his fields.[2] He was often his own blacksmith, cooper, shoemaker and tailor, and the family spun and wove its own clothing. If it sought the services of the village shoemaker or tailor, it was likely to pay him in grain or other products of the farm, and the peasant paid in produce even for the wretched goods of the wandering pedlars, who for a handkerchief might get a quart of grain.[3] The only requirements of the share-tenant's cottage that might send him to market were such indispensables as copper kettles, domestic utensils and farm implements. Carlo Ravizza's good curate of the Brianza "had seen too much how badly money was used by the poor people who are accustomed to see it seldom."[4] On the Plain the wants of the farmhands were even simpler. The women wove linen in winter. Wages were paid for the most part in the products of the farm and among the wage-workers very little money changed hands.[5] "The cultivators of the fields like to make their purchases in kind rather than in money, and so, for example, pay the dairyman a determinate part of the grain which they have milled." In the linen country, "that product serves as an object of exchange with the traders in stuffs, who in this manner obtain large profits."[6]

None of the nine provinces of Lombardy was self-sufficing or self-contained in its agricultural economy. The provinces of the Plain, where the population was relatively sparse, produced a surplus of wheat, maize, and rice; nevertheless they imported some from other provinces. Pavia differed from the rest of the provinces in the Plain in producing less wheat than it consumed, because of its concentration on rice and dairy-farming; and in the triennium 1825-1827 Mantua harvested less wheat than its inhabitants required. The provinces of the Hills, Como, Brescia, Bergamo, and Milan, although the last three named had a section in the Plain, were dependent on the others to make up a deficit in their production of cereals, owing no doubt to the hungry maw of their numerous towns and cities. On the other hand, the northern provinces, led by the Alpine province of Sondrio, raised livestock in excess of their needs

---

[2] Spreafico, p. 166.
[3] *Annali*, 1847, XCIV, 82.
[4] Ravizza, p. 78.
[5] Cattaneo, MS notes in M. R. M., Fondo Cattaneo, cartella 127, plico 21.
[6] Jacini, p. 285.

ˋ supply the consistent deficiency of the lower provinces in
and hogs. Nevertheless all of the southern provinces sent
to interprovincial markets—probably within the zone of
...ı which they were located.[7] In general there was an inter-
...ange of cereals and livestock between the northern and southern zones
of agriculture and some lateral movement across provincial lines.[8] The
domestic trade in these commodities greatly exceeded the trade in them
with foreign countries. For example the quantity of wheat imported by
the provinces from each other in 1822-1824 was more than twenty times
the amount they drew from abroad; and the quantity that they sent to
each other more than three times the amount that they exported to other
countries.[9] The cities great and small, led by Milan, drew to themselves
the main lines of movement in comestibles.[10] In addition to agricultural
products local manufactures, particularly low grades of cotton, silk and
woolen textiles, were moved from the districts where the several industries were concentrated to the domestic consumers who provided
their chief market. In general, because of the high tariff wall between
Austria and the neighboring states and the competition of German and
Bohemian manufacturers in the transalpine markets within the Monarchy, the internal trade of Lombardy-Venetia was much more con-

[7] The deductions in this paragraph refer to the six years between 1822–1827
and are derived from a statistical comparison of the two triennial periods 1822–
1824 and 1825–1827 contained in a series of reports to the Government from the
provincial authorities in A. S. M., Presidenza, Atti segreti, busta 516, cartella 6.
The local importation of cereals in the face of a surplus and the exportation of
cattle in spite of a deficit probably indicate a faulty organization of the market.
When Napoleon remarked with surprise the difference in the price of grain in
different Departments of the Kingdom of Italy, Eugene replied: "There have
never existed and there do not yet exist great commercial relations between one
department of the Realm and the other." Eugene to Napoleon from Rimini,
October 13, 1810, cited by Tarlé, p. 96.

[8] The following figures will give some indication of its volume:

Triennium 1822–1824

	Wheat	Minuti (chiefly maize)
Importation across internal lines	2,354,883	2,716,372 some metriche
Exportation	697,999	1,075,818 some metriche

[9] In "minuti" the provinces imported from each other seventy-seven times as
much as they drew from abroad and shipped to each other four times as much as
to other countries. Report cited above, note 7. The Province of Bergamo in 1835
was importing large quantities of grain, maize, rice, wine and oil. Annali, 1837,
LIV, 315.

[10] In 1841 it was estimated that there was a movement of 20,000 sacks of grain
a week to Milan from Mantua, of 5,000 sacks more from San Benedetto, Piadena,
Bôzzolo and Casal Maggiore, and of 12,400 sacks from Cremona, Brescia, Vérola
Nova, Orzi, Soresina, Castel Leone and Crema. Politecnico, 1841, IV, 439.

siderable than traffic in imports and exports or than commerce in transit.[11]

The dense population of Lombardy overtaxed the capacity of the soil to supply it with foodstuffs. There was a constant and considerable importation of cereals, especially of wheat and maize,[12] and of wine and liquors.[13] Sea-food, citrous fruits, olive and fish oil were brought in from the Mediterranean through Genoa.[14] The dairy farms of the Plain, unable to replenish their herds from the Mountain provinces of Lombardy alone, imported cattle from the pastures of Switzerland. A very important category of consumption goods that had to be brought in from abroad consisted of so-called "colonials"—that is, tea, coffee, drugs, spices, sugar and dyes.[15] Lombardy had to buy from foreign manufacturers most of the finer textiles which its population used, linens from England, silks from Naples, England and France, cottons from England, Switzerland, France, Germany and Austria.[16] On its markets also appeared large quantities of ordinary woolen cloth and a variety of metal goods manufactured in Germany and in the other provinces of the Austrian Monarchy.[17] Local manufacturing industries imported their machine equipment[18] and eventually iron for the construction of

[11] Cattaneo affirmed in 1836 that the proposed railroad between Milan and Venice would have to depend on passengers rather than freight, on short trips rather than long ones, and on internal trade rather than foreign. Foreign and transit traffic would come only with the victories of free trade. Summary of arguments in "Ricerche sul progetto di una strada ferrata da Milano a Venezia," *Annali*, 1836, XLVIII, 304–305. In 1841 the Chamber of Commerce of Milan found the traffic between Lombardy and the neighboring Italian states extremely limited, owing "to the heavy import duties" imposed by these states. M. C. M., Camera di Commercio, cartella 173, November 27, 1841.

[12] In years of dearth some wheat was imported from Russia and Egypt. M. C. M., Camera di Commercio, cartella 172, June 20, 1817.

[13] According to a table translated from "an English sheet" in 1834, wine and liquors were imported to a value of 12,425,000 francs out of a total import balance of 45,550,000 francs. Animals accounted for 8,200,000 francs, "colonial" goods for 5,250,000 francs. *Annali* 1834, XXXIX, 85.

[14] *Annali*, 1836, XLVIII, 298; report of the Chamber of Commerce of Milan to Count Spaur regarding the commerce of Lombardy with Genoa, M. C. M., Camera di Commercio, cartella 173, May 20, 1843. Linseed and olive oil were imported from the Kingdom of the Two Sicilies. *Ibid.*, cartella 172, July 17, 1817.

[15] M. C. M., Camera di Commercio, cartella 173, No. 807, April 26, 1826; *ibid.*, cartella 173, May 20, 1843.

[16] M. C. M., Camera di Commercio, cartella 173, May 20, 1843; *Annali*, 1847, XCI, 154-159. In 1855 most of the local supply of patterned cotton goods was coming from Austria and the states of the Zollverein. Frattini, p. 110.

[17] Reports of the Bergamo and Brescia fairs, *Annali*, 1827, XIII, 334-335; Bulletino, 1833, pp. 323, 497; 1835, XLVI, 163-165.

[18] "Anyone who exercises a mechanical art, or has a spinnery or manufactory active in the province of Milan has to resort to foreign markets at every turn

machinery in the new shops set up late in the period.[19] The Brescian tanneries imported their hides from Trieste,[20] the woolen manufacture its wool from Naples and the Levant, and the growing cotton industry had to import all of its material: raw cotton from Naples and the United States and yarns from England.[21]

In return, Lombardy exported silk, dairy products, rice and some grain; linen thread, low-grade cotton, silk, wool, linen and hemp textiles, wrought iron and firearms, worked leather goods, carriages, paper, books, furniture, and a few miscellaneous items of perfumery, colored tiles, and crystal.[22] It shipped cheese and butter to Parma, the Papal State, Naples and the region of Genoa.[23] Cattaneo estimated that in 1836 the export trade in cheese was worth from eighteen to twenty million francs.[24] With the exception of the trade in cheese and silk, none of these exports gave any signs of particular animation or growth, and some, such as the trade in linen and iron, were declining.[25] The minor products of Lombard industry found their way into Parma, Modena, the Papal State, Piedmont and Naples, amid the grave difficulties raised by the protective tariffs and the transit regulations of these states, and to the fair of Sinigaglia and the ports of Trieste and Genoa.[26] Brescian

---

and provide himself abroad not only with entire machines of every new kind . . . but also with spare parts of iron machinery to replace those which are daily broken or wear out." "Programma della Società d'Incoraggiamento delle Arti e Mestieri di Milano," *Annali,* 1842, LXXII, 293. There are frequent references to machines purchased in England and France.

[19] See, for example, petitions of the manufacturers to import pig and scrap iron duty free, M. C. M., Camera di Commercio, cartella 816, May 20, 1845; September 9 and 19, 1846.

[20] They "bring from Trieste 500,000 raw hides which they tan and return to be sold at Trieste and Sinigaglia." *Annali,* 1837, LII, 75.

[21] M. C. M., Camera di Commercio, cartella 173, July 21, 1827; November 15, 1843; Frattini, p. 93. The importance of spun cotton practically disappeared after the development of the local spinning industry. See Frattini, p. 93.

[22] This list is based on a variety of notices in the *Annali,* the archives of the Chamber of Commerce of Milan, and the MS notes of Cattaneo.

[23] To Parma in small quantities. References to these exports will be found in M. C. M., Camera di Commercio, cartella 173. In 1843 the amount of butter that went to the Genovesato was 1962 metric quintals, the amount of cheese 9,000 metric quintals.

[24] *Annali,* 1836, XLVIII, 297. The cheese exported was mainly so-called Parmesan, or hard cheese, made in Lodi, Pavia and the lower Milanese. But Cattaneo noted in 1844 that the *stracchino* or soft cheese of Gorgonzola was beginning to enter the export trade. M. R. M., Fondo Cattaneo, cartella 127, plico 21.

[25] *Annali,* 1834, XLIII, 70; *Politecnico,* 1839, I, 103.

[26] The data available do not reveal what proportion of the shipments to Genoa were for local consumption and what for shipment abroad, but with the exception of silk waste (*cascami*) the amount that went abroad does not seem to have been great.

firearms were sold to the Austrian Government, and for a while shipments of them went to Greece to arm the revolutionists ;[27] some paper
manufactured in Lombardy made its way to Turkey ;[28] some of its linen
thread went to Germany, Genoa and Spain ;[29] and some of its wrought
leather to Corfu.[30] This foreign trade was of no great significance. The
master export of Lombardy, that which towered over all others and
involved the community in trading relations with Europe at large, was
silk.

If the production of silk in Lombardy grew by leaps and bounds, its
value increased still more rapidly, with the phenomenal expansion of
the European and American market.[31] After the collapse of the Continental System London became the chief consumer of Italian silk as it
had been before the Napoleonic wars. In fact as late as the 'twenties it
absorbed practically all of the local supply, enjoying a monopoly which
grew onerous as the silks of Bengal and China, imported by the East
India Company, crowded into the London market and threatened to
break the price. But an alternative outlet was developing at Lyons,
whose demand for crude silk increased in spite of the rapid extension of
silk culture in France itself.[32] Still other markets were opening and as
early as 1829 Lombardy was exporting silk to France, Switzerland,
Germany, Russia, and Portugal, as well as to England.[33] The Lyonnais
market was presently rivaling that of London.[34] The other continental

[27] This profitable trade was cut off by a decree. A. S. M., Presidenza, Atti
segreti, cartella LXIX, 1824.

[28] *Annali,* 1833, Bulletino, p. 320.

[29] R. Ciasca, "L'evoluzione economica della Lombardia dagli inizi del secolo
XIX al 1860," in *La Cassa di Risparmio delle Provincie Lombarde,* p. 374;
Politecnico. 1839, I, 103.

[30] *Annali,* 1833, Bulletino, p. 324.

[31] Cattaneo estimated in 1836 that the quantity was increasing at the rate of
8 per cent a year, and that in the few preceding years its value had increased
more than 100 per cent—"so that we ourselves are stupefied and almost frightened
by it." *Annali,* 1836, XLVIII, 296. According to one estimate, based on the
"Official Registers," the quantity exported increased from 4,578,886 lbs. in 1829,
valued at 77,841,062 Milanese lire, to 7,266,533 lbs. in 1841, valued at 142,042,388
lire. A. Balbi, *Miscellanea italiana* (Milano, 1845), pp. 249–250.

[32] "It quadrupled between 1815 and 1850." Artz, p. 184.

[33] *Annali,* 1829, XX, 262.

[34] The steady advance of the demand from Lyons is noted in the *Annali,* 1835,
XLIII, 118, and in 1837 the exportation to Lyons was greater th͏͏
London, London taking 673,500 lbs. (of 12 oz.) of crude silk and
twists, while Lyons took 607,900 lbs. of raw silk and 619,500
Annali, 1838, LV, 116.

markets, including Austria, rapidly gained in importance,[35] and the proportion of the increasing output sent to them grew until in 1855 it was estimated that Germany and Switzerland alone were absorbing more than one-half of the total quantity exported.[36] For some years after the Restoration the bulk of the silk of Lombardy had been exported crude—that is, after having undergone only the first stage in the process of manufacture.[37] But as the market expanded and changed in character and a silk-twisting industry developed in Lombardy, the proportion of spun silk exported grew until much the larger part of the output was in that form. To England the silk continued to go chiefly in the crude state, to France in about equal proportions of crude and wrought silk, to the other markets in the form of twists.[38] By 1848 the inferior grades of crude silk had been almost entirely pushed out of the London market by the cheaper silks of the Orient, and the French consumption of Italian silk was in a threatening decline,[39] but the production of silk continued to be the great export industry of Lombardy.[40]

In the first half of the nineteenth century Milan and Bergamo still obtained a commercial advantage from their location at the foot of some of the great Alpine passes which were the gates of Italy, and the traders of Lombardy derived their profit not only from internal traffic and the movement of imports and exports to and from the Lombard market but also from commerce in transit on which a swarm of drivers, innkeepers, and shippers flourished. Lombardy lay across the lines of traffic between the Italian states on the south, the ports of Trieste and Genoa, through which Switzerland and Germany still largely provided themselves with "colonial" products, and the transalpine countries, which were both markets for Italian silk and the sources of supply of much of the manufactured goods consumed in the Italian states. Lombard merchants

[35] The table cited in the previous note shows 8,800 lbs. of crude silk and 1,228,000 lbs. of twist exported to Germany and Switzerland in 1837. In 1838 1,714,000 lbs. of twist were sold to Germany and Switzerland and 174,500 lbs. of twist went to Vienna from Milan alone. Another 24,200 lbs. went to Vienna from Brescia. The bulk of the silk taken by Vienna was produced in Venetia—amounting, in 1838, to 302,000 lbs. shipped from Verona and Vicenza and Udine. *Annali,* 1839, LIX, 111.

[36] According to this calculation 5/40 was going to London, 7/40 to Lyons, 1/40 to Russia, 1/40 (plus) to Vienna, while 4/40 (plus) was being consumed by the looms of Lombardy itself. Frattini, p. 58.

[37] See below, pp. 83–85.

[38] M. C. M., Camera di Commercio, cartella 564, September 17, 1830. The export tables in the *Annali* bear out this statement. The characterization of the exports to Lyons is based on the tables for 1837-1838 in the *Annali,* 1839, LIX, 111.

[39] M. C. M., Camera di Commercio, cartella 564, February 15, 1848.

[40] The average annual export was estimated in 1855 at 4,549,145 lbs., exclusive of the quantity (400,000 lbs.) exported to Vienna. Frattini, p. 55.

and shipping agencies distributed goods from Genoa destined for Venetia,[41] transported to markets north of the Alps silk shipped overland from Romagna and Tuscany, handled shipments to and from Trieste to Switzerland and Western Germany, and manufactures coming from Neufchatel, Switzerland, the Low Countries, and the German states on their way to Central Italy. Owing to a superior commercial organization and the advantages of the Splügen road, they also negotiated much of the traffic in "colonial" goods coming from Genoa and Trieste bound for Switzerland and Germany, though their advantage in handling this was in time impaired by the improvement of the route through Arona and the St. Gothard and Bernardino passes, and was menaced with extinction by the railroad that Charles Albert began to build from Genoa to Arona in 1844. From 1815 to 1848 the merchants of Milan were continually preoccupied with the preservation of this "rich branch of industry," threatened by the rivalry of alternative routes and by the vexatious transit regulations and dues imposed by the Austrian Government.[42]

The main lines of traffic in Lombardy were fixed by the geographical situation just described. The great east and west route was from Milan to Venice through Bergamo, Brescia, Desenzano, Verona and Padua. West from Milan went the line to Turin through Buffalora, south the highroad to Genoa through Pavia and Novi and over the Apennines. The highroads to the north were determined by the position of the St. Gothard and Splügen passes. The main road from Milan to the St. Gothard went to Sesto Calende at the foot of Lake Maggiore, and the main road to the Splügen through Como to Chiavenna. The Austrians also built a military road through the Valtellina (1820-1825) which crossed the Stelvio pass into the Tyrol and was used to some extent by shippers and passengers but which remained of secondary importance.[43] To the Splügen there was an alternative route which omitted Milan, shunting through Bergamo and Lecco the traffic from

---

[41] Even before the customs line on the Mincio, between Lombardy and Venetia, was abolished (June 15, 1822), "copious and incessant shipments" were made from Genoa to the Veneto through Lombardy. M. C. M., Camera di Commercio, cartella 173, No. 807, June 23, 1826.

[42] The foregoing description is based on the reports and petitions of the Chamber of Commerce of Milan and a detailed article on the transit trade of Lombardy by "L. A." in *Annali*, 1844, LXXIX, 283-292.

[43] In 1835 there was a weekly diligence service over this road from Milan to Innsbruck. *Annali*, 1835, XLV, 129. For a time the Stelvio route seems to have carried the bulk of the silk shipped from Bergamo and Milan to Germany, England and Russia, but only because of the transit regulations that then embarrassed the Splügen. *Annali*, 1844, LXXIX, 290-291.

Venice-Trieste and from the Romagna and Tuscany.[44] Sesto Calende and Como were the two main gateways of the traffic of Lombardy with Europe and Milan and Bergamo its two main points of distribution.

The development of these routes and of their rivals played an important part in the economic strategy of the period and became an object of lively interest to the Milanese trading community. The Austrian Government, prompted by military considerations, built a road to the Splügen, which offered great advantages to Lombard commerce.[45] It led to Chur (Coira) on the upper Rhine, the distributing point north of the Alps for Switzerland, Germany via Frankfurt-am-Main, and the Low Countries. Through Milan and over the Splügen road passed for a time not only the golden stream of Lombard silk, together with the trade between Europe and the Romagna, Modena, Parma and Tuscany, but also the main current of traffic between Genoa and North Central Europe,[46] and some of that to and from Trieste and the Levant.[47] But through trade on this route was grievously hampered by transit dues and also by the subtle classifications imposed by the Austrian tariff to prevent contraband.[48] The dangerous effect of these regulations began to be keenly felt by the Lombard traders when the road over the St. Gothard pass was opened to wagons in 1831 and the rivalry of the Piedmontese on this and the Bernardino route became serious.[49] Milan shared in the traffic coming from the north over the St. Gothard and the Simplon, a stream which divided at the foot of Lake Maggiore between Arona, on the road into Piedmont, and Sesto

---

[44] Opened up by the road which the Austrians laid from Lecco to Colico at the head of Lake Como. *Annali*, 1836, L, 282.

[45] For the arguments advanced by the Milan merchants in favor of this road, see the memorial of the Chamber of Commerce, M. C. M., Camera di Commercio, cartella 821, March 10, 1817, October 13, 1818, September 6, 1821, November 15, 1823.

[46] M. C. M., Camera di Commercio, cartella 822, May 12, 1829.

[47] *Annali*, 1844, LXXIX, 283.

[48] Memorial of the Milan Chamber of Commerce, M. C. M., Camera di Commercio, cartella 822, May 29, 1829. In 1848 the Chamber was still petitioning that "the regulation in force regarding the procedure in the matter of transit goods be revised and made much less rigorous." *Ibid.*, cartella 822, January 23, 1848.

[49] The danger was anticipated as early as 1817. M. C. M., Camera di Commercio, cartella 821, March 10, 1817. By 1832, when the St. Gothard had been opened to wagons and steamboats were operating on the Rhine as far as Mannheim, the Chamber was pressing for a reduction or abolition of transit duties to offset the advantages offered by the Piedmontese tariff and enable Milan to "attract anew" the transit of Italy. *Ibid.*, cartella 822, August 28, 1832. The Chamber was still complaining of the transit duties on the Gothard route in 1843. *Ibid.*, cartella 564, March 10, 1843.

Calende, on the road to Milan.[50] In fact, owing to the superior efficiency of the Lombard transports,[51] much even of the trade to and from Genoa took the Splügen route and passed through Milan. But the diversion of this traffic to the line from Genoa to Arona, within Sardinian territory, was an object steadily pursued by the Sardinian Government and one in which Charles Albert became especially interested. The improvement of the St. Gothard road and a road built along Lake Maggiore from Pallanza to Bellinzona[52] increased the attractiveness of this route. When Charles Albert planned the railway system of his kingdom (1835-1845), he projected a road from Genoa to Arona which was to be prolonged to Chur on the Rhine over the Lukmanier pass.[53] Work was begun on the Genoa end of the line and a tunnel was started through the Apennines at Giovi. The whole plan was the commercial side of Charles Albert's challenge to Austrian dominance in Upper Italy. Shrewdly providing for a connecting line that ran to the Lombard frontier at Novara, it offered a standing challenge to Austria to come to the aid of the shippers of Lombardy by linking the Milan-Venice road, begun in 1840, with the Sardinian net. The projected line from Genoa to Arona awakened grave concern among the merchants of Milan, who pressed the Austrian Government to meet the threat to their interests by building a railroad from Milan to Genoa and another from Milan to Sesto Calende.[54]

Meanwhile Milan was disturbed to see that not only was part of the overland traffic from Trieste and northeastern Italy passing through Bergamo and Lecco to the Splügen,[55] but that a very large part of it was being entirely diverted to the line through Bolzano to Innsbruck via the Brenner pass, while some of it was even coming through France to

[50] See preceding note and *Annali*, 1836, L, 292.

[51] M. C. M., Camera di Commercio, cartella 822, May 12, 1829; August 28, 1832; *Annali*, 1844, LXXIX, 287.

[52] M. C. M., Camera di Commercio, 1829, cartella 822, May 12, 1829.

[53] C. Vidal, *Charles-Albert et le Risorgimento italiano, (1831–1848)* (Paris, 1927), pp. 184–186.

[54] Count Visconti d'Aragona immediately petitioned the Government for authorization to construct these lines. Carlo Ilarione Petitti, *Delle strade ferrate italiane e del migliore ordinamento di esse* (Capolago, 1845), p. 261, note 1. The petition met with no response and the merchants grew impatient. In 1848 the Chamber of Commerce of Milan complained that the Sesto Calende road "has been pending since 1837 as a paper project with the Aulic Councils in spite of the desires of commerce and the unanimous accord of the Lombard Dicasteries regarding its appropriateness." Memorial of January 23, 1848, supporting the petition "of various merchants," M. C. M., Camera di Commercio, cartella 822.

[55] *Annali*, 1836, L, 282; M. C. M., Camera di Commercio, cartella 564, May 10, 1843; *Annali*, 1844, LXXIX, 284. This circumstance tending to inflame the jealous rivalry between Milan and Bergamo is part of the background of the historic controversy that arose between Milan and Bergamo as to whether the Milan-Venice railroad should pass through Bergamo or Treviglio.

Genoa and from there shipped to the seaports of Central and Southern Italy.[56] These changes aroused particular anxiety because they were viewed in the light of a larger question then being widely discussed in Italy—namely, what routes across Europe would be taken by the traffic through the Mediterranean, again brought to life by the development of commerce between England and the Orient via Egypt. It may be assumed that such preoccupations played no small part in fixing the attention of the Lombard public on the revolution that was going on in the economic life of Europe and nourished the discontent of its merchants and shippers with a government whose policies condemned them to suffer the loss of their share of the carrying trade.

The facilities which Lombardy offered for the internal movement of commodities in bulk were exceptional. Loaded on barges they were towed, or they placidly drifted with the current, along its rivers, lakes and canals, or, heaped on carts, were drawn by white oxen, horses or mules over the remarkable network of good roads, national, provincial and communal, with which the French and Austrian Governments had endowed the region. The period saw the important canal from Milan to Pavia finished and opened to navigation.[57] The Po was of little use as a highway, both because of difficulties of navigation which had not been corrected and of the customs regulations of the states on its banks which, in spite of vigorous and repeated complaints from Milan, had never been regularized in accordance with the agreements of the Congress of Vienna.[58] In the total mileage of its navigable waterways Lombardy outranked contemporary Belgium and France.[59] The system

[56] M. C. M., Camera di Commercio, cartella 822, August 28. 1832; *ibid.,* cartella 564, March 10, 1843; *Annali,* 1844, LXXIX, 284–287.

[57] The Pavia canal was opened August 16, 1819, and carried 2,000 barges and 60,000 tons of merchandise a year. *Politecnico,* 1841, IV, 428.

[58] A barge took six days to descend the Po from the Ticino to its mouth, twenty-nine days to ascend. The steamboat would have offset this difficulty, but repeated attempts to establish steam navigation were defeated by the five customs lines through which the vessel had to pass and the eighty different posts at which the right of visit and search was exercised. *Politecnico,* 1841, IV, 410; 1842, VI, 424. For complaints regarding the customs on the Po, see report of the merchants of Milan regarding the best tariff policy to be pursued by the Government, M. C. M., Camera di Commercio, cartella 172, December 4, 1814; also letter of the Marchese Visconti d'Aragona to Count Luigi Porro, published in the *Conciliatore,* No. 2, 85–87; *Politecnico,* 1842, VI, 424–425; *Guida di Milano* (Bernadoni, 1830), pp. 360–362; *ibid.,* 1832, p. 422; *Annali,* 1840, LXV, 136–141.

[59] With 974,000 metres of natural, 220,000 metres of artificial more or less navigable water. The ratios per kilometre of linear surface were Lombardy 55, Belgium 48, France 15. In canals alone the ratios were Great Britain 17, Belgium 15, Lombardy 10, France 7. The Naviglio Grande, patriarch of all European canals, carried 3,600 vessels a year, with a cargo of more than 100,000 tons—two-thirds from Lake Maggiore and the rest local traffic in bulky commodities. "Prospectus of the Internal Navigation of the Lombard Provinces with some Notes on their Irrigation," *Politecnico,* 1841, IV, 406, 415–416.

of roads and bridges was pushed forward rapidly by the Austriaɪ.
after the Restoration and was the pride of local patriots. One of these
exclaimed as he contemplated the 3,294 miles of communal roads built
between 1814 and 1833: "Now we can say that they [the Lombard
roads] have almost reached the maximum of perfection. . . . Lombardy
has in a short time become the leading country in Italy, having the best
and most numerous roads that are known."[60] Besides this internal net,
the through lines described above were furnished with paved highroads.[61] By 1848 two short railroads had been finished, one between
Milan and Monza, opened August 18, 1840,[62] the other a section of the
much-agitated Milan-Venice trunk line, the tract from Milan to
Treviglio, on which trains began to run on February 17, 1846.[63]

Diligences were operated on schedule over regular runs by the firm
of Franchetti.[64] In the second quarter of the century regular services
for both freight and passengers were considerably improved. In 1827
a service of *"velociferi* and fast diligences" was added, on the initiative
of a private company consisting chiefly of noblemen,[65] whose business
was soon afterwards taken over by the Government.[66] In 1830 mail left
Milan for Venice every day, but was taken by a messenger, except on
Wednesdays and Saturdays, when it went by a mail-coach.[67] By 1839 at
least, and perhaps earlier, there was a daily operation of diligences between Milan and Venice.[68] In 1834 a stagecoach left Milan three times
a week for Paris via Turin.[69] By 1838 there was a stagecoach service

[60] Giuseppe Sacchi, *Annali,* 1833, Bulletino, p. 5.

[61] The most important were the road along Lake Como from Lecco to Colico,
the road from Chiavenna to the Splügen pass, the tract linking the Splügen road
with Colico, and the Stelvio road through the Valtellina. *Annali,* 1836, L, 303–305.

[62] *Annali,* 1840, LXV, 386.

[63] *Guida di Milano* (Bernadoni, 1847), p. 42.

[64] Franchetti seems to have been the stand-by among the local transportation
agencies. See quotation below, note 83.

[65] Duke Carlo Visconti di Modrone, Pietro Falugi, Count Vitaliano Borromeo,
Marquis Alessandro Visconti d'Aragona, Count Francesco Sant' Antonio and
Engineer Giuseppe Bruschetti. M. C. M., Camera di Commercio, cartella 569,
April 21, 1827.

[66] Notification of August 27, 1827, No. 10584–3407C, in *Raccolta degli Atti del
Governo e delle disposizioni generali emanate dalle diverse autorità in oggetti si
amministrativi che giudiziari* (Milan, I. R. Stamperia, 1815 ff.), XXXVIII, 83.
The vehicles were thenceforth called *"diligenze celeri erarali."* D. and G. Sacchi,
L'Arti e l'industria in Lombardia nel 1832 (Milan, Da Placido Maria Visaja,
1832), p. 198.

[67] "Corriere." *Guida di Milano* (Bernadoni), 1830, pp. 43 ff. At present the
"corriere" carries passengers as well as mail.

[68] *Almanacco della provincia Bresciana per l'anno 1839* (Brescia, B. Minerva,
1838), pp. 165–169.

[69] The trip took ten days. *I. R. Almanacco delle provincie del Regno Lombardo-Veneto soggette al governo di Milano,* 1834, pp. 412–413.

ʿermany, as well as one to Paris, one to Rome and one
re was as yet none to Bologna, Florence or Naples.[70]
t Milan daily for Vienna, Berlin, Paris, Genoa, Rome
assengers for Como travelled to Monza by train and
a stage which connected with steamboats on the lake.
wenty-five omnibuses were operating in the streets of
ᵧ this date the shipping houses had developed a service
of express convoys of merchandise for Venice, Vienna, Poland, Russia,
Lyons and London, and there were scheduled dispatches of silk for
London five times a week, either via Lyons or the Rhine.[72]

By such means of transport it took a passenger nine hours to get
from Milan to Brescia,[73] thirty-six hours from Milan to Venice (a distance of one hundred and sixty miles).[74] The Milan-Venice diligence
rolled along day and night, rumbling through the streets of Brescia at
3.45 in the morning and arriving at Mestre, for the ferry crossing to
Venice, the next morning at 1.30.[75] In 1830 it took five days to go from
Milan to the Austrian capital. The passenger left Milan at 5.30 Satur-
day morning, reached Verona Sunday noon, was at Treviso by midnight, and at Udine for lunch on Monday, arrived at Tarvis at 10.15,
where he spent the night, proceeded at 6 a. m. on Tuesday and arrived
in Vienna at 6 a. m. on Thursday, after a voyage longer than is now
necessary to cross the Atlantic, and in a state of exhaustion that can
easily be imagined.[76] By 1845, the completion of a railroad from Vienna
to Bruck enabled him to save eighteen hours on this journey.[77] Letters,
on the other hand, could reach Milan from London in five or six days,[78]
and in 1839 news from New York was published at Milan within a
month; from Marseilles (brought "by steamship") within six days;
from Messina within eleven days.[79]

Merchandise moved more slowly. In 1838 it required from eight to
nine days to get packages of books from Turin to Milan, two months
to get them from Milan to Turin.[80] Shipments of goods between Milan

---

[70] *Annali*, 1838, LVIII, 80–81; 1840, LXIV, 110.
[71] *Guida di Milano* (Bernadoni), 1845, pp. 58–59.
[72] *Ibid.*, p. 61; M. C. M., Camera di Commercio, cartella 564, March 22, 1844.
[73] *Almanacco bresciano,* 1839, p. 169.
[74] *Annali*, 1835, XLIV, 315, note 1.
[75] *Almanacco provinciale per l'anno bisestile 1844* (Bergamo, Sonzogni), p. 171.
[76] *Guida di Milano* (Bernadoni), 1830, p. 43.
[77] *Ibid.*, 1845, p. 26.
[78] M. C. M., Camera di Commercio, cartella 564, March 10, 1843.
[79] *Foglio commerciale di Milano,* May 15, 1839, No. 39. *Notizie estere.*
[80] This timing is the result of an experiment conducted by the *Annali universali di statistica.* The delay in the westbound shipment was due to the Piedmontese Customs at San Martino. *Annali,* 1838, LVIII, 80–81.

and Florence were regularly two months en route.[81] On the other hand, express dispatches of silk from Milan were so well organized by 1844 that they reached London via Lyons in from twenty to twenty-two days, via the Rhine in from thirteen to fifteen days, and by special service via Basel and from there to Calais by diligence in only twelve days.[82]

There was therefore a general and marked improvement in the regularity, frequency and speed of communications within the old system of conveyance still prevalent, particularly of communications inside of Lombardy-Venetia and on the routes to the north. Connections with the rest of Italy continued to lag behind those with Europe, a subject of frequent lamentations with the progressive publicists.[83] It seemed a scandal to them that as late as 1840 there was no service of diligence between Milan and Florence,[84] a service which they could announce as partly established only in October 1841;[85] and when the Congress of Italian Scientists met at Naples in 1845 it was necessary to get the news of their proceedings from the German papers, "as if they had gone to China."[86]

With regard to the local organization of commercial business the question of greatest interest from the point of view of the present study is to know what classes of the Lombard community were brought most directly into contact with the foreign market, and who were therefore likely to be sensitive to the influences that were affecting it. But even

[81] A statement based on the experience of the shipping houses of Airoldi of Milan and Conti of Florence. *Annali,* 1839, LXII, 103–104.

[82] M. C. M., Camera di Commercio, cartella 564, March 22, 1844.

[83] "When one reflects that to get a parcel of goods from Naples, Rome and Florence to Milan and vice-versa requires an infinite time and a heavy expense, while from London, Paris and Vienna one receives shipments in a few days and at limited cost," it would seem, observed the editors of the *Annali,* that Italian express companies do not know their business. *Annali,* 1833, Bulletino, pp. 274–275. After describing the stage-coaches of England and the diligence services to Venice, Piacenza, Novara, Novi and Vienna, the editors exclaimed impatiently: "But what are these means compared with those which daily multiply in France, England and Germany? It is truly grievous that not only are there no diligences from Milan to Florence and from Rome to Naples, but that such services are not multiplied. . . . We hope that Franchetti will not be with us for eternity and that other entrepreneurs will appear who will have the courage to organize easy transports throughout the length and breadth of Italy; it being however impossible to speak except with praise of the regular service of our existing diligences." *Annali,* 1835, XLIV, 315, note 1.

[84] *Annali.* 1840, LXIV, 110. "Shipments are organized with such expedition, with such celerity, that they take from forty to fifty days to go two hundred miles . . . and this in the fine season, and precisely in 1839 when one can travel thirty miles an hour!" *Ibid..* 1839, LXII, 103.

[85] *Annali,* 1841, LXX, 115.

[86] *Annali,* 1845, LXXXVI, 118.

the most elementary facts of that organization are obscure and hard to get at.

It is clear that the number of wholesale merchants trading in a large way was small. In Milan, between 1836 and 1846, it varied from forty-nine to fifty-four, as compared with about 1,750 retailers.[87] At Bergamo the group engaged in wholesale trade would seem to have been considerably larger, without being numerous.[88] The intervention of a licensed broker was necessary to give legal regularity to a contract. The broker brought the parties together, made a record of the terms of contract, which he deposited in the local archives, acted as umpire in the execution of the terms, and was authorized to see to it that no goods dangerous to health or dishonestly obtained were exchanged.[89] The number of brokers licensed to negotiate in each community was fixed by law. Thus, at Milan there were only eighteen brokers authorized to deal in silk. The requirements of the trade outgrew this limitation. In 1839 the *Politecnico* described the situation in terms that throw an interesting light on the habits of the local trading community. At the moment when the great silk crop had to be moved the indispensable eighteen had "to travel from one village and market to another to carry on negotiations with producers and spinners, while several *thousands* of proprietors seek to dispose of their goods with the harvest imminent." In the meanwhile the traders in Milan were left in urgent need of their services. "In a city where merchants do not love to gather at the bourse," the writer continues, "nothing can be gained by the passive

[87] Statistica dell'industria privata dall'anno 1836 al——, Sommari," M. C. M., Ragioneria municipale, cartella 4 (1834 ff.). Some idea of the complexion and position of the trading group in Milan can be got from the occupational directory which appears in Bernadoni's contemporary *Guide di Milano:* principal merchant shippers; commissioners and principal warehouse merchants in colonial goods. woolens, cottons, threads, etc.; principal merchant manufacturers; bill changers; agents of exchange; commodity brokers; brokers or mediators for the Royal City of Milan; principal manufacturers, merchants and artists; notaries; architects, engineers, surveyors and foremen; painters, sculptors and engravers; masters and professors of music, dancing and fencing; the "Messers Accountants."

[88] The *Annali* in 1837 gave the following figures, without indicating the scale of operations of the merchants concerned. It is probable that the categories of wholesale merchants overlap and that they do not correspond to those on which the number for Milan given in the text were based. All that can be inferred with certainty is that the class was comparatively small.

Wholesale merchants in silk	58
in iron	139
in woolen and cotton cloth	48
in linen and cotton textiles	5
in cheese	100
Shippers and commissioners	35

Annali, 1837, LIV, 321.

[89] *Raccolta degli atti del Governo. Atti,* No. 11, 1816, XXVII, 419–433.

broker, since a broker must run repeatedly from one end of the city to the other to complete a contract. . . . The fact is that for every *broker with a license,* at least *four* are known *who have none,"* but the contracts negotiated by these unlicensed brokers, however reliable, did not "carry with them that authenticity almost notarial which the law accords only to those with license."[90]

Trading was carried on in authorized markets and periodical fairs.[91] At Milan there was a Bourse, in the Piazza de' Mercanti, with officers named by the Chamber of Commerce, and open daily from noon until 3 p.m. It would seem that the Bourse was not frequented by the merchants.[92] Grain could be traded in the capital only on the market of the Broletto.[93] The official supervision of trade was completed by Chambers of Commerce in the principal trading centers. Their members were nominated by the merchants of the community and appointed by the Government and their expenses were paid by local "commerce." The Chambers were charged with the registration of the merchants, bankers and manufacturers in their districts and in general with the tutelage and promotion of the economic interests of their communities. The Chambers had summary jurisdiction in disputes between merchants and were the agency to which a merchant must apply for a decree of sequestration or arrest against the person of another merchant.[94]

Silk was the commodity around which the commercial interests of Lombardy chiefly revolved. The great bulk of this product was traded by the wholesale merchants of Milan and Bergamo and found its main outlet through Milan.[95] At Milan were some hundred old firms that

[90] *Politecnico,* 1839, II, 380–381. The journal was in favor of a number limited only by the needs of the trade and the number of reliable applicants.

[91] The official lists of these appear in the annual *I. R. Almanacco.* A comparison of the number in 1834 (pp. 384–388) and that in 1843 (pp. 427–431) shows only slight changes. In the Province of Bergamo, besides the ancient fair of the city, there were nine hundred and seven local fairs in the fifty-one communes, where cattle and farm products to be traded with neighboring provinces were brought to market. *Annali,* 1837, LIV, 324.

[92] In 1837 Cattaneo spoke of "the lack of a bourse" at Milan. *Annali,* 1837, LIV, 205. It would seem that the motive of the traders in fearing the Bourse was to avoid giving publicity to their business. But a contemporary observed that no secrets were kept by "the public brokers, who without restraint or consideration of any sort when they meet in the cafés, which for them take the place of a Bourse, carry on open and scandalous auctions." G[iulio] F[ortis], "Dell'erezione di un monte depositario di sete nella città di Milano," *Annali,* 1837, LII, p. 190.

[93] *Raccolta degli Atti del Governo, Circolari,* 1816, XXVI, 42–43.

[94] The constitution of the Chambers is in the *Bolletino delle leggi della Repubblica Italiana* (Milan, 1802), Anno I (1802), p. 15. *Costituzione della Repubblica italiana, titolo* XIII, 101, modified by an Act of 1811, in *Bolletino delle leggi del Regno d'Italia,* No. 145, June 27, 1811, Pt. 1, 654–657.

[95] *Politecnico,* 1939, II, 379; Bowring, *Statistics,* p. 104 (on the basis of information furnished by Czoernig, Secretary of the government of Lombardy).

were dedicated to this trade.[96] They bought the silk through brokers in the form of raw silk, the product of mills operated by the proprietors themselves or of spinners to whom the wholesale merchants advanced the capital necessary to finance this elementary stage of the industry. An increasing part of the local output was exported in the form of silk thread. In some cases the merchants themselves carried on the industries of reeling and thread-making. It seems indeed to have been through their initiative that the silk-spinning industry made such notable advances during the first half of the nineteenth century.[97]

Almost all the silk produced was sold in foreign markets.[98] It is evident that some of the firms employed in this commerce specialized in shipping. Some important firms had magazines at Milan in which to store the silks before shipping them abroad;[99] and the commissioners of foreign firms appeared on the Lombard market to make their purchases. But in the second half of the eighteenth century the practice arose of sending the silk to foreign markets, especially at first to London, before it was purchased,[100] and in our period a good part of the product went abroad in search of purchasers. The actual practice was reflected in the fact that a part of the silk exported was shipped by way of Lyons to try the market there before that of London.[101]

One of the much-discussed defects in the organization of the Lombard silk trade was that the traders were unable to wait for a favorable market, whether for lack of adequate facilities for financing the commerce, or for lack of an effective representation of their interests abroad. As soon as the silk was put in deposit at London, the Lombard merchants found themselves at the mercy of the English bankers and buyers. The solution of this problem was partly attained when Italian silk found other markets. Its complete solution required a better organization of the credit system,[102] and the development of more rapid and effective means of transportation. "The railroad extended into other parts of Europe can render us this service," observed Cattaneo, "giving

[96] "We have a round hundred of houses that trade in silk, and many of them are heavily subsidized by foreign markets or hold commissions from these." Cattaneo, "Alcune ricerche sul progetto di un Monte di sete," *Annali,* 1937, LIV, 210.

[97] See below, pp. 85–86.

[98] Seven-eighths, according to G[iulio] F[ortis], *Annali,* 1837, LII, 188.

[99] "The big merchants have their own means of storage." Cattaneo, *Annali,* 1837, LIV. 209.

[100] De Carli, "Sull'ora proposta erezione di una Banca di Sconto in Milano," *Annali,* 1833, XXXVIII, Bulletino, 415, 428.

[101] M. C. M., Camera di Commercio, cartella 564, March 22, 1844.

[102] See below, pp. 140–143.

the shipment of silks such promptness that their habitual concentration on a distant market will no longer be necessary," and they can be accumulated at Milan until it is known which market abroad offers the greater advantage.[103]

Besides there was not at Milan a central office of "seasoning" to assure and certify the quality and classification of the silk destined for export. This defect of organization was blamed as the cause of the loss of ground that Lombard silks suffered in the international market during our period in competition with silks from other sources.[104]

It was the wholesale merchants, then, who were most directly in touch with the foreign demand for silk and who financed the shipping and marketing of this prime export. The proprietors are represented in contemporary reports as out of touch with the foreign market, holding their crops for prices fixed by tradition, which did not allow a margin of profit wide enough to enable the spinners to turn out a product of requisite excellence, or to permit the merchants to meet the competition of the cheaper Asiatic silks on the London market.[105] On the other hand, the proprietors responded to the expansion of the foreign market by rapidly extending and improving their cultivation and preparation of the silk.

The importation of raw cotton became an increasingly important business and in this case the Lombard importing houses had their own agents in the American market.[106] But in general the trade of Italy with the United States seems to have been carried on through English commissioners.[107] The small amount of trade which Lombardy carried on directly with the Levant was negotiated through local Greek or Jewish firms or through the commission merchants of French and English

[103] "Alcune ricerche sul progetto di un monte delle sete," *Annali*, 1837, LII, 197.
[104] *Annali*, 1837, LII, 197.
[105] The first sharp protest of the merchants against this attitude of the proprietors was the Marietti Circular, described in Chapter II, where the campaign of the journalists to awaken the proprietors to their wider interests is also described.
[106] "Our merchants of Milan, furnished with vast capital, send their agents to New Orleans, purchase provisions of raw cotton at the local prices and without need of passing through third hands in the ports of Liverpool and Havre, call into the port of Genoa their ships loaded with their cotton which they sell directly to the spinneries not only of the Lombardo-Venetian Kingdom but even of Piedmont and also of Southern Italy." Report of the Milan Chamber of Commerce to Count Spaur, M. C. M., Chamber of Commerce, cartella 173, November 15, 1843.
[107] Luigi Serristori, "Commercio tra l'Italia e gli Stati Uniti dell'America settentrionale," *Annali*, 1841, LXVIII, 221–223.

houses.[108] In some branches of commerce the Lombards were represented abroad by Genoese houses, in Nice, Marseilles, Barcelona, Cadiz, Lisbon, London and Amsterdam,[109] with which they had relations of long standing. Indeed a good share of the foreign trade of Lombardy was carried on through the Genoese organization.[110]

Fairs, such as those of Bergamo, Brescia, Pavia, and Verona—once famed throughout Europe—still played a part in the commercial life of Lombardy. The fair at Pavia had become exclusively a market for horses and cattle used on the dairy farms of the Plain.[111] The Brescia fair was chiefly a local market for silk.[112] The Bergamo fair was a market for silk and also for trading in soap, iron, cotton and linen textiles, and in woolens from Austrian Germany, all of which found their way through this exchange not only to the rest of Lombardy-Venetia but to the other Italian states.[113] Most of the languishing trade of Lombardy with the Levant was carried on through the annual fair at Sinigaglia, near the port of Ancona in the Papal State.[114]

[108] The Chamber of Commerce of Milan was dissatisfied with this situation and in 1820 recommended that the Government send young Italians, "sons of manufacturers and merchants" "who combine with commercial knowledge the principles of the political and economic sciences," as consuls to the Near East. M. C. M., Camera di Commercio, cartella 172, January 21, 1820. The Austrian Government subsequently established consuls-general at Alexandria (Giuseppe Acerbi) and Smyrna (Pietro Questiaux). The merchants were asked to send them samples of their wares. Printed notice of the Milan Chamber of Commerce, April 24, 1826, *ibid.*, cartella 173. The samples were not forthcoming, in spite of the efforts of the Chamber. *Ibid.*, No. 1565, August 10, 1826.

[109] *Ibid.*, No. 807, June 3, 1826.

[110] In the trade of Lombardy with Genoa there was an excess of imports over exports, as Lombard importations from Genoa included great quantities of goods brought from overseas. But the trade of Genoa with France and England was passive, while that of Lombardy with those countries produced a favorable balance owing to its exports of silk, so that it was convenient to both parties that the Lombard merchants should settle their balances in Genoa with drafts on France and England. M. C. M., Camera di Commercio, cartella 173, May 20, 1843.

[111] *Annali*, 1828, XV, 325.

[112] This is evident from the annual reports of it in the *Annali.*

[113] For example, in 1827, 70,000 to 80,000 lbs. (Troy) of silk were sold at the Bergamo fair; 40,000 pieces of German cloth, sold for 4,608,000 francs, as compared with only 8,000 pieces of local manufacture; and 20,000 pieces of cotton goods, sold for 460,800 francs. *Annali*, 1827, XIII, 334-335. The Bergamo fair was reported annually in the *Annali.*

[114] To explain why the Lombard merchants failed to come forward with samples of their wares to be sent to the Austrian consuls newly established at Alexandria and Smyrna, the Milan Chamber of Commerce explained that rather than risk sending their goods on the long voyage to the Levant, "they prefer to go with their merchandise to the fair at Sinigaglia, where they obtain a modest sale and enjoy the advantage of being paid in ready cash." M. C. M., Camera di Commercio, cartella 173, No. 1565, August 10, 1826. From 1831 to 1836 the total sales at the fair of Sinigaglia rose steadily from 42,000,000 francs to over 100,000,000 francs, the goods chiefly coming from the Austrian Monarchy. Article translated from the *Commercial Register*, in *Annali*, 1837, LIV, 257-258.

However conservative in spirit, the Lombard trading community felt the need of a better adjustment to the commercial life of Europe. One obstacle to this the merchants found in the protectionist customs policy of their Government. The rigorous Austrian system of tariffs, which limited their markets, burdened their exports and particularly interfered with their transit business, drew repeated criticisms and complaints from the Milan Chamber of Commerce. From the first the merchants took their stand with the liberal economists in favor of free trade, and some of their memorials read like pages from the *laissez-faire* economists of the period. Refusing to support the petition of a local manufacturer for protection, they wrote: it "would tend in the end to a system favorable to monopoly, contrary to liberal ideas in favor of commerce. Industry and perfection develop only from a noble rivalry between manufacturers."[115] Again in 1819: "If one had to reason theoretically regarding the interests of commerce, it would be obvious to answer that all limiting laws either in the way of prohibition on the introduction [of goods] or of excessive import duties are fatal to it, so much the more when there is an absolute need of the raw materials, but also when there is need of the raw material in a modified form." They proceed with a statement of the law of the territorial division of labor. The price, they conclude, "always tends to an equilibrium and when this does not exist, efforts to elude the law flow from it."[116] From 1814 the Chamber declared itself in favor of a policy of light export duties on the surplus products of Lombardy, such as silk, cheese, linen, hemp and rice, and light import duties on the materials of industry,[117] and argued against the prohibitive system of Austria whenever an excuse for presenting its views occurred.[118] In 1824 the Government drew a howl of pain from the Milan Chamber when it prohibited the importation of certain articles and ordered the merchants to dispose of

[115] M. C. M., Camera di Commercio, cartella 172, July 29, 1816.
[116] *Ibid.*, February 8, 1819.
[117] Report of the Chamber to Governor Marshal Bellegarde, *Ibid.*, 1814. Asked to report on the changes desirable in the existing tariffs in 1823, the Chamber replied that it would "not occupy itself in reporting the general desire born in all to see both the import duties and the export duties diminished in the whole tariff, with due regard to the local circumstances of Lombardy, a country everywhere open and bordering on foreign states, where contraband could not be prevented except with a huge force." *Ibid.*, cartella 173, No. 190, June 12, 1823.
[118] They opposed it on the ground that (1) it provoked reprisals; (2) reduced the money in circulation and injured consumers; (3) made manufacturers lazy and inefficient; (4) restricted the scope of commerce; (5) produced contraband. *Ibid.*, cartella 173, No. 2709, March 12, 1834. In 1838 they reported to the Chamber of Commerce of Venice regarding their trade with Belgium that "the present [prohibitive] system of finance is destroying also this important trade so profitable to the countries through which it passes." *Ibid.*, April 23, 1838.

their existing stocks within three months.[119] The merchants were continually preoccupied with the effect of Austrian policy on the transit trade. Reporting on the condition of the transit trade in 1834 the Chamber remarked: "Commercial science which has made immense advances in this century teaches the encouragement of the transit trade in foreign goods with every favor." They repeatedly urged a relaxation and simplification of the rules that governed the passage of the frontiers by goods in transit and favored the complete abolition of transit dues, to enable them to hold their own in this branch of commerce against the competition of Piedmont and France.[120] The closing of the customs post for goods in transit at Sesto Calende in 1842 provoked them to strong and repeated protests.[121] In 1834 in a long and carefully fortified memorial the Chamber urged the Monarchy to abandon the prohibitive system altogether and join the German Zollverein, as a move that would advance not only the interests of Lombardy but the true economic interests of the whole Empire.[122] One is left in no doubt of their free trade proclivities. When local manufacturers developed, they weakened somewhat, but advocated protection only as a temporary aid to infant industries,[123] expressing a preference for technical education as the best means of enabling Lombardy industry to cope with its foreign rivals.[124]

The Government made a persistent effort to divert the traffic of Lombardy from Genoa to Trieste. This was a policy which ran counter to the commercial habits of Lombardy and which the Milan Chamber of Commerce dared to oppose. Trieste was the darling of Austrian commercial policy. Austria sought to develop it as the chief outlet and port

[119] "Ruin . . . desolation . . . disaster . . . anguish" are some of the words with which they described the effect. The Chamber expressed itself as "venerating the sublime views of His Majesty for the system excluding foreign goods, and does not dare to lift its brow to make observations of any sort regarding it. But as to the *manner* of obtaining the full execution of this system," the Chamber implored a modification which would give "the poor merchants" at least three years to accommodate themselves to the order. The Government allowed them nine months and they returned thanks in a most obsequious memorial on behalf of "so many families saved from disaster." *Ibid.*, cartella 814, No. 4996/P, October 12, 1824; cartella 822, January 21, 1825.

[120] *Ibid.*, cartella 173, No. 190, June 12, 1823; cartella 822, May 12, 1829; May 4, 1834.

[121] The Chamber made representations to the Provincial Delegation June 19, 1842, January 18, 1844, November 20, 1846, and on August 6, 1847 petitioned the Governor. Receiving no response they extended their views in a long and indignant memorial dated January 23, 1848. *Ibid.*, cartella 822.

[122] *Ibid.*, cartella 173, No. 2709, March 12, 1834.

[123] *Ibid.*, May 10, 1841.

[124] Letter of President Mylius of the *Società d'incoraggiamento per le arti e i mestieri di Milano*, signed also by its secretary Carlo Cattaneo. and indorsed by the Chamber, asking for continued financial support of the Government, *Ibid.*, cartella 823, July 25, 1846.

of entry of the provinces of the Monarchy north of the Alps and to attract to it the transit commerce of Germany and northern Europe with the Levant and eventually with the Indies. In the second quarter of the century Trieste rapidly rose to first rank among Mediterranean ports.[125] Its gains, it would seem, were in large part due to its success in capturing the trade in "colonial" goods.[126] In 1836 the incorporation of the Austrian Lloyd, a company financed by Rothschild to operate steamships between Trieste and the Ionian Islands, Greece, the Archipelago, Smyrna, Syria and Egypt, was announced at Milan as Austria's bid for a share in the resurrection of trade between Europe and the Orient through the Mediterranean.[127] Its vessels, all steamers of more than three hundred tons, began their runs in 1837.[128] Subsequently the company multiplied its services between Trieste and the Adriatic ports of Italy, binding Austria closer to Central Italy through Ancona.[129] When the portentous success of the German Customs Union brought Austria face to face with a crisis in its commercial policy Metternich decided to turn his back on the Zollverein and use Trieste as the means of bringing to heel the Italian states, where the movement for a union similar to the Zollverein was gaining a formidable strength.[130]

[125] According to one estimate, based on statistics that are probably not irreproachable, Trieste had by 1838 passed Genoa and Constantinople and stood second only to Marseilles in the tonnage of ships entering its port. The enthusiastic commentator remarked that the movement of ships at Trieste yielded place by only one-third to the movement observed at New York in 1824. *Annali*, 1838, LV, 296–298. The following figures taken from the annual reports of the commerce of Trieste published in the *Annali di statistica* give a rough measure of its growth. (The figures exclude coastwise vessels.)

	Arrivals	Departures
1825	779	665
1832	1046	998
1835	1691	1730
1837	1731	1688
1839	1858	1807
1843	1412	1463

[126] According to the estimates of the Austrian statistician Czörnig the importations of skins, olive oil, wool, hemp, dyewoods and sugar through Trieste more than doubled between 1816 and 1835, while those of cotton and coffee tripled and almost quadrupled. Czörnig calculated the average total of imports and exports for 1814–1827 at 171,000,000 Austrian lire. The minimum (1820) was 120,000,000 lire, the maximum (1826) 228,000,000 lire. "Statistical Notes on the Maritime Commerce of Trieste" (from an article by Czörnig in the *Lloyd Austriaco*, May 15, 1836, reproduced in the *Gazzetta di Milano*, June 7, 1836), *Annali*, 1836, XLVIII, 333–335.

[127] *Annali*, 1836, XLIX, 323–325.

[128] *Ibid.*, 1837, LII, 90–92.

[129] *Ibid.*, 1838, LVI, 231–232.

[130] See below, pp. 208–209. For the crisis in Austrian policy and the circumstances determining its outcome, see Alfred Stern, *Geschichte Europas von der*

In 1826 the Austrian Government made a move to divert to Trieste a larger share of the overseas commerce of Milan.[131] The Chamber of Commerce of Milan sharply protested that "such a ruinous measure" would do violence to the old and profitable relations of Milan and Genoa, and cut into their already diminishing transit business. Venice, which had been linked with Trieste by a service of steamers, was to profit by the scheme proposed but the anxious merchants of Milan showed no sympathy for Venice. Its port was inconvenient for the docking of ships and its port regulations were severe. It was poor policy, they argued, to rehabilitate one province by ruining another, and they reviewed the history of Venice to show that her wealth and glory had always been those of a vampire and were now irretrievably lost, owing both to circumstances and to the character of the Venetians. Let the Venetians face the fact that their port would "always be tributary to the port of Trieste, and therefore, condemned to exercise only a commerce at second hand." "In short," they concluded, the loss of Lombardy would be "a fatal holocaust, which would be offered as an immolation to the *risorgimento* of Venice."

It is impossible to say what extent municipal sentiment and mere inertia entered into this sharp reaction. Actually Lombardy imported a good share of its supply of "colonials" through Trieste, and shared, as has been pointed out above, in the transit trade between that port and northern Europe.[132] Until the 'forties at least Trieste seems to

Verträgen des 1815 bis zum Frankfurter Frieden von 1871 (Stuttgart und Berlin, 1894–1924), V, 68–81; Ciasca, *Programma*, pp. 365–370. The political fears underlying Metternich's commercial policy are apparent from his instructions to the Austrian ambassadors at Turin and Florence to bring pressure on Tuscany and Sardinia to prevent the granting of privileges to the French company seeking to establish steamship lines between Marseilles and the ports of Italy in 1831. See Sandonà, *Il regno Lombardo-Veneto* (Milano, 1921), p. 275.

[131] By a modification of the tariff system, raising the existing duties on all goods imported at any point on the frontier of Lombardy-Venetia except Trieste and Venice, justified as an act of reprisal against the Sardinian Government for its navigation act of January 17, 1825, and also "more broadly . . . to cause [the commerce of Venice] to rise again from the state of debasement produced by the political vicissitudes which it has suffered." M. C. M., Camera di Commercio, cartella 173, No. 807, April 26, 1826.

[132] The exports of Lombardy-Venetia to Trieste were only 16 per cent of its importations through that port. The average annual imports were valued at 28,500,000 francs, the average exports at 5,000,000 francs. Cattaneo, citing a statistical table published in the *Giornale di Trieste, Annali*, 1836, XLVIII, 298. "Milan provides itself alternately at Trieste and Genoa, I suppose in about equal proportions, and serves as an emporium for shipments from Genoa to the neighboring Lombard markets. This explains why Milan will always make every effort to favor its relations with Genoa; but since these relations are opposed by the invincible nature of the land, they cannot awaken serious fears for the Austrian ports." "L. A.," discussing the effect of the projected railroad lines on the transit trade of Lombardy, *Annali*, 1844, LXXIX, 290.

have been a more efficient port than Genoa.[133] The Austrian Government dropped the measure proposed in 1826, but none the less continued to pursue a policy centered on Trieste. The trunk line of the Lombardo-Venetian railways projected in 1836 was to run from Milan to Venice, and the Austrian Government not only refused to provide a connecting line with the Piedmontese system and Genoa, so much desired in Lombardy, but the *Lloyd Austriaco,* officialy inspired, declared that the discussion of it as desirable was "an act of rebellion" on the part of any subject of Austria.[134] When the Government in 1844 proposed that Milan ship its silk to England by steamships out of Trieste, the opposition of the Chamber of Commerce of Milan was as firm as it had been in response to the measures proposed in 1826.[135] The Milanese continued to feel that their port was Genoa.

The rivalry of Trieste and Genoa was invested with a larger significance for Lombardy and for Italy with the return to the Mediterranean Sea of the line of communication of England, and potentially all trading Europe with the Orient.[136] The steamship was the new commercial instrument that produced this momentous revolution. The merchants of Calcutta and Bombay, eager to get dispatches to and from the home country more promptly took the initiative in experimenting with it. The trial voyage of the steamship "Enterprize" around the Cape of Good Hope in 1826 demonstrated the handicap to which a steam vessel was subject from the lack of proper coaling stations on the old route.[137] By 1838 the connection by steamship between Indian ports and Suez, established some years before, had become fairly regular. The new vista in which the Levant was placed by the prospective shift in the life line of the British Empire had its diplomatic effect in quickening the interest of the English in the eastern end of the Mediterranean and in the dissolution of Turkey, and the interest of the English in the transit of the Levant eventually became one of the chief determinants of British foreign policy. Meanwhile efforts to complete the inside line of communication with India by steam were being pushed forward. In 1836 the British hopefully explored the practicability of passing it through Mesopotamia to the head of the Persian Gulf, but the expedition ended

[133] "When two cargoes of cotton leave Alexandria the same day, one consigned to Trieste and the other to Genoa, it happens that the cotton consigned to Trieste has already reached Turin while that consigned to Genoa has just begun its quarantine." "L. S[erristori]," *Annali,* 1840, LXIV, 236.

[134] January 25, 1846, reprinted in the *Gazzetta di Milano.* Vidal, pp. 198–199.

[135] M. C. M., Camera di Commercio, cartella 564, March 22, 1844.

[136] For a comprehensive account of this revolution, see H. L. Hoskins. *British Routes to India* (Philadelphia, 1928).

[137] The *Annali di statistica* published a full account of the voyage and took note of the fueling problem. *Annali,* 1826, IX, 69–71.

in failure.[138] By 1835 a regular service of steam packets had been established between the home country and Alexandria,[139] and with the failure of the expedition on the Euphrates the attention of the British finally settled on Egypt and the Isthmus of Suez.[140]

The first rich prize created by these events was the "India mail," and the development of railroads on the continent incited the continental states to bid for it. It was first captured by the French, who in 1835 established a service of fast packets between Marseilles and Alexandria, touching at Nice, Genoa, Leghorn, Civitavecchia, Naples, Malta, and Syra.[141] Passengers for the East and the India mail travelled by packet from Dover to Calais and partly by rail and partly by diligence to Marseilles, to be placed on board the Alexandria steamer.[142] As soon as the Germans began to build railways, Austria saw a chance to divert the India mail fom Marseilles to the shorter route through its rising port of Trieste. In 1845 the Austrian Lloyd started its direct service of steam packets between Trieste and Alexandria. As the contest developed, it was dramatized by the English newspapers, and watched with the keenest interest by the continental journals, including those of Lombardy. The London *Times,* the *Standard,* and the *Morning Herald* backed a race between their correspondents from India to London over the two rival routes, and the governments whose territory was traversed placed every facility at the disposal of the contestants.[143] As yet the prize con-

---

[138] Hoskins, Chapter VII.

[139] A monthly service between England and Malta and another between Malta and Alexandria.

[140] The Mesopotamian expedition was reported by the Lombard journals. *Annali,* 1835, XLV, 150–151; 1836, XLVIII, 301; *Rivista,* 1841, IV, Pt. 3, 384. The British did not abandon their interest in the alternative route, even after the Suez canal was in their possession. See E. M. Earle, *Turkey, the Great Powers and the Bagdad Railway,* pp. 195–202.

[141] Hoskins, pp. 126, 223. Torelli, *Pensieri,* says 1837. Mail went from Paris to Suez in twenty-two days and eight hours; passengers in twenty-six days. *Annali,* 1840, LXV, 265. A correspondent writing from Malta in 1840 was "stupefied" by the changes steam navigation had brought to that island in ten years. He declared himself "in ecstasies over such incredible and incessant movement as that which steam had given to navigation, and the advantages they have been able to draw from this sublime invention." He found three steamship lines touching there—the French, the English and the Austrian, and reported that forty steamers were then engaged in these various services, which had awakened Malta from "its long sleep." "P," in *Annali,* 1840, LXIV, 112–113.

[142] The *Annali di statistica* reproduced an article from the *Revue brittanique* which declared: "One cannot hide the fact: the relations of England are in the hands of France." *Annali,* 1839, LXI, 165.

[143] In the fall of 1842 Captain Bloomfield had been sent by the British Government to test the route London-Trieste, with a view to its use for the India mail. He made the trip from London via Ostend, Cologne, Frankfort, Munich, Augsburg and Innsbruck to Trieste in 135 hours and 25 minutes. *Annali,* 1843, LXXV,

sisted only of passengers and mail, but in 1843 a cargo of tea, rice and indigo arrived at Trieste in the Austrian brig "Pylades"—the first to be brought directly from India to that port; and a canal through the Isthmus of Suez was being widely discussed in the journals of Italy as a means of completing the revolution.[144]

The position of advantage in which the Italian peninsula was being placed was evident to all, and after 1835 Charles Albert began a series of moves to put Genoa in competition with Marseilles and Trieste. One was a railroad connecting Genoa with the Rhine over the Lukmanier pass, to be followed by one over the Mt. Cenis to France; another was the mail contract which Sardinia made with the Peninsular and Oriental Steamship Company in February, 1847.[145] All of these events and their significance for Italy were being discussed in the Italian journals, and plans for a pan-Italian railway which would carry the India mail through the length of peninsula to Brindisi were eagerly agitated.[146] It was seen that to profit by their position on the re-opened way to the Orient the Italians must take concerted political action and build a national railroad system.[147] Amid these developments the Lombards, stranded between Genoa and Trieste, with their main railroad planned to run east and west, and with no north and south lines in prospect, were faced with the outlook not only of losing their traditional transit traffic, but of being left on one side by the new lines of intercourse through the Mediterranean. They had therefore motives of a very practical nature for drawing closer to Piedmont and for listening attentively to voices like those of Balbo and Petitti, which warned the Italians that unless they took prompt and united action they would be left aside by the great stream of commerce that was once more passing their doors and lose their one remaining chance to take a place among the leading nations of the modern world.

120–121. Waghorn's trip via Trieste, backed by the *Times*, was reported in the *Annali*, 1845, LXXXVI, 253–254. Waghorn went from Trieste to London in 99 hours and 45 minutes, arriving at London at 4.15 p.m. on October 31 with mails that had left Bombay on October 1. Baldwin's trip via Marseilles, backed by the *Standard* and the *Morning Herald*, was reported by the *Annali*, 1846, LXXXVII, 116–117. Baldwin arrived with the mails in 27 days, or 60 hours less than Waghorn had taken, in spite of bad weather.

[144] See, for example, *Annali*, 1826, IX, 69–71; *Rivista*, 1842, V, Pt. 3, 115; Ciasca, *Programma*, pp. 433–448; 508–509.

[145] Vidal, pp. 183–189; 207–208.

[146] See below, pp. 209–211. The route for the India mail via Brindisi was completed in 1870 and Brindisi remained the principal port of transit for the India mails until 1914. Hoskins, p. 411.

[147] See Ciasca, *Programma*, pp. 433–455.

A review of the commercial history of Lombardy between 1814 and
48 leaves the impression that, while its commerce, particularly in
lk, was expanding considerably and reflecting the influence of a livelier
tempo in the commercial life of Europe, its merchants as a class were
slow to move. Steeped in the traditions of a community preponderantly
agricultural, they were prompt to resent any interference with their
traditional practices, but slow to strike out on new lines. Their dignified
conservatism is reflected not only in the sarcasm of the progressive
publicists and the efforts made by these to coax or lash them into action,
but in their reluctance to seek new markets even when spurred by the
Austrian Government. In 1816 the Government proposed that they
develop their trade with Brazil by availing themselves of the opportunity to send some samples of their exports offered by an official visit
which "an Austrian frigate and some brigs" were about to make to that
country. But the Chamber of Commerce received no response from the
merchants to its request for samples.[148] In 1817 the Government tried
to stimulate their trade with Spain, but the Chamber replied with a
memorial that showed only a vague and languid interest.[149] The Chamber
petitioned Austria to send consuls of Italian blood to the Levant to
foster trade with Asia Minor and Egypt, but when this step had been
taken, the merchants could not be induced to provide them with samples.[150] In 1843 an attempt of the Government to interest them in trading with Algiers was met with a complacent expression of indifference.[151]
Cattaneo declared with withering irony that "if a group of our merchants happened one evening to speak among themeselves of the project
of forming the East India Company and conquering the trade with
the East and the realms of the Mogul, the next morning they would
be ashamed to remember it in order not to be thought crazy."[152] If the
modern spirit of enterprise had here and there produced a stir in the
economic life of Lombardy, it had made little difference in the attitude
of the mercantile class. They remained passive in a changing world.

[148] M. C. M., Camera di Commercio, cartella 172, November 29, 1816; January 20,
1817. This incident is described by Pugliese, "Iniziative," p. 426.
[149] M. C. M., Camera di Commercio, cartella 172, No. 1200/P, May 21; May 27,
1817.
[150] Ibid., cartella 173, No. 1565, August 9-10, 1826.
[151] Ibid., November 15, 1843.
[152] Annali, 1837, LIV, 187.

CHAPTER IV

LOMBARD MANUFACTURING INDUSTRY

T HE manufacturing industry of Lombardy was unimportant in comparison with its agriculture or even with its commerce. According to a rough estimate of the time, about one-third of the population was engaged in manufacture in 1840, but a large proportion of those who were thus employed were also tilling the soil.[1] During the period industry did not undergo a revolution in Lombardy or threaten the preponderance of agriculture; but it made enough progress to justify hopes for the future, so that Frattini could say in 1855: "Lombardy is a country eminently agricultural, but this does not prevent it from being at the same time modestly industrial and from having the power to become more so."[2]

The policies of Napoleon left Lombard manufacturing industry in a state of depression.[3] Napoleon cut off its raw materials, damaged its markets, and ruthlessly exposed it to the competition of French manufacturers, with the object of converting the North of Italy into "an economic colony of France." Lombard manufacturing industry was in a state of demoralization on the eve of the Restoration and the manufacturers of Lombardy as well as its merchants hailed with joy the collapse of the Napoleonic system.

During the first half of the century in Lombardy, as in the rest of Europe, textiles and metal goods were the chief manufactures. The textile industry included the spinning and weaving of silk, wool, cotton, linen and hemp. The metallurgical industry worked in iron, copper and bronze, producing from the latter statues, gilded ornaments and church bells. There was some manufacture of jewel work in gold and art work in crystals and leather.[4] "Silk, cotton, iron, furniture, jewelry, paper

---

[1] 800,000 out of a total population of 2,524,000. Giuseppe Sacchi in *Annali*, 1842, LXXIII, 240.

[2] Frattini, p. 220.

[3] For these policies see Tarlé, *Le blocus continental*.

[4] An indication of the products most esteemed for quality of workmanship is to be found in the advice given local manufacturers in 1833 to send to the industrial exposition of Vienna in 1834–1835 works of fine art, jewelry, leather boxes, fine weaves of silk, worked leather, straw hats and inlaid furniture. Note of the editors, *Annali*, 1833, Bulletino, p. 33. The prizes awarded to Milanese manufacturers were for silk fabrics, objects of bronze, woodwork, confectionery,

and carriages" were the manufactures that contemporary observation, solicitous of the industrial standing of Lombardy, regarded with pride.[5] These, if linen be added, formed the backbone of Lombard manfacturing industry.

Manufacturing industry in Lombardy was almost entirely confined to an East and West belt which embraced the Hill zone described in the first chapter and the upper edge of the Plain—a region of small farms, large towns and cities, and dense population, between the great irrigated estates of the lower Plain and the patchwork quilt of tiny farms in the folds of the Mountains. In this middle belt were the outlets of the mountain valleys and their mines and the entries to the Alpine passes, and here were the cities that were the centers of trade and the reservoirs of capital—Brescia, Bergamo, Como, Milan. In this belt most of the silk was grown; and water power was provided by the canals and rivers flowing from the mountains into the Plain—a circumstance less important to industry at the time of the Restoration than twenty years later when water-driven machinery was to become a considerable factor in the manufacture of textiles. Water power and a dense population were also to be found in the Mountain zone, but their industrial potentialities remained undeveloped. More naturally in the lower Plain, with its high farming, there was little manufacturing, except in Lodi and Crema which produced Parmesan cheese and the Province of Cremona which spun and wove a quantity of linen and before 1848 began to play a part in the manufacture of silk and cotton.

To the mind of the reader familiar with economic history the "manufacturing region" thus defined will not suggest the visible signs of the presence or absence of industry familiar to us—neither smokestacks nor even great mills, not to mention mill-towns and "black districts." Except for the silk-reeling mills that were springing up on the farms or collecting in the country towns, it would generally be necessary to go into the peasant's cottage or to watch the string of horses or wagons on the road to town to detect the presence of industrial activity, for the manufacturing industry of the region was widely and increasingly diffused through the countryside as the part-time occupation of the peasants and their families. A smoking furnace on the mountainside or a

---

woolen felt, cotton stuffs, percussion guns, typographical work and embroidery. *Annali*, 1836, XLVII, 86–88. To make the inventory of Lombard manufactures complete one would have to add paper, printing and book-making and various other titles—some, articles of consumption, such as cheese, sugar, felt hats, illuminating gas, pottery, porcelain, and carriages, a product for which Milan enjoyed a widespread reputation; others, auxiliaries of a growing industrial life, such as soap, dyestuffs, machines and chemicals.

[5] Frattini, pp. 220 ff.

mill rising on the bank of a running stream or in the suburbs of a commercial city, was still an infrequent sight. Nevertheless the region embraced a very considerable industrial activity.

The most important manufacture, that of silk, was widely distributed throughout the industrial belt.

To understand this industry one must have in mind the steps in the transformation of silk from the spider-web filament spun by the silkworm itself into the fabrics finally marketed.[6] In the process of preparing the warps and wefts of which these fabrics are woven, there are three distinct stages which, taken together, correspond to the process of spinning in the other textile industries. The first is that of unwinding the filament from the cocoon and winding it on a reel. In this stage of the process a number of filaments, almost invisible when single, are brought together to form a strand. The skeins of silk thus created are the crude silk (*seta greggia*) of commerce; and for some time after 1814 this crude silk was much the most important surplus product of Lombard industry. The next stage is that in which several of these strands are united, at the same time receiving a preliminary twist. The skeins are then cleaned. There remains the more elaborate process of "throwing" or twisting the strands to give them the strength to serve as wefts and warps or organzines. It is important, then, to distinguish between the reeling-mills (*filande*), which produced the crude silk shipped abroad in ever increasing abundance and the twisting or spinning mills (*filatoi*), which were a different kind of establishment, with its own machinery, producing wefts and warps. Quite distinct from either of these stages was the process by which the two forms of silk waste were reduced to an article of commerce. The first of these forms is the floss (*strusa*) which must be removed from the surface of the cocoon to find the head of the continuous filament which forms the bulk of it. Another form is the *strazza*, the tough and gummy sack (*cascame*) in which the worm encloses itself before it begins to spin, and which is left when the filament has been unwound. These *struse, strazze* and *cascami* contain the same precious material of which the filament is composed, but not being formed in a continuous thread have to be reduced to fibres by a process of carding and spinning, similar to that applied to the fibres of cotton, linen or wool. This ruder material was the basis therefore of a special industry—one which seems to have been set up in Lombardy for the first time during the first half of the last century. Such are the steps in the preparation of silk yarns for weaving. Finally, quite

---

[6] The reader is advised to consult some brief description of this complicated process, such for instance as that in the Encyclopedia Britannica, as only the principal steps can be indicated here.

separate and independent from these preparatory steps, remains the manufacture of silk textiles.

In the Napoleonic era the manufacture of silk was the leading industry of the region and was concentrated on the production of crude silk and silk yarns rather than weaving.[7] Sericulture and silk-winding were geographically allied: the Departments of the Napoleonic Kingdom of Italy in which the most silk was produced were those in which the winders were most numerous.[8] The winding of silk was a village industry, scattered through the silk-breeding districts and largely carried on by peasant families as an auxiliary occupation. After the Restoration this branch of the industry continued to preponderate.[9] Some of the silk-winding may have been carried on in private houses;[10] but in general it was done in a mill or *filanda,* equipped with vats and with simple machinery for turning the reels. The multiplication of these mills has already been noted as a phenomenon that accompanied the rapid extension of mulberry plantations between 1814 and 1848,[11] until there was scarcely a village in the silk-growing districts in which rustic Pippas might not be seen passing on their way to work.

It pleased me, wrote a contemporary observer, to see the active tumult of the silk-winding mills: that rural industry employing a population of women in an airy edifice, from which one looks out across a stretch of lake to a background of mountains, amid the hum of voices and recurring songs, and the continuous screeching of a hundred reels loaded with soft and lucent floss.

One Sunday morning, contrary to usage, I saw in action the winding-mill of a proprietor with whose family I had contracted a friendly acquaintance. I entered: the young winders, clean and adorned, were intent on tying up and reuniting the threads which they were unwinding from four cocoons afloat in the boiler, and which mounted and wound themselves on the reel moved by a restless little girl. From time to time one of the young women would yield her place to this girl to give her practice in the work of drawing the silk, while she applied herself to the less important business of winding it on the reel. Other women saw to refilling the baskets of cocoons near the winders. When

[7] In 1810 the exports of these from the whole region embraced in the Kingdom of Italy were worth four times as much as the exports of silk textiles. Tarlé, p. 252.

[8] The Departments centering in Bergamo, Brescia and Como. *Ibid.,* p. 71.

[9] In 1829 crude silk was still "the main nerve of Italian silks." *Annali,* 1829, XX, 21. In 1841 a writer on the "Nuovo metodo di trarre la seta, detta trama filata," declared: "A very large portion of our silk goes abroad in the crude state." *Politecnico,* 1841, IV, 471.

[10] Francesco Lencisa, describing the silk industry in Piedmont in 1831, included in his estimate 12,000 heaters (*fornelli*) in private houses, the apparatus costing with its appurtenances about 40 lire. *Annali,* 1831, XXIX, 146–147.

[11] See above, pp. 43 ff.

the reels were full, all together took away the spools full of silk; they inspected the skeins, carefully cleaning them or taking away the little lumps, the bits of impurity, the broken heads, and putting aside what little of the silk was dirty and torn; then they carried the skeins shining with a fine golden yellow to dry in a large and airy chamber.[12]

The extension of silk-culture intensified the manufacture in the districts where it had already existed—that is, in the Provinces of Brescia, Bergamo and Como,[13] and also disseminated the industry in the Plain which turned to the breeding of silkworms after 1814.[14]

The multiplication of reeling mills was a direct and necessary consequence of the extension of sericulture. Meanwhile, the second stage of manufacture, object of an industry independent of agriculture and one which had scarcely existed in Lombardy at the time of the Restoration, had made great progress and in 1855 six-sevenths of all the silk exported from Lombardy was reported to be in the form of wefts and warps.[15] Most of the silk waste, the *strusa* and *cascami*, was exported raw, to be manufactured abroad. In 1833 an industry based on the use of this waste had been established in Lombardy.[16] But "to our shame,"

[12] Ravizza, pp. 243–244.

[13] In Brescia the silk industry developed rapidly after 1800, especially in the decade 1810–1820. By 1825 there were 1149 reeling mills in the province. *Annali*, 1833, Bulletino, pp. 317 ff. In the province of Bergamo the number of winding mills grew from 80 in 1806 to 202 in 1837 and 412 in 1854. Tarlé, p. 121; *Annali*, 1837, LIV, 320; Frattini, p. 57. In the district of Lecco, there were 1034 silk-winding mills in 1842. *Annali*, 1842, LXXIII, 248. In the province of Como there were reported to be 400 "heaters" (*fornelli*) for winding silk in 1830. Review of C. Cantù, *Nuova Guida al Lago di Como* (1830), *Annali*, 1832, XXXI, 116.

[14] Thus in the province of Milan, where in the Napoleonic era very few silk-winders had been employed, there were 208 winding-mills by 1855, and as many as 675 winding-mills had been set up in the province of Cremona. Frattini, p. 57.

[15] *Ibid.*, p. 65. In 1844 silk twisting was declared to have "begun to improve among us only in the past few years." Giulio Sarti, "Sullo stato del setificio in Italia," *Politecnico*, 1844, VII, 520. In 1833 there were 86 throwing mills in the province of Brescia (*Annali*, 1833, Bulletino, p. 317), as compared with 87 in 1855; 94 in the province of Bergamo in 1837 (*Annali*, 1837, LIV, 313–336), and 110 in 1855; 82 in the province of Milan in 1845 (M. C. M., Camera di Commercio, cartella 556, August 26, 1845), as compared with 93 in 1855. The number of spindles for twisting silk in the province of Como seems to have grown from 2,550 in 1830 (review of C. Cantù, *Nuova guida ol Lago di Como, Annali*, 1832, XXXI, 115) to 162,000 in 1855. The figures for 1855 are from Frattini, p. 65.

[16] A manufactory at Monza, owned by Pietro Campana and Pietro Gos, which turned *cascami* into a thick fabric for bed coverings, employing the idle hands of the peasants in winter (*Annali*, 1833, Bulletino, p. 391; *Ibid.*, 1838, LVIII, 215), and one at the Porta Comasina, Milan, founded by Gaetano Venini and Gaetano Piccaluga, who invented a process by which they turned the waste into a floss that was reported to be hardly distinguishable from the best silk. *Annali*, 1833, Bulletino, p. 391. In 1855 there were still only three mills in Lombardy for the reduction of *cascami*, one at Milan (with 512 spindles), another at Bergamo (with 1000 spindles), and another at Cremona, not in operation. Frattini, pp. 90 ff.

wrote Frattini in 1855, most of the 2,472,220 lbs. of *cascami* produced annually is still exported in the crude state.[17]

As for weaving, the other great branch of silk manufacture, Lombardy had lagged behind Lyons at the beginning of the century. The industry was concentrated in Milan and Como; but "there were not more than five hunded looms in the few manufactories that Milan could count in 1816," and these were producing only for the lower classes. The Jacquard loom, which wove patterned silks, had yet to be introduced. Under the shelter of a prohibitive tariff, some able foreign manufacturers established themselves in Lombardy and the industry began to expand. By 1844 the total number of looms in Milan had increased to 4,000 and those of Milan and Como combined to 8,000, and "the most complicated stuffs . . . for every use and of all dimensions" were being turned out.[18] Nevertheless the number of Jacquard looms was less than one-fifth of the total in 1855—an indication that the product chiefly consisted of simple and less expensive fabrics.[19]

The other branch of the textile industry that underwent a notable expansion in Lombardy between 1814 and 1848 was the spinning and weaving of cotton. In the time of Napoleon, while the use of cotton fabrics supplied by England, Switzerland, Saxony, and France was already widespread in North Italy, local manufacture was only in its beginning.[20] The spinners seem to have been concentrated in the neighborhood of Brescia and the weavers in the districts of Milan and Cremona.[21] In 1810 there were three manufactories "of very considerable size" at Milan and Intra (Lake Maggiore), and "small manufactories of ordinary cotton goods" scattered through several Departments of the Kingdom of Italy.[22] Released from the restrictions of the

[17] Frattini, p. 91.

[18] The facts just stated are from an article by Angelo Piazza, "Cenni sul setificio," *Rivista*, n. s., 1844, II, pt. 2, 276–286. Piazza had successfully directed two of the largest manufactories of Milan and was about to give a course on silk weaving under the auspices of the Society for the Encouragement of the Arts and Crafts of Milan. *Ibid.*, pp. 265–275. In 1830 there were already 1200 looms in operation in the province of Como. Review of C. Cantù, *Nuova guida al Lago di Como, Annali*, 1832, XXXI, 116.

[19] Frattini, p. 70. Frattini gives 4,431 as the total number of looms in Lombardy. The discrepancy between this and the larger figure given by Piazza in 1844 is probably due to the fact that Frattini counted only the looms employed in manufactories.

[20] Tarlé, pp. 303–304.

[21] The statistics of the Napoleonic era are unsatisfactory because they lump cotton spinners and weavers together with those that spun and wove linen and hemp. In 1806 there were 19,871 weavers of cotton, linen and hemp in the Departments centering in Milan and Cremona, and 33,096 spinners around Brescia. Tarlé, pp. 298–299.

[22] According to the Viceroy Eugene. Tarlé, p. 314.

Napoleonic régime, the Lombard cotton industry expanded rapidly between the Restoration and 1848. As it grew, the industry tended to concentrate in the Province of Milan, particularly around Gallarate, Busto
Arsizio and Monza—the district in which the great textile factories of
North Italy are to be found today.

Some reports of the Chamber of Commerce of Milan in 1819 give a
picture of the still struggling industry and its difficulties shortly after the
Restoration. The Chamber was arguing for a reduction of the tariff
on the importation of spun cotton. This tariff protected the spinning
industry, but the supply provided by the local spinneries was entirely
inadequate "in comparison with the consumption of cotton fabrics
[which is now] most extensive and universally adopted." The spinning
then being done in Lombardy was confined to ordinary grades of white
cotton and left unsatisfied the demand for the finer grades, which could
be introduced only at a cost that destroyed the profits of the weavers.
The spinning industry was woefully deficient in equipment. The machines that existed were small affairs of from 50 to 100 spindles and
were operated by hand. The plants equipped with this simple machinery
were to be found near Milan in Gallarate, Busto, Lecco and Chiavenna.
The rest of the spinning, and that the greater part of it, was done "by
the peasants in the winter season, but not very extensively, in spite of
the incitements public and private given for so many years to awaken
this branch of the industry." Even at this early date some improvement
was noted. In 1820 the Chamber admitted "that the national machines
for the spinning of cotton had been somewhat increased . . . while . . .
a manufactory has been established at Legnano and another is being
constructed at [MS illegible, probably] Torre." But these establishments, the Chamber maintained, made no sensible difference in view of
the vast quantities consumed. The spinners could hope to profit only
if they introduced water-driven machinery, but this was too expensive
in Lombardy for the production of ordinary fabrics because of the
competitive demand of agriculture for the use of running water. The
Chamber declared the industry to be further handicapped by its inferi-
ority in the use of dyes. "In the Lombard dyeworks no dyeing of
foreign cotton is done on commissions, since in Genoa and in other
places near the Realm there are dyeworks which have been brought to
the highest degree of perfection. Very few of the dyeworks can apply
themselves to dyeing in red, because the Lombard industry cannot compete with foreign industry in producing bright and fast red dyes. . . .
Our dyeworks therefore serve only for the dyeing for internal consumption, and very little for dyeing in red." Here is a picture of a weaving
industry tied down by the tariff to a struggling and still rudimentary

spinning and dyeing industry—so handicapped that "the commerce of speculation" was declared by the Chamber to be "annihilated in this branch of traffic."[23]

But in the next twenty years cotton weaving prospered in Lombardy.[24] In spite of the duties on cotton yarns great quantities were being imported from England.[25] The spinning industry underwent a corresponding expansion, thanks to a number of water-driven factories that sprang up in the Province of Milan. In 1836 a writer in the *Eco della Borsa* observed: "It is only a few years since the spinning of cotton was introduced, and already the factories of the firm of Andrea Ponti and others of first rank contend with the leading French and English establishments."[26] By 1842 there were twenty-six establishments for spinning cotton and they were almost all large plants.[27] By the end of the period this new industry had risen to a place of importance in local manufacturing economy second only to that occupied by the manufacture of silk.[28] Meanwhile the weaving of cotton fabrics, which remained a household industry, continued to expand.[29] On the eve of 1848 this weaving industry was still limited to the production of coarse cotton cloth.[30]

There was a widespread manufacture of linen in Lombardy, and although it suffered from the competition of cotton,[31] the industry made an ambitious spurt towards the end of the period. The raw material was supplied in abundance by local agriculture. In the eighteenth

[23] Report of the Chamber of Commerce of Milan to the Delegation of Milan on the effect of the tariff on cotton yarns, February 8, 1819; report of the same to the Provincial Delegation of Milan, August 2, 1820. M. C. M., Camera di Commercio, cartella 172.

[24] In 1832 there were reported to be 9,890 looms in operation in the province of Milan, producing some 304,000 pieces of ordinary cotton goods, and 4,300 looms in Cremona, Mantua, Bergamo and Brescia producing 107,500 pieces. It was calculated that these were employing 50,000 persons. *Annali*, 1832, XXXIV, 221 (misprint in the original text for 321).

[25] 577,200 packages of 10 English lbs. each. *Annali*, 1833, Bulletino, p. 232.

[26] Quoted in *Ricoglitore italiano e straniero*, 1836, Anno II, 680.

[27] G. Sacchi, reviewing Giovanni Frattini, *Sulla filatura e tessitura del cotone in Lombardia e principalmente nella provincia di Milano nel 1845* (Milan, 1846), in *Annali*, 1846, XC, 272.

[28] *Pronipote del Vesta Verde*, 1849, p. 80. See also Merlini, *Il passato, il presente e l'avvenire dell' industria manifatturiera in Lombardia*, pp. 30 ff.

[29] In 1845 it was estimated to be employing in the province of Milan alone 99,000 men, women and children at 71,000 looms, and consuming 25,844 tons of cotton. M. C. M., Camera di Commercio, cartella 127.11. The date is uncertain, but is probably 1844. The figures are of little absolute value because of the large number of cottage laborers who might easily escape accurate enumeration. The calculations of Frattini in 1845 gave a very different result. See *Annali*, 1847, XCI, 145–159.

[30] *Annali*, 1847, XCI, 157.

[31] *Annali*, 1833, Bulletino, p. 323; *Politecnico*, 1839, I, 103.

century the Plain, on the left bank of the Po between the Adda and the Mincio, was famous for its production of flax, and Crema and Cremona were reported in 1806 to be producing enough linen "to provision Italy and France."[32] The chief export was then in the form of threads, whose quality gave them a wide foreign market. The spinning and weaving were diffused through the countryside. Even in districts in which the peasants did not grow flax, as in Brescia and Bergamo, they bought it and in the idle winter days the women gathered in the stables to spin and weave it, both for home use and to add something to the money income of the family.[33] Such continued to be the prevailing character of the industry throughout the first half of the nineteenth century.[34] But a notable attempt was made in the 'forties to modernize the manufacture of threads, and between 1839 and 1848, after several failures and amid a considerable stir of public interest, two great linen-spinning mills were successfully established in Lombardy.[35]

Wool spininng and weaving was a more ancient industry in the North of Italy than the manufacture of silk or cotton; but it had fallen far behind silk as an export industry even before the French invasion. The Spanish Wars of 1808-1809 cut off the supply of merino wool and seriously injured the manufacture of the finer grades of cloth at Bergamo, Como and Milan,[36] but the industry had continued to play a considerable rôle in the production of coarse textiles for the home market. After the Restoration, however, the market for these was damaged by a flood of cheap woolen cloth manufactured in the transalpine provinces of Austria, and the industry showed no signs of progress before 1848. The manufacture of woolen blankets occupied some 2,200 of the peasants of Brescia, especially in winter.[37] There was also one considerable plant in the Province of Brescia which manufactured woolen and other textiles of a finer grade,[38] and the most important establishment of the French period, that of the Signori Guaita at San Martino, near Como, a manufactory with a centralized workshop, survived and was suffi-

[32] Tarlé, p. 318.
[33] Ibid., pp. 319–320.
[34] "The industry remains for the most part in the hands of the peasants." Politecnico, 1839, I, 103. See also Jacini, p. 223.
[35] The founding and history of these mills can be followed in the Annali, 1833, Bulletino, pp. 214–215; 1838, LVI, 350–351; 1840, LXIII, 335–347; 1842, LXXIII, 245; 1843, LXXV, 72–73; Politecnico, 1839, I, 103; 188–191; and in M. C. M., Camera di Commercio, cartella 569, June 14, 1841; cartella 173, January 29, 1844; cartella 569, December 24, 1846 and March 27 and September 18, 1847.
[36] Tarlé, Chapter IX and summary, pp. 292–295.
[37] Employed by 90 firms, they produced from 30,000 to 36,000 blankets, worth 900,000 Austrian lire, and marketed in the Veneto and the surrounding states. Annali, 1833, Bulletino, p. 323.
[38] That of the Bellandi Brothers at Pratalboino. See below p. 106.

ciently up-to-date to make an impression on travellers.[39] A local revival
of wool weaving in the Province of Bergamo was reported in 1837,[40]
and a wool spinnery operated by a joint stock corporation was set up at
Linate near Milan at about the same time.[41] But these were isolated
cases, and the woolen industry was regarded as on the decline.[42]

Mining and the metallurgical industry, though of some local importance, were declining in the first half of the nineteenth century. The
exhaustion of the supply of wood in the Lombard mountains had occa-
sioned alarm even before the French invasion and had caused the Austrian Government to offer a prize in 1789 for the discovery of coal in
Lombardy. In the Napoleonic era the shortage of wood and the low
level of chemical and hydraulic technique were felt as serious handicaps
on the industry.[43] The dearth of fuel contnued to prevent a full and
systematic exploitation of the metals of Lombardy in spite of various
efforts of private enterprise and of the Government to renew the for-
estation of the region and to find substitute fuels.

The metallurgical industry was localized in the vicinity of the mines,
that is, in Brescia, Bergamo and Como. The Brescian iron industry
showed no signs of prosperity in the period after the Restoration. In
1825 four of its twenty-five mines had fallen into disuse.[44] There were
two bronze foundries at Brescia for the casting of church bells, for
which a market was provided by the passion in Lombardy for the beau-

---

[39] D. Bertolotti, *Viaggio ai tre laghi*, pp. 14 ff. Lady Morgan to whom the
silk and cotton industry of Como seemed a slight affair, wrote: "The cloth
manufactory of Messrs Guaita in the neighborhood of the village of San Martino,
is of some consideration." Lady Sidney Morgan, *Italy*, I, 308. Guaita was the
first to introduce the flying shuttle into Lombardy. Melchiorre Gioia, *Dettati
sulle manifatture nazionali e tariffe daziarie*, II, 32, note. 1.

[40] *Annali*, 1837, LIV, 320–321.

[41] *Politecnico*, 1839, I, 103. The company proposed to add "a complete manufactory of woolen cloths of various and elegant kinds." In 1841 the Fratelli
Preyssl had in operation a manufactory at Milan described as a great factory for
spinning and weaving woolens, with a dyeworks. *Annali*, 1841, LXIX, 198.

[42] Giuseppe Sacchi so described it in a survey of child labor in local industry
in 1842. *Annali*, 1842, LXXIII, 245.

[43] Tarlé, p. 335. Even then Carinthian steel, though subject to an import duty,
was found to be cheaper than the local product. *Ibid.*, pp. 339–340. The dearth
of wood under the Napoleonic régime faced the Bergamasque and Brescian
workers with a crisis and forced them to resort to the use of coal imported from
Istria. *Ibid.*, pp. 113–114.

[44] The local manufacture of iron was then employing six blast furnaces, with
540 operatives, 94 shops, with 1260 operatives, and two steel foundries, with
30 operatives. The outstanding iron mill, that of Signor Luigi Torre at Vobarno,
was equipped with six forges, four other "great fires" and a "cylindrical [rolling]
machine," and employed 270 men, including the woodcutters. This plant also
manufactured copper and supplied the navy at Venice with copper sheets and
strips. *Annali*, 1833, Bulletino, pp. 317 ff.

tiful chimes that still delight the traveller on its lakes and in its hills,[45] and a local manufacture of firearms, sustained by a standing order of the Austrian Government for guns and by the home market, had a limited foreign market which fell off when the Government prohibited the exportation of arms to the Greek revolutionists.[46] The Brescian metallurgical industry was suffering from the competition of the manufacturers of Carinthia, the exclusion of its products from the Papal State and the scarcity of charcoal.[47] The metallurgical industry at Bergamo, based on the iron ore extracted from its mountains, was subject to the same limitations. In 1837 it consisted of fourteen blast furnaces and a number of small ironworks, engaged in producing nails and excellent agricultural implements.[48] Some iron and copper were extracted and manufactured in the mountains of Lecco and Como.[49] The traveller Davide Bertolotti was much impressed by the sooty iron and copper forges that he found in the steep mountain valleys above Lecco, "wondered at the manner of work of these bronzed Steropes," and lamented that there was not "some mechanical device to spare the terrible human labor involved."[50] At Dongo, on Lake Como, visiting the furnaces and forges of the Signori Rubini, near the mines located there, he found iron being smelted and wrought "with the best methods used beyond the Alps, and where one can see fine cylinders of iron produced which do not yield in strength to those made abroad."[51] At Milan there was a considerable manufacture of art objects in bronze.[52] In the

[45] A contemporary measured the increasing prosperity of the peasants during the period by the number of new bells swung in the campanili of the parish churches. Spreafico, p. 168. It was a kind of expenditure not always regarded with complacency by the advocates of "progress," for example, Ravizza.

[46] Summary of the reports of the police delegates of the various provinces of Lombardy, A. S. M., Presidenza, Atti segreti, cartella LXIX (1824). In 1825 the industry was divided among 76 shops, which employed 776 operatives, 230 at the forges and 546 in the manufacture proper. *Annali*, 1833, Bulletino, pp. 317 ff.

[47] *Ibid.*

[48] *Annali*, 1828, XVII, 313; 1837, LIV, 320.

[49] In 1842 there were 17 iron foundries and 6 copper foundries at Lecco. *Annali*, 1842, LXXIII, 248.

[50] Bertolotti, pp. 247–248.

[51] *Ibid.*, pp. 225–226.

[52] In 1829 there were 50 shops in the city engaged in this industry. M. C. M., Camera di Commercio, cartella 555. In 1855 the development of the manufacture of bronze statuary was signalized as one of the notable achievements of the period 1814–1848. Merlini, p. 31. The bronze foundry of Viscardi, formerly Manfredini, near Milan, was regarded as one of the most remarkable in the Austrian Empire, "rivaling those of Paris and Munich and ranking with the best in Europe. From it came the monumental statues of the Arch of Peace [Milan] and the statues that adorn Turin, Monferrato, Grätz, etc." A. Balbi, *L'Austria e le primarie potenze*, p. lxxi.

'forties shops of some importance for the manufacture of railway equipment and of machines of all kinds were established at the capital.[53]

A mining and metallurgical industry on the decline, but of considerable importance; a manufacture of woolen and linen yarns and coarse fabrics that was stationary or declining; a manufacture of raw silk, silk warps and wefts, spun cotton and of ordinary grades of silk and cotton textiles, expanding rapidly—such are the chief positive data which the available statistics yield regarding the main outlines of Lombard manufacturing industry between the Restoration and the middle of the century. In the midst of this activity there was an extension of silk weaving to a limited manufacture of fine fabrics, a traditional manufacture of paper, leather, hats and carriages, and some skilled handicraft in the production of jewelry, fine metal work and fancy leather goods, and of guns, hardware and agricultural implements in the small shops of Bergamo and Brescia. Before the end of the period auxiliary industries were to appear, particularly chemical and dye works and machine shops.

Two of the characteristics of the principal industries have already become apparent. One is the close dependence of manufacturing on the extractive industries, that is, on mining and agriculture. Only in the case of cotton manufactures was the local industry based on a supply of raw material entirely imported from abroad. Dependent largely on local supplies Lombard manufacturing industry was passive with reference to agriculture and commerce. There was no industry in Lombardy before 1848 that forced the pace on either of these other forms of economic activity, unless one should include in manufacturing industry the vast and growing production of silk. Even in this case the art of transformation received the impulses that shaped it from the enormous pressure of the foreign demand. It was the demand created by the markets of England, France, Switzerland and Germany that multiplied the reeling-mills in the Lombard villages; and it was the change in this demand, particularly the closing of the London market, that stimulated in Lombardy the second branch of this industry—the art of silk-throwing, the conversion of crude silk into warps and wefts. In general the manufactures of Lombardy grew directly out of its agriculture; the atmosphere that its industrial life breathed, high and low, was that of a community of agriculturists. Industry had to yield precedence to agriculture in obtaining both labor and capital. Manufactures took root and flourished in the interstices, so to speak, of an agricultural order. The exception to this rule was the spinning and weaving of cotton—an industry that imported its raw material and flourished on a

[53] See below, pp. 114–115.

combination of elements in part extraneous to agriculture, namely: abundant labor, power-driven machinery and a high tariff that gave it a local market for cheap cotton goods.

The other characteristic that has already become evident is that manufacturing in Lombardy was a diffused industry. It is true that, except for cheese making, it was almost entirely confined to the zone of the Hills, the upper Plain and the Cremonese; but within this zone it was largely carried on in the cottages of the peasants and in the rural villages, as a supplement to agricultural occupations.[54] Even mining and the metallurgical industries were carried on in great part by peasants in their spare time. In the two industries that were expanding notably, there were opposite tendencies in the matter of diffusion. The manufacture of raw silk spread still further through the countryside with the extension of sericulture and the erection of reeling-mills near the sources of supply.[55] The spinning of cotton, on the other hand, while it did not concentrate in the cities, tended to localization near the water-power sites of the Milanese, and in the last decade of the period linen-spinning began to obey the same influence.

Lombard manufactures were chiefly the work of unskilled hands, of the hands of peasant men and women, who laid aside the hoe to take up the loom or to go to the silk-winding mill. The cunning expertness that had made Italian handicraft brilliantly famous in the Renaissance was still present but it was no longer dominant. Such native skill as remained was a matter of family tradition. Its ancient custodians, the guilds, had disappeared in the eighteenth century, swept away by Enlightenment as an obstacle to Progress; and the art of manufacture was not taught in the schools. Labor was left free, but unorganized and untaught. The important manufactures of Lombardy, except silk, which for the most part was exported after merely being wound, owed their market to other elements than skilled handicraft. They were coarse and ordinary grades of goods, chiefly for home consumption by the lower classes.

The principal industries, the manufacture of textiles and metals, seem to have been for the most part in the stage of wholesale handicraft.[56]

[54] For example, the weaving of cotton was performed (in 1839) by 52,000 looms "scattered in the peasants' houses." *Politecnico*, 1839, I, 38. In some communes of the province of Milan (1855) there was a loom for weaving cotton in every peasant's house. Frattini, p. 105. They were "kept in motion for the most part in the season of the year when agriculture is idle." Jacini, p. 223.

[55] "The manufacturing activity of our country, passing from the woolen to the silk industry, has in large part abandoned the city and come to establish itself in the countryside," observed Jacini in 1855 (p. 17).

[56] This classification is based on that worked out by Professor N. S. B. Gras, *Industrial Evolution* (Cambridge, 1930).

This statement is a characterization of the prevailing form of manufacturing organization. There was probably some retail handicraft in the larger towns and cities, and there was certainly a good deal of manufacture for immediate use in the countryside and the rural villages.[57] M. Tarlé observes that in the Napoleonic era the establishments called *fabbriche,* that is, manufactories, "are often only a kind of *bureau des commandes* which distribute the works to the peasants of the vicinage and receive the manufactured products destined for commerce." In general, "Napoleonic Italy knew neither strong concentrations of workers in the manufactories, nor important agglomerations of workers in the cities." "Little shops of artisans, tiny manufactories, modest *bureaux des commandes* which employ some thirty or forty operatives are the rule," except in the textile industry and even in this they were the prevalent form of organization.[58] The glimpses of manufacturing organization that can be obtained from the descriptions and statistics available for the period from 1814 to 1848 are sporadic and unsatisfactory, but they indicate that an organization under *fabbriche,* that is, under firms of merchant manufacturers employing the labor of peasants at home with their own implements, remained the rule in the textile industry of Lombardy throughout the first half of the century.[59]

The organization of industry varied of course in the different branches of manufacture which stood in various relations to the organization of trade. Parmesan cheese was manufactured on the latifundia of the Plain and seems to have been bought up for sale in the cities and for export by commissioners through the medium of brokers who visited

[57] A glimpse of this is given in Spreafico's account of the Brianza, *Politecnico,* 1844, VII, 165.

[58] Tarlé, pp. 81–82.

[59] Its prevalence in the spinning of cotton during the first decade after the Restoration has already been indicated. In Cremona (1822) the cotton looms of the four considerable firms of that province were active "for about six months of the year in the respective houses of the workers." A. S. M., Presidenza, Atti segreti, cartella XLVII (1822). In Como (1822) there were 31 firms engaged in silk weaving. "About a thousand looms are located in the city and towns of Como supplied with work by the . . . manufacturers and merchants of silk according to the commissions that come to them. More than a thousand silk weavers are occupied in active work when huge commissions occur." *Ibid.* The *Politecnico* reported in 1839 that the linen weaving industry "remains for the most part in the hands of peasants who make very coarse weaves." As the product was exported, it must have passed through the hands of wholesalers, but there is nothing to indicate to what extent the merchants controlled the manufacture. *Politecnico,* 1839, I, 103. The woolen blankets made in Brescia (1825) were woven by the peasants, under the direction of 90 firms, which exported them to the Veneto and surrounding states. In Brescia (1825) the weaving of woolen textiles was organized by 64 firms, and there were 75 auxiliary shops for the preparation of the cloth (whether owned by the manufacturers or not is not indicated). *Annali,* 1833, Bulletino, pp. 317 ff.

the farms.[60] The production of soft cheese was concentrated at Gorgon-zola to which the clotted milk was shipped from the dairy farms of the Plain.[61] Linen spinning was carried on by peasant families, who in the districts that did not raise flax bought the raw material, and, it would seem, did not generally produce for regular orders but sold their surplus thread to commissioners of the wholesaler travelling through the countryside.[62] On the other hand at Salò in Brescia this industry was directed (in 1825) by twenty manufacturing firms, employing the spare time of peasant families according to the commissions which they received.[63]

The silk winding industry was concentrated at the time of Napoleon in the silk producting districts and the winder and his family were peasants "who worked most often in the villages for any purchaser or any manufacturer of silk who came to take their silks," in order to export them or to convert them into fabrics.[64] When the manufacture of crude silk expanded after 1814, there seems to have been a change in the organization under which it was carried on. The new reeling-mills, some of them equipped with boilers heated by steam, were built and operated in many cases by the proprietors, who sold to the shipping houses of Milan and Bergamo; in others, as at Bergamo and Brescia, merchants bought the cocoons and manufactured the raw or twisted silk for export.[65] Even in the Napoleonic era the weaving of silk had been concentrated around the commercial cities, notably Milan.[66] When the manufacture of twisted silk developed, the mills sprang up near the commercial outlets of Lombardy rather than in the silk producing districts.[67] Such facts point to the intervention of the merchant capitalist in these fields of manufacture.

---

[60] But see also Jacini, pp. 269–270, who notes a tendency to the separation of cheese-making from dairy-farming on the Plain.

[61] See above, p. 43.

[62] The picture of this industry given by Tarlé, pp. 319–320, for the Napoleonic era is repeated by Jacini in 1855. "The women [of the Hills and upper Plain] in winter, when the cotton and silk industries do not offer employment, spin in the stables, on their own account or on commission, the small amount of linen they have collected during the year, but still more what they buy and what comes from the linen-producing country of the lower Plain." Jacini, p. 223.

[63] Annali, 1833, Bulletino, pp. 317 ff.

[64] Tarlé, p. 69.

[65] Annali, 1833, Bulletino, pp. 317 ff.; 1837, LIV, 319–320.

[66] Tarlé, pp. 69–70.

[67] In 1847 Brescia was spinning not only the 260,000 lbs. of reeled silk drawn from the province but importing 30,000 lbs. from other provinces to feed this branch of the industry. Bergamo was importing one-third of the total amount of raw silk twisted in its mills. M. C. M., Camera di Commercio, cartella 173 (1847). Frattini, p. 65, gives the following table for 1855:

Mining and metallurgy required a greater investment of capital in fixed equipment. Nothing is clear regarding the organization of these industries except the size of the manufacturing units. At Brescia in 1825 the average number of persons employed in the iron mines was only 11 per mine.[68] The average number of persons employed in the six blast furnaces of Brescia was 90—a surprisingly high figure for the period. On the other hand the shops for working the metal were small affairs, employing from 13 to 15 operatives.[69] In the manufacture of paper at Salò, another industry requiring the use of a fixed equipment, there were 1,100 operatives employed by 44 plants equipped with 76 vats for reducing the wood pulp. The most important tanneries of Brescia (in 1825) employed a number of operatives that varied from 40 to 70 according to the season.[70]

Contemporary publicists invariably hailed the appearance of more advanced forms of manufacturing organization employing a large fixed equipment as worthy of special remark, so that the fact that references to them are few, and are heavily emphasized, may be taken as evidence that small establishments in which the capital employed was largely invested in the commercial side of the business were the rule. For instance Brescia, from which most of the examples of this form of organization just cited have been drawn, was regarded by contemporaries as an "industrial" region. The Province of Bergamo, which was referred to as *par excellence* the industrial district of Lombardy, was reported in 1837 to have 18,056 manufacturing units, employing 57,405 persons. This gives the microscopic ratio of 3.5 operatives to each unit. The report containing this information was drafted to emphasize the industrial activity of the region. Inasmuch as it mentions specifically the few considerable manufactories that existed, one may assume the prevalence here and elsewhere of a great number of small establishments.[71]

	Filatoi	Spindles
Milan	93	18,765
Bergamo	110	330,000
Brescia	87	12,291
Como	210	162,000
Cremona	2	256
Mantua	17	1,103
Lodi	2	300
Pavia	2	4,532
Sondrio	2	392

[68] *Annali*, 1833, Bulletino, pp. 317 ff.
[69] *Ibid.* In the arms manufacture 776 persons were employed in 76 shops.
[70] *Ibid.*
[71] The memoir in question was drawn to support the case for the construction of the Milan-Venice railway through Bergamo instead of Treviglio. *Annali*, 1837, LIV, 313–336.

The information available regarding the organization of manufactures in the capital city is more abundant and it confirms the conclusion just stated. If Milan is to be considered an economic metropolis, it was a metropolis still in the commercial stage of its development. It did not become an industrial center during the first half of the century. Reports on the state of its manufacturing industry in 1830 and 1833 yield a picture of small scattered shops, producing for the retail trade or serving the commerce of the city, and a limited number of larger establishments operated by merchant manufacturers.[72]

Very little of the mechanical equipment used at Milan in 1833 was not of a kind that might be set up in a small shop. There were only two power-driven machines in the city—a polisher and a hydraulic press. About half of the manufacturers employed fewer than 10 adult operatives, men and women; 59 more employed from 10 to 25. Only 13 firms employed 100 or more operatives. Some of these, including the three largest establishments (with 253, 279, and 310 employees), were engaged in the manufacture of silk stuffs. These relatively large figures cannot be considered as indicating a concentration of labor in centralized shops. The organization of the noted silk manufactory of Innocent Coizet may be taken as representative. It chiefly employed scattered looms, not owned by the firm, on which the work was directed by overseers (*capi-operai*), whom the firm employed. There were twenty-one of these foremen, and each directed the production of a particular kind of goods—one, "plain stuffs and handkerchiefs," another, "plain stuffs, velvets and plushes," and so on. The greatest number of operatives which any one foreman directed was fifteen. Several directed only two or three. Twelve of the foremen were employed exclusively in management. Besides the foremen, the permanent staff seems to have consisted of five women who sorted silk and five clerks "attached to the establishment." The Chamber of Commerce, discussing the merits of the firm of Coizet in 1829 as a candidate for the rank of *fabbrica privilegiata,* referred to its organization as that "of every well-regulated manufactory"—namely, one that does not keep all of the looms that it employs going continuously, but diminishes or increases the number in action according to the state of the market. "In fact the manufactory Coizet, like any other, does not own most of the looms which it puts to work, as this would require the investment of considerable sums of

---

[72] Report of the Chamber of Commerce, March 28, 1829, M. C. M., Camera di Commercio, cartella 555. In the latter part of cartella 555 and the beginning of 556 are to be found reports of the manufacturing establishments of the city on their condition made to the Chamber in 1833. In 1833, 91 of the 203 manufacturing establishments of the city and its suburbs were producing in part for markets outside the province of Milan.

capital, which would remain unproductive when it was found necessary to restrict operations. And on the other hand it is much more profitable to take it up a little at a time, as the employment of it is required, and so the operatives themselves never lack an opportunity of gain, lending their work by turns to several manufactories by which they are employed according to the needs of the moment."[73] In some of the other silk manufactories there was a nucleus of looms in the manufacturer's workshop which were kept in more or less continuous employment, but even these establishments had a broad periphery of domestic looms, to which they gave temporary occupation in the busy season.[74]

As for the little enterprises, which still held the field in 1833, the notes which the manufacturers made in the margins of their reports shed some interesting sidelights on their organization and their difficulties. One of the two glass makers, who reported himself as employing ten operatives, remarked that his artisans came "every year from the Sardinian State and manufacture the goods in the two furnaces set up, one for glass, the other for crystal." Several of the stocking knitters reported their working force as consisting of "my wife; my son." One of the manufacturers of silk waste (*cascami*) wished "to remark that the summer months are those in which [the firm's] work is at its lowest ebb for the simple reason that the hands are needed in agriculture, and especially the women, of whom only the clerks remain in the establishment in summer: this circumstance is common to all the manufacturers of the same article." Massone and Poggi, manufacturers of combs, remarked: "the manufacture is restricted to only six months of work at the manufactory with machines, the rest being occupied exclusively in marketing the product." Two of the lace-making establishments reported that their workers were not "enrolled, but come and go with changes of the season, etc."; and one small manufacturer in this field made the following note regarding his equipment: "four looms and even six when there are orders to execute, and these looms not my property." A silk manufacturer who was employing one man and one woman sadly reported: "Up to 1827 my manufactory consisted of eight looms in activity and all fabricating hat bands; the demand was

---

[73] M. C. M., Camera di Commercio, cartella 558, January 20, 1829.

[74] The other establishments in Milan that employed more than 100 operatives in 1833 were distributed as follows: one (with 170 operatives) was a print-factory for silk and cotton goods; another (with 220 to 265 operatives) was an enterprise for the reduction of silk waste; one was a simple silk winding mill; two (with 116 and 100 operatives) were manufactories of gloves; and one (with 250 employees) was a brick yard. It will be noticed that the silk industry, in some one of its various branches, accounts for all but the three last-mentioned establishments.

equal to the quantity manufactured; after that the trade went on getting worse from year to year, and at the same rate it was necessary to suspend the looms one by one." Now there was only one in action and the bodeful proprietor expected soon to be driven out of business.

Later reports reveal a growth in the manufacture of silk at Milan and the development of a machine trade.[75] By 1840 linen weaving had taken a place of first rank among the industries of the city, second only to silk in the number of operatives it employed. But the industry developed on the familiar lines of organization and was carried on by "little manufactories each comprising a few looms."[76] The years 1839-1841 showed a very considerable increase in the estimated amount of capital employed in Milan,[77] and the industries of the city felt the influence of this wave of prosperity.[78] But as late as 1846 small shops continued to dominate the field of manufacturing industry in the city.[79] More machinery was being used, but there is no indication that the centralized workshop as revealed in earlier reports had undergone any considerable development, and the steam-driven factory had yet to appear.[80]

[75] "Elenco dei principali stabilimenti industriali colla indicazione del personale impiegato e della importanza degli stabilimenti stessi, non che dei vantaggi e degli inconvenienti che recano alla città nella quale trovansi situati," rassegnato con rapporto 18 ottobre 1840, M. C. M., Ragioneria municipale, cartella 4, No. 3871. In 1840 the silk industry employed 7,000 of the city's inhabitants. There were then some 40 "important" firms (in a total of 140) with "about 1,600" weavers. A number of silk twisting mills had sprung up (39 employing 4,000 men: 35 operated by manpower, 1 by horses, and 3 by water).

[76] "There are about 120 looms in all." These were kept in activity by 39 firms, employing 2,000 persons, among whom "are included those occupied in spinning the flax,"—presumably peasants in the surrounding countryside.

[77] The estimates, in the hand of the President of the Chamber of Commerce, accompanied the annual report of that body on the state of private industry in the city. *Statistica dell'industria privata dall'anno 1836 al Riassunto*, M. C. M., Ragioneria municipale, cartella 4 (1834 ff.).

[78] See above, pp. 37–38.

[79] Report on child labor, including a survey of "all the principal industrial establishments of Milan," M. C. M., Camera di Commercio, cartella 556 (1846).

[80] A questionnaire sent out in January, 1842, to determine how many steam engines there were in Milan in 1841, revealed only 2—"a hot and cold machine" owned by a pharmacist and a machine for stamping fabrics owned by a dyer. A steam engine of 6 h. p. formerly employed by the sugar refinery of Azimonti and Company was found to be no longer in use. Report dated January 7, 1842, M. C. M., Ragioneria municipale (Statistical Division), cartella 50, Atti al No. 23,200 del 1841.

CHAPTER V

INDUSTRIAL PROGRESS

I N the first half of the nineteenth century Lombard manufacturing industry made no great advance beyond the stage of wholesale handicraft. Nevertheless, in spite of the continued prevalence of older forms of manufacture, contemporary publicists, watchfully eager for the economic progress of their country, believed that an important forward movement of industry was taking place. In fact many of them were convinced that Lombardy was being drawn, for better or for worse, into an industrial revolution. The evidence that is available does not make a measured account of that movement possible, but it does reveal changes which contemporaries might well regard as symptomatic of an impending transition in the industrial life of the region.

One important change was the tendency of certain industries towards regional concentration. The development of a silk twisting industry carried on in mills set up near the commercial outlets of Lombardy, while the silk winding mills remained diffused through the silk growing districts, has already been noted. But the most important case in point was the localization of cotton spinning in the Province of Milan, particularly at Monza and in the district around Gallarate, Legnano, and Busto Arsizio. It is important because it was produced by the attraction of water-power sites and led to the construction of large power-driven spinneries from which the great textile factories now in the district can trace their lineal descent. The industry in the 'forties is in sharp contrast with the picture which it presented on the morrow of the Restoration. Then it was lagging behind the demand, equipped with a few small spinning machines of from 50 to 100 spindles, and incapable of producing fast dyes. It was even then concentrated in Gallarate, Busto and Lecco, but was for the most part carried on sporadically by the peasants in winter.[1] By 1840 seventeen great mechanical spinning mills had appeared in the Province of Milan alone.[2] By 1845 Lombardy as a whole had twenty-eight cotton spinneries—two of them, with 10,500

[1] See above, pp. 86–88.
[2] Giuseppe Sacchi, in *Annali*, 1842, LXXIII, 244.

spindles, set up since 1842.[3] This enormous development of the cotton spinning industry had taken it out of the cottage. In the 'forties all of the plants were of considerable size. Only four had fewer than 1,000 spindles; some had as many as 8,000 to 10,000.[4] The explanation of this development and of the concentration of the industry along the Olona and Lambro rivers is to be found in the application of mechanical power. All but one of the mills were driven by water. In one of them, at Solbiate, a steam engine provided the power when water was lacking. The only mill not power-driven was an enterprise at Gallarate, with 4,500 spindles, moved by men.[5] In these mills the problems of the factory had emerged—not only the problem of factory discipline and technical education, but of child labor, long hours and unhealthful surroundings.

Cotton spinning had been lifted from languor into busy importance with the introduction of power-driven machinery and at least one step had been taken to supply the lack of fast dyes. In 1841 a company that had erected a spinning mill at Torre set up nearby a dyeworks where "with the new methods a fine Robbia red, very durable, is obtained." The company promised soon to produce an equally excellent blue.[6]

Cotton weaving, an industry four times as important as cotton spinning if measured by the estimated value of its product in 1847, was like spinning a manufacture independent of agriculture, and had concentrated in the Province of Milan.[7] It had also undergone a considerable expansion.[8] But it had remained decidedly a rural industry, still in the stage of handloom weavers and wholesale handicraft.[9] Only one of the

[3] These spinneries operated 101,644 spindles, produced 29,306.50 quintals (of 100 kilos each) of thread, and employed 3,186 operatives. Sacchi, in *Annali*, 1846, XC, 271. In the Province of Milan alone the spinning industry turned out a product worth 4,368,252 Austrian lire. It was estimated that in 1847 the sum invested annually in cotton spinning and weaving taken together amounted to 23,626,720 Austrian lire. G. Sacchi, in *Annali*, 1847, XCI, 154.

[4] The average number of spindles per plant in the province of Milan was 3,886; the average number of operatives 135.

[5] G. Sacchi reviewing Frattini, *Sulla filatura e tessitura del cotone, Annali*, 1846, XC, 272.

[6] 30 operatives were employed, directed by one G. D. Schnel-Griot. *Annali*, 1843, LXXVIII, 329.

[7] In 1855 the province had 15,600 of the total of 17,014 looms. Frattini, p. 106. In 1845 Busto Arsizio and Monza had 10,790 looms or three-fourths of the total of 14,504. G. Sacchi, reviewing Frattini, *Sulla filatura e tessitura del cotone, Annali*, 1847, XCI, 148.

[8] In 1832 there were only 10,800 looms in the Province of Milan. *Annali*, 1832, XXXIV, 221 (misprint for 321 in the original text).

[9] Giuseppe Sacchi estimated in 1847 that the industry was giving at least part-time employment to 29,000 persons. *Annali*, 1847, XCI, 149. "The majority of them are agriculturists who do not always work at the loom in the summer season." M. C. M., Camera di Commercio, cartella 127.12.

firms by which the manufacture was directed had looms that were driven by water.[10] The fact that the only two firms that are known with certainty to have used improved machinery in weaving were also firms operating power-driven spinning mills suggests that the introduction of machinery into the field of weaving resulted from the impulse given by the new-born factory industry in the field of spinning.[11] A writer in the *Annali* announced in 1847 "with true complacency" that of the total of 138 firms engaged in cotton weaving "only four have great factories where the employees work together. These enterprises count only 629 looms, of which 75 are operated by mechanical forces."[12]

Thanks to the development of the cotton spinning industry the Province of Milan had begun to present some of the aspects of a modern industrial district. Another part of Lombardy which seemed to contemporary observers to be undergoing a similar transformation was Lecco. By 1842 the proportions of the population of Lecco engaged respectively in agriculture and manufactures had been reversed. Of a population of 9,133, 4,603 were reported to be industrial workers, and 2,296, or one-fourth of the total population, children occupied from twelve to fifteen hours a day. These operatives were variously employed in 17 iron foundries, 6 copper foundries, 1,034 silk winding mills, 42 silk twisting mills and a cotton spinnery. The large place which silk winding mills occupy in this list leads one to suspect that many of the operatives counted as mill hands were not properly speaking factory wage-workers but peasant women and children employed in their spare time. It can only be said that the situation in Lecco impressed contemporaries as symptomatic of a coming industrialism. "The example of the Lecco district destroys to a great extent the rooted idea that Lombardy is all agricultural and little industrial. Agriculture is indeed the prevalent condition of the country, but industry, lodging and concentrating in certain localities, has almost suppressed agricultural life and taken its place. The benefits and evils of industrialism already exist among us, and exist with all their economic and moral consequences."[13]

Occasional glimpses of the internal organization of some of the larger manufacturing units afford illustrations of the forms which the centralized workshop or the factory was assuming in Lombardy. The establishments described were in each case exceptional, either in size or

---

[10] A small establishment, operated by Sioli, Dell'Acqua and Company at Vaprio, employing 70 looms. *Annali*, 1847, XCI, 148.

[11] The two firms referred to were those of Andrea Ponti (Gallarate) and Turati and Radice (Busto). *Ibid.*

[12] *Ibid.*, p. 151.

[13] Giuseppe Sacchi, "Sulla condizione dei fanciulli occupati nelle manifatture," *Annali*, 1842, LXXIII, 249.

type, and may be taken as representing the particular manufacture concerned in its most advanced form of organization.

The silk weaving establishment of the firm of Osnago was the largest in Milan in 1833 and one of the largest in Italy.[14] It kept in action 300 looms and employed "about 925 persons."[15] Its operations were divided between Milan and Como. At Milan about half of the looms employed were housed in two separate shops, one containing 38 looms—30 common and 8 Jacquard, the other 17—9 common and 8 Jacquard. The operations were directed by a foreman (*capo-fabbrica*). In these permanent quarters 150 persons were employed. In addition "Signor Osnago offered to show from 50 to 55 looms kept in activity by the firm and scattered through the city." His staff included 14 *capi-fabbrica,* and the firm employed 304 persons in all at Milan. "All of the aforesaid looms," the report here cited declares, "operate on a piece-work basis, as do those of the firm of Delacroix and others." At Como the firm had a warehouse but no central shops. It employed "63 looms scattered through the city and the neighboring villages, and under the supervision of four directors who take the silk from the warehouse, have the pieces woven according to the orders that are received, then supervise the work." The firm also owned a steam winding mill at Cavenago, which assured a supply of silk of just the quality needed—in other words, had taken a step towards vertical integration of the manufacturing process.[16] At the top of the silk weaving industry, then, was an establishment that had a permanent organization of foremen, and owned a warehouse, a winding mill, and two small central shops, in which the looms were moved by hand and 150 operatives were employed on a piece-work basis. It did not own the rest of the equipment which it employed, and kept an elastic and not a great amount of capital invested. It had not, in short, entered the stage of the fully developed central workshop, but recruited

[14]*Prospetto statistico della condizione delle manifatture e fabbriche attualmente attive nella città di Milano,* M. C. M., Camera di Commercio, cartelle 555–556. "This manufactory," runs a report on it made in the same year (1833), "can boast of being the first in all Italy, as much for the number of individuals who are employed in it, as for the fact that it embraces the fabrication of all kinds of silk stuffs." *Ibid.,* cartella 558 (1833).

[15] These figures were presented by the proprietor himself to support his petition to be accorded the rank of *Fabbrica privilegiata.* His indefiniteness in reporting the number of persons employed is probably significant of the fact that the proprietors were not in a position to state the number of looms regularly employed by their elastic organizations.

[16] The mill in question was a *filanda a vapore*—not a steam-driven mill, but one in which steam was used to heat the water in which the cocoons were immersed to detach the filament.

and mobilized a variable number of independent weavers for the execution of piece-work.[17]

A very complete picture of the manufacture of woolen cloth at Follina, in the Veneto, can be given,[18] and it is especially interesting as an illustration of conditions in a local industry that was in process of transition to the capitalistic-mechanical stage of manufacture. The industry had been founded by the monks of Chiaravalle. The mill constructed by them had passed into the hands of a Signor Colles, and in its modern amplified form was located near the cloister of the suppressed monastery. Besides this plant there was another large manufactory at Follina owned by a Signor Andretta and several small establishments. The two "large" establishments dominated the wool weaving industry of the district.[19] They turned out a greater quantity of cloth per loom than the small shops, but they did not economize labor at the looms.[20] The small firms produced less "because they are not accustomed to operate all year round, but at intervals." It may be inferred that the larger plants were in continuous operation. It is useful to note, wrote the author describing the mills,

> first, that in indicating the number of workingmen . . . account is taken only of those who are constantly occupied and not of those who work outside the manufactory; second, that even though the manufactory of Colles is provided with the best machines for spinning wool, it does not cease to have a good quantity of it produced by hand, and this to give work in the long winter evenings to the women of the country-

[17] For a description of the even less fully developed central plant of the important firm of Innocente Coizet at Milan, see above, pp. 97–98. Another manufactory, that of Giovanni Gilat, employed 14 Jacquard looms. "An approximate estimate having been made of all the persons employed on the looms operating in the manufactory of the firm, and those working outside the same on its orders, there might be about 120 in all, counting weavers, spinners, tenders of the looms, and all the others in service." M. C. M., Camera di Commercio, cartella 564, January 29, 1827.

[18] F. Sanseverino, "Delle fabbriche di pannilana in Follina nella provincia di Treviso, 1840," *Annali*, 1841, LXVII, 222–229.

[19] The following table shows their relative position:

	Number of operatives	Looms	Yards of cloth produced
Colles	350	40	60,000
Andretta	350	32	60,000
Small firms	100	10	12,000

[20]

	Product per loom	Average number of operatives per loom
Colles	1500 yards	8 3/4
Andretta	1850 "	10 30/32
Others	1200 "	10

The difference between the two large firms is attributed to the fact that Colles specialized in producing finer grades of cloth.

side, who do not figure in the number of operatives indicated; third, that the little firms, not being equipped with wool spinning machinery have what they need spun by hand, and that these women spinners do not figure in the number of operatives; fourth, that the Andretta factory, instituted only recently, has all or almost all of its spinning done by machinery. Both the Colles and the Andretta manufactories are furnished with the best machines made in England, in France, in Belgium, and in Germany, and also in Italy on the best models.

Some of the old machines were kept by Colles in a kind of museum. Samples of ancient Florentine models, old English combing machines, and superannuated looms were preserved to "keep before the thought the picture of the progress of the human mind applied to industry."

The machinery of the Colles plant displaced the labor of 1,662 persons, if one takes "into account those who are saved at the looms, which now for the most part occupy one operative instead of two; the improvement of the fulling mills and the presses for smoothing the cloth, which save labor by speeding up the work."[21] Other operatives (about 10 in number) were employed who were not counted because engaged in operations not theretofore practiced, such as those of the steam-machine that glossed the cloth. There were several old-style shearing machines in the factory, but these were soon to be displaced by "machines similar to one of the four indicated which were recently introduced into the manufactory, and the like of which does not exist," remarks the reporter, "in any of the factories of Italy"—machines which tripled the speed of operation.

The industry was located in a village of 1,200 inhabitants. The operatives came also from the neighboring villages. Our witness remarks that, contrary to the prognostications of pessimists, Follina was one of the cleanest and most prosperous towns of the Veneto. Its population had escaped economic injury from the displacement of labor by the factories because the flourishing agriculture of the region absorbed the surplus labor. The workpeople, he continues, were not the sickly lot that might have been expected. They enjoyed pure air, good wages and short hours, working eleven hours a day in summer and nine in winter. The author turned to England for his standard of comparison: "All praise to our

---

[21] The statement here made about the saving of operatives at the looms is in conflict with the figures given above from the same source, above, note 20. The mechanical equipment of the Colles plant was as follows:

	Operated by:	Supplanting:
18 spinning machines	18	1080
8 combing machines	4	560
4 machines to shave the hides	8	22
	30	1662

manufacturers," he exclaimed, "who show themselves much more humane than those of England, where a law was necessary to limit to fourteen hours the daily work of the operatives, while before that they were compelled to work as much as sixteen hours."

Here was a manufacturing district where a marked concentration had occurred, drawing groups of over three hundred operatives into continuous employment in shops equipped with machinery. A cottage industry of indefinite proportions still continued but had been largely displaced by central workshops. Power-driven machinery had not appeared, but the industry had entered the stage of the centralized workshop. A factory district and an industrial proletariat were emerging.

The evidence available yields also a picture, unfortunately less complete, of a textile manufactory at Pratalboino, in the Province of Brescia, that of the Bellandi Brothers, which was engaged in the weaving of linen, wool and cotton textiles. Its product consisted of simple and patterned fabrics, especially table-linen and cotton goods, bed covers and carpets. The "rich proprietor," Signor Alessandro Bellandi, was vice-president of the Imperial and Royal Chamber of Commerce of the province.[22] His enterprise centered in "an edifice constructed for the purpose," which housed "a highly organized distribution of 90 and more looms, including 7 Jacquard machines which executed the finest damasks." The establishment also kept "almost at its disposal 70 other looms and sometimes more in various homes of the district, and in neighboring districts, which are occupied more or less fully according to the demand." One hundred and fifty persons, mostly men, were employed in the central shop; "but if one considered all of those associated with them for other tasks which cannot be performed inside the establishment, such as spinning the linen, bleaching and dyeing, one might very well count more than 400 persons who are kept in daily employment."[23] As in the manufactories of Colles and Andretta at Follina, concentration in the mill had begun but was incomplete, and the process of vertical integration had not been carried so far as in those establishments. The plant was employed solely in weaving; the spinning and other auxiliary processes were still carried on outside the central workshop.

Instructive glimpses can be caught of a few of the larger foundries and metal-working shops. Reference has already been made to the

---

[22] *Annali*, 1833, Bulletino, pp. 167–168. In 1835 Bellandi was awarded Second Prize by the Athenaeum of Brescia for the manufacture of new products. He was then lending his services free as Deputy of the Provincial Congregation; "he is a philanthropist at every opportunity; he employs his means to mitigate the rigors of the lot of poor artisans," *Annali*, 1836, XLVII, 85.

[23] F. L. . .na, "Importanza della fabbrica dei Fratelli Bellandi in Pratalboino (Provincia di Brescia)," *Annali*, VII, 1826, 173–175.

traveller Bertolotti's impression of the ironworks of the Signori Rubini at Dongo, on the upper part of Lake Como, near the mines located there which contained "rich veins of iron carbonate intersected with veins of copper."[24] In 1841 this firm was officially awarded a gold medal for improvements in its plant. "The furnace of first fusion is a huge affair, to which is applied with profit the hot air created by the combustion of the charcoal. The furnaces of second fusion are operated likewise. The bellows are of great size." The firm had brought in several foreign founders and modellers to instruct its operatives, and had increased their output while economizing fuel, so dear in Lombardy.[25] Glimpses of two metallurgical works at Milan, established towards the close of the period under survey, give some idea of the scale of operations in that branch of manufacture. One was a mill constructed to make railroad equipment. The firm was reported as having set up "a vast mill" with "two blast furnaces," operated by ten workingmen and six boys, besides a factory superintendent. It imported the pig iron which was used. The other firm, which was seeking permission from the government to import scrap iron, had set up a shop with two furnaces, capable of turning out daily 1,000 kilos of iron, from which were drawn 900 kilos of "finished iron." The blasts were operated by horses; but these were shortly to be replaced by a steam engine. The mill employed 25 or 30 adult operatives. The report of the Chamber of Commerce referred to it as "a fine and large mill. When finished it will be capable also of producing steam engines."[26]

The foregoing survey leaves no doubt that, in spite of certain tendencies towards a higher degree of organization, wholesale handicraft was still prevalent in Lombard manufacturing industry. The central workshops noted in the textile industries were incompletely developed and at best represented a loose and elastic form of capitalistic organization in which the commercial interest still had the ascendancy over the technical and manufacturing interest. On the other hand, in the spinning of cotton and linen and the twisting of silk, and to some extent in the manufacture of machinery, the power-driven factory was beginning to take shape. In these fields an industrial capitalism was detaching itself from agriculture and commerce and binding a group of wage-earning operatives continuously to the wheels of industry.

[24] See above, p. 91.
[25] *Annali*, 1841, LXIX, 198.
[26] The data regarding both shops, directed respectively by Giacinto Recalcati, and the firm of Balleydier, are drawn from reports of the Chamber of Commerce of Milan to the Intendant of Finance, September 19 and December 11, 1846, M. C. M., Camera di Commercio, cartella 816. The Balleydier shop was established in 1844.

The metal and machine works of the factory type were the modest affairs just described. Of the new cotton spinneries there is no complete description, but it is possible to form a rough idea of their size and characteristics. The largest (in 1849) was a factory equipped with more than 10,000 spindles, and employing (in 1855) 400 operatives.[27] This was the plant mentioned above which was equipped with a steam engine to supply power when the water was low. The next most extensive plant was that which has grown into one of the largest cotton manufactories of Italy—that of C. Cantoni at Castellanza, which in 1855 was employing 257 operatives.[28] On an average the spinneries in the Province of Milan were equipped (in 1845) with 3,886 spindles each and employed a working force of 135 men, women and children.[29] A mill at Torre, near Pordenone, built about 1842, was driven by a turbine waterwheel of 100 horsepower,[30] but the power plants of the new spinneries averaged (in 1855), only about 22 horsepower.[31] Built on low ground by the rivers, the spinneries were located in unhealthful sites and were in general badly ventilated,[32] though in some factories care was taken to disinfect the workrooms and look after proper ventilation.[33]

In the case of some of the firms that operated spinneries, a tendency to vertical integration was manifesting itself. The firm owning the spinnery at Torre just mentioned operated a dyeworks, and several of the large firms with mechanical spinning mills were also extensively engaged in weaving.[34] But only one weaving establishment had installed power-driven looms.[35] In general the manufacturers continued to employ large numbers of fullers, dyers, printers, and weavers in the

[27] A manufactory owned by Andrea Ponti at Solbiate Olona. *Pronipote del Vesta-Verde*, 1849, p. 62, note. It employed (in 1855) 227 men, 63 women, and 110 children under 14 years of age. Ponti also had a small spinnery at Gallarate. Frattini, p. 102.

[28] This establishment was under construction in 1849, at a cost of half a million lire. *Pronipote del Vesta-Verde*, 1849, p. 80.

[29] Giuseppe Sacchi, reviewing Frattini, *Sulla filatura e tessitura del cotone, Annali*, 1846, XC, 271. By 1855, if Frattini's statistics are to be trusted, the average number of spindles in the province had grown to 4,043. Frattini, p. 102.

[30] The flow of water on the site was capable of developing 1,000 h. p. *Annali*, 1843, LXXVIII, 328.

[31] Frattini, p. 102.

[32] *Ibid.*, p. 104.

[33] Note by Giuseppe Sacchi on the establishment of Candiani at Olgiate, *Annali*, 1846, XC, 275.

[34] The largest of the cotton spinners, Andrea Ponti, also employed the greatest number of looms engaged by any one firm in cotton weaving (1,624 in 1845). This firm and that of Turati and Radice, also owners of a mechanical spinnery, together employed one-fifth of the total number of looms active in weaving cotton in the province of Milan in 1845. Giuseppe Sacchi, reviewing Frattini, *Annali*, 1847, XCI, 148.

[35] *Ibid.*

countryside, feeding to the looms of the peasant-weavers the product of their mechanical spinneries. In only one case (in 1849), that of the largest manufactory, was there a central workshop connected with the cotton weaving industry.[36]

In the twisting as distinguished from the reeling of silk, an industry that sprang into being in Lombardy during the period under survey, water-driven mills were established, some of them employing "from 100 to 200 operatives, of whom the majority are girls," wrote Giuseppe Sacchi in 1842. "If the mill is operated by water, the work is sometimes uninterrupted; if by animals or men, it goes on only by day."[37] A twisting mill of 10,000 spindles was considered exceptionally large.[38] By 1855 four-fifths of the silk twisting mills were driven by water-power and a few by steam.[39]

The only old and established industry, closely connected with agriculture, in which the factory was introduced before 1848 was linen spinning. Three water-driven mills were put in operation between 1839 and 1848. They were of about the same size and power as the larger cotton spinneries.[40] Watched with hopeful interest by the patriotic liberals as an augury of the progress of Italy in the ways of civilization, these enterprises had a struggle to survive. Before 1848, with Government

[36] ". . . Only the firm of Andrea Ponti in Gallarate has there a local workshop for the preparation of the threads produced by its own establishment at Solbiate, in which about 184 women are employed continuously, who then distribute the cotton for weaving in the manner previously indicated,"—that is, to domestic looms. *Pronipote del Vesta Verde*, 1849, p. 83.

[37] *Annali*, 1842, LXXIII, 243.

[38] G. Sarti, "Sullo stato del setificio in Italia," *Politecnico*, 1844, VII, 522. A good deal of the work was still put out to women working at home. M. C. M., Camera di Commercio, cartella 556, August 26, 1845.

[39] Frattini, p. 66.

[40] The first to get started was on the Brembo river, at Villa d'Almè, Province of Bergamo. *Annali*, 1840, LXIII, 341, note of editor. In 1855 this plant had 4,132 spindles for drawing, and 386 for twisting the thread, and was driven by a water wheel of 100 h. p. Frattini, p. 122. The first samples of its output were tested at Milan in 1842 and found to be as good as the English product. *Annali*, 1842, LXXIV, 277–278. The second plant was on the Adda river, at Cassano, province of Milan, and was put into operation on December 22, 1842. *Annali*, 1842, LXXV, 72–73. The firm, headed by Paolo Battaglia, was capitalized at 1,250,000 lire. M.C.M., Camera di Commercio, cartella 569, June 14, 1841. When Battaglia died in 1846, the plant was taken over by Cusani and Co. who enlarged its equipment, bringing the total number of "machines" up to 4,000 and proposing to increase its output from 45,000 to 90,000 lbs. a month. They employed 250 men and women in the factory and planned to expand their force to 350 when new machinery was installed. M. C. M., Camera di Commercio, cartella 569, March 27, 1847. In 1855 they were operating 6,000 spindles, with a motor of 140 h. p. Frattini, p. 122. The third factory was at Melegnano, in the Milanese.

d,[41] only two had been measurably successful and the third was perating in 1855 at less than half of its intended capacity.[42] Regarding the handicaps of the industry the Chamber of Commerce of Milan reported in 1847 : "The beginnings of mechanical spinning were expensive and difficult, many prejudices had to be overcome in these provinces accustomed for centuries to the use of linen spun by hand, and the order and discipline, the habit of using machines, and the skill of the operatives were not to be obtained except after long and persevering efforts."[43] The fact that two of the promoters of the first of these factories to be projected belonged to firms engaged in cotton spinning suggests that the impulse to introduce power-driven machinery into the linen spinning industry came from the success of the new cotton mills.[44] But the linen industry had to cope with a force of tradition that was absent in the case of cotton spinning.

In general it will be observed that the industries which remained in the stage of wholesale handicraft or failed to pass beyond the centralized workshop were branches of manufacture well established in Lombardy before the Restoration, and furthermore were industries in which manufacture was closely dependent on a local extractive industry—either mining or agriculture. The branches in which the power-driven factory appeared were cotton spinning, which was not associated with local agriculture, silk twisting, which was a new industry in Lombardy, linen spinning, which seems to have been influenced directly by the mechanical spinning of cotton, and the manufacture of such metal products as were directly auxiliary to a gradually developing industrial life. An important factor retarding the progress of manufacturing industry would therefore seem to have been the weight of custom, and the conservative habits of a community preoccupied with agriculture.

The territorial concentration of certain industries—their drift away from the sources of supply towards the commercial outlets and power-sites of the region, conspicuous in the case of the new industries of silk and cotton spinning—was a sign of progress toward a more highly de-

[41] In the form of an increase of the duty on imported threads. The Chamber of Commerce of Milan, supporting their petition for help, declared them to be in the "sad condition of keeping at work a number of spindles far below their capacity." M. C. M., Camera di Commercio, cartella 173, January 29, 1844. The protection sought was granted on July 29, 1846. *Ibid.*, cartella 569, September 18, 1847.

[42] The mill at Melegnano. Frattini, p. 122.

[43] M. C. M., Camera di Commercio, cartella 569, March 27, 1847.

[44] The mill at Melegnano, though the last to go into operation, was planned in 1839. Note on "The Introduction of New Industries into Lombardy," *Politecnico*, 1839, I, 103. There is a full description of the plans of organization, naming the leading promoters, an article entitled "Delle imprese per la filatura meccanica del lino," *Politecnico*, 1839, I, 188–191.

veloped manufacturing industry. Another sign of this is to be found in
the development of centralized workshops and power-driven factories,
and of firms of manufacturers extending their organization into two or
more related branches of manufacture, of which glimpses have been
caught. Other indications of the growing importance of manufacture
in the economic life of Lombardy are available. One is the accumulation
of machine equipment and the use of mechanical power. Another is the
development of auxiliary industries such as the local manufacture of
machines and chemicals. A third is the emergence of the labor problems
characteristic of modern industrialism.

In regard to the introduction of machines the evidence available is
fragmentary, but it yields some facts that are of value in estimating the
movement of local industry towards heavier capitalization. Largely in
the hands of handicraftsmen and peasant operatives, manufacturing in
Lombardy was carried on chiefly with instruments owned by the
artisans. There is evidence that this simple mechanical equipment increased very considerably during the first half of the century with the
expansion of manufacturing activity. The number of silk looms, for
example, grew by leaps and bounds.[45] There is also evidence that the
technical equipment was improved by the introduction of more
complicated machines. In the extensive industry of silk winding
the most important improvement was the introduction of the Gensoul
method of heating the boilers by steam instead of by separate fires.
These were uneconomical because of their large appetite for fuel,
inefficient because of the difficulty of maintaining a high and uniform temperature, and damaging to the health of the operatives.
The Gensoul method was introduced into Lombardy in 1815 by
Count Dandolo, "that man destined by Providence to put Italian silk
in competition with those of Asia in the markets of Europe and
America."[46] Lombard inventors made some improvements on this
process.[47] By the middle of the century some of the winding mills were

[45] According to Angelo Piazza the number in the Province of Milan increased
from 500 in 1816 to 4,000 in 1844. "Cenni sul setificio," *Rivista*, n. s., 1844, II,
Pt. 2, 282. Frattini estimated that the total number in Lombardy increased from
about 1,000 in 1816 to more than 4,000 in 1855. Frattini, p. 70. Piazza on the
other hand gave 8,000 as the total number in Milan and Como alone in 1844.

[46] F. Lencisa, "Sopra l'industria della seta," *Annali*, 1831, XXIX, 135. Pugliese
gives Porro the credit for introducing the method. It is true that in 1816 Count
Luigi Porro and Antonio Robaglia were granted exclusive use of it for five years.
Raccolta degli atti del Governo, 1816, XXVII, *Circolari*, No. 108, August 25,
205–206.

[47] Described in the record of a litigation between G. Leonardi and Felice Botta,
two Milanese inventors, and one Bruni, defending his patent, A. S. M., Presidenza, Atti segreti, 1823, cartella LX. Lencisa stated in 1831 that "boilers of
the Milanese type are now used in Piedmont as the best adapted to the perfection
of the manufacture." *Annali*, 1831, XXIX, 136, note 1.

not only heated but driven by steam.[48] But the use of steam for either purpose was still very limited, and as late as 1855, of the total of 3,088 winding mills in Lombardy only 144 had steam-heated boilers.[49] The introduction of machinery and of power-driven mills into the field of silk twisting has already been noted. Mechanized silk spinning progressed so rapidly that in 1844 an observer declared that "twisting by hand will shortly be confined to the working of inferior silks and to few others."[50] In the weaving of textiles the most important mechanical innovation was the Jacquard loom which permitted the weaving of patterned fabrics. The invention was first smuggled into Milan from Lyons in 1818 and Jacquard looms began to multiply after 1825 when an adequate local manufactory was established in Milan.[51] The number of Jacquard silk looms increased to more than 700 in the Province of Milan alone, and to more than 800 in all Lombardy (1855). As was natural in an industry devoted largely to producing the lower grades of silk fabrics, the Jacquard looms remained only a minor fraction of the total.[52] The appearance of mechanized workshops in the field of wool weaving has already been described. The woolen manufactories of Brescia, especially those in the Valgandino and at Schio, badly shaken by the competition of the cheap German-made cloths that flooded the annual fair at Bergamo, were compelled about 1830 to apply themselves to the manufacture of finer grades of cloth "with the introduction of machines of foreign invention."[53] Before 1840 the Brothers Preyssl set up at Milan a "great manufactory" for spinning and weaving woolens, with a dyeworks, and installed new French and English machinery.[54] A considerable introduction of mechanical equipment can be attributed to the new cotton and linen spinneries described above. In metallurgy shops with improved machinery developed at Dongo and Milan. The mechanization of the local manufacture of paper made some progress. As early as 1823 the Chamber of Commerce of Milan reported that

[48] The largest were of considerable size. The most important, that of Torriani at Monza, was equipped with 100 steam heated boilers. There were others that employed more than 300 operatives. *Pronipote del Vesta Verde*, 1849, pp. 76 ff.

[49] The Province of Como had been the most progressive in the introduction of steam boilers and had 62 steam-heated *filande*, with 4,178 reels, out of a total of 412, with 8,796 reels. Frattini, p. 57.

[50] Giulio Sarti, reporting to the Sixth Congress of Italian Scientists at Milan, *Politecnico*, 1844, VII, 520.

[51] Angelo Piazza, "Cenni sul setificio," *Rivista*, n. s., 1844, II, Pt. 2, 281.

[52] One-fifth, according to Frattini, pp. 49, 70.

[53] Report on the Bergamo Fair of 1833, *Annali*, 1833, Bulletino, p. 497.

[54] The product had been so improved by their efforts as to "exclude" foreign goods from the local market. The Preyssl Brothers received a silver medal at the industrial exposition of Milan in 1839 and a gold medal two years later. *Annali*, 1841, LXIX, 198.

"the paper mills of Lombardy have increased in number, and some of those already existing are extensive, and have doubled their production of paper, besides perfecting it by means of new machines and cylinders of the Dutch type."[55] In 1830 it was announced that a mechanical paper mill, with an English-made cylinder continuously operating to press the paper, had been set up at Varese—the first of its kind in Italy.[56] Steamboats plied Lakes Como and Maggiore after 1826. By 1848 steam locomotives were pulling trains on the two short lines from Milan to Monza and Treviglio; a gas plant had been set up to illuminate the capital;[57] and the sugar refinery of Azimonti and Company was using high-pressure tubular boilers.[58]

The Austrian Government did not remain indifferent to the need of Lombard industry for improved equipment. In 1817 it freed from duty the introduction of machines and of steamboats and their accessories and exempted from taxation the use of combustibles necessary to obtain steam.[59] Nevertheless in 1855 the duties on steel and machinery, "of which we are immensely in need," were named among the chief hindrances to the progress of manufactures.[60] The Government held an industrial exposition every year at the Brera in Milan, awarding prizes for inventions and improvements, and in 1830 opened there a permanent exhibition of machine models, open on Mondays for inspection by mechanics and artisans.[61] In 1841 the Imperial and Royal Institute of the Arts and Sciences was reorganized and thereafter held sessions in alternate years at Milan and Venice to stimulate technical progress with its awards. But these efforts proved unsatisfactory.[62] Lombardy trailed behind all the other provinces of the Austrian Empire except Venetia in the number of patents for inventions and improvements taken out between 1821 and 1844,[63] and in 1839 the *Politecnico* sadly affirmed that "the steam engines in Lombardy can still be counted on the fingers."[64]

[55] M. C. M., Camera di Commercio, cartella 814, August 5, 1823.
[56] G. Sacchi, "Ragguaglio intorno alla pubblica esposizione degli oggetti d'industria in Lombardia nell'anno 1830," *Annali*, 1830, XXVI 107; *ibid.*, 1840, LXV, 82–83.
[57] In 1844, by Roux and Co., which received a monopoly of the right to lay pipes in the streets not to expire until 1880. Frattini, p. 212.
[58] Four, with 100 h. p. *Annali*, 1847, XCIV, 74.
[59] "Prescrizioni onde ottenere il privilegio esclusivo per la navigazione coi battelli a vapore," Notificazione, December 27, 1817, *Raccolta degli Atti del Governo*, XXIX, Pt. 1, 341–348.
[60] Frattini, p. 111.
[61] *Annali*, 1831, XXVIII, 313–314.
[62] For an able discussion of their inefficacy, see Pugliese.
[63] Adriano Balbi, *L'Austria e le primarie potenze*, p. xxxiii.
[64] *Politecnico*, 1839, I, 48.

The efforts of the Government were applauded and supplemented by patriotic citizens, though some of the leading publicists were reserved in their enthusiasm for mechanized industry, with its train of human misery.[65] Count Federico Confalonieri and his friends, inspired by an eager enthusiasm for progress, bought in England the engine for a steamboat and Christian and Hill machines for spinning linen and hemp, and tried to encourage their use in Lombardy. But the steamboat had to be given up, and machinery did not take hold in the linen industry until twenty years later. The application of machinery and modern chemical processes to industry was consistently urged by the liberal journals and was one of the objects of the Society for the Encouragement of the Arts and Crafts formed at Milan by a group of public-spirited citizens in 1841. In 1842 the Society offered a gold medal to the person who would establish in the Province of Milan a factory for the manufacture of machinery and spare parts, to relieve those who practiced a mechanical art or had a spinnery or manufactory active in the province from the necessity of buying their plant or replacements abroad.[66] A similar society for the promotion of industry got under way at Bergamo in 1847.[67]

The new machines introduced into Lombard industry during the period were largely imported from abroad. There are frequent references to the importation of machinery from the Low Countries, Switzerland, France and England. The value of English machines sold in Italy increased from £929 in 1825 to £2,918 in 1826 and £5,704 in 1827.[68] One of the best indications of the growing demand of Lombard manufactures for technical equipment is to be found in the local manufacture of machines. One of the first machine shops was a manufactory of Jacquard looms established in Milan in 1825, which was soon not only able to supply the demand of local weavers but was exporting its product to other parts of Italy.[69] Before 1837 a Signor Stefano Dufour had set up "an extensive manufactory" for the construction of textile

---

[65] For example, Giuseppe Sacchi, one of the most consistent advocates of progress, disagreed sharply with the author of a book at Naples which complained that his country employed too little machinery. Machinery, he argued, would come as it was needed and as the intelligence and condition of the population permitted of its profitable employment. In Italy machinery must be introduced only gradually. "Notizie del nuovo gabinetto di macchine per uso d'arti e mestieri aperto in Milano nell'I. R. Istituto delle Scienze ed Arti," *Annali*, 1831, XXVIII, 313–314.

[66] "Programma della Società d'Incoraggiamento," *Annali*, 1842, LXXII, 291.

[67] The *Società industriale bergamasca*, projected in 1844 by Gian Battista Berizzi in the Agronomical and Technological Section of the Milan Congress of Scientists. *Rivista*, n. s., 1847, V, Pt. 1, 743–746.

[68] *Annali*, 1828, XVI, 196–198 (from a report to Parliament).

[69] Angelo Piazza, "Cenni sul setificio," *Rivista*, n. s., 1844, II, Pt. 2, 281.

spinning machinery of all kinds.[70] In 1846 the Chamber of Commerce of Milan reported to the Intendant of Finance that the firm of Bouffier and Company was establishing a shop for the manufacture of all sorts of "machines, utensils, apparatus for use in industry and the arts." The Chamber's opinion throws an interesting light on the conditions affecting the local manufacture of machines. The firm, they believed, would have to exclude from its program machines of much importance. "The situation of the city, its remoteness from a seaport, the condition of its customs sanctions, the sphere and scope of its manufactures, the quality of the national iron whether hammered or cast, is such that a factory assuming too great proportions would have difficulty in finding the conditions of success." But, they added, the firm had a good start in a contract with the new gas company to furnish the equipment necessary for the illumination of Milan.[71] Taken in connection with the metal works set up at Milan in 1844 and 1846, equipped to manufacture railway supplies, these enterprises indicate the firm establishment and perhaps the growth of a local market for machinery. Its strength can be inferred from their success and the subsequent multiplication of such works. In 1855 there were seventeen establishments engaged in manufacturing machinery, led by Bouffier and Company.[72] They were turning out a great variety: hydraulic motors and their spare parts, sugar and tobacco machines, steam engines, spinning and winding mills, boilers, pumps, paper machines, oil and flour mills, hydraulic presses, threshers, railway mechanisms, looms and factory equipment. The local manufacture was criticized as still deficient, in failing to produce large machines for sugar refineries, centrifugal pumps, "continuous machines" for paper mills, spinning jennies, locomotives and rails,[73] but in view of the recent establishment of the industry, its success may be taken to indicate the organic development of Lombard manufacturing industry.

Another auxiliary industry whose growth towards the middle of the century marks the development of an industrial organism capable of supplying its own needs was the manufacture of chemicals. Acids were being manufactured in Lombardy as early as 1818.[74] Nevertheless in

---

[70] "Solenne distribuzione dei premi di agricoltura e di industria in Milano nel 1837," *Annali*, 1837, LII, 326.

[71] M. C. M., Camera di Commercio, cartella 816, August 3, 1846. In 1849 Bouffier and Company were reported to be in a flourishing condition, employing continuously 120 operatives and turning out machinery valued at 360,000 lire a year. *Pronipote del Vesta Verde*, 1849, p. 90.

[72] The other important establishments were Schlegel and Company, Edoardo Suffert, and two railway shops at Monza and Treviglio.

[73] Frattini, p. 161.

[74] Notice of the establishment by E. C. Bonelli and Co. of a manufactory of acids at Lezzeno (Lake Como), *Conciliatore*, November 19, 1818, No. 23, p. 92.

consumption of acids in Lombardy was considered
a local manufacture of chemical products.[75] But by
'hemical manufacture had sprung up, and in that
.ablished for the manufacture of stearine candles,
, in quantity boric, acetic, citric, nitric, oxalic, sulphuric
.ic acid, rock alum, bicarbonate of soda, ammonium and
.csium carbonate, sulphates, soap and candles,[76] and Frattini, dis-
.ussing the condition of the dyeing industry in 1855, declared that as far
as acids were concerned the factories of Milan were adequate to supply
the necessary.[77]

Power-driven factories were not numerous in Lombardy in 1848,
but the factory had established itself as an institution, and had already
created a labor problem, which the liberal publicists viewed with grave
anxiety, contemplating its growth in the baleful light of its magnitude
abroad. The condition of industrial labor as reflected in their discussion
of this problem and of its possible remedies sheds additional light on the
state of manufactures in Lombardy.

Labor was free from legal restrictions. The guilds had been abolished
in 1787,[78] and the efforts of the employers to obtain a renewal of some
of the discarded legal disciplines during the Napoleonic era had fallen to
the ground.[79] But labor, set free by the hand of despotic Enlightenment,
was deprived not only of the discipline but of the technical training
which the guilds had insured. What survived was preserved solely by
tradition and habit. The result was unsatisfactory and the period following the Restoration was agitated by the problem of training labor in a
modern technique and by the problem of discipline, which grew serious
with the development of centralized workshops and factories.

These problems were grave, for the labor force to be trained consisted
largely of men, women and children who had never known any other
discipline than that of the rural family. When the new cotton spinneries
were set up in the late 'thirties the manufacturers resorted to a variety
of devices for solving them. One means that they employed to insure an
industrious character was to require a certificate of good behavior from

[75] Report of the Chamber of Commerce of Milan favorable to the petition of
Kramer and Company, manufacturers of print fabrics and metal cylinders, to be
allowed a remission of the import duty on acids, M. C. M., Camera di Commercio, cartella 173, No. 7106, December 16, 1825.
[76] Report of Antonio Pestalozzi on the establishment of Luigi Massari, July 9,
1847, M. C. M., Camera di Commercio, cartella 569.
[77] Frattini, p. 130.
[78] Carlo Tivaroni, *Storia critica del Risorgimento italiano* (Turin-Naples, 1888–
1897), I, 132. Tarlé (p. 51) attributes their abolition to the Napoleonic régime.
[79] Tarlé, pp. 84–85.

the parish priest.[80] To break the operatives to the unaccustomed routine of the factory, the manufacturers used the common device of imposing fines for violation of the factory rules.[81] The Lombard manufacturer of silk regarded with longing the organization of apprenticeship at Lyons, where every operative had to be provided with a book (*livret*) containing a signed record of his employment and his conduct. At Milan, left free, the workingman did not apply himself steadily; he was undisciplined, drifted from job to job, and learned his art mechanically and in a haphazard fashion.[82]

But the problem of factory discipline was only in its infancy; the centralization of industry had not advanced far enough to give it more than a superficial importance. Much more urgent was that of technical training. This was not only a question of introducing and diffusing a knowledge of modern technique, but of breaking the spell of custom and rule-of-thumb, deep almost as life in this agricultural community. The Austrian Government provided Lombardy and Venetia with a system of free and compulsory schools, in which a remarkably large attendance was in time secured. But the special secondary schools in which at least the elements of a technical education were given reached only a small number of boys and girls and the progressive writers of the time complained bitterly of the curriculum, and especially of that of the gymnasia, where the boys were bound to a useless study of the classics. For many years the only vocational training offered in Lombardy was given in the trade schools of various charity asylums and in Sunday and holiday schools that sprang up here and there, some in the new cotton factories, others in connection with the remarkable educational movement that founded the so-called *asili d'infanzia,* or pre-schools for poor children.[83] The first important steps to remedy the situation were taken by private initiative. When the Government failed to establish promptly technical schools at Milan and Venice which it had promised for some years as an integral part of the public school system, several private technical schools sprang up at Milan. The Society for the Encouragement of the Arts and Crafts of Milan, a coöperative enterprise of public-

[80] This was the practice of the firm of Candiani at Olgiate and of Fumagalli and Strucchi at Peregallo. G. Sacchi, in *Annali,* 1846, XC, 275. These firms employed (in 1855) 226 operatives—78 men, 79 women and 69 children. Frattini, pp. 102–103.

[81] At least one of the cotton manufacturers required a deposit equal to two weeks' wages as a pledge of good behavior. The deposit was returned only after the operative had served the firm for a year.

[82] Angelo Piazza, "Cenni sul setificio," *Rivista,* n. s., 1844, II, Pt. 2, 284–285. Frattini in 1855 urged that the operatives be required to have a conduct record, to give the manufacturer better control of his working force. Frattini, p. 83.

[83] See below, pp. 214 ff.

spirited merchants, industrialists, proprietors and professional men, launched in 1841, devoted itself at once to the diffusion of applied science. Its president, Enrico Mylius, who was the soul of the enterprise, founded within the Society, on a liberal endowment, a school of industrial chemistry, and added a further sum to equip it with a laboratory. The founder intended the school for the instruction of industrial foremen and operatives; but Professor Kramer, who gave the lectures, found himself facing an audience of more than 300 which included some workingmen but consisted largely of cultivated persons who were eager to know more of the recent progress of chemical science; and he was compelled to give the course a popular character.[84] But the laboratory served the original purpose. In 1847 the professor took five of his best pupils on a tour of observation in Germany, Prussia, Belgium, Holland, England and France to demonstrate the progress of industrial chemistry.[85] The school turned out practical chemists and teachers of chemistry, and it worked in the closest harmony with the Milanese industrialists.[86] By 1846 the Society for the Encouragement of the Arts and Crafts was giving four free courses for the technical instruction of workingmen—that in chemistry, one in industrial physics, one in applied mechanics, and another, conducted by Angelo Piazza, master silk weaver, on the art of manufacturing silk.[87] These courses were attended by more than four hundred and fifty listeners and gained such a reputation that the Chamber of Commerce of Como requested Piazza to give his course on silk weaving in that city. At the same time the newly founded Industrial Society of Bergamo opened free public courses in metallurgy and other arts.[88]

Meanwhile the Government, lagging behind the progress of public interest, had at last got its two higher technical schools afloat, founded at Milan and Venice in 1841 and 1843. They offered a three-year course designed to give a training for industrial and commercial life. "All the teachings are applied to industrial life," Giuseppe Sacchi reported in 1847, "and the precepts are continually tested by practical experiments, by the exposition of illustrative tables, and by assiduous visits to the principal manufactories." In 1846, 432 students were attending the school at Milan, 154 enrolled in the obligatory courses and 278 in the optional courses in French and German and technical chemistry. The engineer Baraldi, director of the Milan school, was also giving a free

[84] *Annali*, 1842, LXXII, 286. See also Pugliese, pp. 423–433.
[85] G. Sacchi, in *Annali*, 1847, XCIII, 195–196.
[86] Pugliese, p. 433.
[87] *Rivista*, n. s., 1847, V, Pt. 1, 84–94.
[88] *Annali*, 1847, XCIII, 196.

evening course of lectures, popular in character.[89] The stir of interest in all these courses showed that a public consciousness of a long standing need had been awakened, and the schools at least made a beginning towards its fulfilment. But in 1855 Frattini complained that the Lombard silk industry still rested on an empirical basis, with only one school of silk weaving in existence at Milan to correct it.[90]

The potential industrial army of Lombardy was free and imperfectly skilled. With the advent of factories in the cotton industry a social problem at once arose. As in England the cotton operatives were set to work in ill-ventilated rooms, where they breathed air charged with moisture and irritating cotton dust.[91] In the district of Lecco both children and adults were kept at work fourteen hours a day under such conditions that the population could hardly furnish its annual military contingent.[92] But the side of the labor problem that seemed to contemporaries the most menacing was the employment of children in industry, and this danger was not confined to the new factory industry of cotton spinning but had existed for some time in the use of children in the silk mills. Giuseppe Sacchi estimated that in 1840, 37,800 children were employed in the various manufacturing industries of Lombardy.[93] In the new cotton industry even the practice of employing batches of children taken from the poor houses had lifted its ugly head.[94] In the silk reeling mills each woman was "assigned a girl to turn the reel and keep the heater lighted." These girls were from five to twelve years of age and worked from twelve to fifteen hours a day.[95] In this branch of industry the evil was not so serious at its worst because the mills were active only three months in the year, the period during which the crop of cocoons was being reeled. It was more serious in the twisting mills

[89] G. Sacchi, in *Annali*, 1847, XCIII, 195 ff.

[90] Frattini, p. 80.

[91] Frattini, who in 1845 questioned the darkness of the picture that Giuseppe Sacchi had painted in the *Annali* of the conditions of labor in the industry, admitted in 1855 that the mills were usually on low ground and ill ventilated. Frattini, p. 104.

[92] G. Sacchi, in *Annali*, 1846, XC, 281.

[93] *Annali*, 1842, LXXIII, 242. Sacchi got at the number through the use of school statistics with which he was thoroughly conversant. In Lecco 2,296 children, or one-fourth of the total population of the district, were employed in industry from 12 to 15 hours a day. *Ibid.*, 249. In 1845, 1,645 of the 3,168 cotton spinners of Lombardy were children—600 boys and 465 girls. *Annali*, 1846, XC, 275.

[94] In the years 1834–1839, in the district of Busto Arsizio, 405 children from the foundlings' home in Milan were put to work in the cotton spinneries. *Annali*, 1846, XC, 283, note 1.

[95] G. Sacchi, in *Annali*, 1842, LXXIII, 242.

where a majority of the operatives were girls and the activity of the mills became continuous with the growth of the industry.

> The rooms are often damp and ill protected against changes in the weather. The nature of the work is such as to render a child a machine or worse than a machine. The children are for the most part employed to tie broken threads and sometimes to aid those unhappy persons who, with the weight of their bodies and the motion of a beast of burden, turn the mechanical drum." There were 15,000 such children Giuseppe Sacchi reported in 1842, "consuming the flower of life for a daily wage of 20 to 24 centesimi in a branch of industry which yields the country 45,000,000 lire a year.[96]

The mills took the children away from school; what was more alarming to enlightened observers of this conservative community, they threatened the life of the family replacing its paternal discipline with that of a hierarchy of foremen, either indifferent to morals or men of bad character.[97]

The Milan Chamber of Commerce reflected a much less gloomy view of child labor in a report which they presented to the Government in 1846.[98] The report has a disagreeable tone of complacency, but it states at the outset one condition for which due allowance must be made in any attempt to weigh the social problem created by local industry. "The work-people, young and old, go home and sleep under the paternal roof or in the bosom of the family; they have hours for dinner and for evening recreation, they retire before sunset from the manufactories and so can find sufficient repose. Their parents may at will stipulate with the manufacturers the hours that the children must dedicate to elementary instruction, the abundance of which offers such facilities at Milan." The Chamber further reported that very few children under nine were employed in the city of Milan;[99] that the work was "harmless and simple," and that "no damage to their health was to be feared." The

[96] *Annali*, 1842, LXXIII, 244.

[97] *Ibid.* The preamble of the act regulating child labor in the factories of Lombardy referred to grave abuses, slack surveillance, and work "*precocious* and *excessive* and also performed in *modes* and *places pernicious* to health and physical development." *Circolare alle I. R. Delegazioni provinciali*, entitled "Discipline per ovviare agl' inconvenienti derivanti nelle fabbriche manifatturiere da un precoce impiego dell' opera dei fanciulli e dall' eccessivo esercizio delle loro forze," in *Raccolta degli Atti del Governo*, LX, Pt. 2, 405–406. The whole problem of child labor in Italian factories was reviewed in a report of Cesare Correnti for the investigating commission appointed by the Congress of Scientists at Lucca in 1843. It was read at the Milan Congress in 1844 and reproduced in part by the *Rivista*, n. s., 1844, II, Pt. 2, 577–582.

[98] M. C. M., Camera di Commercio, cartella 556, November 24, 1846.

[99] The number of children employed in the larger industrial establishments of the city was reported as 226; those under 9, 78.

working day was "not greater than ten hours long in winter, with an hour more for dinner, and twelve hours in summer, plus two hours for dinner." As artificial lighting had not yet been perfected, one is tempted to translate this last remark to mean that a maximum use of the Lombard sunlight was made, according to the season.

It must be remembered that such conditions as those just described, although they well might alarm the publicist as a symptom of what was to come, were still confined within relatively narrow limits. The only manufactories that could have produced a considerable geographical dislocation of labor were the cotton and linen spinneries located on the Olona, Lambro, Adda, and Brembo rivers, and there is no evidence that even these produced mill towns. Outside these spinneries and a few silk twisting mills, the description which Giuseppe Sacchi gave of cotton weaving may be taken as a general picture of the life of the peasant artisan of Lombardy. The weavers, he wrote,

> while they pursue the life of the artisan remember always to be country people, and preserve the habits and occupations of such. During the winter and the rainy season, when the farmer can accomplish nothing in the fields, our manufacturers of cotton industriously apply themselves to their looms. . . . In this industry they are often aided by the family. . . . As soon as the heat of the sun dries the soil in spring . . . the weaver rolls up his web, and putting away the shuttle, takes the hoe and the sickle and goes with the other peasants to govern the fields inherited from his elders. . . . [Thus] industry is associated with agriculture, and these two modes of life, which are elsewhere rivals and often enemies, are with us always kept sisters and friends.

The happy results, he continued, are florid health, and personal independence from "the servitude of the factory" on one hand, and from "the servitude of the glebe" on the other. "Meanwhile," he concludes, "we must cordially thank the promoters of this industry in Lombardy because they have procured us all the benefits that it can give, while avoiding the economic and moral evils which, alas! too much disturb other populations."[100]

Indeed, the observers of the time are in general agreement that the Lombard manufacturers showed no disposition to push the exploitation of labor to the limit, as did their English contemporaries. The social atmosphere of the country, still patriarchal and gentle, linked with the fact of a well protected market and the absence of acute competition, was against exploitation. Giuseppe Sacchi, who represented the section of public opinion fully aroused to the danger by a knowledge of conditions abroad and determined to forestall a repetition of them in Lom-

[100] *Annali*, 1847, XCI, 152–153.

t fail to note the measures taken even by the cotton
sure the welfare of their employees. The firm of
iate, he observed in 1846, employed no children under
shment was cleaned and ventilated daily and disin-
.cre used. The regulations were enforced by a director with
ur assistants, "who treat their subordinates with much kindness." In
several of these new factories the fines imposed for breaking factory
rules went into a fund for the benefit of sick operatives, and some of
the manufacturers had set up mill schools to instruct the children in
reading, writing and religion.[101]

In 1843 the Government issued a decree regulating the employment of
children in factories.[102] Factory owners were forbidden to employ
children under nine years of age. A child must be fourteen years old
to be employed where conditions were dangerous to life or health. He
must have had at least two years of elementary instruction "unless the
owner of the factory provides this in the same"; otherwise until he
reached the age of twelve, he must be allowed two hours a day to attend
the free schools. A child under twelve could not be employed under any
condition for more than ten hours a day, or children from twelve to
fourteen years old for more than twelve hours. Their conditions of
employment must besides leave "at least eight hours for sleep, and
always avoid keeping them while at work in uncomfortable positions,
except for short periods, and under regulations with which the inspectors will be charged." Night work for children under twelve, corporal
punishment and promiscuity of sexes in the factory, were forbidden.
The inspectors were to be accompanied by the public doctor on their
rounds.

Contemporary opinion recognized the need of industrial labor for
some form of self-organized protection against the dangers of its new
position. The form that received the widest discussion and approval was
the workingmen's Mutual Aid Society, some examples of which had
sprung up spontaneously.[103] The aim of these societies was to promote
"the morality and concord" of the workingmen and to provide a fund

[101] Giuseppe Sacchi, reviewing Frattini, in *Annali*, 1846, XC, 277.

[102] November 10, 1843, proclaimed in a Circular to the I. R. Provincial Dele-
gations, December 11, 1843, in *Raccolta degli Atti del Governo*, LX, Pt. 2, 405–
410. The Government had already regulated the use of steam engines to the
extent of calling the attention of manufacturers to their legal liability for "the
perfection and solidity" of their machinery. *Ibid.*, 1837, XLVIII, Pt. 2, 262–263.

[103] The Italian name was *Società di mutuo soccorso*. The *Pio Istituto Tipo-
grafico*, founded in 1804, the most flourishing organization of the kind in
Lombardy, is described in the *Rivista*, n. s., 1843, I, Pt. 3, 353–355.

for the relief of sick, indigent and aged members. The societies sought work for members who were unemployed and undertook to discipline those who failed in the faithful performance of their duties. One of the editors of the *Rivista europea*, Gottardo Calvi, proposed that the national Congresses of Italian Scientists should undertake to stimulate and regulate this movement by drafting a model constitution, and the *Rivista europea* threw its pages open to a discussion of the question and solicited information about such societies in Italy and abroad. Calvi's proposal was immediately opposed on the ground that in lending support to the movement the Italian Scientists would be interfering with the principles of *laissez-faire* and hampering the free expansion of industry.[104] The Lucca Congress in 1843 nevertheless appointed a committee headed by Calvi himself to collect information. Calvi prosecuted his idea vigorously in the *Rivista* throughout the year 1844 and presented a report to the Congress which met in Milan in that year.[105] In the discussion the proponents of the mutual aid society were careful to emphasize the fact that no return to the *compagnonnage*, in bad odor because of the disorders to which it had given rise in France, nor to the guild, was contemplated. The organization of labor in the form proposed was advocated both as an act of justice to labor and as a timely precaution against a menace to the existing social system, but in a spirit of extreme conservatism. Encouragement was to be extended to labor as an act of charity, the fulfillment of a debt of honor to the struggling poor; and the organization to be set up was to be safeguarded by the appointment of a wealthy patron, who was to supervise the use of its fund. There is no doubt that a free organization of labor would have been vigorously opposed.

As to the share of labor in the profits of industry it is possible to make only a few broad statements. The statistics available are fragmentary and at best would be inconclusive with regard to the material welfare of the industrial operative because employment in industry was so largely a supplementary occupation. In the textile industry, the weavers, working at their handlooms, were better paid than the spinners, working in shops and factories. Industrial labor in general received higher wages than field labor. Also it would appear that, in terms of

[104] The opposition came from Count Ilarione de Petitti, the well known Piedmontese Liberal, who voiced it at once in the Congress and later in Valerio's journal *Letture di famiglia*. *Rivista*, n. s., 1843, I, Pt. 3, 358–364; 1844, II, Pt. 1, 166–180.

[105] "Delle Società di Mutuo Soccorso esistenti in Italia," Rapporto al VI Congresso scientifico di G. Calvi," *Rivista*, n. s., 1844, II, Pt. 2, 710–723.

money, industrial operatives were better paid in Lombardy than in France.[106]

Some of the more ambitious manufacturing enterprises that sprang up in Lombardy before the middle of the century required a greater investment of capital than the individual capitalist or the traditional partnership could command. The favorite device for mobilizing these larger sums was the *società in accomandita*. Corporations were associated with speculation, which the leaders of local opinion regarded with aversion and dread.[107]

It is clear from the foregoing survey that Lombardy remained industrially backward during the first half of the nineteenth century, outdistanced by England, Belgium, France, Switzerland, and parts of Germany and of the Austrian Empire.[108] The arrival of certain of its industries at the threshold of the factory stage of production does not mean that the factory system had come or that conditions were yet ripe for it. In England that system crystallized only when various slowly maturing elements, human, economic and technical, reached a certain point of development in combination, then fused and interacted to

[106] Some contemporary estimates of day wages (in Austrian lire):

		Men	Women	Children
Cotton spinning:	1845	.75—2.50		.20—.50
	1855	1.50—2.00	.88	.40—.50
Silk winding:	1842			.15—.30
	1855		1.00—1.20	
Girls tending reels—			.50— .60	
Silk spinning:	1855	Plain—2.30—3.00		
		Patterned—3.30—3.60		
Woolen industry:	1842			.24

The figures for 1842 are from G. Sacchi in *Annali*, 1842, LXXIII, 242, 244–245. Those for 1845 are from Sacchi's review of Frattini, *Sulla filatura e la tessitura di cotone*, in *Annali*, 1847, XCI, 150. Those for 1855 are from Frattini.

Sacchi said that the wages paid in the cotton spinning mills in 1845 were "sufficient and in most cases even generous," and were higher than those paid for field labor. We know that the tenant of the Brianza was obliged to give his labor to his landlord at the rate of 40 Italian centesimi a day in winter and 60 in summer, while agricultural day laborers received 70–75 centesimi a day in winter; 90 centesimi to 1 franc in fall and early spring; while "in the great fury of the cocoon harvest the price is doubled." Spreafico, pp. 149, 163.

In France Villermé estimated the wages of men employed in manufactures at 454–785 francs a year, of women at 252–264 francs, and of children aged 14-16, working 14 hours a day, at 200–260 francs. Sacchi, "Studi sulla pubblica beneficenza," *Rivista*, n. s., 1846, IV, Pt. 2, 418.

[107] See below, pp. 131–134.

[108] The total value in 1841 of the industrial products of Lower Austria was estimated at 107,844,000 florins, of Bohemia at 141,680,000 and of Lombardy at 122,964,000. The ratios per inhabitant were calculated to be 78 for Lower Austria, 47 for Lombardy, and 34 for Bohemia. A Balbi, *L'Austria e le primarie potenze*, p. lxv. 1 florin was worth 3 Austrian lire.

produce a rapid transformation of the social order. Lombardy possessed a dense, industrious and sober population,[109] and this potential supply of labor was not restricted as in Germany by the survival of guild regulations. Lombardy also had a supply of industrial metals not as yet fully exploited. But its potential labor force was still firmly rooted on the land, and too many other elements were lacking or in a state of immaturity to justify the hope of a speedy industrial transformation. One was the deficiency of technical skill and of the means of imparting it. Another was the scarcity of fuel. The supply of wood was running short and Lombardy-Venetia was unprovided with the coal measures which the English found in their soil to supply that defect. With fuel scarce and dear, the iron industry languished and the steam engine was a luxury. A fundamental condition lacking for the evolution of a concentrated industry was the stimulus of an extensive market. The manufacturers of Lombardy lived in a Europe cut up by the high tariffs of the Restoration and were encircled by the prohibitive system of Austria. They had a free market only in the states of the Austrian Monarchy, where they could make little headway because of the established position of their competitors in Bohemia and Lower Austria. The only market left that might support a mass production was that created by the demands of the lower classes of Lombardy-Venetia. But these demands were simple and were largely self-supplied by the peasants. This market, fenced in for the benefit of local industry by a high tariff, did actually suffice to float a factory production of cotton and a large-scale, if still somewhat primitive, manufacture of cheap textiles, but it was too narrow a basis to support an extensive structure of mechanized industry. Only the semi-manufactured silk of Lombardy broke over the barrier, thanks to the advantage conferred by the climate and traditions of Italy.

Even had Lombardy been endowed with a tradition of technical skill, with coal mines and an extensive market, there would still have been lacking in the class possessing capital the daring, the spirit of enterprise, which had been stimulated in England by the commercial adventuring of the seventeenth and eighteenth centuries and by the dislocations resulting from the revolution in English agriculture. How different the experience of the Lombards! After the quasi-medieval stupor of the Spanish régime in the seventeenth century, they had been prodded into economic consciousness by the Austrian Government and their own enlightened thinkers in the eighteenth, and had found in the production of silk an

---

[109] Carlo Cattaneo remarked in 1839 that Lombardy had a larger population of males of the industrial age (20 to 60) than almost any other continental country. *Politecnico*, 1839, I, 47.

interest that drew them once more into the economic life of Europe beyond the Alps. The subsequent Napoleonic régime, however stirring, had reduced their country to an economic appanage of France. There was nothing in this history to prepare them for bold economic initiatives. The capital remained in the hands of the conservative proprietary class who gave the tone to Lombard society. When it began to accumulate in other hands, it tended to seek safe and solid investment in land, which conferred on its owner the universally desired respectability of proprietorship. The one manufacturing industry which was subjected to strong stimulation by an outside market, the production and winding of silk, was in the possession of the landed proprietors. They found it growing on their hands; it had an effect on them, and imparted an impulse of energy to the whole economic community. But given its agricultural auspices, there is no reason to wonder that silk-production remained a passive, and failed to become an aggressive industry. Foreign merchants sought out the silks of Lombardy, and the local community did not succeed, in the period before 1848, even in effecting an organization to finance the trade in silk, or in freeing this trade from dependence on foreign wholesalers.

This prudence and caution, the spirit of the landed proprietor permeating the economic life of Lombardy, was the subject of universal lamentation among the publicists who wished to see their country play a livelier part in the life of the times.[110] The Lombard manufacturer, wrote one of these publicists in 1855, "can only in rare cases count on the capital of our wealthy citizens, first, because in Lombardy this is not abundant, then because one loves rather to invest it in proprietorship, and finally because we have not yet conquered that kind of opprobrium in which Castilian ignorance for several centuries held those who dedicated themselves to commercial speculations."[111] The only industries in which the factory made any headway, silk twisting and cotton spinning, were industries free from the routine of peasant life. Even among the progressive publicists the *spiritus capitalisticus*, the spirit of

[110] Carlo Cattaneo, the greatest of them, never tired of inveighing against "the cold and sterile life of the little proprietor, which in some provinces has substituted for our trafficking and opulent forbears a generation of gentlemen who devote their lives to giving a little income the appearance of prosperity." *Annali*, 1836, XLVIII, 292–293. "The influence of this spirit of stagnation, resulting from the great division and universality of landed possession, insinuates itself into and saturates our whole mercantile system; since with us every wretched trader wants to be a proprietor at any cost, and to some degree takes on the thoughts and manners of one." "Alcune ricerche sul progetto di un monte delle sete in Milano," *Annali*, 1837, LIV, 186.
[111] Frattini, pp. 80 ff.

the daring and unscrupulous entrepreneur, was in bad od\
Lombardy.

Nevertheless, the period of ten or fifteen years just preceding
Revolution of 1848 witnessed a definite forward movement of indus\
The part of this study that deals with the thought of the period will
show to what extent this movement was a conscious one. Suffice it to
say here that from 1824 on a group of publicists writing for various
journals which they founded sought to promote it, confronting the
public with a picture of Lombard industry, comparing it with that of
the rest of Italy and of Europe, encouraging its promoters, criticizing
its defects, and sponsoring improvements. Presently concerted action
began to be taken to remedy shortcomings. In 1837 the public subscribed the large sum of 3,000,000 Austrian lire to the stock of a Company for the Excavation of Mineral Combustibles,[112] whose purpose was
to search the soil of Lombardy-Venetia for coal and to exploit its resources of lignite. In the following years the periodicals rang with
rumors and echoes of the eager hunt, which if successful would remove
one great handicap from the progress of local industry. In 1841 the
Society for the Encouragement of the Arts and Crafts of Milan was
founded to stimulate needful industries and provide technical instruction
for industrial operatives. The Society manifested such initiative and
independence that the Government began to oppose it. Its program and
its success mark the fact that the leaders of the Lombard economic community had been educated to a consciousness of the defects and potentialities of industry and had reached the point of taking stock of itself.

The important concrete signs of progress were the advent of
mechanized spinning, the cautious but steady extension of the principle
of stock ownership as a means of mobilizing industrial capital, and the
development of auxiliary industries such as the manufacture of dyes,
chemicals and machinery. However modest these beginnings, they
signified that the days of a purely parasitic industrialism were past and
represent the first steps towards a manufacturing organism free from
the domination of agriculture.

---

[112] *Società dei combustibili fossili.*

CHAPTER VI

CAPITAL AND CREDIT

T HE investment and movement of capital and the mechanism by which capital was mobilized in Lombardy during the period 1815–1848 can as yet be traced only in broad outlines. The whole subject would repay close investigation.

The central fact has already become evident: that the bulk of the accumulated wealth of the community was invested in real estate and the operations of agriculture, and was in the possession of the proprietors of land. Cattaneo's careful estimates led him to the conclusion that the capital invested in the Lower Milanese alone amounted to no less than a billion francs.[1] As the reader of the preceding chapters is aware, an increasing amount of productive capital was being invested, during the second half of the period 1814–1848, in the equipment of railways and industrial plants. As early as 1821 the disposition of the nobles to invest their money, "formerly hoarded in chests," not only in agricultural improvements but in commercial and industrial "speculations" was noted, and this new disposition was attributed to the example of the government under the French régime, which had put much of its revenue from taxation into public works.[2] According to official estimates verified by Jacini, "the aggregate of capital employed in commerce and industry, less wages," was 381,069,880 Austrian lire. This sum, though considerable, was less than a sixth of the capital value of real property, which was approximately 2,424,444,000 lire.[3]

The chief productive uses into which capital seeking investment flowed before 1848 are indicated by the figures just given. Aside from the income subtracted by taxation and loans for use by the Austrian government, some of which passed into the construction of canals, roads, and bridges in Lombardy, that part of the "national" income which became fixed in construction or capital improvement was invested, with overwhelming preponderance, in agriculture, that is, in the planting of mulberries, in the construction of silk-reeling mills, in irrigation and drainage, and in reclamation of uncultivated land and of that

---

[1] *Istituzioni agrarie*, pp. 46–50.
[2] Lady Morgan, *Italy*, I, 190.
[3] Jacini, *La proprietà fondiaria*, 3d. ed. (Milan and Verona, 1857), p. 139. It must be remembered that the former figure includes capital invested by foreigners.

acquired from the communes. A substantial quantity of capital must have been absorbed by the building operations that were transforming Milan during this period.

Between 1840 and 1848 a good deal of capital, a considerable portion of which seems to have come from abroad,[4] was invested in local railway, mining, and manufacturing ventures.[5] But the bulk of surplus income continued to find investment in land and its requirements as an instrument of production.

As for circulating capital, a considerable quantity was required for agricultural operations, especially on the great estates of the Plain. But the chief demand for circulating capital was to meet the requirements of foreign trade, above all to finance the annual production and movement of silk. This demand was not only a heavy one, but increased by leaps and bounds, particularly between 1814 and 1841, when the value of silk exported from Lombardy rose from 37,771,203 to 152,597,193 Milanese lire.[6]

The negotiable forms of capital which existed in Lombardy during the period under discussion were mortgages, the securities of stock companies, the bonds of the government, bills of exchange, and, of course, cash.

The mortgage was solidly enthroned as chief among the instruments by which a degree of negotiability could be imparted to capital wealth. By 1854 the value of mortgages on real estate had reached the sum of 600,000,000 lire.[7]

The overwhelmingly prevalent use of the mortgage as security rested on the preponderance of agriculture as the basis of Lombard economy, and the consequent need for long-term, rather than short-term credit. But a strong preference was accorded to the mortgage in obtaining credit not only for agricultural improvements, but also for every sort of capitalistic undertaking. Cattaneo attributed this to the penetration of the whole business world by the habits and cautiousness of the dominant class of landed proprietors, which he described as fixed in the soil like "an old plant that aspires only to a comfortable motionlessness."[8] In 1821 the Chamber of Commerce, denying its support to a proposed Traders Bank organized as a limited liability company, declared that

[4] See below, notes 22 and 23.
[5] Reflected in heavy withdrawals of savings from the Savings Bank. See, for example, the editorial note on the report of this bank, *Annali*, 1841, LXXII, 71–73; also an open letter to the director of the *Eco della Borsa* by Cesare Cantù, *Ricoglitore italiano e straniero*, 1837, Part 2, pp. 512 ff.
[6] Adriano Balbi, *Miscellanea italiana*, pp. 249–250.
[7] Jacini, *Proprietà fondiaria* (3d. ed.), pp. 137–139.
[8] *Annali*, 1837, LIV, 107.

the guarantees of such an institution, to enjoy public confidence, should consist of the only sound security, "that of land and the mortgage."[9] The promoters of the ambitious project of a Silk Bank (*Monte delle sete*), in Milan, launched in 1836, devised a reserve fund of 3,000,000 lire guaranteed by the deposit of mortgages to insure the credit of the proposed institution.[10] The Savings Bank (*Cassa di Risparmio*) of the Lombard Provinces, the one important banking institution created in this period, lent its funds to individuals only on the security of mortgages. Cattaneo described the Lombard business community as "suspicious of every investment that does not include a title-deed, certificate of mortgage, ample margin, and complete acquaintance with the persons concerned."[11] It appears that the merchants made a practice of advancing money to producers on deposits of silk,[12] and that private bankers would discount the notes of wealthy and recognized proprietors on their signatures, even without endorsement.[13] The fact remains that the chief instrument of credit for obtaining the use of money was the mortgage. Only with serious difficulty could a Lombard merchant obtain advances unless his credit was visibly guaranteed by land and buildings.

"This profoundly rooted prejudice of ours . . . requires every good commercial house to have large possessions in land and houses; which means keeping perpetually idle half of its forces in order to be permitted to employ the other half in trade." The merchant had to "keep his own money invested in land at 3 per cent to have *credit,* that is, the privilege of managing precariously in commercial operations a little of other people's money borrowed at 5 or 6 per cent or at an even much higher rate." Milan, Cattaneo exclaimed bitterly, is "a city where many of the traders themselves have hardly any respect for a trader except in so far as he is not a trader."[14]

Even the system of obtaining funds on the security of mortgages was open to serious criticism. Such loans had to be obtained, for the most part, from private capitalists. A writer of the *Annali di statistica* in 1846 went so far as to declare that, given the lack of credit institutions, the difficulties surrounding a loan on mortgage were such as to make its use only a last resort. "Capital borrowed on mortgage at 5 per cent is an excessive burden for the object of an agricultural speculation; but there is much more to pay, outside the legal terms: there is a payment to be made to the mediator, who is often one of the

---

[9] M. C. M., Camera di Commercio, cartella 569, 6 August 1821.
[10] See Cattaneo's attack on this proposal in *Annali*, 1837, LIV, 190–199.
[11] *Annali*, 1836, XLVIII, 330.   [13] *Ibid.*, p. 206.
[12] *Ibid.*, p. 178.   [14] *Annali*, 1837, LIV, 205.

lenders; there is too often a loss in the contract between the money
[actually] paid and that specified in the terms of the loan; there are all
the expenses of the accountant, of the notary, of the papers of hypothecation; there are the stamps, the delays"; and above all, the dread of
the consequences if the loan is not paid.[15] Money was lent on mortgages for short terms, usually five years, but there was a general tendency to the prolongation of the loan. Even the Savings Bank was not
able, until 1862, to introduce rules for a regular amortization of such
loans.[16]

A more flexible form of negotiable wealth was introduced into this
credit structure based on the mortgage by the shares sold to float the
joint stock companies launched during the period to finance enterprises
in insurance, banking, transportation, and gas-lighting, and, to a limited
degree, manufacturing industry.

The preferred device for mobilizing the considerable sums of capital
required by such enterprises was the *società in accomandita*, a stock
company in which some of the shareholders were subject to unlimited
liability. The limited liability company, the "corporation" of American
business, although hailed and vigorously recommended by liberal publicists as a fine expression of "the spirit of association," was viewed with
suspicion by the business community.[17] But it established itself firmly
in the field of insurance, banking, and public services. In 1845, even
though only eight of the twenty-seven stock companies at Milan were
true limited companies, they had a much larger capitalization than the
companies *in accomandita*.[18] With a single exception,[19] all were destined

[15] Agostino Perini, "Degli ostacoli che si oppongono al progresso dell'agricoltura," *Annali*, 1846, LXXXVII, 129–130. Jacini referred to the "procedural defects" attending the process of hypothecation. *Proprietà fondiaria* (3d. ed.), p. 136.
He discusses them at length in his final chapter, *ibid.*, pp. 386–405.

[16] *La Cassa di Risparmio*, p. 279.

[17] The Chamber of Commerce of Milan repeatedly advised the Government
against permitting the formation of limited companies in the field of manufactures.
Such a form of organization, "not known except to the laws of France," was
suitable only for such a business as the operation of diligences, where success was
assured by the type of service to be rendered. In the case of an industrial undertaking, the promoter should be required to show that his object was a clearly
defined manufacturing enterprise which excluded the idea of commerce; the
project should be submitted to the police, a time prescribed within which the
whole sum subscribed must be paid and a guarantee given that subsequent purchasers of shares, and the names of the new shareholders would be communicated
to the police. Finally, no change in the statutes of the company must be made
unless authorized." M. C. M., Camera di Commercia, cartella 569, 4 November
1822; *ibid.*, 27 June 1823; and also 1825.

[18] M. C. M., Camera di Commercio, cartella 573, 1845.

[19] The Società dei combustibili fossili (coal company), with a capital of 3,000,000
Austrian lire, a semi-public enterprise.

for insurance, banking, postal services, steam navigation, and railways. Readers familiar with the history of the industrial revolution in England will remember that, there also, limited companies did not pay an important part in founding the great manufacturing industries and will not be surprised that they were extended very slowly and cautiously into the development of industrial enterprises in Lombardy.

The company *in accomandita* was the means preferred for financing new industrial enterprises in which large expenditures for plant were required.[20] But even the companies *in accomandita* were surrounded with precautions against the peril of irresponsibility. For example, in the notice of the projected mechanized linen spinnery to be set up at Melegnano, with a capitalization of 1,600,000 Austrian lire *in accomandita,* it was made clear that the managing owners might not "participate with personal liability in any other enterprise." They owned six of the one hundred shares of stock and could not alienate them during their administration.[21]

How much wealth was in circulation in the form of company securities at the end of the period it is impossible to state with confidence. Some indication of its amount can be found in the nominal capitalization of the twenty-one companies whose seat was Milan in 1845,[22] roughly 70,000,000 Austrian lire.[23]

---

[20] For example, the adventurous linen-spinneries organized shortly after 1830 were companies *in accomandita.*

[21] *Politecnico*, 1839, I, 188–191.

[22] Twenty-seven companies were operating in Milan in that year. Six were foreign corporations.

[23] The Austrian lira, of 100 centesimi, was worth 114.8 centesimi in Italian lire, 88 centesimi in Milanese lire (Sandonà, p. 268). The following table reflects the distribution of commercial and industrial investment in 1845:

Transportation:	
Diligences	100,000 lire (Italian)
Steamboats	100,000 lire (Italian)
Ferdinandea Railway Company	50,900,000 lire (Austrian)
Milan-Monza Railway	3,660,000 lire (Austrian)
Mining:	
Coal Company	3,000,000 lire (Austrian)
Peat-mining	50,000 lire (Milanese)
Manufacture:	
Cylinder Flour Mill	540,000 lire (Austrian)
Sugar refineries:	
Calderara	600,000 lire (Milanese)
Azimonti	500,000 lire (Austrian)
Pirovani	500,000 lire (Milanese)
Comb-Spinning of wool	500,000 lire (Austrian)
Linen and hemp spinning:	
Bazzoni e Compagnia	900,000 lire (Austrian)
P. Bataglia e Compagnia	1,200,000 lire (Austrian)

The securities issued by the joint stock companies were negotiable, and variations in their market price indicate that they were traded, but their negotiability was subject to strict limitations. It was precisely their negotiability, the fact that ownership and control might pass into the hands of unknown persons, that made stock companies seem dangerous to the prudent merchants of Lombardy.[24] Both the negotiability and the diffusion of wealth in company securities was limited by the size of the shares, which was relatively large. Among the twenty-seven companies operating in Milan in 1845 the par value of the shares was, in one case, the Azimonti sugar refinery, 100,000 Austrian lire each; in four cases, 50,000 each; in four others, 25,000 to 36,000 each; and only in four was as low as 1,000 lire. The shares of only two companies, a small refinery of wines, and a semi-public coal mining company, were of a size (100 lire each) that put them within reach of the small investor. In the regulations of the Melegnano linen spinning mill it was stipulated that under no circumstances could the shares (of 15,000 Austrian lire each) be subdivided, and that no share could be alienated by its purchaser until paid up in full.[25] Company securities were not bought and sold on the Bourse at Milan.[26] A further impediment to their circula-

Wine refinery	100,000 lire (Italian)
Stearic candles	150,000 lire (Austrian)
Stearic candles	120,000 lire (Milanese)
Textile prints	10,000 lire (Austrian)
Ironworks at Dongo	550,000 lire (Austrian)
Insurance:	
Life	2,400,000 lire (Austrian)
Fire	3,600,000 lire (Austrian)
Banking:	
Delachi P. Ba and Co.	800,000 lire (Austrian)
Petracchi Tagliferri and Co.	800,000 lire (Austrian)
Swimming School	150,000 lire (Austrian)

M. C. M., Camera di Commercio, cartella 573, 1845. It must be borne in mind that not all of the securities that represented this capitalization were the property of Lombards. In 1837 Cattaneo had warned of the danger that the stock of the proposed Silk Bank "should pass into the hands of foreign bankers as has happened in other enterprises, thanks to our excessive pusillanimity." *Annali*, 1837, LIV, 220. See also Jacopo Pezzato, "Dell intervento dei capitali forestieri nelle imprese di strade ferrate," *Annali*, 1846, LXXXIX, 334–338. ". . . foreign capitalists have made themselves the masters of our railways (later taken over by the Government), of steam navigation on the Po (the Lloyd enterprise) and what is more important of a part of the principal trade and industry of the country, namely silk." Jacini, *Proprietà fondiaria* (3d. ed.), p. 363.

[24] See above, n. 17.

[25] *Politecnico*, 1839, I, 189.

[26] Trading on that inactive scene was limited to "the exchange of commodities, of public securities, and of metallic materials." *I. R. Almanacco*, 1834, p. 272; 1843, p. 297.

tion was raised by the order of the Emperor in 1839 "that in future in the publication of periodical works, journals, and pamphlets, it is forbidden to insert tables indicating the current value of shares, either national or foreign."[27]

A third kind of negotiable lien circulating in Lombardy during the period was the bonds of the Monte Lombardo-Veneto, which represented the funded debt of the Kingdom.

This institution was erected in 1822 for the funding and servicing of the debt inherited from the Napoleonic Kingdom of Italy. Its creditors received bonds bearing interest at 5 per cent, payment of which was a preferred claim on the revenues of the Lombardo-Venetian Kingdom. Income from the sale of public property in Lombardy-Venetia was assigned to the Amortization Fund (*Cassa d'ammortamento*) of the Monte for the redemption of these bonds and extinction of the debt.[28] The public debt increased and in 1841 amounted to 222,000,000 Austrian lire. The certificates of the Monte were a prime security, and, as such, a considerable though diminishing quantity of them were carried in the portfolio of the Savings Bank.[29] In 1830 the Government took advantage of an easy money market to refund these bonds at 4 per cent.[30] They were traded on the Bourse and in the period 1832–37 their market value rose from a minimum of 86 in April, 1831, to above 111 in 1837.[31] In 1844 they had risen to 118. In that year, in consequence of rumors of malversation of the funds of the Monte, communicated under secret orders from Vienna (rumors later verified), the price fell to 105 and never again rose above 111.[32]

Another mobile form of wealth in circulation consisted of bills of exchange. But they did not circulate freely. Discounting of such bills was not accepted practice. If a merchant resorted to the sale of a bill he was assumed to be in financial straits. "The few bills that are discounted," Cattaneo observed in 1837, "are almost all of foreign origin."[33] The circulation of bills was subject to "a grave abhorrence of paper money" in any form which was one of the characteristics of this con-

[27] Notification of the Governor Hartig, 24 June 1839, A.S.M., Presidenza, Atti segreti, 493, cartella 328.

[28] A description of the Monte Lombardo-Veneto and its predecessor, the Monte Napoleone, will be found in Sandonà, pp. 287–311.

[29] See below, pp. 137–139.

[30] A.S.M., Presidenza, Atti segreti, cartella CXXXII.

[31] Riccardo Bachi, "Storia della Cassa di Risparmio delle Provincie Lombarde 1823–1923," in *Cassa di Risparmio delle Provincie Lombarde*, p. 12; *Annali*, 1837, LIV, 207–8, where Cattaneo gives the minimum quotation as 80.

[32] "Un Rapporto Segreto di Stefano Jacini al Conte di Cavour sul Monte Lombardo Veneto" (April, 1859), *Rivista di Storia Economica*, 1936, I, 232 ff.

[33] *Annali*, 1837, LIV, 204.

servative community. "Paper money is the scarecrow that rises before
our eyes in connection with every contract and instrument of credit,"
wrote Cattaneo. "The notary in all his formulas invariably contemplates three great enemies: death, disorder, and paper money; and
sound gold and silver certificates are, in our notarial archives, the sole
symbol of public and private good health."[34] Stefano Jacini testified
to the same effect in a secret *Promemoria* addressed to Cavour in 1859:
"the population of Lombardy-Venetia feels a profound traditional
antipathy for paper money."[35]

Metallic money was the chief form of circulating wealth in Lombardy,
and all efforts to increase the circulation of negotiable paper met with
discouragement and failure. Some paper money, the so-called Certificates of Vienna, may have been in circulation early in the period.[36] It
had been hoped that the notes of the National Bank of Austria would
be circulated in Lombardy, and to facilitate their circulation an Office of
Exchange (*Cassa di cambio*) was created at Milan by the Viennese
bank. But, even though these notes were accepted in payments to the
Treasury, the preference of the Lombards for metallic money excluded
them from circulation and the Office of Exchange was suppressed.[37]
Stefano Jacini informed Cavour in 1859 that Lombardy-Venetia had
been explicitly excluded from the operations of the Bank of Austria.[38]
The preference for hard money was reinforced by the requirement that
a large class of current obligations could be discharged only by payments in cash. "Rents, leases, life annuities, interest payments, anniversary masses for the dead, pensions, taxes and surtaxes on income,
fixed taxes, customs duties are all disbursements payable, by injunction
or stipulation, only in hard money," wrote Cattaneo in 1837. Even if
paper money had been current, the habits of the rural population would
have compelled the proprietor to settle in coin with his tenants, day-
laborers, spinning women, and with the local retailers from whom he
bought supplies.[39] After 1823, when a new coinage was established for
the Lombardo-Venetian Kingdom, the Austrian silver lira (of 20 soldi

[34] *Ibid.*, p. 186.
[35] In *Rivista di Storia Economica*, 1936, I, 243–244.
[36] At an exchange rate to the florin of 2.5 to 1. See Sandonà, p. 265. I base
the supposition that they circulated in Lombardy on the fact that Austrian currency
enjoyed the right of circulation as legal tender in the Lombardo-Venetian Kingdom
along with the currency of the Kingdom.
[37] M. L. de Tegoborski, *Des finances et du credit public de l'Autriche* (Paris,
1843), I, 88, n. 1.
[38] ". . . the Italian provinces are in fact foreign to the operations of that
institution, directly or indirectly—these [provinces] and these alone." Jacini,
Promemoria, p. 241.
[39] *Annali*, 1837, LIV, 187.

or copper coins) soon drove out other coins and "became the sole money in circulation."[40]

The credit institutions of Lombardy in the period 1814–1848, other than the Monte Lombardo Veneto, were the insurance companies, the Savings Bank of the Lombard Provinces, benevolent institutions which advanced money against the deposit of pledges, and, finally, private banks.

Insurance companies not only increased the sum total of investments in negotiable forms: among the risks that they helped to socialize were the risk of capital losses, loss of purchasing power and productive wealth.

Insurance was first made available to the Lombard community in 1824 when the Azienda Assicuratrice di Trieste established a branch at Milan and offered to insure against damage by fire, "to buildings, furniture and merchandise, and against damage by hail to every product of the soil."[41] The kind of insurance that the Lombard farmer needed most was insurance against the hail-storms, formed by the cold air of the mountains, that often flayed the fields with sudden devastation. The Triestine company made some headway and in 1829 had written 162 policies, concentrated in the northern tier of provinces and in Lodi and Crema.[42] Fire insurance was less directly important to the cultivator, the solid construction of whose buildings offered him a reasonable protection. But a company providing insurance against damage by fire, on human life, and life annuities launched at Milan in 1825—saluted by the *Annali* as the first life insurance company in Italy,[43]—acquired confidence and prospered and in 1839 was carrying insurance to the amount of 1,694,442.63 Austrian lire, of which 416,658.20 had been placed in that year.[44] By 1844, in addition to these companies, a company for mutual insurance against hail and the agencies of four extra-national companies were operating in Milan.[45] But in 1833 when the Phoenix Company, Limited, of Leghorn proposed to introduce a type of insurance designed to expand business credit, by "insuring credits, bills of exchange, notes, commercial effects, etc." and petitioned to be allowed to establish a branch in Milan, the Chamber of Commerce repelled the petition.[46]

[40] Sandonà, p. 268.
[41] *Annali*, 1824, I, 277–285.
[42] *Annali*, 1831, XXIII, 103–105.
[43] "Fro . . .ni," "Cenni sull'origine, le basi, e l'utilità pubblica e privata delle assicurazioni sulla vita dell'uomo," *Annali*, 1826, VII, 51–69.
[44] *Annali*, 1840, LXVI, 84–85.
[45] M. C. M., Camera di Commercio, cartella 573, 31 dicembre 1844.
[46] *Ibid.*, cartella 569, 15 May 1833.

A fountain of long-term credit for building and agricultural operations developed in the well-known Savings Bank *(Cassa di Risparmio)*
of the Lombard Provinces, founded in 1823.[47] This bank flourished
from the start and was an object of great pride to local patriotism. The
need for such an institution was immediately revealed by the increase
of its deposits from 299,134 Austrian lire in December, 1823, to
1,566,242 lire by the end of the following year.[48] By 1846 Lombardy
Venetia had twenty-two of the eighty-three savings banks then existing
in Italy,[49] and the Lombard bank with its branches had accumulated
deposits of 17,450,002 Austrian lire.[50] The growing funds of this
prosperous bank were chiefly invested in local agriculture. Investments
were divided into three parts—one put into bonds of the Monte Lombardo Veneto, another in loans to "moral bodies," that is: to the communes and provinces of Lombardy, to "associations constituted for purposes of drainage, defense, or irrigation," and to benevolent institutions;
the third in loans to landowners on the security of mortgages. The bank
obtained legal permission to discount commercial paper, but did not
exercise the right until 1858. The sum of its loans to moral bodies was
never large and the proportion tended to decline. At first the proportion of funds invested in state bonds was more than three times that
lent to individuals. But after 1830 the bank changed its course and
lent an increasing proportion of its funds to proprietors, so that by the
end of 1847 it was lending them 15,324,063.660 Austrian lire or more
than seven times the sum of its investments in bonds.[51] The Savings
Bank founded for other purposes became "prevailingly, almost solely,
the great land bank of Lombardy."[52] The *Annali di Statistica*, reviewing

[47] *Annali*, 1824, I, 272–277. A full and competent history of the bank and the
movements in the business and economic life of Lombardy with which it has
been related was published in celebration of its one hundredth anniversary, a
volume entitled *La Cassa di Risparmio delle Provincie Lombarde nella evoluzione
economica della regione* (Milan, 1924).

[48] *Annali*, 1824, I, 275; 1825, III, 257–259.

[49] Serristori in *Annali*, 1847, XCI, 206–207.

[50] *Annali*, 1847, XCII, 83–85. The Savings Bank of Lombardy alone was richer
in deposits by some millions of lire than those of any other Italian state. Its
deposits in 1844 were 11,916,000 Austrian lire as compared with 8,405,000 lire in
the corresponding institutions of Tuscany, which were incomparably the richest
in Italy after those of Lombardy. Serristori, "Casse di Risparmio dell'Italia,"
Annali, 1844, LXXXI, 217–219.

[51]	31 December, 1829	31 December, 1847
Government bonds	5,394,915.633 Austrian lire	2,141,921.130 Austrian lire
Loans to moral bodies	385,033.350 Austrian lire	848,000.000 Austrian lire
Mortgages	1,687,408.030 Austrian lire	15,324,053.660 Austrian lire

Annali, 1830, XXIII, 220; 1848, XCV, 77–78. For table showing the percentage
division of investment at five-year intervals, see *La Cassa di Risparmio*, p. 167.

[52] Bachi, in *La Cassa di Risparmio*, p. 181.

the history of the bank on the eve of the Revolution of 1848, congratulated the country that the savings of depositors had been "passed on to other more active classes who made them fruitful in agricultural improvements and building enterprises."[53]

The history of the Savings Bank throws an interesting light on the cautious finanical habits of the Lombard community. The bank was not intended to be a commercial organization but an institution of charity. It was founded and directed by the central Commission of Benevolence, a committee of the Central Congregation. This commission had been constituted to administer distributions of grain and work relief during the crisis of 1816–17, when the poor were thrown into acute distress by the disorders attending the Restoration. But it proved difficult to hold the bank to its non-commercial purpose. Its 4 per cent and its air of benevolent security offered an irresistible temptation to the Lombard investor. By 1829 it was suspected that those who were benefiting by the bank were not the poor, but "small capitalists, merchants and proprietors, a number of public employees, and many domestic servants."[54]

The liberal publicists, the directors and the Government disapproved of this development, and in 1830 the management lowered the interest rate from 4 to 3 per cent.[55] But even 3 per cent in such a safe and sane investment attracted and satisfied the speculative ambitions of Lombard investors, and on March 1, 1836, the directors made still another effort to bring their ship back to its course by lowering the maximum limit of single accounts from 300 to 75 lire.[56] The only effect seems to have been to multiply the number of accounts and increase the cost of administration.[57] In 1840 the *Annali di Statistica* was regretting that the Cassa di Risparmio did not follow the example of the similar institution at Bologna and publish a classification of investors by types, "so much the more because there is a rumor, one might say universal, that the greater part of the sums which compose the millions in its treasury come from large deposits made by people who are well-off in order not to have their money in the house."[58] The fluctuations in the sum of

[53] *Annali*, 1848, XCV, 77–78.
[54] *Annali*, 1830, XXIII, 222. "The class of wage-earners and artisans had not attained the degree of foresight necessary to induce them to deposit little sums to succor themselves in the evil day."
[55] Secret report to the Government on the policy of the bank, A.S.M., Presidenza, Atti segreti, cartella CXXXII; *Annali*, 1832, XXXII, 313–314.
[56] M.R.M., Fondo Cattaneo, cartella 127.11. "The motive was that the greater part of the money was the property of rich persons attracted by the easy interest procurable." Another motive, not mentioned in the documents, may have been the anxiety of the directors to make sure of the liquidity of their funds. (Gino Luzzatto.)
[57] *La Cassa di Risparmio*, p. 94.   [58] *Annali*, 1840, LXV, 89.

deposits confirmed this rumor. A considerable decline in 1836 was attributed to the fact that capital was then being diverted to investment in the new railroad and coal-mining companies; and a like reason was found for the slump which occurred in 1841.[59] This curious body of facts and opinions is not only an eloquent revelation of the prudence of Lombard capital—its attachment to a credit which Cattaneo ironically termed "almost canonical"—but testifies also to the need of the region for a commercial banking organization which would offer the security necessary to entice into circulation the considerable reserves of capital that were evidently in existence.

Of private bankers little can be said except that frequent references to them prove that they existed. The official lists of firms for 1836–47 show that about thirty private banks were operating in Milan during these years.[60] None of the Milanese banking firms except the Savings Bank was organized as a limited company, and only two appear on the list of firms organized as companies *in accomandita* in 1845. It seems clear enough that they took part in the financing of commercial transactions, though there are indications that the merchants engaged in the principal branch of commerce, the exportation of silk, either themselves advanced part of the capital required or borrowed it in the foreign markets in which they deposited their stocks of silk. The banks did not issue notes and rarely discounted bills of exchange. It may be inferred from a careful exposition of the mode of operation of banks of deposit and discount that Cattaneo introduced into his discussion of a Silk Bank *(Monte delle Sete)* in 1837, and from the failure of several projects for the establishment of a discount bank in Milan, that the existing banks did not engage in the book transfers of credit characteristic of that type of institution. It may be suspected that they confined themselves to advancing money on the deposit of mortgages or of warehouse receipts for commodities, chiefly silk. The part, if any, played by the local banks in floating the securities of the more ambitious joint stock companies founded during the period does not appear.

From the foregoing description it will be evident that the credit supply of Lombardy was characterized by very limited negotiability. The bulk of it, in the form of mortgages, was of a type notoriously lacking in liquidity. But thanks to the security of mortgage contracts, the supply of the kind of credit most in demand was abundant. The landed proprietor (even without giving a mortgage, if we are to believe

---

[59] Cesare Cantù in an open letter to the Director of the *Eco della Borsa, Ricoglitore italiano e straniero*, 1837, Part II, 512 ff.; *Annali*, 1842, LXXII, 71–73.
[60] "Statistica dell'industria privata dal anno 1836 al—: Sommario," M. C. M., Ragioneria municipal, cartella 4, 1834 ff.

one competent authority) could borrow at 4 per cent.[61] "The supply always meets the demand," wrote Jacini in 1854 in a discussion of loans secured by mortgage.[62] Monetary crises broke out in 1830–31 as a result of the revolutions of those years in France and Italy; in 1834–36 when all Europe was affected by bank failures spreading from the United States and England, aggravated in Italy by an epidemic of cholera; and in 1847–48 as a result of crop failures and a growing sense of political insecurity. But in the intervals it would seem that no monetary stringency or lack of capital for the needs of agriculture, industry, or business was felt except for the purpose of financing the annual exportation of silk. Rejecting in 1821 a proposal of some merchants to establish a discount bank, the Chamber of Commerce declared that in Milan "the money available exceeds the needs of business."[63] Cattaneo testified to the same effect in 1837, attributing the excess of supply over demand to "[our] paltry commercial activity which, especially in winter allows the money of our merchants long periods of sleep."[64]

It can therefore be maintained that institutions providing long-term credit were sufficient to meet this need, especially after a development of the Savings Bank into a farm-credit bank. On the other hand short-term credit was in far less abundant supply. The difference is reflected in the fact that the legal rate on commercial investments was 6 per cent as compared with 4 per cent on loans guaranteed with real property.[65] And the lack of short-term credit was bitterly felt when merchants needed funds to set in motion the annual crop of silk.

In summer and early fall, when the silk crop was being harvested, reeled, and put in trade, money could not be obtained except at rates that provoked outcries against usury.[66]

---

[61] Professor Ciasca, citing Jacini and C. Cattaneo, *Memorie di economia pubblica dal 1833 al 1860* (Milan, 1860), pp. 17, 23, says that ". . . to the landed proprietor, and not to industrialists, loans were made at 4 per cent and 3½ per cent without mortgage and, in rare cases, at 4½ per cent." "L'evoluzione economica della Lombardia," in *La Cassa di Risparmio*, p. 385. This statement is not borne out by the table published by R. Bachi in the same volume (p. 189) which shows that previous to 1832 more than one-half of the loans on mortgages extended by the Savings Bank bore interest at 4½ per cent and a third of them at 5 per cent. From 1832 to 1848 almost all of them were at 4 per cent, but none at a lower rate.

[62] *Proprietà fondiaria* (3d. ed.), p. 136.

[63] M. C. M., Camera di Commercio, cartella 569, 6 August, 1821.

[64] *Annali*, 1837, LIV, 204.

[65] *Annali*, 1837, LIV, 178. With periodic variations, of course. In 1830, for instance, on an easy money market, the rate seems to have been 4 per cent. Bachi, *op. cit.*, p. 102.

[66] Carlo Cattaneo, "Alcune ricerche sul progetto di un Monte delle sete," *Annali*, 1837, LIV, 233; also documents in M. C. M.

First of all, the traders in silk were called on to advance capital to the spinners, many of whom, as we have seen, were proprietors who had set up reeling mills on their own estates. "The spinners," wrote Cattaneo in 1837, "seek capital not when the silk is ready to ship, but present themselves with hands empty at the beginning of the season." In relation to the capitalists they are *"a type of household workers,* who receive pay for the work performed, rental of the holdings, the price of fuel, and the hire of the machines, while the provider of funds receives interest on the capital lent, with a premium for his risk, and with the speculative profits of purchase, sale and commissions."[67] Once the silk was brought into the Milanese market, a large part of it was sold to commissioners of foreign houses. But it was a common practice of the Lombard traders to ship silk to foreign markets in search of a buyer. To finance this transaction the exporters, unable to obtain money in Milan at reasonable rates, or unwilling to have it known in Milan that they were short of funds,[68] accepted advances from foreign importers and bankers, secured by the deposit of their silks. If opportunity for an advantageous sale was delayed, the Italian merchants were either driven to a forced sale or compelled to purchase more silk in the Lombard market in order to increase the value of their pledges. "How many are the forced purchases made for this purpose," a writer in the *Annali* in 1837 exclaimed, "and how many the houses that are thereby ruined!"[69]

Discussion of improvements in the credit system naturally turned on the problem of obtaining a more elastic supply of commercial credit. The success of the rural banks of the German states called attention to the advantages that such banks would offer in financing agricultural improvements, and their introdutcion into Italy was recommended by the *Annali di Statistica,*[70] but there was no serious agitation of the proposal in Lombardy before 1848.[71] The reforms that were vigorously

[67] *Annali*, 1837, LIV, 233–234.
[68] There are a number of references to this motive in the contemporary discussions of the project of founding a Silk Bank at Milan.
[69] G[iulio] F[ortis], "Dell'erezione di un Monte Depositorio di Sete nella Città di Milano," *Annali*, 1837, LII, 191. Pasquale De Carli, who had launched a project for the creation of a Silk Bank in Milan as early as 1823, described the situation in his "Osservazioni sull'ora proposta erezione di una Banca di Sconto in Milano," *Annali*, 1833, XXXVIII, Bulletino, pp. 413–30. It is more fully described in the masterly essay of Cattaneo, "Alcune ricerche sul progetto di un Monte delle Sete," *Annali*, 1837, LIV, 177–234.
[70] 1836, XLIX, 105.
[71] Jacini argued strongly for such banks in 1854, largely on the basis of their success in Germany. *Proprietà fondiaria* (3d. ed.), pp. 395 ff. The only land bank established in Italy before 1848 was the highly successful Monte dei Paschi di Siena. Serristori, *Annali*, 1846, LXXXIX, 79.

agitated and that reached the stage of at least preliminary action were directed toward repairing the inelasticity of short-term credit.

Several attempts were made to create a bank of discount. In 1821 the firms of Mirabaud and Co. and Kramer and Co. petitioned to be allowed to launch one organized in the form of a limited stock company. The Chamber of Commerce disapproved, chiefly on the ground that a limited liability company would not inspire the necessary confidence. They also declared that Milan did not need such an institution, though they admitted that the city might profit by one organized with adequate guarantees.[72] Another attempt was made in 1833 by a group of wealthy proprietors and merchants.[73] This time the Chamber of Commerce was a little less cold to the idea, expressing itself, in a by-opinion of that year, as favorable at least to the "creation of a National Bank of Discount . . . once commercial circumstances improved."[74] The *Annali* lent its support, taking the view that a bank of this type is "imperiously necessary to commercial interests of every sort in our provinces."[75] In 1847 still another project for a discount bank was afoot.[76] But none of these projects was realized.

The most serious defect of the credit system, its inelasticity, was increasingly felt with the growing demands of the trade in silk. Every summer the system was stretched beyond its capacity. The only activity of Lombard commerce that had a vigorous rhythm was placed at the mercy of foreign capitalists. It seemed absurd that this annual crisis should arise when capital was abundant in Lombardy and needed only to be mobilized to meet the annual need by an improvement in the organization of credit.

The simple and obvious remedy was a silk deposit bank, issuing loans on receipts for deposits of silk made in its warehouse. Such a *Monte delle sete* had existed at Milan before the Napoleonic régime, as a branch of the Monte di Santa Teresa, and had demonstrated its benefits.[77] It disappeared with the old Austrian régime. In 1824 the Chamber of Commerce proposed to revive it, but the Government disapproved.[78]

From the '20's onward the air was full of projects for a silk bank. In 1825 Pasquale De Carli, a banker, sought permission from the Government to found a "Monte Banco Sete," with certain privileges and a subvention from the Treasury. The authorities were favorable, but

---

[72] M. C. M., Chamber of Commerce, 6 August, 1821, cartella 569.

[73] *Annali*, 1833, Bulletino, p. 430, n.

[74] M. C. M., Camera di Commercio, 15 May 1833, cartella 569.

[75] 1835, XLIV, 296.

[76] Notice copied from the *Eco della Borsa* in *Annali*, 1847, XCI, 97.

[77] De Carli, *Annali*, 1833, *Bulletino*, p. 415; Jacini, *Promemoria, op. cit.*, p. 218.

[78] Dispaccio della Camera Aulica del 10 November, 1827, cited in *La Cassa di Risparmio*, p. 211.

refused to let the public administration take any part in the enterprise.[79] In 1826 the central Commission of Benevolence, under whose direction the Cassa di Risparmio had just been so successfully launched, asked for permission to create a Monte delle Sete as a means for investment of the funds of the Cassa. But the mere rumor of this proposal seems to have started a mild run on the Savings Bank.[80]

Di Carli had received too much support for his scheme to be easily discouraged, having obtained the signatures of "106 leading merchants and landowners" as underwriters—whose place "was later taken by the small number of founding members," Cattaneo suspiciously observed some years later.[81] In 1833 De Carli was still persevering and hopeful, publishing in that year a pamphlet in favor of his plan, which was reprinted by the *Annali*.[82] The project was revived in 1836–37, with the support of that enterprising and expansive personality, Giuseppe De Welz, banker, engineer, and journalist.[83] A rather grandiose institution was projected and stock was sold. It was not only to be a Silk Bank, making loans on deposits of silk at 4 per cent, but was also to issue bank notes, discount bills of exchange, invest in public securities, provide a warehouse for the holding of silk, and engage in sales, with the idea that its operations would in time convert Milan into a great emporium not only for silk but for other commodities as well. In two masterly articles in the *Annali* Cattaneo attacked the scheme as far too inflated and ambitious for the community, but at the same time supported vigorously the idea of a Silk Bank which should engage in the credit transfers of a deposit bank, and, endowed with the privilege of discounting bills of exchange, gradually habituate the Lombards to that practice.[84]

The project came to nothing. Its failure, and that of all attempts to create a commercial bank in Lombardy before 1848, can be attributed to the inveterate conservatism of the business community and to its distrust of credit not secured by property in land.

---

[79] *Annali*, 1833, Bulletino, p. 413. De Carli had asked for a monopoly, and buildings donated by the state, as well as a subsidy.

[80] *La Cassa di Risparmio*, pp. 211–212. Permission was denied. The Committee was invited to draw up a new project, but in 1829 they abandoned the idea. The Savings Bank did not ssume this function until 1870. *Ibid.*, p. 214.

[81] *Annali*, 1838, LVIII, 316.

[82] "Sull'ora proposta erezione di una Banca di Sconto in Milano: Osservazioni di Pasquale De Carli (Milano, Tipografia Felice Rusconi, 1833); *Annali*, 1833, XXXVIII, Bulletino, pp. 413–430.

[83] See below, pp. 172–173. Salvatore Pugliese describes the part played by De Welz in the silk bank project, "Iniziativi per promuovere l'attività economica in Lombardia nella prima metà del secolo XIX," in *La Cassa di Risparmio*, p. 443.

[84] "Alcune ricerche sul progetto di un Monte delle sete," *Annali*, 1837, LIV, 177–234; "Sulla nuova proposta di un banco in Milano per sovvenire ai depositi di seta ed altri valori e per lo sconto," *Annali*, 1838, LVIII, 311–325.

PART II

THOUGHT AND ACTION

INTRODUCTION:
"A Conspiracy in Open Daylight"

THE reader of the foregoing chapters will already have observed that the economic changes taking place in Lombardy between 1814 and 1848 were closely watched and subjected to continuous comment by a chorus of thinkers who were using public journals to report the facts and express their opinions. In other words, a movement of thought took place in Lombardy during the period as well as movement in the economic and social sense.

This movement of thought was a phase of that which found political expression in what may be called "the primary works" of the Risorgimento—the well-known series of books, tracts and articles by Gioberti, Cesare Balbo, Massimo d'Azeglio, Count Petitti, Camillo Cavour, Luigi Torelli, Giacomo Durando and others, in which the political program of the moderate liberal party took concrete form on the eve of the first war for the independence of Italy, the national rising of 1848–1849.[1]

The strategic aim of the moderate liberals manifested in these writings was to frame a platform on which all the active elements in the nation, including the princes, could unite with a fair prospect of immediate practical results. Their writings were opportunist, but they were all characterized by an underlying conviction that there was a necessary relation between economic and social progress and the achievement of unity of action and political emancipation. While these writers openly professed the political independence of Italy as their objective, they put first certain economic, social and moral reforms. These were summed up by d'Azeglio in 1847 to include: the promotion of industry and agriculture by free associated effort and by the application of technical

---

[1] Vincenzo Gioberti, *Del primato morale e civile degli Italiani* (Brussels, 1843); Cesare Balbo, *Delle speranze d'Italia* (Paris, Didot, 1844; 2d. ed. Capolago, tipografia Helvetica, 1844); Carlo Ilarione de Petitti, *Delle strade ferrate italiane e del migliore ordinamento di esse* (Capolago, 1845); Cavour's review of this book in *La Revue nouvelle*, May 1, 1846; Luigi Torelli, *Pensieri sull'Italia di un anonimo Lombardo* (Paris, L. R. Delay, 1846); Massimo d'Azeglio, *Degli ultimi casi di Romagna* ("Italia," 1846); Giacomo Durando, *Della nazionalità italiana* (Paris and Lausanne, 1846).

knowledge; the extension of railroads on a national plan; free trade; a free press; popular education directed by laymen; and a lay philanthropy uniting rich and poor.[2] These were put forward as objectives for which the public could work within the bounds of legality and in coöperation with the more enlightened princes, but it is important to note that they were also represented by d'Azeglio and the other liberal writers as embodying the demands of a new type of civilization that had been spreading through Europe since the French Revolution. The argument of the liberals turned on the assumption that a fundamental change in European economic and social life had taken place and that this movement made a "liberalization" of the political order necessary to the maintenance of the peace and stability of Europe. If the Italians failed to respond to the demands created by this movement they would lose their place in the march of European civilization.[3] But over against the danger was set a shining hope, namely: that once aligned with the progress of civilization the nation would be working with the support of an irresistible force.

As a result of the widespread discussion that followed the publication of Gioberti's *Primato degli Italiani* (1843) and Balbo's *Speranze d'Italia* (1844), the moderate liberals could by 1847 agree on a minimum program of political adjustments which the condition of Italy seemed to require immediately. One was the formation by the Italian states of a customs-union similar to the German Zollverein. Another was the abolition of the censorship. Another, about which they were prudently indefinite, was some measure of representative government. They quite definitely insisted that the time had come for the practice of a higher political morality, and they called on princes and people alike for the abandonment of force and fraud—of conspiracy and insurrections on the part of the people; of espionage and the policing of thought, and of such immoralities as the lottery, on the part of the princes. The consistency of the whole program is to be found in the end to which it was directed, namely: that an enlightened public opinion might assume in Italy the empire that it was gaining everywhere else in civilized Europe, for "public opinion," said d'Azeglio, "is the dominating force of the modern world."[4]

These writers based their hope on the Italian princes. Lombardy-Venetia was excluded. The only hope for this most richly endowed

<hr/>

[2] Massimo d'Azeglio, *Proposta d'un programma per l'opinione nazionale italiana* (Florence, Le Monnier, 1847), reprinted in *Scritti e discorsi politici*, ed. M. De Rubris (Florence, 1931), I, 213–269.

[3] *Ibid.*, p. 254.

[4] *Degli ultimi casi di Romagna* (in *Scritti*, ed. De Rubris), I, 72, 89.

and civilized part of Italy seemed to be the expulsion of Austria by the united effort of the rest of the nation, or, as Balbo suggested, by some future crisis in Europe that would divert Austria's attention to the Balkans.

The shower of constitutions precipitated by events in the spring of 1848 seemed to clear the way for the realization of the moderate program throughout Italy, and the ideas of the moderates dominated the first phase of the revolutionary movement of that year in the peninsula. When the campaign of Charles Albert, King of Sardinia, failed, the moderate liberals were discredited and the revolutionary nationalists gained the upper hand. The violence of revolution was followed in 1849 by a violent reaction. But after 1856 the ideas of the moderates regained the ascendancy, thanks to the strong hand of Cavour, who shared these ideas and had played an important rôle in propagating them even before 1848, and in Piedmont they became the working principles of Cavour's national policy in "the Great Decade" between 1851 and 1861.

In the literature of moderate liberalism that appeared on the eve of the Revolution of 1848 Lombardy was represented by only one writer, Luigi Torelli. But Lombardy was not only ripe for that program but had shared fully in paving the way for its general adoption. Investigation of the movement of ideas in this part of Italy that lay immediately under the shadow of foreign domination reveals the fact that its patriotic thinkers had taken the same direction as those of Tuscany and Piedmont and that in the formative period of the liberal movement, that preceding 1843, when there was as yet no public discussion of political objectives, Lombardy might claim to have led the nation in d'Azeglio's "conspiracy in open daylight," for it contributed not only the earliest but three of the ablest and most aggressive patriotic journals; it initiated the liberal program of popular education; and in Romagnosi it gave Italy the thinker in whose mind the fundamental idea that inspired Italian liberalism received its first strong and mature expression and from whose activity and influence it received its first great practical impulse. In Lombardy, then, the early, non-political phase of Italian liberal thought can be studied to unique advantage.

CHAPTER I

NATIONAL JOURNALISM, 1818-1824

THE *Conciliatore* (1818–1819), the *Annali universali di statistica* (1824–[1848]), the *Politecnico* (1839–1845), and the *Rivista europea* (1838–1848) are the conspicuous and recognized champions of liberal nationalism among the journals of Lombardy in the period between the Restoration and 1848. But these journals were not isolated. They were closely related to a movement which by the end of the period had created an extensive and active journalism initiated and sustained by private association and enterprise—a journalism which as far as the censorship and the intellectual conditions of the region would permit was a free organ of public opinion.

A widespread extension of independent journalism was a characteristic phenomenon of the age all over Europe. In Italy journalism had been sporadic in the eighteenth century, somewhat more common but without the character of a public force under the French régime. After 1814 in Lombardy as elsewhere in the Italian peninsula, the field of political notices continued to be monopolized by a privileged gazette—the *Gazzetta di Milano*.

Immediately after the Restoration the Austrian Government, with the object of creating "an Italian sentiment favorable to Austria,"[1] made an ambitious attempt to extend its domination over the journalism of thought and literature in the peninsula by means of a subsidized journal, the famous *Biblioteca italiana*.[2] The patriot-poet Ugo Foscolo was offered the direction of the enterprise by the Austrian Commander Bellegarde, but Foscolo would have nothing to do with it or with the new régime and withdrew to England. A certain Giuseppe Acerbi, a Freemason and explorer of some reputation, was finally chosen. Steered away from politics and economic questions, the new journal was devoted to the criticism of literature and thought. It was in the *Biblioteca itali-*

---

[1] Rosi, *L'Italia odierna*, I, 860. See also Italo Raulich, *Storia del Risorgimento politico d'Italia* (Bologna, 1920–1925), I, 94–97.

[2] *Biblioteca italiana, ossia Giornale di letteratura, scienze ed arti, compilato da una società di letterati. Anno* I, Vol. I, Jan., Feb., Mar., 1816 (Milano, presso Antonio Fortunato Stella). With *Anno* II, Vol. V, Jan., Feb., Mar., 1817, the journal was announced as compiled *"da vari letterati,"* and to be had at the "Direzione del giornale, Contrada de' Tre Monasteri, No. 1254."

ana that Madame de Staël published in 1816 her article on "The Manner and Utility of Translations," which was the trumpet call to the furious war between Romanticists and Classicists in Italy.[3] Even such patriots as Silvio Pellico and G. B. Niccolini at first applauded the journal and Acerbi had Vincenzo Monti and Giordani as collaborators. But the *Biblioteca italiana* failed to win a public. It contained too many abtruse and erudite articles to be popular. Then its Teutonic patrons clumsily let the authority of the Government be used to force the journal into circulation, and stirred up a hornet's nest of protests from the communes of Lombardy, which had been required to subscribe.[4] The distinguished collaborators fell into discord; Monti withdrew in a huff of jealousy, and poor Acerbi was left alone. At the end of 1817 this zealous man was petitioning to be allowed to set up a press to print the *Biblioteca italiana* in his own house, not only "for reasons of economy," he writes, "but also from jealous regard for the secrecy which experience has so often found to be necessary in a literary-scientific Journal under the immediate supervision of the Government."[5]

The *Biblioteca italiana* continued to maintain a dignified existence and in time came to resemble the journals that the liberals were publishing. As late as 1835 it was issued in editions larger than those of any of its rivals.[6] But the Government lost interest in the journal when it proved to be an instrument unsuited to its original purpose. The later numbers contained articles by such patriotic writers as Romagnosi, and to this extent the *Biblioteca italiana* became genuinely Italian, in spite of its taint of birth. In 1841 its remains were decently interred in the "unofficial" section of the *Giornale dell'Imperiale e Reale Istituto*

[3] *Biblioteca italiana*, 1816, I, 9–18.

[4] A. S. M., Presidenza, *Atti segreti*, 493, carta 331. The communes had been given to understand that they must advance the money for the subscriptions. The commissioners wished to know "if these journals evidently useless for communes inhabited solely by peasants can be sold to their advantage." They had been "*scolded*, taxed with negligence, and *menaced* [by the editor] in a letter truly indecent and anything but urbane" for not disposing of the allotments that had piled up on the local Commissioners. The Government as early as January 1817 appointed an investigator who recommended conciliation and suggested that the management of the journal should buy up the superfluous numbers at half or even less of the specified price.

[5] *Ibid.*, carta 343, December 31, 1817. With Vol. X (1818) the title page of the *Biblioteca italiana* announced that the journal was henceforth to be had at "Cassa Caj dirempetto al Borgo Nuovo."

[6] For instance, in December 1835, 750 copies were printed as compared with 500 of the *Indicatore lombardo*, 300 of the *Ricoglitore italiano e straniero*, and 500 of the *Annali universali di statistica* in March 1835 (the nearest date for which a figure is available). A. S. M., I. R. Uffizio di Censura, carta 111.

Lombardo, which began to appear in that year in a small edition of from two hundred to three hundred and fifty copies.[7]

The effort of the Austrians to capture the field of Italian literary and philosophical criticism not only failed; it called into existence the *Conciliatore* (1818–1819),[8] the precursor of a line of independent journals which eventually took the direction of Italian public opinion completely out of the hands of Austria. By 1818 the *Biblioteca italiana* was obviously in difficulties. The founders of the *Conciliatore* seized the opportunity to prove that a similar journal, free of official patronage and openly proclaiming its independence, would succeed.[9] The journal was conceived and edited by a circle of young nobles and men of letters, who made the youthful Piedmontese dramatist Silvio Pellico editor-in-chief, and who met and pooled their effervescent ideas in the liberal salon of the Milanese Count Luigi Porro-Lambertenghi, while a number of the same group, under the leadership of the brilliant and ill-starred Count Federico Confalonieri, were plotting to awaken their country from sleep by introducing steamboats, gas-lighting, popular schools and an up-to-date civic center which was to enlighten while it entertained and embellished Milan.

If the *Biblioteca italiana* was ponderous, the *Conciliatore* was gay. It came out once a week, in a single fold, on azure-tinted paper, and with youthful vigor of spirits took up the cudgels for Romanticism and "the spirit of the century," reviewing books, praising economic and scientific "improvements," promoting steam navigation and "Lancastrian" schools, hinting at politics in witty parables, and boldly proclaiming its patriotism. It is known as the first Italian review that championed Romanticism. But its full title: *Il Conciliatore, foglio scientifico-letterario* reflects the broader aim of its writers. Besides such *literati* as Pellico, Giovanni Berchet and Ermes Visconti, its collaborators included the economists Giuseppe Pecchio and Adeodato Ressi, the historian-economist Sismondi, the ex-Jacobin physician Giovanni Rasori, the jurisconsult Giandomenico Romagnosi, and the young nobles Luigi Porro-Lambertenghi, Federico Confalonieri and Ludovico De Breme, who financed and protected the journal and who saw it as one element of a social program. In the "Introduction" or manifesto the editors avowed as their object the general good of Italian society, conceived in a new sense which the times required. The day

---

[7] *Ibid.,* 493, carta 112.

[8] *Il Conciliatore: foglio scientifico-letterario* (Milan, Vincenzo Ferrario, No. 1, September 3, 1818—No. 118, October 17, 1819. No. 119 was printed without date.) In 1929 the manuscript of two additional numbers was found and printed at the expense of the Commune of Milan.

[9] Cesare Cantù, *Il Conciliatore e i Carbonari* (Milan, 1878), pp. 82–83 *et passim.*

was past, they declared, when public opinion in Italy was an insub̲
tial web spun by "the literary sects and the academies."

Italy and Lombardy in particular is an agricultural and commercial country. Property is much divided among the citizens, or tends to be; and wealth circulates equably so to speak through all the veins of the state. Aware of this truth of fact, the *Conciliatore* has felt that it could not without blame fail to speak of good methods of agriculture, of the invention of new machines, of the division of labor, in short of the art of multiplying wealth: an art which turns to the profit of the state, but which in large part is abandoned by its very nature to the talent and activity of private persons. . . . But it is not enough to make universally known the good principles of economic science, to facilitate the application of them. Industry guides its steps along the line of needs which either diminish or multiply or change in objective according to the moral habits and the vicissitudes of peoples. And we shall therefore procure as far as possible, to follow and make known from time to time the varied movement of such habits and of manners as well, to furnish our readers as many bases of fact on which to support their conjectures and our theories. This will be the statistical and scientific part of the Journal. . . . Sometimes, to serve the purpose proposed, we shall have to give the picture of the customs of this or that country, of this or that social class. Again we shall have to speak of the discoveries of a chemist or a traveller, as those which can open new combinations or new roads to industry. Sometimes in fine we shall have to occupy ourselves with those principles of legislation, which transfused in various guises into the institutions of ancient and modern peoples, powerfully coöperate, not less than nature itself, to temper their character and fix their customs. . . . Nevertheless the severity of those objects would render our Journal too heavy, if we did not propose to temper it perpetually, as we already intimated, with smiling studies of literature.

It must be admitted at once that the *Conciliatore* did not measure up to its promises as an economic and scientific journal. It is true that, scattered among the literary and historical reviews and articles that form the bulk of its contents, are to be found a number that deal with economic progress: articles extolling the initiative of noble gentlemen in agricultural improvements; discussing the effect of economic progress on the nature of empires and the balance of power; presenting the principles of protection versus free trade; calling attention to the good results obtained from the application of mechanical and chemical science to industry in France and to the possibilities of the steam engine in navigation and industry; signalizing various mechanical inventions and hailing their introduction into Lombardy; explaining to the reader the uses of the bill of exchange. But these articles are obviously the work of amateurs in the field into which the *Conciliatore* was seeking to direct the public mind—that which we should today call the sociological field. It was in literature that the writers of the *Conciliatore* were at home, and it was as the champion of Romanticism that the journal earned its fame. Twice a week, for a little over a year, with exuberant earnestness and dancing in the ever-tightening hobbles imposed by the censor, its young writers renewed their argument for a literature vitally related to the needs and feelings of the times. But they were hindered not only by the censorship but by their unpreparedness from coming to close grips with the life of their age and people.

The writers of the *Conciliatore* were branded by their enemies as Romanticists at war with Classicism. But, throughout, they insisted that their Romanticism was something lifted above the schools. Romanticism, for them, was the spirit of a literature which, however inspired by classical examples, had its roots in the needs, the feelings, the faith of the present. In that sense Dante, Petrarch, Parini, Monti writing the *Basvilliana*—in short, all the great Classicists—were Romantic. Add that for the *Conciliatore* the present was not confined to Italy. To live in it one must be in touch with all contemporary humanity, which the *"Conciliatori"* believed to be responding to a new impulse of life and in the midst of a great transformation. Summing up the case of the journal against the academicians, De Breme wrote: "It is enough that they write beautiful verse, no matter whether they are Classicists or Romanticists; exclusive systems are always injurious." "Italy is still asleep, as everyone knows, in the philosophy of Aristotle and meantime the thought of Europe goes on. . . . There are current in the world so many ideas, so many concepts, so many notions that the Italians have not yet clothed with shape . . . and so for morals, economics, metaphysics, domestic life, these have not words and forms to be found in our Dictionary. . . . For us it is much less urgent to speak as Cardinal Bembo did, or as do certain modern bonzes of the Holy Crusca, than to share fully in the benefit of human culture and intellectual civilization. . . ."[10]

From the Austrian point of view there was danger in this conviction of the *Conciliatore* that to have a great literature the Italians must know the life of their times, for an essential condition was perfect freedom to interrogate the age abroad and at home. Berchet, masquerading in the cloak of the German critic Bouterwek, emphasized his author's point that if Italian poetry as a whole was less original than its painting and excelled in style rather than in thought it was because great poetry

---

[10] Review of V. Monti, *Proposta di alcune correzioni ed aggiunte al Vocabolario della Crusca*, Article IV, *Conciliatore*, September 16, 1819, No. 109, p. 441.

is impossible in a country where thought is not free. "It seems that Herr Bouterwek means," he added, slipping his comment into apparently innocent parentheses, "that the frequency of such thoughts and reflections [as are inspired by the contemplation of man and of nature] can be the fruit only of a free and frank consideration of moral phenomena, of public events, of the misfortunes, the hopes, the wishes, the remorses and the improvements etc., of a nation; and that the free expression of such considerations has not always been in the power of the poets of Italy. . . ."[11]

To have a great literature, then, the Italian "nation" must be free to commune not only with Europe—that is, with the new young pulsating Europe of the Romantics: it must be free also to commune with itself! This might be merely a literary doctrine, but with what dangerous implications it bristled when declared by a rebellious generation! Sometimes the very language of rebellion got past the censor.

> Every time we speak of political economy, of fraternal alliance between the peoples, of the need of a literature essentially liberal, of Lancastrian schools, of the diffusion of *lumières,* of the means of speeding the progress of human knowledge, and other like subjects, experience teaches us to hear near at hand a buzz of malediction on our heads from the missionaries of darkness and the *frères ignorantins* of the peninsula. . . . If in trying to serve as best we can the Italian Nation, the *Conciliatore* necessarily runs the risk of displeasing the individual, let him not complain of us but of his own self-consciousness and of opinions of his own perhaps too much in discord with those of the Nation and of the century; let him complain of himself for having chosen to follow with the few the worn-out pennon of obscurantism, instead of the fine flag of patriotism to which the heart of the many is loyal.

If the editors of the *Conciliatore* had been content to flood their pages with notices and reflections of the liberal literature of Europe and aggressively champion Romanticism, would they have been tolerated by Austria? Perhaps not. But more probably it was the social implications of their philosophy that brought the Austrian Government down on both their paper and themselves. They left their readers in no doubt what these implications were. The first step towards civic consciousness was to gain a knowledge of the nature and progress of contemporary civilization, and therefore, though none too effectively, the *Conciliatore* sought to provide its public with statistics. "The publicity of statistics," wrote Giuseppe Pecchio reviewing Chaptal's *De l'industrie*

---

[11] "Grisostomo" [Berchet] on Bouterwek, *Geschichte der Poesie und Beredsamkeit*, Article III, *Conciliatore*, November 12, 1818, No. 21, p. 83.

française, "is the most efficacious means of increasing and propagating in the proprietor, in the merchant, in the creditor of the state instruction, emulation, confidence, a feeling of the national force." But the young men of the *Conciliatore* believed in action too. They urged the nobles to abandon their social parade and interest themselves in agricultural improvements, in the patronage of mechanical inventions useful to industry, in savings banks; most of all, in the education of the poor, specifically by introducing Lancastrian schools of mutual instruction. An interest in education would call for social action on the part of the nobles; it could be advocated as a means of saving public money; furthermore, it promised well as a means of exposing even the lower classes to the influence of a progressive civilization. Advocating the production of books for popular consumption—the next step to be taken if the poor were to profit by their education—the *Conciliatore* observed that, "As long as these books do not exist as useful interpreters between the learned and the unlearned, the discoveries in chemistry, in mechanics, in agricuture, the confutation of errors, of prejudices will penetrate only slowly and late into the lower classes of society for lack of the means of communication. . . ." In short, it was evident that the writers of the *Conciliatore* were looking forward to a revolution in the aristocratic society of their country. The "proprietor and the merchant are two brothers . . . property and industry are two sisters," ran an article that appeared on March 28, 1819. The author went so far as to assert that the superiority of the noble as such was a feudal prejudice.

> There is nothing ideal in the positive interests of society, and he is the most precious to it who renders it the most service. Would you wish perhaps to compare the impudent man who wearies the great cities with the grave weight of his opulent nullity, and that respectable merchant who for the interest of his country renders the four ends of the earth tributary to its commerce or that industrious manufacturer who in his immense factories occupies, nourishes and sustains, he alone, a whole village and sometimes a population of ten, twelve and even fifteen thousand operatives?

Seen in its connection with the movement for a civic awakening for which Confalonieri stood sponsor, the *Conciliatore* could not fail to arouse the Government to repressive action. "The Blue Sheet" was repeatedly maimed and mutilated by the censor, and in mid-October, 1819, was abandoned.[12]

---

[12] Ludovico De Breme, one of its collaborators, in a letter to Confalonieri dated November 13, 1818, described the mutilation of the *Conciliatore* by the Governor, Strassoldo—sometimes in his own handwriting—which had already begun. Cantù, *Conciliatore*, p. 58. On November 4, 1819, Confalonieri wrote to Baron de Staël: "Our *Conciliatore* was reduced to silence by open violence,

Another "non-privileged" journal that dared to hoist a liberal flag was launched in Milan during the period preceding the revolution of 1821—the *Annali di commercio*, which first appeared in July 1816.[13] From the beginning it struck a note which must have sounded very dangerous in the freezing silence of the Restoration. It proposed to compare the commercial life of Italy with its past glories and with the commerce of contemporary nations, and dared to observe that "everything changes in the world, which was never in any respect stable." "Italy, as everyone sees very well," said the editors in the first number, "even if divided between various governments, finds itself strictly bound by reciprocal needs and infinite relationships." As a remedy for the languishing commerce of Italy they proposed a commercial treaty between the Italian states—in short, a customs-union. In principle the *Annali di commercio* favored free trade. "Commerce is a reciprocal advantage which is the greater the freer [trade] is"; this they affirmed to be the conclusion of "the *science* of commerce." If the prosperity of England's commerce was in contrast with the languor that afflicted the rest of Europe, the secret was the use of machinery: machinery applied to manufactures and a "gigantic commerce" went hand in hand. By way of recommending to their readers the latest mechanical novelties of the age, the editors published an account of the steamboat, accompanied by a diagram. One is not surprised that on January 11, 1817, they had to announce with regret that, as the result of "unforeseen circumstances," they were unable to publish their last numbers. Their ambitious undertaking dwindled into a trade sheet, and even this, in 1818, was being harried by the censor.[14]

---

as the result of one of the so numerous agreements of the most holy act of Frankfort." G. Gallavresi, *Il carteggio del Conte Federico Confalonieri ed altri documenti spettanti alla sua biografia* (in *Biblioteca scientifica*, serie *Carteggi*, II-III, Milano, 1910–1913, published by the Società nazionale per la storia del Risorgimento italiano), II, Pt. 1, 161. An account of the pressure exercised on the *"Conciliatorii"* by the Government will be found in *Dal 'Conciliatore,' introduzione e commento di* Pier Angelo Menzio (Turin, 1919), pp. 25–36.

[13] *Annali di commercio, arti, manifatture e mestieri* (Milano, Visai, 1816). After January 11, 1817 when the journal became merely a collection of commercial notices, the publisher was Placido Maria, "Stampatore-librajo nei Tre Re." There is a file in the Archivio Civico di Milano.

[14] *"Annali di commercio, arti, manifatture, e mestieri*, Anno 3°, Nos. 10, 11, 12, and 13, *Admittitur, omissis deletis."* A. S. M., I. R. Uffizio di Censura di Milano, September 1818, No. 2426.

CHAPTER II

NATIONAL JOURNALISM 1824-1838

IN 1814 a periodical called the *Spettatore italiano e straniero* was founded at Milan. It was merely an Italian popularization of the *Spectateur*, published at Paris by M. Malte-Brun[1] and it would hardly be worthy of mention but for the fact that it led to something of the greatest importance in the history of Italian journalism, after a series of metamorphoses which will be noticed presently. The *Annali di commercio* and the *Conciliatore* remained the only two serious attempts at independent journalism in Lombardy before the crisis of 1821; and neither of these took strong enough root to survive official disapproval. But shortly after that crisis independent journalism acquired a remarkable vigor. By 1830 fifteen periodicals, besides the official *Gazzetta,* were coming from the presses of Milan.[2] In view of the tendency of the liberal press to identify progress with applied science, it is a fact of great interest that seven of the fifteen were "scientific" periodicals, or, as the phrase then ran, journals of "useful knowledge" (*cognizioni utili*). Five of these issued from the publishing house of Francesco Lampato, founder and director of the *Annali universali di statistica,* and were entitled "Annals"—of Medicine, Agriculture, Arts and Crafts, Pharmacy, and Jurisprudence.[3] Three years later the number of jour-

---

[1] *Le Spectateur, ou Variétés historiques, littéraires, politiques et morales.* See the publisher's preface of the *Nuovo Ricoglitore,* 1825, I, by Ant. Fort. Stella.

[2] *Annali,* 1830, XXV, 93.

[3] *Annali,* 1830, XXIII, 71. After 1827 two of these sister journals were used to effect a division of labor with the *Annali di statistica,* that journal thereafter watching for important publications regarding agriculture, but leaving reviews to the *Annali di tecnologia* and the *Annali universali di agricoltura, di economia rurale e domestica, di arti e mestieri* (1825 ff.). *Annali,* 1827, XIII, 357. According to Massarani, Lampato's list of periodicals included the *Annali d'agricoltura e di tecnologia* (which seems actually to have been two journals, as stated in the contemporary list cited above); the *Annali di fisica, chimica, e scienze affini,* the *Annali di medicina e chirurgia,* the *Giornale di giurisprudenza,* the *Bolletino dell'industria e del commercio,* and the *Eco delle letterature straniere.* Tullo Massarani, *Cesare Correnti* (Rome, Forzani, 1890), pp. 58–59. (The *Bolletino* to which Massarani refers seems to have been merely the extra volume of the *Annali di statistica* published separately in 1833, with the title: *Bulletino di notizie statistiche ed economiche di invenzioni e scoperte italiane e straniere.*) The full title of the *Eco* was: *L'Eco, giornale di scienze, lettere, arti, commercio e teatri, compilato in italiano, inglese e tedesco* (Milano, 1828–1835). It would seem that in 1838 Lampato was also directing the publication of a journal called *La Moda,* with the collaboration of Cattaneo. On October 12, 1838 he wrote

nals published in Lombardy had grown to twenty-two. No division o\
the peninsula, except the Kingdom of the Two Sicilies, credited with\
twenty-four, was publishing as many journals at the time. The Pon-\
tifical State came third with fourteen; Piedmont, yet to be awakened,
followed with ten; and Tuscany lagged far behind with only six.[4]

The popularity that "useful knowledge" was gaining in Italy at large
is reflected in the fact that in this same year, 1833, there were twenty-
three journals in the peninsula devoted to "physical, economic and moral
science," out of a total of ninety-two.[5] Comparisons with the number
of journals devoted to other subjects emphasize the tendency. In Lombardy, as compared with eight journals dedicated to "literature, the
theatre, and variety" there were no less than six journals of "useful
knowedge." The *fogli politici e di annunzi*, largely official, still led the
field, with thirty-two in all Italy, though with only six in Lombardy;
but the outcropping of independent journals, and their tendency to seek
the channel of *cognizioni utili*, is the notable fact. A contemporary
commentator was of the opinion that the most popular journals were
those devoted to medicine and sanitary science; second, those dedicated
to pastime; and next those whose subject was the exact sciences and

---

Cattaneo: "Vi mando i numeri della Moda a tutto ieri"; and October 29:
"Ho ricevuto il 2 art. ed c'è già stampato e pubblicato nella Moda, e nei nostri
Annali. . . ." M. R. M., Fondo Cattaneo. Another journal of useful knowledge active in 1830 was the *Giornale di medicina*. The whole list of journals
published in Lombardy in 1830 comprised, in addition to those named above,
the *Gazzetta privilegiata*, the *Biblioteca italiana*, the *Ricoglitore*, the *Indicatore
lombardo*, *I Teatri*, the *Censore universale di teatri*, the *Corriere delle dame*.
Another medical review, the *Indicatore bibliografico delle scienze mediche*, was
published at Monza. *Annali*, 1830, XXV, 93.

[4] The total number published in Italy was then 92. Lombardy and Venetia
together, with 32, accounted therefore for more than one-third of the total.
Annali, 1833, Bulletino, pp. 244 ff. In 1842 Lombardy-Venetia was still holding
its position in the front rank of Italian journalism if one may judge by the subscription list of Vieusseux's famous *Gabinetto di lettura* at Florence in that year.
The distribution of "literary" journals on that list was as follows:

Sardinia	7
Lombardy-Venetia	18
Modena	3
Parma	2
Lucca	2
Pontifical State	10
The Two Sicilies	15
Tuscany	10

Rivista, 1842, V, Pt. 3, 218.

[5] A writer in the *Annali* remarked that whereas a few years before Italian
journalism had been languishing, "our progress has been rapid and great." He
noted the founding in recent months, in the diocese of Como alone, of three new
journals concerned not with "turbid political subjects, but with bloodless and
beneficent agrarian and economic doctrines." *Annali*, 1833, Bulletino, pp. 463–465.

economics.[6] The whole picture reflects a veritable Risorgimento of journalism in Italy before the third decade of the Restoration had passed and in this movement Lombardy was in the lead.

Of the fresh crop of "non-privileged" journals that sprang up in Lombardy in the very midst of the grim reaction following the crisis of 1821, the one that overtops all the rest in an account of the Italian national movement is the *Annali universali di statistica*, which was launched in 1824 by a modest and enterprising publisher named Francesco Lampato.

One would wish to know more about this remarkable man. He had been an Intendant in the Grand Army of Napoleon,[7] and when the Empire collapsed held the office of Chief Intendant in the Ministry of War of the Provisional Government set up at Milan in 1814.[8] In launching the *Annali di statistica* he had the backing of "wealthy citizens, notably of Azimonti and Viscontini, ardent in seconding his efforts."[9] To the credit of his energy as a publisher it can be said that in 1833 eight of the twenty-two journals then being published in Lombardy were edited in his *Società degli editori degli Annali Universali*.[10] For twenty-five years he carried on his staff the most notorious liberals of Italy, from Melchiorre Gioia and Giandomenico Romagnosi to Cesare Correnti, Carlo Cattaneo, Luigi Serristori, Giacomo Giovanetti and Camillo Cavour. He had a sense of humor, as well as energy and principles, and was on intimate terms with at least one of his distinguished collaborators, Carlo Cattaneo, whose contributions he freely criticized.[11] In spite of the manifest liberalism of his staff, his journal was able to escape the pruning knife of the censor until 1826 and was never subjected to it except occasionally.[12] A man of deeds and not of words, Francesco Lampato proved himself to be a master strategist of liberal patriotism.

[6] *Ibid.*, p. 244.

[7] Massarani, *Correnti*, p. 58. Massarani in ch. II, gives the best existing description of the *Annali*.

[8] When he assumed that office in the revolutionary government of Lombardy in 1848, the *Annali* announced that he had been recalled "to the post from which he was taken in 1814 at the moment of the ill-starred Austrian occupation." "Avviso del compilatore degli *Annali di statistica*," signed "L'Intendente Primo al Ministero della Guerra—Francesco Lampato," *Annali*, 1848, XCV, opposite p. 230.

[9] Massarani, *Correnti*, p. 59. Luigi Azimonti was a capitalistic sugar-refiner and friend of Romagnosi.

[10] See above, note 3.

[11] These facts are revealed in his letters to Cattaneo, M. R. M., Fondo Cattaneo.

[12] Volume VII, No. 19, January, 1826, was passed by the censor as "*admittitur, omissis deletis,*" likewise Vol. XVII, No. 51, 1828. Other numbers censored were those for June and August, 1833; October and November, 1836; April–May–June, 1837; April–June, July–September, 1839. After 1839 the record is defective. A. S. M., I. R. Uffizio di Censura, busta 493, Nos. 108-112.

The *Annali di statistica* was ostensibly merely a journal of "useful knowledge," designed to provide Italian readers with a kind of periodical which had become common in France. It came out in sober octavo leaflets, printed in small, close-set type. What could seem less dangerous to the existing order than a journal bearing the title: *Annali universali di viaggi, geografia, storia, economia pubblica, e statistica?*[13]

In the prefatory note to the first number, the publishers (*editori*)[14] announced it to be their intention to offer a rapid but meaty analysis of the most important works appearing in Italy or abroad on the subject of "public economy"[15]—"which may bring at once entertainment and instruction in a century in which reason would seem to be extending its empire always further over the old as well as the new world." So the *Annali* was not to be merely a statistical journal. Its interest in statistics would be directed to the illustration of the progress of reason characteristic of "the century"! If the reader needed any further hint that Lampato was nourishing a liberal and patriotic purpose, he had it in the editor's choice of collaborators. At first the only ones Lampato could enlist were "good Giambattista Carta, a thoroughly proven patriot," and Luigi Ferrari, both his "former companions in office" under the French régime.[16] Presently he secured the coöperation of Pietro Custodi, Secretary-General of Finance in the ex-Kingdom of Italy, and the economist Melchiorre Gioia.[17] Gioia was a conspicuous patriot, who had held office as an economic expert under the revolutionary French republics in Lombardy and had been driven into exile by the government of the Kingdom of Italy in 1810, and who had returned to Milan after 1815—a survivor of eighteenth-century thought incarnate.[18]

[13] With Volume II, October–December 1824, the title became: *Annali universali di statistica, economia pubblica, storia e viaggi*; with Volume VI, October–December 1825; *Annali universali di statistica, economia pubblica, storia, viaggi e commercio,*—the form that was retained until 1848.

[14] A note on terms is necessary because of a lack of correspondence between Italian journalistic practice and our own. The publisher was known as the "editore," and usually acted as the managing director ("direttore" or "compilatore"). The group whom we should call the editorial staff were known as "collaboratori," and one or more of these might determine the policy of the journal, as in the case of the American newspaper. Thus Romagnosi became what we should call editor-in-chief of the *Annali*, though Lampato, its publisher continued to be its "Director" or managing editor. In the same way Carlo Tenca eventually became the directing editorial force in the *Rivista europea*.

[15] Note the avoidance of the term "political economy" which the *Conciliatore* had used freely.

[16] Massarani, *Correnti*, p. 58.

[17] *Ibid.*; also Giuseppe Sacchi, "Gian Domenico Romagnosi," *Annali*, 1835, XLV, xl.

[18] For an account of Gioia's philosophy and influence, see Julien Luchaire, *Essai sur l'évolution intellectuelle d'Italie de 1815 à 1830* (Paris, 1906), pp. 74–81.

Then in 1827 Lampato placed the *Annali* in the hands of a man who lent it the weight of a philosophy and the force of a personality so powerful as to make of the journal an agency of national regeneration. This was Giandomenico Romagnosi.

When he took charge of the *Annali* Romagnosi was almost seventy, having been born in 1761, at Salsomaggiore in the Duchy of Parma and Piacenza.[19] He was educated with Gioia in the Collegio Alberoni, a mission school at Piacenza. The atmosphere of the school was theological, but his vigorous mind found itself at the touch of French eighteenth-century thought when he came by chance on Charles Bonnet's *Essai analytique sur les facultés de l'âme,* acquiring it from a fellow-student in exchange for a handsomely bound Virgil.[20] Delighting in "the felt and naked truth of things"[21] rather than abstractions, he turned to physics and mathematics, and while a student joined in the search then going on for the laws of light and electricity, making his own experiments with both. He had hardly received his degree from the University of Parma in 1786 when he was called to public office in the Principality of Trent, first acting as a kind of Podestà under the Bishop, and later as Secretary of the local Council set up by the French when they overran the Tyrol. He continued to follow his interest in natural science, and discovered the identity of magnetism and electricity sixteen years in anticipation of the conclusive experiments of Oerstedt. At the same time he was testing by observation and practice the principles of jurisprudence, which were to be the chief occupation of his mind for many years and the subject of his best-known works.

In 1802 he accepted the invitation of the University of Parma to occupy its chair of Public Law. Four years later the government of the Kingdom of Italy summoned him to Milan to assist in framing the new Code of Civil Procedure. There he occupied a position of conspicuous honor and influence in the public life of the Napoleonic kingdom as official consultant, author, journalist and teacher of jurisprudence, first at the University of Pavia and after 1809 in a special chair of high legislation in the capital.[22]

[19] The data from which the following sketch is drawn were drawn chiefly from three sources, namely: Cesare Cantù, "Giandomenico Romagnosi," in *Italiani illustri* (3d. edition, Milan, 1879), I, 517–593; Giuseppe Sacchi, "Gian Domenico Romagnosi," in *Annali,* 1835, XLV, v-1; and L. G. Cusani-Confalonieri, *Giandomenico Romagnosi: notizie storiche e biografiche, bibliografia e documenti* (Carate Brianza, 1928).

[20] He seems to have kept the book by him always. On his deathbed, he signed his will on a copy of Bonnet. Sacchi, p. xiv.

[21] A phrase which Romagnosi uses in the Preface in his *Genesi del diritto civile.*

[22] As consultant of the Council of State while it was drafting the Civil Code, Romagnosi kept the minutes of its deliberations and had the task of reducing

After the Restoration he continued to teach at the capital until the Austrians abolished the special schools in September 1817. Thereafter Romagnosi lived on at Milan, giving private lessons and acting as legal consultant. The young patriots of the *Conciliatore* obtained his collaboration in their enterprise; in August 1818 Porro even made an effort to get him to act as editor-in-chief.[23] His association with the *Conciliatore*, and Silvio Pellico's testimony when on trial that he had sought to make a Carbonaro of Romagnosi, resulted in an indictment for political conspiracy, and the now venerable jurisconsult was brought to trial at Venice on June 12, 1821.[24] The clerk of the court made the following record of his appearance: "tall, stout, coloring good, nose and mouth regular, beard gray at the temples, red wig." The clerk noted that his thigh and right leg seemed to have been affected by an apoplectic stroke, but Salvotti, his keen prosecutor, said of him: "If his body is full of pain, his mind is free and profoundly sagacious." Although Romagnosi parried shrewdly and serenely Salvotti's sharp thrusts, he did not hesitate to reveal the robust and temperate liberalism that was characteristic of his mind. Admitting having had a conversation with Pellico, he professed to have forgotten the details of it and remarked that "in any case he could not have failed to answer Pellico— with the authority of Bacon and other distinguished thinkers—that the 'sects'[25] do not make changes that are extensive and efficacious, and that the Italians are immature for liberty, which requires a therapeutic education very different from that offered by the sects." When Salvotti attacked him for his liberal writings, Romagnosi replied that they were purely theoretical, and "a wise government does not persecute opinions but only deeds." The Commission judging his case was forced to declare the trial "suspended for lack of legal proofs." But Salvotti was not convinced that the influence of the formidable mind with which he had just measured his own uncommon powers was not a menace to the dominion of Austria. In summing up the whole series of trials

---

its conclusions to good form. Romagnosi also took an important part in revising the Penal Code, which was never put into effect. Meanwhile he held the office of Consultant to the Ministry of Justice. At the same time he edited the *Giornale di giurisprudenza amministrativa e civile*, whose purpose was to explain the new system of laws and facilitate their execution. During this period he published a number of works that were the outgrowth of his public activities and his lectures.

[23] "Porro intends to invite him to become editor-in-chief, in place of Monti: we have already decided to see him about it." Pietro Borsieri to Ludovico De Breme, August 17, 1818, in Cantù, *Conciliatore*, p. 44.

[24] For the documents of the trial and Romagnosi's able defence, see A. Luzio, *Il processo Pellico-Maroncelli* (Milan, 1903), pp. 129–140; 417–419; 467–472.

[25] The term commonly used to describe the secret societies, particularly the various branches of the Carbonari.

conducted by the Venetian Commission, he lingered, still suspicious but baffled and mystified, on Pellico's testimony that Romagnosi, trying to dissuade the young man from further association with the Carbonari, had declared that he himself held in his hands "the threads of Italian unification." What did that mean? Was it perchance that "opinion," and not the "sects," was the key to the Italian problem?[26]

An examination of Romagnosi's pupils by the police yielded no compromising evidence.[27] Nevertheless, in a decree of September 24, 1822, the Government, declaring that it was clear from the trials at Venice that Romagnosi "professes principles which do not permit him to be entrusted with the instruction of youth," withdrew his authorization to give private lessons.[28]

Stricken with infirmity and banished from his professional life, Romagnosi was reduced to the verge of destitution. In 1824 when Lord Guilford of Corfù invited him to come to the Ionian Islands and organize the legal studies of the University there, with the promise of a position on the bench and the office of Supreme Consultant at his retirement, he was prevented by the Government from leaving Milan. But, although pushed into a corner, he was surrounded by his young disciples, who flocked to him for instruction,[29] and was graciously protected by a patriotic capitalist, Luigi Azimonti, who became one of Romagnosi's most devoted friends.[30] Such were the conditions under which the doughty old philosopher became associated with Francesco Lampato's journal, and in the midst of poverty, infirmity and suspicion entered on what was probably the most fruitful phase of his career.

Editorial direction of the *Annali* called on Romagnosi to turn his mind to political economy and practical economic issues. If he did so with reluctance, it was not from lack of practical knowledge. When Luigi Azimonti, about to establish his sugar refinery, which was destined to become one of the most important business enterprises of the period,

---

[26] Luzio, *Processo*, p. 484.

[27] The examination of the twenty-year old Carlo Cattaneo on July 21, 1821—reported in Luzio, *Processo*, pp. 417–419—was fruitless, one feels, largely because of the wary coolness and loyalty of the disciple. It could leave no doubt in a suspicious mind that Romagnosi had expounded the principles contained in his work *Della costituzione d'una monarchia nazionale rappresentativa*, published anonymously in 1815 when the French Charter was under discussion. Cantù, *Italiani illustri*, I, 564.

[28] Cantù, *Conciliatore*, p. 131.

[29] G. Sacchi, "Intorno alla dottrina di Romagnosi sulla libera concorrenza," *Rivista*, n. s., 1847, V, Pt. 1, 619.

[30] The documents of this fine episode are in Cusani-Confalonieri. During Romagnosi's last illness Azimonti requested the Castelli family to provide clean changes of linen for the old man at Azimonti's expense without letting Romagnosi know who had paid for them.

sought Romagnosi's advice in 1822, he wrote: "I have spoken to G. D. Romagnosi of my project; the vastness of his knowledge, even in the industrial and financial line, is stupendous, admirable; and then what modesty, what goodness!"[31] But Romagnosi had little sympathy for the classical economics represented in Italy by Gioia, though he admired Adam Smith and thought him the one economist outside of Italy worth reading. His disciple, Giuseppe Sacchi, later reported him as grumbling when in 1822 a little group of his young admirers gathered about their venerable master to seek instruction in "the new science," that "those blessed economists . . . do not seem to me to be sufficiently disposed to assimilate the splendid heritage of our ancestors"; they had made of political economy a science "all belly, and have forgotten the noblest parts of man, the head and the heart." For him "the name economy itself signified order, and the science must therefore be called the doctrine of the social order of riches."[32]

Once absorbed in his new task Romagnosi came to love the *Annali*. He contributed to other journals at the same time, but he called the *Annali* "his own journal," "in which he sought to have deposited the notices appropriate both to the history and the progress of civilization."[33] He himself poured into it a continual stream of articles, reviews, and "observations," which, while chiefly concerned with economic themes such as industrialism and its social effects, insurance, commerce and commercial policy, and discussions of statistics which were intended to give greater scientific validity to their use by Italian writers, touched on subjects ranging from education and geography to ancient astronomy, ritual architecture, and the history, the books, and the present condition of the East, a subject in which Romagnosi was particularly interested.[34] He published serially in the *Annali* his treatise *On the Nature and the Factors of Civilization*[35]—the theme which in all its phases was the chief interest of his mind. But Romagnosi's great strength lay in his power to attract and stimulate young minds. A kind of Socrates,

[31] Cusani-Confalonieri, p. 30.

[32] G. Sacchi, "Intorno alla dottrina di Romagnosi sulla libera concorrenza," *Rivista*, n. s., 1847, V, Pt. 1, 621.

[33] Cesare Cantù, in *Ricoglitore italiano e straniero*, 1835, Anno, II, Pt. 2, 458.

[34] His notes on India in the *Annali* were the fruit of researches that he was making in the history of India "in continuation of the work of William Robertson." "He was meanwhile collecting the materials for a great work on the history of ancient civilization." On his death-bed, as he signed his will, he said with a smile: "It would grieve me not to be able to do the ancient part of civilization." Sacchi, in *Annali*, 1835, XLV, xxxviii, xxxix, xlv.

[35] *Sull'indole e sui fattori dell'incivilimento*, first published in the *Annali* with the title: "Che cosa è l'incivilimento?," *Annali*, 1832, XXXI, 129–140; 241–260; XXXII, 17–36; 145–194.

he inspired with ardent devotion a group of young men that included some of the best of the generation coming of age about 1830—most eminent among them Carlo Cattaneo, Giuseppe Ferrari, Cesare Cantù, the cousins Giuseppe and Defendente Sacchi, and the fiery Cesare Correnti. Gathering these young disciples about him as collaborators he converted Lampato's periodical into the organ of a philosophy of patriotic social action. When he died in 1835, Giuseppe Sacchi with the aid of Cattaneo, Ferrari and Correnti, carried the *Annali* on in the Romagnosian tradition,[36] and through them and others whose minds were formed by kindred conceptions his influence passed into the *Politecnico* and the *Rivista europea*, the other two great liberal journals of Lombardy during this period of the Risorgimento.

The significance which Romagnosi gave to the *Annali* in the minds of his younger collaborators appears in a letter written by Cesare Correnti in which he told, years afterwards, how he had been drawn into the editorial circle of Lampato's journal.

> Forty years ago when we were in the dawn of happy presages, and life was ardent in our heads and poetry in our hearts, our venerable master G. D. Romagnosi had begun to make us see how this science of statistics might be a weapon less worn and blunted than historical lamentations and poetical anathemas manipulated by many, so well—and so uselessly! For this reason, I resigned myself, an impatient conscript, to the discussion of averages, tables and numbers, which gave us a chance to talk in jargon and in a cipher, and to withdraw ourselves from the mutilations of the censorship, accustomed as it was to sniff only at phrases and epithets. The thing was done. Numbers spoke their language only to those who knew how to read their hints: true language of mutes. Sometimes these guesses piqued the curiosity; sometimes was heard in them an echo of poetry, a response more intimate and intellectual than the casual jingle of rhymes.[37]

The type of journal that Romagnosi and his followers produced is indicated by its full title: "Universal Annals of Statistics, Public Economy, History, Travels and Commerce." It was not a statistical journal in the rigorous sense of the term. In addition to statistical notices of population, commerce, industry, agriculture, education and scientific inventions, it published original articles, reviews, reports of

---

[36] In his notice of Romagnosi's death, Lampato said: " . . . it only remains for us to assure the public that the doctrines of Romagnosi will always be the guide of these *Annali*." *Annali*, 1835, XLIV, opposite p. 144. Lampato wrote in 1847: "The doctrines of the *Annali di statistica* will always be in accord with the maxim of free competition and opportunism which our master Romagnosi preached." *Annali*, 1847, XCIII, 197–198.

[37] Massarani, *Correnti*, pp. 62–63, note 1.

academies and scientific bodies, and notes on current events. Excluding from its scope philosophy, literature and the fine arts, and forbidden to speak of politics, the *Annali* devoted itself to giving the serious reader a panorama of the social and economic life of the time. Naturally the picture of Lombardy that was produced was the fullest and most detailed. The journal kept close watch over the agriculture, commerce and industry of Lombardy, its population, its philanthropic institutions, its educational system. But from the first Italy was assumed to be a national entity and the picture of Italian life and institutions was made as complete as the conditions allowed the editors to make it. They sought and found collaborators in other parts of Italy: Serristori and Ridolfi in Tuscany; Giovanetti, Petitti and Cavour in Piedmont. They complained of the difficulty of bringing Naples into focus but they made a valiant effort to do so.

They represented Italy as an economic whole but they wished their readers to see it in a European perspective. They presented all the facts they could cull regarding the progress of other countries that seemed to bear on their chief objective, which was to draw the life of Italy into the main current of contemporary civilization. Beyond the horizon of Europe their eyes sought that of the world both to the East and the West. The pages of the *Annali* were sown with reviews of travel books. Under the stimulus of Romagnosi the writers of the *Annali*, and later those of the *Rivista europea*, devoted especial attention to the British empire in India. The world beyond Europe remained somewhat indistinct, but it is interesting to observe in passing that the readers of the *Annali* were kept well informed about the phenomenal economic progress of the United States.

The picture of civilization that the *Annali* presented was that of a world in movement, and the editors did not remain, nor were they willing that their Italian readers should remain merely spectators of the movement that they were depicting. They tirelessly urged their public to take part in it. The first volume supplies the keynote. Reviewing the notice of the establishment at Milan of a fire and hail insurance agency, the editorial commentator besought the public not to oppose this new device just because of its novelty. On this basis, he said, we should have neither of "the boldest new discoveries—the uses of steam applied even to navigation, and the profit drawn from gas for the so numerous and almost prodigious illuminations produced by it." He wished that he had "the voice of Stentor to cry against the blind opposition which is wont to be made against things of recent origin," and appealed to men of substance and wealthy proprietors, pointing out to them the smiling prospect for the investment of money, as little regarded in Italy as is

[also] that of commercial speculations." Reminding them of the Italian past, of the Venetians, the Florentines and the Genoese, he extolled the dignity of investments "in mercantile companies, in factories, in banks, in exchange operations, in mechanical and chemical enterprises and other such."[38] This blast is somewhat naïve, but it illustrates the point that, far from being detached observers, the collaborators of the *Annali* were partisans of progress.

In short, the *Annali*, though professedly a journal of statistics and useful information, was not a trade journal. An example of its statesmanlike policy in seeking to direct public opinion is the series of articles which it devoted to the London silk market. As we have seen, that market had come virtually to enjoy a consumer's monopoly of the product as a consequence of the unalert drifting of the Italian proprietors and merchants. Romagnosi seized the opportunity presented by this situation to awaken them to their true position, applying directly to the taproot of Lombard economy the realistic knowledge of the world and its progress for which the *Annali* stood and incidentally giving a lesson in liberal economic opportunism. In 1827, the year in which Romagnosi assumed editorial direction of the journal, the *Annali* established a service of information in the great English mart and began to publish reports on the quarterly public sales of silk by the East India Company at London, with editorial comment on the conditions affecting these and words of warning and advice to local producers and merchants. The editorial comments were written by Romagnosi himself while he lived, and after his death in 1835 by Carlo Cattaneo.[39] Silk touched the pocket nerve of every class of the community, and Romagnosi and Cattaneo took full advantage of their opportunity to drive home the lesson that the practical interests of Italy were bound up inextricably with the progressive and mobile civilization of the West of Europe. Its legislative crises, the vicissitudes of its economic expansion and its politics, the panic of 1837 in the United States, the riots of the Spitalfields silk spinners, the wave of disturbance produced by the French Revolution of 1830 all affected sharply and directly the prosperity of Lombard gentlemen and shipping houses.[40]

The reports from London revealed that the preferred position of Italian silk in the London market was threatened by the importation of

---

[38] *Annali*, 1824, I, 283.

[39] *Annali*, 1836, XLVIII, 85, where Cattaneo said regarding the series: "He [Romagnosi] was the first to give courage to the friends of the country and to prepare the way for our redemption from the silk monopoly."

[40] *Annali*, 1829, XIX, 153–155; 1829, XX, 3–23, 97–99; 1829, XXI, 50–67; 1830, XXV, 99–110; 1831, XXVII, 321–330; 1831, XXIX, 88–94; 1834, XXXIX, 309–316; 1837, LII, 336–337.

silks from Bengal and China.[41] Reporting the increasing sales of Oriental silk in London the writers of the *Annali* at first sounded a note of alarm—perhaps in part for its moral effect on their complacent fellow-countrymen. Later, while still inciting them to liberate themselves from the British monopoly and to organize their production and trade so as to gain freer control of it, they dwelt on the fact of a rapidly expanding world market, relating this with repeated emphasis to the mechanization of the manufacture of silk, the consequent lowering of retail prices, and an increase in the consumption of manufactured silk that was likely to go on indefinitely.[42] In the long run the competition of Asiatic silk virtually closed the London market to the inferior Italian grades, and towards 1848 the *Annali* began to reflect some concern about the fate of the finer grades as well.[43] But the confidence with which the editors had insisted that the manufacturing industry, expanding with the march of European civilization, would continue to absorb the increasing product of Italy at good prices was justified by the event. In 1833 Romagnosi expressed the wish that the Italians could find markets for silk nearer home than London, to render the trade more flexible and less expensive. "We recognize, alas!," he wrote, "that today in the face of inveterate habits our opinion to this effect resolves itself into a pious wish."[44] But the reports of the *Annali* showed Italian silk making its way steadily into the other markets of Europe.

In its articles on silk the *Annali* sought to illuminate the whole situation of the industry, following up its reports on the London market with statistics of the production and marketing of silk in the other states of Italy, watching sharply an experiment at Philadelphia in the production of raw silk,[45] and conducting veritable journalistic campaigns for measures which were proposed as a means of strengthening the position of the Italian industry in the face of world competition.[46] In all this

---

[41] The British had begun to cultivate the silkworm in India when their continental supply was cut by the Napoleonic wars. The plantations in India had needed time to mature, but in the 'twenties the quantity of silk they were sending to England was already considerable.

[42] Citations seem unnecessary. The reader who wishes to pursue the subject will find a report on the silk trade in the number of the *Annali* that immediately followed each of the quarterly sales in London.

[43] Dr. Gera, "Sul setificio," Rapporto della Commissione letto nella Sezione di agronomia e tecnologia al IX Congresso degli Scienziati a Venezia, settembre 1847, *Annali*, 1847, XCIV, 257–263.

[44] *Annali*, 1833, Bulletino, p. 35.

[45] *Annali*, 1831, XXVII, 331; 1832, XXXII, 110.

[46] One was the establishment at Milan of a silk bank to finance the trade. Another was the extension in Italy of the manufacture of finished threads from the raw product and vigilance in maintaining the all-important advantage of quality enjoyed by Italian silk; still another the adoption of improved methods

discussion the *Annali* dealt with the interests of the Italian silk industry and trade without municipal partiality. For example, it hailed the decree of Charles Albert which liberated the exportation of raw silk from Piedmont as a triumph of good principles, although its effect would be to bring the Piedmontese product into fuller competition with that of Lombardy. In the faith of these writers national patriotism and liberal economic policies went hand in hand. In short, the articles on silk in the *Annali* were bound to have a more telling effect than any amount of abstract discussion in awakening the Italian public to its position in a changing world and habituating it to think of the concrete interests of Italy in terms of liberal economic doctrine and patriotic statesmanship.

The writers of the *Annali* consolidated their position on the terrain which the *"Conciliatori"* had announced their intention to occupy when they proposed to speak "of good methods of agriculture, of the invention of new machines, of the division of labor, in other words, of the art of multiplying wealth." But while the *Conciliatore* perished within a year and a month, the *Annali* survived with very little interference from the censor, though no less liberal or patriotic in spirit than its short-lived predecessor. Adapting themselves more successfully to the conditions under which Italian journalists had perforce to operate, the writers of the *Annali,* some of them "impatient conscripts," buckled down to the task of attaining a mastery of applied economics, until they learned to speak with authority the language of their times and of their country's needs. As for the response which they met from the public, the mere survival of a periodical that was neither a literary review nor simply a useful trade sheet is one evidence of it. The number of copies that were put in circulation usually varied between 350 and 500, and went as high as 600 for some few issues—figures that compare favorably with those for the other substantial periodicals of the time.[47] The authority acquired by the *Annali* with the business community of Lombardy-Venetia was such that the Chamber of Commerce of Venice in 1843 quoted it in an official report of the Austrian Government.[48]

---

of production and an abandonment of the ignorant complacency with which the local proprietors held out for high prices regardless of the state of the market, thus cutting the profits of struggling local manufacturers and endangering the whole position of Italian silk in its world market.

[47] A. S. M., Carte dell' I. R. Uffizio di Censura, Nos. 108–112. (After 1839 the records are fragmentary.)

[48] Supporting the adoption of a Customs League in Italy, the merchants of Venice wrote: ". . . the distinguished and talented Colonel Serristori does not believe that it would be difficult of execution, and takes the Germanic Union as a model, as one reads in the *Annali universali di statistica.*" Archivio di Stato di Venezia, Camera di Commercio, 193, IV, 1.

This is not the only evidence of the circulation of the *Annali* outside of Lombardy.[49] The esteem in which it was held at home is reflected in references to it by some of its contemporaries. Cattaneo referred to it in his *Politecnico* as the journal "whose temperate publicity" made it the source to which those who were interested turned for reliable news about the progress of the Milan-Venice railway.[50] The *Rivista europea,* discussing the examples in Italy of "special journals directed with the constancy and foresight of a social institution," cited as "first among them all, as being supremely well disciplined and directed to its end, . . . the *Annali di statistica,* the oldest perhaps of the non-privileged journals."[51]

The *Annali* dominated the section of Lombard journalism whose avowed object was the diffusion of useful knowledge. Around it were grouped the various *Annali* fathered by Lampato himself which have been mentioned. Their predecessors in the field had been a *Giornale di chimica, fisica, scienze naturali, medicina ed arte* published at Pavia between 1815 and 1827, and a less specialized journal, the *Giornale di agricoltura, delle arti, e del commercio,* which had been established in 1807 and of which Dr. Antonio Cattaneo seems to have been the compiler in 1823.[52] Lampato projected a purely technical journal into the same field as that of Cattaneo's journal with the title of *Annali universali di tecnologia, d'agricoltura, industria, economia rurale e domestica, arti e mestieri.* By 1833 this had been condensed into an agricultural journal, the *Giornale agrario lombardo-veneto.*[53] Another agricultural journal of the period was the *Biblioteca agraria,* which in 1826 set out to publish twelve tracts that would aid in applying the new discussions of science to agriculture, but which ran to twenty-four volumes.

Less a journal of science and nearer to the field of useful information professedly occupied by the *Annali di statistica,* was the *Raccolta pratica*

---

[49] We know that it was on the subscription list of the famous *Gabinetto di Lettura* of Vieusseux at Florence in 1842, in honorable company with the *Revue de Paris,* the *Revue des deux mondes,* the *Revue Britannique,* the Edinburgh and Westminster *Reviews,* the *Revue du Nord,* and the Italian *Rivista europea, Museo, Omnibus,* and *Album. Rivista,* 1842, V, Pt. 3, 213.

[50] *Politecnico,* 1841, IV, 351.

[51] *Rivista,* n. s., 1845, III, Pt. 2, 740. See also *ibid.,* 1845, IV, Pt. 2, 234–235, where in a long review of the *Annali* and its record the writer remarks that "the present *Annali* is not unworthy of such a past, the direction continuing in the honorable founder whom a Parisian journal recently saluted as the uncorrupted Nestor of Italian journalists. Certainly in Lampato's journal a greater elegance of form could be desired; but the substance is excellent and above all Italian."

[52] Ciasca, *Programma,* p. 189.

[53] Compiled by Ignazio Lomeni, and published by the *Società degli Annali Universali delle scienze* (1834–1838, 10 v.).

di scienze e d'industria, published at Como from 1832 to 1838. It was
a popular, though technical magazine which lived largely on borrowings,
and showed little or no editorial bias beyond a desire to see the most
recent inventions applied to an improvement of the art of living in
Italy.[54] In a "question and answer" section of the *Raccolta* the questions ranged all the way from inquiries as to the best way of drying
marshy land to that of a reader who desired "a brief treatise on the
manner of behaving oneself with good morality and prudently." But
not content with imparting useful information in detail, the editors interested themselves in broader social questions, advocating, for example,
the alienation to individuals of the remaining communal lands in
Lombardy.

A foil to the sobriety of the *Annali di statistica* in the contemporary
journalism of useful knowledge is *l'Ape delle cognizioni utili* which
began to appear in 1833, and acquired great popularity.[55] *L'Ape* (The
Bee) was founded by a conspicuous and enterprising character, Giuseppe
De Welz, "native of Como." A merchant by profession, he acquired
his reputation as a propagandist of "up-to-date" business methods. He
arrived in Milan in 1828 after having made a sensation in the Kingdom
of Naples as a hustling promoter of capitalistic enterprise and publisher
of books, of which the two most important bore the titles: *The Magic
of Credit Unveiled* (1824) and *The Prime Element of Commercial
Force.*[56] For De Welz the magic principle of progress, which he proclaimed as an evangel, was "the spirit of association." Entering the
field of Lombard journalism with a magazine that boasted of its cheap-
ness, De Welz sought an audience among the people "that are between

[54] In their Introduction, 1832, the editors promised "extracts from the best
books and journals, and particularly from the *Giornale delle cognizioni utili*
which is published at Paris." The articles on agriculture would be drawn from
their own experience or from "that of a practical farmer of their acquaintance,
and very renowned, although he has written nothing."

[55] The full title is *L'Ape delle cognizioni utili, ossia Scelta delle migliori notizie,
invenzioni, cognizioni e scoperte relative al commercio, alle arti, all' agricoltura,
economia rurale e domestica* (Milano, tipografia del commercio, 1833 ff.). The
journal was published in one *fascicolo* a month, of 32 pp. in 8vo.

[56] *La Magia del credito svelata. Istituzione fondamentale di Pubblica Utilità
offerta alla Sicilia ed agli altri stati d'Italia,* 2 vols. (Naples, 1824); *Primo
elemento della Forza commerciale, ossia nuovo metodo di costruire le strade di
G. L. MacAdam. Traduzione dall'originale inglese di G. De Welz offerta alla
Sicilia ed agli altri stati d'Italia* (Naples, 1826). Professor Macchioro has recently
stripped of reliable support the commonly accepted view that the author of the
two books was a minor Neapolitan economist, Francesco Fuoco, though Fuoco
may possibly have helped De Welz to compile them. Aurelio Macchioro,
"Francesco Fuoco o Giuseppe De Welz?", *Giornale degli Economisti e Annali di
Economia,* Jan.–Feb. 1964, pp. 3–33. *Primo elemento* was given an extensive review by Melchiorre Gioia in the *Annali,* 1827, XI, pp. 101–115.

the unlearned and the learned"—more specifically, "proprietors, merchants, renters, master artisans, country curates, etc." Here at last was a journal frankly for the bourgeoisie. De Welz immediately printed six thousand copies and set up twenty agencies of distribution in Italian Switzerland and throughout the peninsula. Six thousand was too many, but the *Ape* continued to appear in editions greatly larger than those of any of its contemporaries.[57] It offered its readers useful information suited to every taste, from new ways of making watermelon preserves and simple recipes for ink to methods of sweeping chimneys in the country and improving cattle breeds. But besides a cornucopia of practical advice De Welz had principles, and he used his paper to trumpet them. One was the principle of association; another, that industry was the basis of prosperity; another, that "the right of property belongs to the nature of man." All of these were in accord with the principles of the *Annali*; but De Welz believed in a prohibitive system of tariffs as the proper means of developing a self-sufficing industrialism in Italy. Like the writers of the *Annali* De Welz used a practical type of journalism to advance his ideals, and the *Ape* carried on continuous campaigns in behalf of protectionism, the development of the silk industry and particularly a silk bank, and the local search for "mineral combustibles"; and in 1834 began a vigorous promotion of railways, illustrated with pictures of trains, stations, etc. The *Ape* offered also moral instruction suitable to the times in a kind of Poor Richard's Almanac under the rubric *"Economia generale."* Nor was the journal lacking in a patriotic flavor, although political articles were "absolutely excluded." The editor declared it to be his chief aim to promote industry in Italy, not in any one section of it; in 1835 he published Pietro Verri's dialogue *Sulla patria degli italiani;* and among his various campaigns he proclaimed one against dialects. Indeed the whole program of the *Annali*, in a homely and more practical form, is to be found in the *Ape*, except free trade. The exception is important for it marks the lack in the *Ape* of the doctrinal consistency, the quiet and confident faith in liberalism in all of its implications, that distinguished the *Annali*.

Another journal of useful information, the *Economista*, entered the field in 1841. The *Economista* was the organ of Dr. Antonio Cattaneo. It was handsomely illustrated with color-plates and accurate drawings. Technical in character it was a high-grade magazine of useful information. Its advent and success may be taken to mark the increasing inter-

---

[57] The edition for February–March 1837 was 2500; for April 1838, 1500. For May 1838 the figure dropped to 200—perhaps an error in the manuscript; for December 1838 to 800. In March 1839 it was back to 2500. A. S. M., I. R. Uffizio di Censura, busta 493, carta 112.

est in technical knowledge that manifested itself in Lombardy towards the middle of the century. Still another journal was launched into this field in 1844, the *Spettatore industriale, studi e notizie di tecnologia, igiene e letteratura.*[58] This journal assumed the unfulfilled obligations of the *Politecnico* to its subscribers when the *Politecnico* was merged with the *Rivista europea* in 1845.[59]

With such journals should be associated such publications as the scientific annual entitled *Memoria popolare di notizie attinte a scienze fisiche* (Milan, Cavaletti, 1846), modelled on the "celebrated *Bureau des Longitudes,* to which Arago owed much of his fame" by a group of "active young men" impatient of "distant hopes."[60] Learned periodicals of the type of the French *Journal des savants,* or of the contemporary publications of the academies in other states of Italy were conspicuously lacking in Lombardy. The Institute founded by Napoleon became moribund after the Restoration. When it was revived in 1841, the undistinguished *Giornale dell' I. R. Istituto Lombardo* contained the proceedings of the Lombard Section. Meanwhile the Brera was the official scientific and artistic center of Milan and the "Acts" of the "solemn distribution of industrial prizes" at the Brera were published annually and reviewed by the journals.

On one side of the field of the journals of useful information, the side of the purely practical, several trade journals sprang up. The *Giornale utile: con gli arrivi e partenze e tariffe di moneta* began to issue from the press of Bernardoni in 1819. The *Annali di commercio* had been driven to take the form of a trade sheet in 1817. In 1831 the weekly *Termometro mercantile e d'industria* was announced as its successor. It ran until 1839, carrying from time to time articles on fashions, the theatre, economics and the book-trade. The most important of the business journals was the *Eco della borsa.*[61] The *Eco* did not direct the attention of business solely to business notices. In 1839 the publisher declared that his object would always be "to familiarize the minds of our capitalists with the power of credit and the spirit of association," thus fulfilling "the double purpose of making the progress of other nations a matter of popular knowledge in Italy, and diffusing at the same time the knowledge of its commercial and territorial resources." This sounds very much like the purpose of the *Annali* in a more limited form, though in a congratulatory notice of the first numbers in the

[58] Milan, Marenesi e Macchi, 1844. I have found only the volume for 1844.
[59] Antonio Monti, "La prima serie del 'Politecnico' di Carlo Cattaneo (1839–1845)," in *Rivista d'Italia,* June 15, 1925, Anno XXVIII, 808.
[60] *Rivista,* n. s., 1846, IV, Pt. 2, 751–752.
[61] Full title: *Eco della borsa, ricchezze territoriali, interessi del commercio, progressi dell'industria* (Milan, Bernadoni, 1836–1860).

Annali, the *Eco della borsa* was criticized for giving more attention to news from other countries than to notices of Italy.[62] The Government, on the other hand, had watched the birth of the *Eco* with some anxiety. Although the police could report nothing to the discredit of its founder, Michele Battaglia, who was secretary of the Milan Chamber of Commerce, the censor thought that he had enough such journals to watch when his overburdened office was under orders to be especially vigilant.[63] Though the Government gave Battaglia its consent, it ordered him to drop the title *L'Avvenire* (The Future) which he had chosen for his projected journal.[64] In 1837 the censor called Battaglia to account for poaching on the preserves of the *Gazzetta privilegiata* by publishing in the *Eco della borsa* notices that he could have obtained only from the official records of the Chamber of Commerce.[65] The *Eco* confined itself faithfully for the most part to notices appropriate to a comprehensive trade journal; but its articles sometimes had a flavor that might well cause the censor to sniff and remember his reluctance to see the *Eco* published. For example, an article on "Italian Industry in the Middle Ages" published in 1839 ended with these words: "Thus Italy in the Middle Ages nourished germs of such marvelous inventions that other people took them from us, proclaiming them as new things; thus it produced powerful and creative intellects which had everything to do with the history of human progress."

In contrast with the *Eco della borsa* the *Foglio commerciale e d'industria* compiled twice a week by Ludovico Hartmann from 1839 to 1846 confined itself to business notices, dry of all editorial comment.

At the other extreme from the trade journals the field cultivated by the journals of useful information bordered on that of literature and entertainment. In 1833 the journals of "pastime" published in Lombardy were the *Censore universale di teatri,* the *Corriere delle dame,* and *I Teatri.* The *Corriere milanese* published from 1814 to 1822 by Pirotta had belonged to the same class.[66] The *Censore* and the *Corriere delle dame* were presently merged to form the *Bazar: giornale di novità artistiche, letterarie e teatrali,* which ran from 1841 to 1847. A typical number of the *Bazar* contains a section on art, bibliographical notes, a

---

[62] *Annali,* 1837, LII, 209–210.

[63] This was in 1833 when Battaglia first sought license to publish. Although he received it, he declared that he found himself too busy to prosecute the enterprise. A. S. M., I. R. Uffizio de Censura, busta 493, carta 331.

[64] On the ground that under this title "there have been circulated in France writings and periodicals which are opposed to the maxims of sane politics." *Ibid.*

[65] *Ibid.,* carta 332.

[66] This journal may have had a longer life. The only run of it that I have found is in the Biblioteca nazionale at Rome.

"Courier of the Theatres," a section on "spectacles in Milan," a charade. Another journalistic enterprise of the same type began with the *Ape italiana* (The Italian Bee) in 1819. In 1828 it became the *Vespa* (The Wasp) and then was transformed into the *Farfalla* (The Butterfly). In the first number of the *Bee* the publishers promised "beautiful and pleasant things; indeed," they said, "it is our wish that the *Italian Bee* may rest its wings not seldom in the boudoirs of the gentle ladies." They proposed to bring their readers extracts from the new books of every nation, gentle poems and notices regarding the fine arts, and a portrait with every volume. Like the *Bee* the *Butterfly* sought especially the favor of "gentle and cultivated ladies." "All my efforts will be directed to please and I shall always narrate things pleasant, delightful, instructive and new," the publisher Bettoni announced in his first number. Similar in character though perhaps a trifle more dignified in spite of its name, was the *Pirata* (The Pirate), which declared an intention to offer "original articles almost exclusively" since "of translations you have those who supply you with plenty."[67] The *Pirate* paid most of its attention to the arts of entertainment, especially music— "the favorite part with you perhaps, the part most vital in our modern societies."

Illustrations were used by the hustling De Welz in his *Ape delle cognizioni utili,* and they were also introduced into the journalism of pastime. The first pictorial periodical at Milan was the *Cosmorama pittorico* launched in 1835. It devoted itself to the illustration of "physics and extraordinary phenomena," zoölogy, anatomy and physiology, mechanics and steam navigation (which latter was represented in the first number by a picture of the "Charles Carrollton" of the "Citizens Canal Line for Philadelphia"), "steam carriages," and diving. Other subjects brought to life by text and engravings were botany and chemistry, "useful cognitions" and inventions, archaeology and ancient and mediaeval history; "Naples and its Environs, and the *Lazzaroni*"; biography embellished with portraits; "women and their actions"; "temples sacred and profane"; "ancient and modern Italian monuments"; fine arts; "geography and voyages," illustrated by a reproduction of Géricault's revolutionary painting "The Raft of the Medusa"; "remarkable cities, places and buildings"; "roads and mountains"; "castles"; "customs of various peoples." A cosmorama indeed! but, be it noted, one of a world that was astir with new inventions—one of the most profitable of which, the editors remarked, was that of making "pictorial journals."

[67] *Il Pirata, giornale di letteratura, belle arti e teatro* (Milan, Radaelli, 1835–1848).

What is noteworthy is the tendency of these journals of pastime to assume a liberal and Italian character, and at the same time to fall in with the penchant of the age for useful information and for evidences of "the progress of the century." Indeed it becomes very difficult to draw a line between journals that were intended to be merely entertaining and those with a more serious purpose. In the *Bazar* the first article on the "Arts" was an appeal for Romanticism; the leading review, one of a work on the French Revolution. The sixth and seventh numbers contained a "double tribute" to the memory of the suspiciously liberal journalist Defendente Sacchi, one of the collaborators of the *Annali,* and all the numbers were sprinkled with notices of railways and other useful public improvements. The editor of even the gay *Italian Bee,* on wing for "the boudoirs of the gentle ladies" declared that "the useful arts must not be excluded, but rather received with festivity and honor"; and the *Butterfly,* for all its protests of having no object but to divert, contained an account of "the industrial objects in the Brera" by Giuseppe Sacchi, editor of the *Annali,* and declared that in the field of the arts it would "reason briefly of the inventions and discoveries relating to social convenience which may be made in Italy or abroad"; it would not fail—this serious *Butterfly!*—"to visit the factories of our country in order to construct an impartial report of the progress of our industry." The *Pirate,* in spite of its avowed predilection for music and the arts, declared its sympathy with the local movement of commerce, industry and inventions, and offered "a free ticket to its columns" to notices of "trade, the mechanical arts, useful inventions, objects of noveltry of all sorts, and the crafts." The *Pirate* carried theatrical notices not only from Milan but from all parts of Italy. It is interesting to observe that while there were notices from Paris, there were none from Vienna: this journal like all the other independent ones had its back turned on Austria. Furthermore, the readers of these journals seeking pastime found themselves reading articles by the liberal writers of the *Annali* and of the other free journals, notably by Giuseppe and Defendente Sacchi and by Romagnosi himself. In its section on "Biography" the *Cosmorama pittorico* presented portraits and pen-sketches of Monti, Parini, Beccaria, Jacquard, Giovanni Alessandro Brambilla, and when Romagnosi died in 1835 carried a full front-page portrait of him, with a two-page tribute by Defendente Sacchi in which the great liberal thinker was ranked with Galileo in the Italian hall of fame.

In the field of literary journalism in Lombardy, in the period that lies between the extinction of the *Conciliatore* in 1819 and the founding of the *Rivista europea,* the two periodicals of greatest consequence were the *Indicatore lombardo* and the successive metamorphoses of the

Ricoglitore, from which the *Rivista europea* itself emerged in 1838. There were other serious reviews of literature, such as the *Minerva Ticinese, Giornale di scienze, lettere ed arti e notizie patri*, published at Pavia from 1829 to 1831; *La Bilancia, Giornale di scienze, lettere e arti* (Milano, Manini, 1838 ff.); and *La Fama, Rassegna di scienze, lettere, arti, industria e teatri* (1836–1877), which, in 1840, was being compiled by none other than Carlo Tenca. As the titles indicate, neither of the latter was a purely literary review. Every review of the period felt bound to make its bow to science and the useful.[68]

The *Indicatore lombardo* began in 1829 as "a periodical magazine of select articles taken from the most accredited Italian, German, French and English journals," concerning "the physical sciences, literature, the fine arts, the industrial arts, agriculture, geography, commerce, etc." The founder and publisher was Giacinto Battaglia, then aged twenty-six years, who had already made himself known to the public as joint editor of the *Giornale dei Teatri* and then as sole editor of the *Vespa*, and who was eventually to direct the *Rivista europea*. In the *Indicatore* Battaglia immediately proclaimed his belief in "the immutable progress of things" and in the present age as the dawn of "a new splendid era." Had young Battaglia been reading Mazzini? Whether he had or not when he wrote this preface, in 1830 he borrowed from the *Antologia* of Florence Mazzini's famous article "D'una letteratura italiana" and recommended it to his readers as the work of "a young Italian of singular talent."[69] The office of the *Indicatore* was to familiarize Italy with the progress of other nations "more favored than [Italy] by the concourse of a variety of circumstances." Despite the breadth of scope proclaimed in its Introduction, the *Indicatore* remained largely a receptacle for literary borrowings, and there is no reason to suppose that it was a particularly effective journal; but its purpose was both liberal and patriotic.[70]

Much the same can be said of the *Ricoglitore* in its successive metamorphoses. The *Ricoglitore* grew out of the *Spettatore italiano e straniero* (1814–1818) already mentioned. At first the *Spettatore* had lived on borrowings from the French of M. Malte-Brun; but at the end of a year the editor, Antonio Stella, had sought to convert it into an

---

[68] The *Fama* published an appendix entitled *Gabinetto di scienze, arti e industria*, each number of which contains either the description of a piece of "modern" mechanism, with a plate, or an article on some inventor, with his picture.

[69] *Indicatore*, 1830, III, 293–329.

[70] ". . . the *Indicatore* [is] the least insipid journal of our city," wrote the patriot Antonio Trotti to Constanza Arconati, April 10, 1833. A. Malvezzi, *Il Risorgimento italiano in un carteggio di patrioti lombardi 1821–1860* (Milan, 1924), p. 87.

"original Italian journal" and the "metamorphosis was completed when, shortly afterwards, M. Malte-Brun ceased to publish the parent magazine."[71] In 1818 the *Spettatore* gave way to the *Ricoglitore*,[72] directed by Davide Bertolotti, the popular traveller, often quoted by the *Annali*. In 1825, still under the ownership and "literary superintendence" of Bertolotti, the journal was given the sweeping title *Nuovo Ricoglitore: ossia Archivi di geografia, di viaggi, di filosofia, di economia pubblica, di eloquenza, di poesia, di critica, di archeologia, di novelle, di belle arti, di teatri, di feste, di bibliografia e di miscellanea,* and Stella assumed responsibility for the punctual appearance of the magaizne and promised that other collaborators would be associated with Bertolotti. The *Nuovo Ricoglitore* was lighter and offered more of a "variety" show than the *Indicatore*. But its *italianità* was even more pronounced. In Volume I the Venetian patriot Tommaseo replied to the criticism of Manzoni's *Adelchi* made by an anonymous "Censor":[73]

> . . . It is very true that Italian literature is miserable and municipal; that we are more occupied with words than with thought. But does it follow from this forsooth that we must enrich ourselves from the spoils of others, and make conquests with our genius in the poetry of every people? . . . We have no need of conquests. If imitation has degraded us, let us enter into ourselves, let us listen to the voice of the heart, let us remember that we are Italians, not followers of Italians, and then of necessity we shall be sufficiently great, without need of learning even for an hour, to teach many centuries. . . .

Enough of "Cosmopolite Literati": "the Italians must breathe only Italian air."[74] These are strong words, but Tommaseo returned to the charge with words even bolder, in reply to "Censor's" criticism that the theme of the *Adelchi* was not a fit subject for tragedy.

> Who are those unfortunate Kings? The invaders of Italy. What is the occasion of their killing? Their injustices. What is the effect? The liberation of Italy? No: but the yoke of a new invader. With the destinies of the Lombard domination become entwined the destinies of the Italian people. . . . The theme is a powerful Realm founded by force, shaken by injustice, dissolved by treason, by force destroyed; and the subject is not worthy, not capable of tragedy? The theme is the

---

[71] Antonio Fortunato Stella, Preface to the *Nuovo Ricoglitore*, 1825.
[72] This seems to be the journal of which Ciasca gives as the title: *Il Raccoglitore, ossia Archivi di viaggi, di filosofia, di storia, ecc.* (Milan, Batelli e Fanfani 1818–1820). The *Ricoglitore* referred to in the text ran from 1818 to 1825.
[73] The criticism attacked by Tommaseo seems to be the review of the *Adelchi* that appeared in the *Biblioteca italiana*, 1824, XXXIII, 322–337; XXXIV, 145–172. See especially XXXIV, 150.
[74] *Nuovo Ricoglitore*, 1825, I, 267–272.

almost fatal servitude of a whole nation; and are not the misfortunes
of a nation to be regarded as more lamentable than the misfortunes of
a man? If Manzoni was the first to place on the boards this new
subject of pity and terror, ought the Italians to hold it against him?

This quotation gives the tone of the *Nuovo Ricoglitore*. The names of
the authors whose writings it gave to the public would alone suffice:
not only Tommaseo, but Giovanni Battista Niccolini, Giacomo Leopardi,
and Angelo Brofferio.

In 1834 the *Nuovo Ricoglitore* became the *Ricoglitore italiano e
straniero, ossia Rivista mensile Europea*.[75] Like its predecessors the
new review professed itself to be "progressist" and humanitarian in
spirit. Among the collaborators whose names appeared in the *Ricoglitore italiano e straniero* were Giuseppe and Defendente Sacchi, Cesare
Cantù, Tullio Dandolo, and Gaetano Barbieri. The magazine developed
into a review chiefly concerned with history, literature and philosophy,
with occasional scientific articles. One of the interests to which the
editors consistently devoted their pages was education, publishing full
accounts by Giuseppe Sacchi of the progress of the schools of Lombardy
and contributions on the same subject by Tommaseo and Raffaele
Lambruschini. A section was regularly dedicated to *"Benemeriti Italiani"* who had died in the current year. In 1835 this necrology was
introduced with these words: "Again this year we consecrate a few
references to those illustrious Italians who contributed by their work
and writings to the greater increase of the nation's glory. Such a statistical picture is of absolute importance in a time when an effort is
being made to have it believed abroad that Italy sleeps a profound sleep,
and that letters, the arts and the sciences have ceased to have a cult
among us." By way of keeping the living Italy before its readers, the
Ricoglitore presented reports from such widely scattered points as
Padua, Rome, Naples, Modena, Novara, Cremona, Schio, Bagnone,
Modica. Not content with talking about Italy as an emotional abstrac-
tion, the *Ricoglitore* made an effort to picture it as "a local habitation"
as well as "a name."

[75] Professor Antonio Monti says that this review was the successor of the
Indicatore lombardo. Monti, *"Politecnico,"* p. 794. But the dates of that journal
are 1829–1837; and the indications are clear that the predecessor of the *Ricoglitore italiano e straniero* was the *Nuovo Ricoglitore* (Milan, Stella, 1825–1833).

CHAPTER III

NATIONAL JOURNALISM, 1838-1848

THE independent journalism of Lombardy gained in depth and force in 1838 when Giacinto Battaglia launched the *Rivista europea,* and when, a year later, Carlo Cattaneo left the *Annali* and founded the *Politecnico.*[1]

Cattaneo was one of Romagnosi's most gifted pupils.[2] He had caught, as none of the others had, his beloved master's vision of human progress and had adopted his ideas of the means by which civilization advances, though on specific questions the young man did not hesitate to dissent publicly from Romagnosi's views, as in his independent diagnosis of the future of the Italian silk industry in the articles that he wrote on that subject for the *Annali.* Cattaneo had an imagination that was stirred as Edmund Burke's was by the vast consecutive operations of humanity, and—probably directed to the theme by Romagnosi[3]—found in the irrigatory agriculture of Lombardy, built up around a system of canals by centuries of accumulated investment and coöperative effort, an expression of vitality and capacity for civilized living in the Italian race—an achievement to him more marvelous and stirring than any work of art, being a work in which the genius of a great people was the artist. Cattaneo's innumerable manuscript notes on every aspect of this theme and on the trade and industry, the history and the social habits of Lombardy give some measure not only of the tenaciousness of his mind but of the completeness of his identification with every fibre of

---

[1] Monti, *"Politecnico,"* pp. 788–821. An illuminating analysis of the editorial relationships and historical significance of the *Annali,* the *Politecnico* and the *Rivista europea* will be found in Tullo Massarani, *Carlo Tenca e il pensiero civile del suo tempo* (Florence, Le Monnier, 1907), pp. 18–27. Massarani was a participant in the activities of the group of journalists concerned, but his characterization needs to be corrected by the fuller historical perspective that we now enjoy.

[2] "I learned to know Signor Romagnosi only in the past month of November," said Cattaneo in July 1821 when questioned by the police seeking evidence against Romagnosi. "Interrogatorio" published by Luzio, *Processo,* pp. 417–419. Cattaneo was then twenty years old.

[3] Immediately after being barred from his profession in 1822 Romagnosi turned to a study *Sulla condotta delle acque* which was published in 6 vols. (1822–1825). Not content with the hasty publication that it received, he was working it over into a new treatise just before he died. G. Sacchi, in the *Annali,* 1835, XLV, xxviii.

his country's life—an identification that was never pedantic or provincial because it was passionate with the ardor of a powerful imagination.

When Cattaneo resolved to found a journal of his own in 1839, his immensely active mind had for some years been dominant in the counsels of the *Annali*. His most masterly contributions, marked by solidity of knowledge and a characteristic courage in criticism and dissent, were his articles on the choice of routes for the proposed railway connecting Milan and Venice,[4] and his discussion of the project of a Monte delle Sete, or Silk Bank, at Milan.[5] He was no doubt a restless bedfellow on the editorial board of the *Annali*. In 1833 Lampato modified the structure of the journal at his behest.[6] In January 1839 Cattaneo was ready for a new departure in journalism. He seems to have wished to convert the *Annali* to his purpose, which was probably to give a greater

---

[4] "Ricerche sul progetto di una strada di ferro da Milano a Venezia," *Annali*, 1836, XLVIII, 283–332. Cattaneo became secretary of the Milan Commission which in conjunction with one representing Venice presided over the construction of the road, and threw his knowledge and dominating personality into the bitter and humiliating controversy over the question whether the line should pass through Treviglio or Bergamo. Cattaneo saw it as a question whether the road should be bold and direct or bent to serve municipal interests that took no account of the future. Unable to make his views prevail with the Commission he resigned office and was replaced with a nonentity. Lampato to Cattaneo, October 12, 1838, M. R. M., Fondo Cattaneo, 115, plico III, b, No. 12.

[5] "Alcune ricerche sul progetto di un Monte delle sete in Milano," *Annali*, 1837, LIV, 177–236.

[6] Monti, *"Politecnico,"* p. 795. Lampato's MS letter to Cattaneo on April 30, 1833, suggests the difficulty he probably had in handling his gifted collaborator: "You have had me make a reform in the *Annali*, and if you do not continue to procure me the notices as begun the thing will remain imperfect. . . . I pray this with assurance also in the name of our common friend Giuseppe Sacchi." M. R. M., Fondo Cattaneo, 115, plico III, b, No. 3. On the back of this letter in Cattaneo's handwriting there is a most amusing experiment in English doggerel verse, entitled "Pecchio and Pudding":

> Only ride twenty miles on a hard trotting horse
> And you'll eat a plum pudding though greasy and coarse
> Go fourscore miles more on a filthy Welsh pony
> And you'll swallow a sirloin rank,   and bony
>   just
> With a cool hundred more (which gives fifty times four is)
> You'd bolt Pecchio himself with his wonderful stories.
> And repeating the dose twice or thrice in a day
>   blown the poor nag
>   strained poor
> And should you go on till you had   nag
>   your nag
> You might venture to bite at the new monthly Mag
>   could   even   even
> You might find some savour   in the new monthly Mag
> And if you go on till you've blown the poor nag
> You'll find savour even in the N. M. Mag.

scientific depth and concentration to its discussions. Lampato backed by the Sacchi cousins opposed this, and seeking to delay independent action on Cattaneo's part offered to put one of the other journals published by the *Società degli Annali* at his disposal.[7] Nevertheless Cattaneo proceeded forthwith to announce the publication of his own journal, the *Politecnico*.[8]

The *Politecnico* published longer and weightier articles than the *Annali*. Its fire was less scattered. But, on the surface at least, it is not easy to define the difference of its purpose from that of the older journal, except for the obvious dominance of a single mind—that of Carlo Cattaneo—over its pages. It is true that a whole section of the magazine, at least in Volume I, was devoted to "Fine Arts and Belles-lettres," which had been excluded from the scope of the *Annali*. But in the third volume (1840) this literary section, which had almost disappeared in the second, was telescoped with those devoted to "Social Art, Studies Economic, Administrative, Legal, Historical, etc.," and "Mental Studies, Methods of Instruction, New Institutes, etc.," and all together show only about the same number of titles as the ample section devoted to science and technology. The criticism of art and letters remained a subordinate occupation of the journal. In his foreword to Volume IV (1841), Cattaneo wrote: "If the first three volumes . . . cannot easily escape the accusation of having been scarce in diverting essays and almost devoid of pleasant literature, we hope that no one will be disposed to put in doubt their tendency to [promote] the common good. . . . We have wished to give an impulse to the lovers of the practical sciences, that they may desire to go on, and with useful writings humble the vanity of a frivolous literature, ranging over against it some of that immense Truth, with which it apparently scorns to nourish itself."

[7] F. Lampato to Cattaneo, January 12, 1839, in M. R. M., Fondo Cattaneo, 115, plico III, b, 15. Professor Monti interprets this letter to mean simply that Cattaneo considered entering the firm in 1839, and that Lampato was communicating the conditions to him. It is evident from the language of the letter that there was some tension at the time between Cattaneo on one side and Lampato and the cousins Sacchi on the other. Cattaneo's purpose matured suddenly. In the preface to Volume II of the *Politecnico* he spoke of himself and his collaborators as having been "brought together almost unexpectedly in an undertaking that had not been premeditated. But on the way we have been finding companions. . . . We shall make every effort to have the Public forget that our enterprise was born almost unexpectedly and without fitting preparation." *Politecnico*, 1839, II, 4, 7.

[8] *Il Politecnico, repertorio mensile di studi applicato alla prosperità e coltura sociale* (Milan, Per Luigi di Giacomo Pirola, 1839–1844, 7 volumes). The January number did not see the light until April. Monti, *"Politecnico,"* p. 802.

Civilized living is an art; it is the art of arts, the supreme expression of the life of a nation:—this was the great conception to which Cattaneo dedicated the influence of his journal. "Not able to satisfy ourselves with the opinion of past centuries which contemplated in art almost solely the manifestation of the beautiful, not bowing to the present opinion which would restrict it almost entirely to the satisfaction of bodily requirements, we have taken as our guide the vast and wise concept of Romagnosi, who in *art* sought to unify the complete and harmonious satisfaction of all the needs that distinguish humanity."[9] But the editor's choice of subjects shows that he regarded as the particular art which above all others his countrymen needed to master that of using the inventions of modern science. Cattaneo declared in his Introduction that the supreme purpose of the journal would be the prompt diffusion of scientific knowledge to meet the pressing needs of contemporary Italian life, and particularly "the need of promoting among us every manner of industry." Seizing on a recent act of the Austrian Government as a hopeful sign, he remarked that the restoration of the Institutes and the promised establishment of technical schools at Milan and Venice gave courage to "that industrial spirit . . . which has for some time been occupied in propagating the use of mineral combustibles, the new method of illumination by gas, and the first sketches of studies on railroads. These are the feeble signs of that new industrial life without which the dense population of these Provinces could not longer preserve its envied prosperity." Flashing on this movement his profound historical sense he added that it was simply a new phase of the industry which operating through centuries had redeemed Lombardy from swamp and wilderness and more recently converted its resources into a wealth of manufactured silk, cotton and iron.[10] While the articles in the *Annali* ranged in scope over Italy, Europe and the world at large, Cattaneo concentrated the force of his journal on his own section of Italy. Lombardy was his passion. In the *Politecnico,* with insignificant exceptions, only the reviews looked beyond Lombardy or Lombardy-Venetia. Anyone interested in the growth of practical patriotism in the free journals of Lombardy will find it interesting that Cattaneo included war among those arts with which the Italians must equip them-

[9] *Politecnico*, 1839, II, 3.
[10] How deep Cattaneo's profoundly poetic imagination plunged beneath the subjects with which his journal dealt appears in the words of depreciation with which he later referred to the *Politecnico*: ". . . Amid that coarse merchandise of locomotives and gasometers and oblique bridges, there escaped me here and there some arguments that have viscera." Quoted by Gaetano Salvèmini, Introduction to *Le più belle pagine di Carlo Cattaneo* (Milan, 1922), p. xviii.

selves for "the harmonious satisfaction" of their needs.[11] The final article on the subject ended with this sentence: "In the application of gunpowder and of the other inventions of the science of war, the primacy will always remain with the nations that cultivate the sciences with the greatest ardor and frankness and confidence. The peoples who fear the light will be overwhelmed by the fire." His countrymen must know how not only to be prosperous but to defend their rights.

It is difficult to measure the extent of the immediate influence exercised by a periodical. The "established celebrity" of the names that Cattaneo associated with the editorial direction of the new journal at once made an impression,[12] but above all others the reputation of Cattaneo himself, "that veritable matador of the critics who deal with questions of public economy."[13] In 1840 Carlo Tenca ranked the *Politecnico* above every other Italian journal,[14] and the *Rivista europea* referred to it in 1842 as deserving "the esteem it so much enjoys in all Lombardy."[15] Judged by the standards of the time subscriptions were numerous, though the number was probably a disappointment to Cattaneo. 8,100 copies of the "Manifesto" were published and 2,000 copies of the first issue of the periodical but in October 1839 the *Politecnico* had only 230 subscribers in Italy and 22 abroad. The number of subscribers in Milan grew from 325 in 1840 to 700 in 1843.[16] As early as the fall of 1841 Battaglia tried without success to tempt Cattaneo to merge his journal with the *Rivista europea*.[17] In 1845 the merger was accomplished and Cattaneo joined the staff of the *Rivista*.

[11] "A. M.,'" "Divisioni fondamentali della scienza della guerra; la Geografia militare; la Politica militare; la Strategia; la Tattica," *Politecnico*, 1839, I, 132–134; "Alcune notizie sulle riforme delle artiglierie," *ibid.*, 1841, IV, 186–189.
[12] The phrase is from the notice of the second number (for February 1839) in the *Rivista*, 1839, II, Pt. 2, 254.
[13] Open letter from Giacinto Battaglia to Angelo Brofferio, May 23, 1841, *Rivista*, 1841, IV, Pt. 2, 279–288.
[14] *Rivista*, 1840, III, Pt. 3, 138–139.
[15] Editorial note, *Rivista*, 1842, V, Pt. 3, 213.
[16] Monti, "*Politecnico*," pp. 806, 808.
[17] Giacinto Battaglia to Carlo Cattaneo, November 18, 1841. ". . . From your kind letter of yesterday I understand that I was misled by the person who gave me to believe that you are weary of busying yourself with the business management of the *Politecnico* and that you would like to disengage yourself from the speculative embarrassments of publication in order to be freer to play the artist. It was on this erroneous assumption that I took the liberty of presenting my proposal of the fusion of the *Politecnico* and the *Rivista europea* which would have rejoiced to gain a new collaborator in you even on special terms of privilege and with the obligation of placing to your credit a portion of the receipts of all the subscriptions to the *Politecnico* which were carried over to my journal." M. R. M., Fondo Cattaneo, 102, plico 4, 1–23.

If the *Politecnico* in a sense evolved out the *Annali,* the *Rivista europea*[18] was more directly in the tradition of the *Conciliatore* and the *Antologia* of Florence. Springing from a fusion of the *Ricoglitore italiano e straniero* and the *Indicatore lombardo,* effected by Giacinto Battaglia in 1838, it was from first to last preponderantly a review of literature. But like all the other literary reviews that sprang up in Lombardy during the period it was swayed by the idea that art is inseparable from the other processes of civilized living and that the progress of Italian civilization in the nineteenth century called for the active diffusion of science and industry.

The *Rivista europea* displays no such unity of conception as that with which Cattaneo dominated his journal. Characteristically it started without an Introduction or declaration of principles, and its pages betray vicissitudes of policy which are reflected in changes of rubrics and in variations in the quality of its contents. These are traceable in part to the difficulties attending any such venture in Lombardy at the time, and in part to the fact that the management and staff did not remain constant. At first the *Rivista* was vigorously managed and directed by Battaglia. Presently Battaglia was complaining of insufficient support from his collaborators and lamenting the troubles with which an Italian editor had to contend. By 1844 he was out of the management and the review came under the direction of the young Gottardo Calvi (1844) and then, in 1845, of Carlo Tenca, with whose name it is commonly associated.[19] Cattaneo had become one of the principal collaborators since the merger with the *Politecnico* in 1845. At the beginning one of the Sacchi cousins, Defendente, had been hostile to the *Rivista,*[20] but in 1840 Giuseppe Sacchi joined its staff,[21] and in 1843, Cesare Correnti, who like Sacchi was a leading writer on the staff of the *Annali* during this period. Giacomo Sega also wrote for both papers. Tullio Dandolo, Giulio Carcano, Michele Parma and the brothers Ignazio and Cesare Cantù had lent their collaboration from the first. In short, if Lombard journalism may be said to have developed a class of publicists between 1814 and 1848, the majority of its leaders sooner or later joined forces

[18] *Rivista europea* (Milano, first series, 1838–1842; nuova serie, 1843–1847). First number: January 15, 1838. There is a brief descriptive study of the *Rivista* by Anna Pettinari, "Contributo alla storia del giornalismo lombardo: La 'Rivista europea' (1838–1848)," in *La Lombardia nel Risorgimento italiano,* 1929, XIV, 75–122.

[19] Pettinari, pp. 91, 103. In 1847 Tenca became proprietor as well as director. *Ibid.,* p. 117.

[20] He subjected it to a bitter attack to which "Zunca" (Ignazio Cantù) replied with withering sarcasm. *Rivista,* 1839, III, Pt. 2, 242–256.

[21] As expositor of "the new science of charity," "which the Italians have created." *Rivista,* 1840, III, Pt. 1, 93.

with the *Rivista europea*. The *Rivista* reflects the weaknesses and difficulties and also the full strength of Italian journalism operating under
foreign domination.

Battaglia launched his new journal without a declaration of principles,
but the *Rivista* speedily demonstrated that its writers possessed them.
Their reply to an attack directed against their enterprise by Defendente
Sacchi at the beginning of its second year declared boldly what at that
time they thought they had done and what they proposed to do.

> The *Rivista europea* is *put to shame* because its collaborators seek
> to give it the widest extension of which it is capable; because they
> follow closely the march of literature in France, Germany, Russia,
> Spain and England; because in a few pages it presents a monthly
> review of the scientific, artistic, typographical, industrial and literary
> events of Europe; because in criticism it is not content with publishers'
> notices . . .; because it speaks of morals and of science; because it
> has praised Vico, Botta, Tommaseo, Arici, Grossi, Scinà, Carrer,
> Leopardi, Barbieri, and others of the same type; because, treating of
> universal libraries and of the economic condition of letters, it has
> sought to remove literature from all vain gossip of words; because it
> discourses of the chief parts of history, philosophy, statistics, science,
> aesthetics, drama; because, dealing at length with Horace, Pindar,
> Lucian, Sophocles, Seneca, Dante, it has shown in the sixteen months
> since it was born anything but indifference and contempt for the
> ancients; . . . because it has not left any important work without either
> a long or short comment; because it has fixed principles regarding
> the classics, language, philosophy, morals (. . . those who wish to
> play the buffoon know how to deride the doctrines of the *Rivista*,
> particularly that of progress, which seems to annoy the hypocritical
> . . .); because, availing itself of the law of a literary republic, it
> believes it can declare what it thinks and believes, whether the tyrants
> are willing or not. . . .[22]

The review was proclaimed by its title to be European and it did
"follow closely the march of literature," and of civilization, abroad.
But as time went by, while it never ceased to be European in outlook,
it assumed a more and more distinctly Italian character.

This was manifested first of all by its preference of original articles
by Italians to borrowings from foreign journals. At the end of 1840
Battaglia had to admit partial defeat on this score and announced that
in 1841 he would resort more often to translations of articles from
foreign reviews. But the journal did not surrender the principle, and
in the end it achieved a greater measure of originality than any of its

[22] "Zunca," in the *Cronaca* for April 1839. *Rivista,* 1839, III, Pt. 2, 242–243.
The parentheses used in the quotation are mine.

predecessors or contemporaries except the *Politecnico*. "Alien on principle we wish to be," wrote its brilliant and active young associate Gottardo Calvi in 1843, "from publishing in this journal versions of writings dictated in foreign idioms and published in journals of other nations, unless they are mere reports of facts or scientific documents, which belong equally to all peoples." Any exception the editors felt called on to justify to those "who most absolutely insist that our journal . . . has to be Italian in spirit and sentiment as well as in purpose and form."

The *Rivista* sought to present to its readers the best that Italy could produce by means of original contributions from living writers in all parts of Italy or by reviews of their work, and by celebrating the great Italian writers and thinkers of the past—always in comparison with the best that was being produced in other countries. At first the *Rivista* carried over as a heritage from the *Ricoglitore* a section celebrating *"Benemeriti Italiani"* who had died in the previous year. The necrology of the first volume included Carlo Botta, Prospero Balbo, who was praised for his abstinence from the Napoleonic régime, the ex-Jacobin Giovanni Rasori, Domenico Scinà, historian, physicist and philosopher, and Giuseppe de Cristoforis, public-spirited naturalist, who had founded in Milan "the richest museum in Italy." The necrology was supplemented in the *Rivista* by a section devoted to "Contemporary Writers of Italy," among whom were immediately included Tommaso Grossi, Carrer, Nicolò Tommaseo, Giacomo Leopardi. Whether by means of such formal presentations or by reviews and comments the leading figures in the contemporary movement of letters and civilization in Italy, including Massimo d'Azeglio, Cesare Balbo, Vincenzo Gioberti, Count Petitti, the Marquis di Sambuy, Antonio Scialoja, Cosimo Ridolfi, Luigi Serristori, Raffaele Lambruschini, Ferrante Aporti, Alessandro Manzoni, Giuseppe Giusti, F. D. Guerrazzi, G. B. Niccolini, were extolled and made familiar to the readers of the *Rivista*.

One of the features of the *Rivista europea* designed to give it a truly Italian character was the establishment of a regular correspondence with other parts of Italy, opening windows on the movement of its civilization wherever this manifested itself in the peninsula.[23] The

---

[23] In 1843 the "Album delle notizie italiane" contained reports from Venice, Naples, Catania, Ferrara, Tuscany, Lucca, Turin, Brescia, Parma, Rome, Padua, Modena, Piacenza, Bologna, Verona, Siena, Borgo San Sepolcro, Ravenna. In the first semester of 1843 there were 55 contributors to this section and that of "Foreign News"—2 in Milan, 9 in Turin, 2 in Florence, 2 in Venice, 1 in Naples, 1 in Pavia, 1 in Mantua, 1 in Corfu, 1 (G. Libri) in Paris. *Rivista*, n. s., 1843, I, Pt. 1, 129 ff., 273 ff., 406 ff.; Pt. 2, 119 ff., 254 ff., 393 ff.; Pt. 3, 117ff., 245 ff., 376 ff.; Pt. 4, 113 ff., 250 ff., 386 ff.

notices sent were not merely of literary interest but covered the journals, the educational, philanthropic and scientific institutions, the proceedings of the academies, the progress of railway construction. The *Rivista* succeeded better than any of its forerunners or contemporaries in presenting Italian civilization in its fullness—not only in the writers of Italy but in its institutions and their development; and it subjected both to criticism that was designed to stimulate a genuine national life.

The *Rivista* was primarily a literary journal and a review of literature. Its point of view in the criticism of literature may be defined as a sober and balanced Romanticism, in contrast with the youthful effervescence and pugnacity of the *Conciliatore*. In the interval between 1818 and 1838, in the work of such writers as Manzoni, Guerrazzi, Giambattista Niccolini and Massimo d'Azeglio, a literature, some of it of the highest order, had given a concrete embodiment to the ideals of the Italian Romanticists and this in itself made a great difference in the position of the two journals. But the doctrine of Italian Romanticism, that good literature, however much inspired by the glories of the past, must be vitally related to the needs of contemporary civilization and the social movement of the age, was used by the *Rivista* as it had been by the *Conciliatore* as the touchstone of literary criticism. It is the idea at the bottom of the searching and rigorous essays in criticism which Carlo Tenca published in the *Rivista*, and in fact was never absent from its pages.[24]

It was natural therefore that the *Rivista* sought to give its public a picture of contemporary civilization in Italy and abroad. It accomplished this result by publishing the letters of its regular correspondents, by sections devoted to current events and scientific and commercial notices, by a large proportion of articles on science, education, philanthropy and economics, and by reviews of books on these themes. Unlike the *Annali* the *Rivista* did not refrain from communicating such political notices as it was permitted to publish.[25] Those of French politics are especially full, and all of them were boldly colored with sympathy for the Liberal party in the French Chambers, and for the cause of

[24] See, for example, Carlo Tenca, "Scrittori contemporanei italiani: Giambattista Niccolini," *Rivista*, 1845, III, Pt. 1, 408–432.

[25] Irritation with the restraint which the editors had to endure transpires in the remark of G. Sega in his "Cronaca politica e Album del Commercio, dell'Arti e dell'Industria": ". . . We discourse as philosophers about politics, as it presents itself concretely in facts and events, and we connect it with its consequences only in so far as they concern human society. Intimate politics belong to men of state. It pertains to them to guide events, to moderate the effects of political action, to protect themselves against its consequences, and our discourses on this theme would be as inopportune as useless." *Rivista*, 1841, IV, Pt. 1, 123.

liberalism and free trade in Great Britain, the triumph of which in 1846 was acclaimed with jubilation in the *Rivista*.[26]

Beginning with 1843 the emphasis of the journal on history and civilization as contrasted with purely literary subjects was accentuated, and such rubrics as "Studies in Moral Science," "Studies in Patriotic History," "Institutions and Public Works," took precedence of those covering literary matters. In 1844, when the Congress of Italian Scientists met in Milan, the *Rivista* was largely given up to the interests represented by the Agronomical and Technological Section of the Congress, which was itself the best mirror and focus of the new and expanding public life of Italy. In 1845, the year in which Cattaneo joined the staff, and probably under his influence and that of Carlo Tenca, the articles published became more serious and weighty, and the "general outlook" sections were reduced to the literary and scientific "Bulletins" and the "Review of Journals." But the magazine continued to incline toward a discussion of science and education.

[26] *Rivista*, n. s., 1846, IV, Pt. 2, 304.

CHAPTER IV

NATIONAL JOURNALISM:
Achievements under Censorship, 1818-1848

WHAT was the influence of this journalism which had made such advances in variety and power since the days of the *Conciliatore?* How much of a public did it reach? The editions of the journals were very small by our standards. Those of the *Annali* ranged between 350 and 500. The *Biblioteca italiana* which was sold under official pressure issued an edition of 800 in 1822 but this was a peak not reached again. De Welz's *Ape delle cognizioni utili* printed 2,500 copies once in 1837 and once again in 1839, and averaged about 1,000. The *Politecnico* got out one edition of 1,000 copies. The *Rivista europea* ran on an average to about 750 copies.[1] The number of readers exceeded the number of subscribers. "In our country," said a writer in the *Annali* in 1833, "it is customary for a subscriber to share [a journal] with his friends and acquaintances; and . . . in the smaller cities where there are reading rooms very few subscribe individually." The writer felt that it was safe to count on ten readers to every subscriber. He calculated that the average edition of an Italian periodical numbered 300, and reached the conclusion that there were 180,000 readers of journals in Italy[2] There were reading rooms in the great cities as well as the provincial towns where the journals were accessible. The most famous was the Literary Cabinet of Vieusseux at Florence, which was virtually an Italian Liberal Club, and which subscribed to all the leading Italian and foreign reviews.[3]

At Milan one was maintained by Lampato's journal, the *Eco delle lettere,* in connection with its offices in the gas-lighted Galleria De Cristoforis. In a proud description of the new Galleria, the *Annali*

---

[1] A. S. M., Carte dell' I. R. Uffizio di Censura, Nos. 108–112. The figures are omitted from the record in cases where the censor applied his pruning knife. In these the phrase "admittitur omissis deletis" takes the place of a number. As numerous issues of such journals as the *Indicatore lombardo,* the *Ricoglitore,* and the *Rivista europea* were censored, and as the records become fragmentary after 1839 when the last named journal and the *Politecnico* were in their prime, any sort of statistical computation based on these manuscripts is impossible.

[2] *Annali,* 1833, Bulletino, pp. 244 ff.

[3] For a list of these available in Vieusseux's Cabinet in 1841 see the *Rivista,* 1842, V, Pt. 3, 213.

characterized these reading rooms, open from dawn until midnight, as "a kind of emporium in which one finds all the journals of Italy, political, literary, and scientific, as well as the most important journals of the other nations of Europe, to the number of almost a hundred."[4]

The periodicals founded by private initiative had not only to make their way against the competition of privileged journals jealously backed by the Government, but had also to overcome the inertia of a community unused to the appeal of journalism, and at the same time to develop a class of native journalists. The dearth of writers of the type required was one reason for the dependence of the Lombard journals on foreign sources—a dependence from which the more patriotic of them valiantly and with increasing success tried to escape. The limitation of their paid-up subscriptions also put them under a financial handicap. Giacinto Battaglia bitterly complained of the difficulties arising from this. The foreign publisher, he said, whether English, French, "or even German," started "with a pile of gold on his lap" with which he could get prompt service from contributors and secure unity of aim in their collaboration, while in Italy he had to beg them; he could not pay them enough, they therefore had other interests and obligations and he had to be satisfied with what they could give him at their convenience and pleasure.[5]

It has become evident from the foregoing review of independent journalism in Lombardy that the more important Liberal journals were not purely business undertakings. The *Annali di statistica* at least, although its director was evidently a man of considerable business enterprise, was assisted by persons of wealth who were in sympathy with its aim. Furthermore, if journals like the *Annali,* the *Politecnico,* and the *Rivista europea* lived and achieved a success in spite of handicaps, their survival must be considered as having been in large part due to the devotion of a group of writers whose fundamental aim was not the success of the journal but the good of their country.

The journals of a liberal and patriotic tendency were subjected to an embarrassment all their own in the Austrian censorship, the shadow of whose wings hovered continually over their pages. A publisher had to have a clean record in order to obtain license to found a journal, and the proofs of each issue had to be submitted to the censor before they might go to press. The report of the censor on Giacinto Battaglia when he sought permission to publish the *Indicatore lombardo* in 1828 will serve to illustrate the scrutiny to which the prospective publisher was subjected.

[4] *Annali,* 1832, XXXIII, 288.
[5] "Ai lettori ed ai collaboratori," *Rivista,* 1840, III, Pt. 1, vi-vii.

. . . He was born in Milan in 1803, is a bachelor, and lives apart from
his mother. He took a regular course of studies and graduated. as they
tell me, from the University of Pavia as an engineer, but finding that
profession little to his taste abandoned it to become a journalist. At
first he was associated with P. Barbieri in editing the *Giornale dei
Teatri.* Disgusted with the said Barbieri he became editor of the
journal *Vespa,* and drew attention to himself in that [periodical] as
well as in a published brochure on the last exposition at the Brera as
inclined to excessively biting criticism, a circumstance that must have
procured him some displeasure.

The censor concluded, however, by saying the Battaglia was a person
of ability and that he knew of nothing against him.[6] The deletions
made by the censor in the proof sheets of the journals, which would
enlighten us fully as to what was thought unfit to print, unfortunately
left no trace in his records. One document left there, however, seems
to deserve quotation as a measure of the unintelligence of the censorship exercised on the journals—or, it may be, of a subtlety in the intention and language of the journalists too fine for the uninitiated ear.
The sentences here quoted in translation are from an article that appeared
in the *Ricoglitore italiano e straniero* in June 1834, which was submitted by the Governor of Lombardy to Count Sedlnitsky, Chief of the
Police Bureau at Vienna, as illustrative of the suspicious tendency of
the journal. They were interspersed with comments by the censor
which I have put between parentheses in italics.

Benefits of such importance are destined to render fruitful the epoch
of the civil risorgimento. A secret voice keeps saying to my mind that
philosophy, demonstrating and sincerely recognizing the facts, is to
receive a great illustration from the Italian genius. Why [this is to be]
every Italian of intelligence must know. The author [whose work was
being reviewed] has perceived a gleam of the era that Christianity is
preparing for the world. His words dwell in my heart as a living
witness of the hope (*one of the three words of the sectaries*)[7] which
the Church kept awake and vigilant. This hope, O Italians! looks
forward to a good [that is] deserved. The disillusion of Rationalism
goes on making greater conquests and establishes itself in the conviction that has no faith in it. Meanwhile the past insinuates itself little
by little to give realization to the present, and the future approaches to
fulfill the destiny of men; meanwhile the time is rapidly approaching
which will put an end to disputes, and will open the way to the energy
of Christian thought in active and universal love. Society (*page 542 of
the Journal*) cannot absolutely find itself in flower and vital and

[6] A. S. M., I. R. Uffizio di Censura, busta 493, carta 333.
[7] An interpolation by the censor. That is to say, the members of the secret
political societies.

informed by efficacious thought except as it repairs to Christianity, and
in this (*bene notandum*) finds rejuvenation. European minds little by
little are subjected to the alternative of exhaustion or agitation, they
no longer breathe a common atmosphere of vitality.[8]

Cryptic words, indeed! "Sublime mysticism and nonsense," we should
be inclined to say, and suspect that the Government's ferret was on the
wrong scent. Certainly other passages could be found, many of which
are quoted in this volume, which seem far more likely to have awakened
feelings dangerous to Austria. The document just cited shows at least
that the Government, if not the public, was anxiously reading between
the lines of the journals and finding a meaning in them that they do not
have at their face value.[9]

The anxiety which the Austrian Government manifested with regard
to the journalistic movement is an indirect and eloquent tribute to its
effectiveness. Independent journalism had struck fresh root with the
Annali and its contemporaries, in the very midst of the cruel measures
with which Austria had disposed of the group of liberals who had
published the *Conciliatore* and it began to achieve its full stature precisely in the 'thirties immediately after the reaction against Young Italy.
No wonder that the Government was anxious! Antonio Salvotti had
given a warning of the danger and of the difficulty of combatting it
when he was prosecuting Pellico and Romagnosi in 1821. "This so-
called liberalism may itself be considered as also a sect though lacking
rites, emblems, lodges; and it is precisely for this reason more dangerous, because one can never seize it with a sure hand, as one cannot seize
words, thoughts and opinions."[10] In 1833 the Government made a
study of the measures that might serve to correct the influence of the
liberal press. The commissioner reported pessimistically that "Reading

[8] A. S. M., Presidenza, Atti segreti, 1834, carta CLXXXVIII.
[9] The *Indicatore lombardo* was under suspicion and being watched at the same
time. The agent reporting on the *Indicatore* stated that he had not failed to
examine the article by Cesare Cantù in the number for January 1833 and to
make its contents known to the Governor. *Ibid.*, No. 1811. The liberals
knew that the *Indicatore* was in danger. Antonio Trotti wrote to Costanza
Arconati at Paris April 10, 1833: ". . . They say that the *Indicatore,* the
least insipid journal of our city, is also about to be put under the interdict, for
the time being they have been satisfied with designating a special censor who is
responsible for it. What stirred up this storm were the articles of Cantù,
author of the *Cenni sulla storia lombarda nel XVII secolo* whom you know."
Malvezzi, p. 87. Cantù was suspected because of his implication in the Young
Italy trials of 1833. The articles referred to would seem to be the series by
Cantù entitled: "Ragionamenti intorno alla storia lombarda del secolo XVII per
servire da commento ai 'Promessi Sposi' di Manzoni," *Indicatore*, 1832, XI, 63–98;
XII, 91–141; 297–312.
[10] "Conclusione finale" of the *Requisitoria Salvotti contro Maroncelli e Compagnia*, in Luzio, *Processo*, p. 484.

has now become a kind of need which reaches even to the barber-shops, nor is there a spring which acts with greater force on public opinion. . . . Even literature has now become a branch of politics, and infinite is the good as well as the evil of it, so much the more that ordinarily indirect action is more efficacious [than direct]," and the censor could do little since he could only check the evil, not stimulate the good. The commissioner offered the brilliant suggestion that to make the *Gazzetta privilegiata* itself more malleable two editors who were not Milanese, Giorgio Edling, then at Paris, and Signor Garofolo, ex-Director-General of the Modena Police, might be added to the staff.[11] The Lombard Government recommended to Vienna that the rules of censorship be tightened and the office removed from "personal influences" by bringing to Milan censors from the German provinces of the Monarchy.[12]

Genuinely alarmed, the Government took some steps to set up a counter-current of public opinion in its own favor. The *Gazzetta* had an "Appendix" which published reviews and other non-official articles and this, it was thought, might be improved. The Government proceeded to overhaul its contract with the publishers, with the object of making that journal more attractive, at the same time requiring the compiler to publish not only official notices but any articles that the Government desired to see published, introducing "dexterously that wise political tendency which up to now has been in large part lacking." A certain Baroli, professor of philosophy at Como, was found ready to write suitable articles.[13] But two years later the hateful seepage of liberal ideas was found in the "Appendix" of the *Gazzetta* itself, introduced by the contributions of Defendente Sacchi. Sacchi had dared to refer to Tommaso Grossi and "the evil-minded Guerrazzi" as "authors of national character," and had spoken of the death of Giandomenico Romagnosi as "a European calamity"(!)[14] The episode illustrates the dilemma into which the progress of journalism in Lombardy was forcing the Austrians. If they did not use native talent in their

[11] Report to Hartig, Governor of Lombardy, April 16, 1833, signed "Caretani," in a folder relating to the renewal of the contract for the publication of the *Gazzetta*, A. S. M., Presidenza, Atti segreti, carta 188.

[12] Letter to Count Sedlnitsky signed Golz, September 28, 1834, A. S. M., Presidenza, Atti segreti, 1834, carta 188, 1811.

[13] One was published in the *Gazzetta* August 20, 1834. The Government arranged for another to combat the influence of Lamennais' *Les paroles d'un croyant*.

[14] Presidenza, Atti segreti, 1835, carta 194. The affair was the subject of a report of the Director General of Police on the offending articles, a report on them to Hartig the Governor, and a report to Sedlnitsky at Vienna discussing "den Censurirung der Appendici der Mailander Zeitung." In 1834 Defendente Sacchi had been characterized by the local police as "der in politischer Beziehung nicht von der besten Seite bekannte Defendente Sacchi." *Ibid.*, 1834, carta 178.

official journalism, their journals would fail to influence public opinion; if they used native talent, they were almost certain to find it infected with liberal and patriotic sentiment.

Another means of exerting a positive influence remained, though it had been tried without success through the *Biblioteca italiana,* namely: to open a channel of journalism for a natural flow of literature and thought between the Italian possessions of Austria and the capital. Such a measure must have seemed particularly important to Austrian officials resident in Lombardy. They could not fail to observe the tendency of the independent journals to turn their backs on Germany, absorbed as these were in the exciting spectacle of "civilization," stage-lighted with veritable *lumières,* that was being displayed in France and England. A journal that might have been expected to cut such a channel of communication was the *Eco delle lettere,* one of Francesco Lampato's enterprises, launched in 1828. Its sub-title describes it: "Journal of sciences, letters, arts, commerce and the theatre, compiled in Italian, English and German." But the influence of the *Eco* was exerted to make known the merits of Italy abroad rather than to recommend Austrian culture to the Italians. The volume in German for 1837–1838, for example, described the art and population of Milan, Petrarch's monument, Italian literature in the eighteenth century, the Rialto Bridge, the dramatic theatre in Italy, the current spectacle at the Scala; and of things German referred only to beer, as a praiseworthy beverage, which the Italians would not despise if they knew something other than "jene braunen, narkotischen, marklosen *Wermuthlader,*" that passes for beer in Italy!

In 1838, the year in which the *Rivista europea* was launched at Milan, a bi-lingual review, the *Rivista Viennese,* began to appear at Milan and Vienna.[15] It was an obvious attempt to forge a cultural link between the two capitals. The title-page of the second volume (1839) carried a sketch of two sisters, one brunette and the other blonde (and obviously Teutonic), seated together. The blonde is holding the head of the brunette in her lap and assuming (very Teutonically and seriously) an attitude of rapt attention. A sample number contains an article on "The Poet Kings of Modern Europe" by Ignazio Cantù; a translation

---

[15] *Rivista viennese. Collezione mensile di articoli originali; traduzioni in versi, e in prosa* (Vienna, A. Strauss, and Milan, Tendler and Schäfer). The *Rivista europea* damned it with faint praise and cheerfully took a fall from its editors for their notice of the *Presagio* as an example of the tardiness of the reports in that journal: "For example they tell you that the *Presagio,* compiled by the *distinguished poet and prose-writer G. B. Cremonesi* [the ironical italics are in the *Rivista*] has served *for three years as the palestra of a band of youths,* etc., whereas everybody knows that this year it is a very different pair of sleeves. . . ." *Rivista,* 1838, I, Pt. 3, 267–268.

into Italian of "Samuel," "*poemetto*" by Ladislao Pirker; two
both German and Italian: "The Cholera Morbus," by Dr. A. (
a fragment of Goethe's *Torquato Tasso*, translated into
Vincenzo Monti; two philological articles, one on the vowel ~~....~~
the Italian and German languages, another on the etymology of Italian
words, both by G. A. Bolza; finally, "Samples of the Dialects of Italy
and of Germany." There is no evidence that this experiment in conciliation enjoyed any considerable success;[16] nor could it be expected to, for
by 1838 the tide of independent journalism was reaching its crest in
Lombardy and it was setting strongly away from Vienna.

In the decade from 1838–1848 Italian journalism became fully conscious of its power to arouse and sway public opinion. The *Rivista
europea* in its section entitled "Review of Journals" held up a mirror
to the growth of journalism in Italy and in 1845 exultantly declared
that the journalists were "a pretorian guard" in the contemporary field
of literature and thought, ruling the intellectual world and making up
everybody's mind for him. The Turin correspondent wrote in 1840 of
the journals of Piedmont: "The best pages published among us in the
past year are in the columns of the journals. Are asylums for childhood or poorhouses projected? The journal becomes their partisan. . . .
Are the streets lighted by gas? The journal tells Italy of the fortunate
outcome of the first experiment. In [the journal] every work published
is discussed, analyzed, judged; the journal exercises a moral influence
against which it would be vain to contend."[17]

Behind this sense of assurance and power lay a fact of the greatest
importance in the development and organization of a true public life in
Italy. It was that in Lombardy and elsewhere in the peninsula, particularly in Tuscany and Piedmont, a class of writers and publishers
had been trained who were using the periodical press as a whole rather
than any single journal as their instrument. They were Italy's first
publicists. Giacomo Durando in his well-known brochure *Della nazionalità italiana* (1846) said of their influence: "There never was any
power that could perform the office of our present press in combatting
repugnances and correcting wrong notions."[18] Forming like-minded

---

[16] I can find no evidence that the *Rivista viennese* was continued after 1840.
Beginning with fascicolo VII (1839) the editor was announced to be G. B. Bolza.

[17] "Corrispondenza: Lettere sul Piemonte. Lettera prima," by Giorgio Barberi,
Rivista, 1840, III, Pt. 2, 302–312.

[18] *Della nazionalità italiana* (Lausanne, Bonamici, 1846), p. 174. Referring
to the group whom he called the "Active-Rationalists," that of which the
liberal journalists were the spokesmen and which they had been largely influential in creating, he wrote: "The enterprise of these last is bristling with
difficulties, since the arena of action is narrow and the elements of it are for
the most part infinitely small, difficult to seize and to manage. . . . Prevented

groups they exchanged visits and open letters of encouragement and criticism across the political frontiers that divided the peninsula. They immediately linked their activity with the Congresses of Italian Scientists when these began to meet in 1839 and from them they received a strong reinforcement. Indeed it was the journals that had created the agenda for this first national representation of Italian opinion, and the journalists reported the sessions with enthusiasm, played an active rôle on its commissions, and carried forward in their pages the discussions that arose in the annual meetings, and when the institution was attacked joined forces to defend it against criticism and to correct its faults.[19]

The particular "campaigns" carried on by this journalism will not seem impressive to the reader of today. Italian journalism, staggering under handicaps, was still far from realizing its full potentialities. But what progress it had made since the time of the *Conciliatore* with its abstract enthusiasm and its voice crying in the wilderness! Hobbled by the censorship and operating on a public limited by inertia and ignorance, it had developed a class of publicists and made them known to each other and to Italy; it had become a major force in shaping a national program of action.

from engaging in great battles they wage guerilla war and . . . disseminating themselves or even, if need be, dissolving their ranks they succeed in gaining ground imperceptibly and without great bursts of noise. Undoubtedly it is owing to their evolution that the terrible reactionary inundation of 1815 was checked at its flood. But to trace the various paths followed by them and to indicate what expedients still remain to them with which to continue the struggle seems to me a subject on which it is better to keep silence than to say little of it." *Ibid.*, p. 392. If Luigi Torelli, a collaborator of the *Rivista europea*, did not mention the Italian journalists in his *Pensieri di un anonimo lombardo* it was probably because he did not wish to increase their difficulties in Lombardy by magnifying their patriotic influence.

[19] An example of this phase of their activity will be found in the efforts of Gottardo Calvi in behalf of a draft constitution for workingmen's mutual aid societies, above, p. 123.

CHAPTER V

EMERGENCE OF A
PROGRAM OF CIVIC ACTION

T HE result of the discussion carried on in the journals whose history has just been sketched was the crystallization of a program of practical measures for the rehabilitation of Italy. It centered on the idea of drawing the Italians into the current of modern civilization. This idea received its first considerable impulse in post-Napoleonic Lombardy from the work of the group of men associated with the *Conciliatore* who, in their non-journalistic activities, were led by Count Federico Confalonieri.

Confalonieri is well known in the history of the Risorgimento because of his tragic association with the plot to free Lombardy from Austria with the help of Charles Albert of Piedmont in 1821.[1] He was tried and condemned for political conspiracy in 1824 and sent to join Silvio Pellico in the Spielberg.[2] The plans that he and his associates made and tried to execute before they let themselves be swept into the tide of direct political action contained in embryo the whole program of Italian liberal journalism. Incidentally their effort illustrates the difficulties amid which that program first took shape.

Federico Confalonieri was born to a position of the highest rank in Lombard society. While he was still very young his life had been violently stirred by the brief rôle he took in the affairs of his country in the crisis of 1814. He had been the leader of a group of young nobles who had shown a distinct but blundering and futile patriotism during the confused events attending the collapse of the Napoleonic Kingdom of Italy. The experience branded Confalonieri and laid him open to the suspicion of the new masters of his country. After a tour of France

[1] There is a life of Confalonieri by A. D'Ancona, *Federico Confalonieri* (Milan, 1897). Important letters and other documents illustrating the work of Confalonieri and his associates are to be found in Cesare Cantù, *Il Conciliatore e i Carbonari*. Confalonieri left a volume of memoirs, written by him in the Spielberg, published in *Memorie e lettere di Federico Confalonieri pubblicate per cura di Gabrio Casati* (Milan, 1889, 2 vols.). His letters have been published by G. Gallavresi, *Il Carteggio del Conte Federico Confalonieri* (Milan, 1911–1913).

[2] The documents of this trial are in A. Luzio, *Antonio Salvotti e i processi del ventuno*, and *Nuovi documenti sul processo Confalonieri* (in *Biblioteca storia del Risorgimento italiano,* serie III, nos. 1–2, 1901, and serie V, no. 5, 1908).

and England, from which he was recalled by the authorities,[3] and another in 1816 through the peninsula, on which he contracted relations
with liberal patriots in the other Italian states and struck up a profoundly sympathetic friendship with Gino Capponi, Confalonieri found
himself desperately bored and unhappy at home. This young patrician
was peculiarly sensitive to the suffocating atmosphere of the Restoration, in which all the active spirits of his generation were condemned
to restlessness. Proud, ambitious, and talented, he had a somewhat
dangerous penchant for the extraordinary. During his sojourn in
Naples in the winter of 1816–1817 he became intimate with Caroline
Jablonowska, aunt of his friend Capponi and wife of the Austrian
ambassador at Naples. She wrote him on March 17, 1817: ". . . promise
me to do nothing without letting me know of it; you have a taste for
the extraordinary which frightens me."[4] Her letters repeatedly strike
the same note.[5] She saw clearly that Confalonieri needed an outlet in
action to steady him. "Your sombre humor, to judge by your letters,"
she wrote him on February 12, 1818, "increases every day, you create
artificial occupations, trying to distract yourself; but why don't you
seek some real ones? You could and you ought to make yourself useful
to your country; for a long time the idea has occupied me. I foresee
all the objections that you can raise, but I find one reason with which
to oppose in advance all your arguments: that of sacrificing every personal consideration to the real advantage of your country. You are certain of procuring for it an immense one in devoting to its service a man
of your name, of your merit, a man whose means are known, and whose
example would carry with it so many others. What do you say to that?
Be circumspect in your answer by post. . . ."[6]

In the spring of 1818 Confalonieri put Caroline Jablonowska's idea
into effect. He set out on a second tour of Europe and visited Geneva,
Paris and London. Absent when the *Conciliatore* was launched in the
fall of that year, he was constantly in touch with its editors.[7] While

---

[3] D'Ancona, p. 43.

[4] Gallavresi, I, 294.

[5] July 3, 1817, she wrote: ". . . I believe in you always, I need to believe
in you, nevertheless this Italian character, this great penetration, this great
finesse, frighten me sometimes. You have everything that is needed to be eminently good or eminently bad." *Ibid.*, I, 315–316. Again, on September 21,
1817: ". . . I beseech you not to try to astound me, it would be useless—you
have only too much taste for extraordinary things." *Ibid.*, I, 343.

[6] *Ibid.*, I, 380–381.

[7] Cantù, *Conciliatore*, p. 57. In the spring of the next year Confalonieri was
bestirring himself on behalf of the *Conciliatore*, writing to Gino Capponi at
Paris, March 3, 1819: ". . . I desire that in your first letter you give me
news of your activity to favor the diffusion of the *Conciliatore*, with every
detail connected with the subject. . . ." Gallavresi, II, Pt. 1, 90.

on his tour he busied himself effectively about the other enterprises of the group that met in Count Luigi Porro's house: having an apparatus made in London for the manufacture of illuminating gas (that symbol of "Progress," feared by Reactionaries and dear to Liberals through all this period); ordering machines for the spinning of linen from the English manufacturer Hill; arranging for the construction by Boulton and Watt of an engine to be shipped to Genoa and installed in a steamboat for the navigation of the Po; answering the request of Alessandro Visconti d'Aragona for the statutes of the famous *Athenée* of Paris to serve as a model for one to be set up at Milan; and gathering practical information about the methods and operation of the so-called "Lancastrian" schools of mutual instruction, which he and his friends proposed to open in Lombardy.[8]

After his return to Milan in January 1819, Confalonieri's correspondence shows him happily absorbed in all these enterprises. The machines arrived. The gas plant, installed in Porro's house, was "a marvelous success: a coal from Savoy, charged with more gas than the best of the English, seems to assure us that we can naturalize this invention among us with advantage."[9] The steam engine was installed in a boat built for the purpose at Genoa. The boat was brought round to Venice,[10] and Confalonieri had a cargo of coal imported from Newcastle, for the boat and the gas-plant, in order to make comparative tests with native coals.[11] He developed a passion for the importation of modern "improvements" from France and England, even to such things as sanitary water-closets and steel pens; and entered into correspondence and negotiations with a view to the illumination of La Scala by gas.[12]

He had sought and obtained the permission of the Government to found schools of mutual instruction (of the so-called Lancastrian type) for the poor children of Milan and formed a society of citizens to support them. Before the end of 1819 two of these schools had been opened in the capital, and plans had been made for others and for the extension of the system to the whole of Lombardy-Venetia.[13] Confalonieri took

[8] Confalonieri to Ugo Foscolo, November 2, 1819, for a *resumé* of "that about which I was occupied in London last year." *Ibid.*, II, Pt. 1, 160. The teaching in the Lancastrian schools was done by student-monitors instructed by the master. The method offered the prospect of reaching large numbers of children with instruction at small expense.

[9] Confalonieri to Capponi, Milan, October 8, 1819, Gallavresi, II, Pt. 1, 147.

[10] In a letter of November 2, 1819, Confalonieri wrote Ugo Foscolo that it was "now happily navigating from Genoa where it was built, to the river for which it was destined, and whose name (*Eridano*) it bears." *Ibid.*, II, Pt. 1, 160.

[11] Confalonieri to Capponi, July 4, 1819, *ibid.*, II, Pt. 1, 121.

[12] *Ibid.*, II, Pt. 1, 176.

[13] *Ibid.*, II, Pt. 1, 129–130.

under his patronage the idea of an Athenaeum, which should be a center for lectures, reading and technical courses; and he projected an association which was to take over the Canobbiana Theatre, and with a subsidy from the Government, develop a permanent company for the representation of Italian comedy.[14] In the same year, out of these schemes flowered one that seems to have appealed to Confalonieri's imagination more than all the rest. It was the project of a great civic center or Bazaar, suggested to his mind by the Palais Royal and the "permanent fair" in Soho Square, London. It was to occupy the square next to the Scala and the Casino dei Nobili. The projected Athenaeum, with a Greek portico, would rise in its center. The Bazaar would include a public garden, with a fountain, and there would be covered passages for promenading in winter and rainy weather. Besides shops, it would contain restaurants and cafés, baths, a theatre, furnished rooms for the entertainment of foreigners, the bourse, bookshops; and "gas illumination would remove from the whole structure the shadows of night." This grandiose anticipation of the modern Galleria Vittorio Emanuele excited Confalonieri's fancy; it caressed his "taste for the extraordinary." He saw in it something more than a resort of elegance and fashion. "The advantages that would result to our city would be not only physical but also moral, and I dare to believe that I do not go too far in saying that this establishment might make a valuable contribution to the progress of our civilization, and, with the easy and increased contact of persons and classes, to the promotion of a public spirit much to be desired. . . ."[15]

It is unnecessary to repeat the story of the disaster that overtook this whole essay in liberalism. Confalonieri wrote to Lady Sydney Morgan on the eve of his own arrest, on December 7, 1821: ". . . From the summit of our hopes, and from the finest epoch which has shone for Italy in centuries, we found ourselves suddenly fallen into the most profound servitude accompanied by shame and dishonor."[16] Of the whole array of projects: the schools, the society for the production of Italian comedy, the Athenaeum, the Bazaar, illumination by gas, the treatment of linen by mechanical processes; steam navigation on the Po, only three actually got under way: the steamboat, gas-illumination, and the schools. None survived. The schools were closed by the Government in January, 1821; gas-illumination remained confined to Porro's house, which was confiscated when he was sentenced for political con-

---

[14] Gallavresi, II, Pt. 1, 149-154, for Confalonieri's petition to the Government for permission to found such a theatre.

[15] Confalonieri to Capponi, July 4, 1819, Gallavresi, II, Pt. 1, 119–123.

[16] Confalonieri to Lady Sydney Morgan, Gallavresi, II, 1, 469–472.

spiracy. The steamboat was the last to go. In August, 1821, Confalonieri wrote to Porro, who had fled the country: "In your Genevan leisure think of something to do with our poor steamboat which lies inactive and derelict, otherwise we lose both capital and patent."[17] That was all that was left of the apparatus of civilization with which Confalonieri and his friends had hoped to introduce an impulse of progress into the stagnant life of their country. The enterprise failed. But taken with the *Conciliatore* it contained in germinal form the program that was to develop steadily until it was openly proclaimed, together with its political implications, in 1844–1848. Its elements were: a journal, Italian in scope, produced by a free association of patriotic liberals; a new and untrammeled literary movement; a program of practical improvements and of popular education, associated with the type of industry, science and philanthropy that was spreading over Europe from England and France; finally, a faith that in these the liberals had found the secret of an irresistible social progress.

As this program developed in the Lombard journals, its fundamental element was an active industry.[18] From the *Conciliatore* to the *Rivista europea* the journalists showed a lively dissatisfaction with the industrial backwardness of their country and manifested a desire that Italy should share the benefits, without the evils, of the Industrial Revolution. This was their fundamental position. The only difference of opinion turned on the relative importance for Italy of agriculture and manufactures—a subject of debate that was carried over into the national forum of the Scientific Congresses.[19] The final conclusion was that for Italy, in view of its industrial infantilism, the question was largely academic. The balance of opinion is fairly represented by the editorial comment of the *Annali* on an article describing the suffering produced by industrialism in England: ". . . the example of England cannot and must not discourage Italian industry, [a reaction] which would be as ridiculous as if one feared the perils of railways while riding on a patient horse."[20]

The journals followed with watchful interest the progress of Italian industry, describing with praise manufacturing establishments that embodied "modern improvements" in equipment and organization, as well

[17] *Ibid.*, II, Pt. 1, 452.
[18] There is a summary of the moderate liberal program distilled from the journalistic and other current literature of Italy as a whole in Ciasca, *Programma*. An account of the activities and achievements of the moderate liberals is to be found in Mittermaier, *Delle condizioni d'Italia* (1845).
[19] *Diario della quarta riunione degli scienziati italiani convocati a Padova, settembre 1842* (Tipografia Prov. Penada), p. 86; *Atti della quarta riunione* (Padua, Seminario, 1843), p. 533.
[20] *Annali*, 1843, LXXVI, 40–41.

as all public and private efforts to stimulate industry. As the journalism of the period grew more mature, it lent its forces to the advocacy of certain general improvements which the progress of industry seemed to require. Among these were the erection of local plants for the construction of machines and machine parts, to obviate the delay and waste of importing these from abroad; the mechanization of the industry of linen and hemp spinning; the exploration of the subsoil for deposits of "mineral combustibles," without which it was already evident that Italian industry would remain subject to an insuperable handicap.[21]

As for agriculture, recognized as the great basic industry of their country, the Italian journalists hoped to bring about its development by the application of the latest findings of science. This involved the task of awakening Italian proprietors to the progress of agricultural technique in other countries, and to their own and the public interest in improvements, the adoption of fertilizers, the substitution of efficient implements for the slow muscles of the peasant, and technical instruction for the actual cultivators of the soil. The journals made it one of their objects to present an accurate picture of Italian agriculture by means of such studies as those of Correnti and Spreafico,[22] and gave the fullest publicity to organizations whose purpose was the progress of agriculture, such as the Accademia dei Georgofili of Florence, the model farm of Cosimo Ridolfi at Meleto, the Agronomical and Technological Section of the Congresses of Italian Scientists, the Agrarian Association founded by Cavour and Balbo in Piedmont, and the other promotional societies that sprang up at about the same time.

An economic revival in Italy, the harmonization of its life with that of progressive Europe, required also a stimulation of commercial enterprise, which the journals continually strove to administer. They saw that this must be accompanied and supported by a reform both of the means of communication, which must be modernized, and the commercial policy of the Italian states, which must be liberalized.

With the roads that the Austrian Government gave their country the Lombard journalists had no fault to find. The *Annali* was full of self-congratulation, and of praise for the Government, regarding the excellence of the Lombard system of roads, maintained "with an expenditure truly regal."[23] At first the *Annali* referred to the local service of diligences with scarcely less complacency,[24] but after receiving notices of

[21] The use made of the journals as sources of information for the first part of this volume renders citations unnecessary.
[22] Frequently cited above, Part I, ch. I.
[23] *Annali*, 1830, XXVI, 316. See also *ibid.*, 1832, XXXI, 88; 1833, Bulletino, p. 5; 1834, XLII, 126–129.
[24] *Annali*, 1827, XII, 274–279.

the adoption of steam-diligences in England, and an envious glance the comfort, speed and safety of the English stagecoaches and inns that served them, a system then in its sunset blaze of glory,[25] the Lombard journalists began to agitate for improvement. As we have seen, they found the Italian services outside of Lombardy scandalously inadequate. Meanwhile, the *Annali* laid before its readers a picture of the improvements being made in those roads in central Italy which were through routes of commerce.[26] The position which Balbo gave to roads and communications as the foundation of "progressive policies"[27] was carried over from the discussion that had taken place in the journals.

In 1835 the *Annali* introduced a special department entitled "New Communications by Means of Canals, Steamships, Iron Bridges and Roads," to keep its readers informed of the progress of these inventions, particularly of the steamship and railroad. The short-lived *Annali di Commercio* called attention to the steamboat as early as 1816. Porro, Confalonieri and the *Conciliatore* had tried to get a steamboat into operation on the Po. In 1826 the engine that Confalonieri had bought from Boulton and Watt for the now derelict "Eridano" was installed in the "Verbano"—the first steamboat on Lake Maggiore, which began her runs on March 3, 1826. In the same year steamboats began to ply Lake Como as well. The *Annali* reported this up-to-date improvement with enthusiasm, and seized on its economic success to point the moral that the introduction of machinery produces an only temporary displacement of labor and is followed by an increase of employment.[28] The journal followed the development of steam navigation abroad as a fresh triumph of science and commercial enterprise, and was joined by the *Politecnico* in urging a solution of the difficulties that in the 'forties still made steam navigation on the Po unprofitable.[29] One gets a measure of the conservatism of the local mind which they had to overcome from a report of the Milan Chamber of Commerce in 1844 on the feasibility of shipping silk to England by steamship. The merchants reached the conclusion that overland voyages by express diligence would always have the advantage of steamships for safety and punctuality.[30]

[25] *Annali*, 1834, XXXIX, 103–106; 1835, XLIV, 314–316.

[26] Letter from "L[uigi] S[erristori]," *Annali*, 1840, LXIV, 350–351.

[27] Balbo, *Speranze* (2d. ed., Capolago, 1844), pp. 221–222.

[28] *Annali*, 1826, X, 28–34; 1828, XV, 219–220. For other references to steam navigation in the *Annali*, see Ciasca, pp. 281–282.

[29] G. Sarti, "Della possibilità e convenienza d'introdurre la navigazione a vapore sul Po," *Politecnico*, 1843, VI, 422–429.

[30] M. C. M., Camera di Commercio, cartella 564.

"But steamboats are already ancient; now come the railroads," wrote a liberal Milanese noblewoman to her brother in 1834.[31] It has been remarked by Professor Ciasca that, for all its confidence in the forward movement of science and industry, at first even the *Annali* eyed the steam railway with diffidence and until 1832, though watching the early experiments with the new invention in England and France with an increasing sense of its significance, was content with the rôle of spectator.[32] Eventually the liberal journalists of the whole peninsula recognized the locomotive as the chief instrument offered by science for the regeneration of Italy. The *Rivista europea* could report in 1845 that the most important question that had been agitating Italian journalism for the past eight years was the railway, and in 1847 declared that the steam engine "is in our judgment the greatest event of the century."[33] As the discussion progressed the journalists steadily approached the conception of Cavour that the locomotive is the greatest of revolutionists, and more powerful than the weight of armies in determining the course of events.[34]

The development of this discussion has been too well reported to need retracing here except in broad traits.[35] In the, thirties it passed from the stage of watching and reporting results abroad to an increasingly urgent advocacy of local and regional lines for Italy. Finally the journalists began to agitate for a national Italian network, and to insist that the lines projected or under construction be directed or linked with a view to the interests of Italy as a whole, and with reference to the position in which Italy had been placed on the rehabilitated route through the Mediterranean as the potential turn-table of trade between Europe and Asia.[36] Professor Ciasca dates the beginning of this phase of the discussion from an article by Cattaneo in the *Politecnico* in

[31] Costanza Arconati to Antonio Trotti from Bonn, June 17, 1834, Malvezzi, pp. 97–99.

[32] Ciasca, *Programma*, pp. 234–236; 336. Typical is the review by "B . . . i" of T. Tredgold, *Practical Treatise on Railroads and Carriages* (translated from the English by T. Duverne, Paris, 1826) : "perhaps the time is still distant when Italy can profit by this kind of resource, already common, as a French journalist expresses it, with the two nations placed at the head of European civilization." *Annali*, 1827, XI, 229.

[33] *Rivista*, n. s., 1845, III, Pt. 1, 761; Broglio's review of Petitti's book on Italian railways, *ibid.*, 1847, V, Pt. 1, 149.

[34] See Cavour's famous review of Petitti in the *Revue nouvelle* VIII (May 1, 1846), reprinted in *Gli scritti del Conte di Cavour, nuovamente raccolti e pubblicati da* Domenico Zanichelli (Bologna, 1892), II, 3–50, where Cavour met with this thesis the objection that a line connecting Milan with Turin would lay Piedmont open to invasion by Austria.

[35] Ciasca, *Programma*, pp. 336–341 and 433–436. For the progress of the discussion in the *Annali, ibid.*, pp. 342–347; 438–444.

[36] Ciasca, *Programma*, pp. 516–521.

1841.[37] It culminated in the long and animated reviews of Petitti's *Delle strade ferrate italiane e del migliore ordinamento di esse* (1845),[38] and in the discussions of the whole ground traversed by the journals which took place in the Agronomical and Technological Section of the Congresses of Italian Scientists (1839-1847).

In the meantime the free journals of Lombardy had been devoting full and eager attention to the construction of railways in Lombardy-Venetia and also in the other states of Italy, but more especially to Charles Albert's railroad policy in Piedmont.[39] They provided an open forum for the bitter controversy that arose over the great Milan-Venice line.[40] Throughout this controversy, so embarrassing and hurtful to Italian patriotism, the *Annali*, the *Politecnico*, and the *Rivista europea* all favored the shorter route through Treviglio; but they patriotically abstained from bitter partisanship and their editorial attitude was governed by a growing impatience for action, and a feeling that Italy was being outdistanced and threatened with the loss of an opportunity on which its destiny might turn. For the reader of the Lombard journals there was nothing new in Cesare Balbo's urgent warning: "Communications rendered easy, speedy, and numerous are not to be regarded as much, they may be everything, in the formation of national policy." The discussion in the journals was important not only because it

[37] Carlo Cattaneo, "Sui progetti di strade ferrate in Piemonte," *Politecnico*, 1841, IV, pp. 143–158, 180. Actually Cattaneo's article in the *Annali*, 1836, XLVIII, 283–332 discussed the bearings of the projected Milan-Venice line on the eventual establishment of a line from East to West through Italy. To connect Odessa and Genoa, Southern Russia and the Atlantic would only require a link of 300 miles through the Julian Alps from Belgrade to Trieste. Meanwhile, the line would find support in the English establishments in Greece and could be related to their plans for communication with India through the Euphrates and the Gulf of Arabia. For the development of a discussion of a national network in the Lombard journals, see Ciasca, *Programma*, pp. 433–436; for bibliography, *ibid.*, pp. 438–444.

[38] See, for example, a letter from Petitti to Balbo referring to the famous *Lloyd di Trieste* article of January 25, 1846, in *Annali*, 1846, LXXXVIII, 95–97, and the lengthy and temperately critical discussion of Petitti's book by Emilio Broglio in the *Rivista*, n. s., 1847, V, Pt. 1, 149–180. Cavour's article "Des chemins de fer en Italie," in the *Revue nouvelle* was a review of Petitti which the author contrived to turn into a review of Balbo's *Delle Speranze d'Italia* as well, and indeed of the whole discussion of railways in Italy.

[39] For full citations of the discussion in the *Annali* and other journals, see Ciasca, *Programma*, pp. 343–347; 438–444.

[40] *Ibid.*, pp. 370–377; G. M. Trevelyan, *Manin and the Venetian Revolution of 1848* (London, 1923), pp. 45–47. The history of this important episode, and particularly of the part which Austrian policy played in it, generally represented as Mephistophelian, needs to be more thoroughly investigated. If Metternich's government was overreaching and thwarting the Italians, it is curious that the journalists of the *Annali* and Cattaneo himself openly rejoiced when the Government took over the construction of the line. For a bibliography see Ciasca, *Programma*, pp. 278–280; 343–347; 371, note 1; and 438–444.

familiarized their public with an instrument of progress, but because it undoubtedly helped to awake both publicists and public to the economic strategies that were to be increasingly characteristic of the nineteenth century. The need of railroads pointed and reinforced at every step the need of a customs league and brought them face to face with the paramount consideration of union and independence.[41]

In discussing the conditions necessary to the prosperity of Italian commerce all the important free journals of Lombardy, except the *Conciliatore* and the *Ape delle cognizioni utili,* took their departure from the principle of free trade. As Professor Ciasca has remarked, by 1830 Italian publicists had come to accept the principle of free trade as axiomatic.[42] Faithful to the tradition of the Italian economists of the eighteenth century, the journalists of Lombardy assumed a position diametrically opposed to the principle of protectionism, which they faced in the Austrian system of commercial regulation. In this attitude the journalists were in complete accord with the merchants of the community, expressing themselves through the Milan Chamber of Commerce, which repeatedly registered protests against the Austrian customs regulations. True again to the tradition of Italian economists, from Genovesi to Verri, the Lombard publicists believed half a loaf better than none, and advocated immediate, partial reforms that seemed practicable, such as treaties of commerce and navigation among the Italian states and between them and the other trading nations of Europe. But the measure on which they all finally settled as the instalment of free trade for Italy that best served their purposes was an Italian customs-union.[43] They began to suggest it early.[44] But it was the German Zollverein that lent

[41] *Ibid.,* pp. 413–416; 433–436.

[42] See *ibid.,* pp. 238–240; 311–312; 416–419. For bibliographical references to the journals of Lombardy-Venetia, see *ibid.,* pp. 241; 314–317; 422–424.

[43] Their refusal to see the Zollverein as anything but a step towards the complete freedom of trade which was with them an article of faith may be illustrated by the following comments. Giuseppe Sacchi, in a note on an article regarding the Zollverein from the *Foreign and Contemporary Review,* sees in it the basis for expecting the liberation of German commerce, for, he says, although the Zollverein is based on the prohibitive system, the economic growth which it will produce will make necessary the abandonment of that system in favor of freer exchanges. *Annali,* 1835, XLVI, 56–58. The reviewer of the standard contemporary treatise on the Zollverein, P. A. de la Nourais et E. Bères, *L'Association des douanes allemandes, son passé, son avenir* (Paris, Paulin, 1841) in the *Rivista europea,* believed that the authors had mistaken the significance of the Zollverein in regarding it as a triumph of protectionism. "In our opinion, it cannot be understood except as procuring the freedom of commerce." *Rivista,* 1842, V, Pt. 2, 148.

[44] In 1816 the *Annali di commercio* advocated a commercial pact between the various governments of the peninsula that would recognize the fact that "Italy, even if parcelled among various governments, finds itself strictly bound by reciprocal needs and infinite relationships." *Annali di commercio,* 1816, No. 1, p. 10.

a cutting edge to their advocacy of commercial liberalism. The *Annali* immediately hailed as an event of good omen for Italy the treaty providing for the completion of the Zollverein in 1834;[45] and the journalists of Lombardy, and of the whole peninsula, proceeded to exploit it to the limit as an instrument of propaganda ideally suited to their purposes.[46] It was a working model of what they wanted, consecrated by immediate success; and it pointed the way from practical needs, which the whole community felt, to moral and political ends, which the liberal patriots ardently desired to achieve. The interdependency of a customs-union and a national railway system, again accentuated by the triumphant experience of Germany, was quickly perceived, and the advocacy of one was utilized to lend force to the advocacy of the other. By 1841 the discussion of an Italian commercial league had gone far enough to bring the Italian public face to face with the crucial difficulty which the presence of Austria on their soil threw in the way of the fulfilment of their desire.[47] Some of the leading journalists were fain to believe that it could be surmounted without resort to violence. The discussion reached a climax with the publication of Balbo's *Speranze d'Italia* (1844) and Petitti's *Strade ferrate italiane* (1845). Both of these writers proposed a peaceful solution, Balbo by the adoption of a half-measure—an Italian League without Lombardy-Venetia; Petitti, by adandoning the League as hopeless and trusting to the effect of a well-planned railway system. But the issue between the Italians and the foreign invader had been made as clear as day by the long and animated discussion in the journals.

The Lombard journalists found a powerful leverage in arguing both for a national railway plan and an Italian customs-league in a development of the European economic revolution that was touching the interests of Italy directly and with an increasing pressure. This was the shift in the line of communication between England and the East from the Cape of Good Hope to the Mediterranean, which began with the invention of the ocean steamship. That all the stages in this momentous

[45] Report from the *Dorfzeitung* of September 4, 1833, of the success of the meeting at Berlin to complete the union on January 1, 1834. "Heaven send that like dispositions may be proposed and adopted for the states of Italy." *Annali*, 1833, Bulletino, p. 463.

[46] For a full account of the progress of this discussion see Ciasca, *Programma*, pp. 354–356; 455–483; 497–540. For bibliographical notes on the journals of Lombardy-Venetia, *ibid.*, pp. 357–358; 465; 466–467; 476–477.

[47] This phase of the discussion was precipitated by a paper of Petitti, read at the session of the *Georgofili* of Florence on December 5, 1841, entitled "Delle associazioni doganali tra vari Stati italiani" and published in the *Atti dei Georgofili*, 1842, XX, 131 ff. Cited and summarized in Ciasca, *Programma*, pp. 459–460.

shift can be followed in detail in the Lombard journals is evidence of the alertness and comprehension of their writers. They were quick to see that Italy had been placed once more on a world highway. The Italians were being swept into the main stream of a traffic through which they had won their leadership of Europe at the close of the Middle Ages. "The steamship lines between Bombay and Suez, Alexandria and Marseilles have reversed the terms of the problem which was solved by Vasco da Gama when he passed the Cape of Good Hope," the *Annali* declared in 1839. With the full development of steam navigation in the Mediterranean "Italy will find herself again in the center of commerce and civilization, after having been for these last centuries relegated to its extremity," Cattaneo wrote in the same year.[48] "Behold a new social revolution in full force," exclaimed a writer of the *Annali* in 1842. "The prestige of the Cape of Good Hope disappears, and the commerce of the Orient resumes its ancient track." The needs of England's vast trade, and her political relations with the Orient, Broglio wrote in the *Rivista europea* in 1847, require communication by steamship and by railways on a line that "will return to the ancient and venerable scenes of civilization, to the shores of the Mediterranean and the Red Sea."

This commercial revolution was charged with hope and danger in equal proportions. Italy, divided and backward, might lose the precious opportunity, and the journalists plied this fear vigorously as an argument for the prompt and sweeping reforms that would put the Italians in a position to profit by their Heaven-sent chance—in particular, a customs-union and a national railway plan, providing the swiftest possible communication from end to end of the peninsula. It was Italy's relation to "the reopened way to the Orient" that Cesare Balbo invoked in the conclusion of his *Speranze d'Italia*, to clinch his argument for the prompt and realistic adoption of an Italian customs league based on free trade. The last pages of his book were an epitome of the ideas of commercial policy that his fellow-journalists in Lombardy had been developing over a period of twenty years. He echoed their argument for immediate action: if Italy stood still she would go backwards, relatively and positively. There was no hope, he said, that the Italians could overtake other nations in capturing the markets of the East. Their one hope lay in seizing the advantage of Italy's position on the new current of trade through the Mediterranean. To attract this trade each port must be made a port for all Italy, and the customs league must be based on the principle of free trade, now axiomatic everywhere. Whatever was to be done must be done quickly. A race was on; the salvation of Italy was a question "of arriving first, of seizing the single advantage that remains for us. Other nations have other advantages, other precedences, more ships, more industries, more markets; we cannot take these from them; we can only seize the advantage which they have not yet seized: freedom of trade. . . . Freedom without the league, or the league without freedom, or the league and freedom without promptness, will not avail."[49]

In the same year that Balbo published his book, Charles Albert began building railways with a view to capturing the India mail for Genoa. He thus placed himself in line with the recommendations of the Liberal publicists and immensely strengthened both his chances of national leadership and the hopes of Italy.

There were two other commercial reforms in the liberal program of 1848 which were related to the demand for an Italian customs-union and which had been agitated by the journals. One was a uniform system of weights, measures and coinage to take the place of the interminable thicket of conflicting standards in which Italian trade was entangled, and the other an improvement in the conditions of the Italian book-trade, and specifically a uniform copyright law.[50] Neither reform was possible without some sort of concerted political action. The intellectuals in particular were aroused by the disorders of the Italian book-trade and the journalists themselves had a direct interest in it.[51] They took what measures they could, and carried the discussion into the Scientific Congresses.[52] The ultimate need, a uniform copyright, was impossible without some sort of union, and gave the literary class a special motive for advocating it.

The liberal journalists invoked an agricultural, industrial and commercial revival; they also believed in education for the masses. All of the independent journals of Lombardy from 1818 to 1848 devoted systematic attention to the promotion of an education that would be at once popular and practical.

[49] Balbo, *Speranze*, pp. 437–452.

[50] See Ciasca, *Programma*, pp. 253–254; 324–327; bibliography for Lombardy-Venetia, *ibid.*, pp. 254; 327–329; 484–485.

[51] The problem was fully and ably discussed by Cesare Cantù in two articles on "Condizione economica delle lettere," *Rivista*, 1838, I, Pt. 2, 35–59; 141–163. The most serious impediments to the trade were the lack of uniform copyright laws and "the subdivision of Italy which prevents the rapid circulation of books in the country itself; and for a good while a shipping house has been considered in vain."

[52] The Lucca Congress in 1843 recommended a book-fair modelled on that of Leipzig. Both the *Annali* and the *Rivista europea* condemned this proposal. For the extensive discussion of the question in the latter, see *Rivista*, n. s., 1844, II, Pt. 2, 612–625.

They diligently praised the Austrian system of public schools, carefully recorded its progress, and held it up to the emulation of the other states of Italy. And well they might, for at that early date none of these, and very few governments anywhere, provided free and compulsory education for the children of their people. Elsewhere in Italy, if exception be made of the universities, education was entirely in the hands of the Church and the family. The Italians of Lombardy could not complain that their education had been slighted in comparison with that of the other nationalities of the Empire.[53] Surveying the Lombard system with enthusiasm in 1830, Giuseppe Sacchi declared that in its schools Lombardy surpassed all the rest of Italy, noting with complacency "the huge total" of their enrollment of 160,962 children between the ages of 6 and 12.[54] When Serristori in 1842 wrote that he had nothing but praise for the Austrian Government for realizing that "a copious number" of schools is required by the progress of industry, Sacchi demurred a little, being keenly interested at the moment in an increase of technical instruction;[55] but he wrote in the *Rivista europea* that thanks to the work initiated under Maria Theresa and Joseph II and renewed after 1814 "the Lombardo-Venetian Kingdom was the first country in Italy to see the problem of an education imparted to all the people through public institutions, with rational methods, and with appropriate books, brought to solution."[56] When the Congresses of Italian Scientists came to take up the educational problem in Italy, the motion adopted was that "as soon as possible the elementary instruction of both sexes be organized and generalized in the various parts of Italy, as it was under-

[53] The ratio of children in school to the total population of the Monarchy was the same in 1827 for Lombardy-Venetia (1–13) as for the Monarchy as a whole, and was excelled anywhere in Europe only by those of Bohemia (1–11), the Austrian Tyrol (1–8), Bavaria (1–8), and Denmark (1–12). Quoted by Giuseppe Sacchi from C. Dupin, *Les forces productives et commerciales de France* (Paris, 1827), *Annali*, 1831, XXX, 98. The article contained the following table of comparison with France:

	France	Lombardy
Communes	37,262	2,237
Communes without elementary schools	14,271	117
	(1/3 of total)	(1/20 of total)
Pupils	1,116,777	117,890
	(1/30 of population)	(1/13 of population)
Expenditure	1,500,000 lire	3,000,000 by the Government
		1,500,000 by the communes

[54] This figure includes the enrollment in private schools. *Annali*, 1830, XXVI, 315.

[55] L. Serristori, "Istruzione tecnica nelle province venete," with note by G. Sacchi, *Annali*, 1842, LXXIII, 184.

[56] "Rivista di opere sull'educazione popolare," *Rivista*, n. s., 1845, III, Pt. 1, 81.

taken twenty-five years ago by the wisdom of the Government
Lombardo-Venetian Kingdom."[57]

It is true that in Lombardy the principle of lay education was subject
to limitations which in part reflected the traditional organization of
Italian society on an ecclesiastical basis. In 1847 only 24,780 of the
251,168 school-children of Lombardy were in private schools, which
included those of the Church. But a large proportion, probably a large
majority, of the rural schoolmasters were almost of necessity priests,
in spite of the existence of the normal schools which the Government
set up for the training of teachers.[58] This was an inevitable result not
only of the intellectual and social dominance of the clergy but of the
meagreness of the stipends, which made teaching a part-time occupation.[59] Moreover, the compulsory feature was not enforced.[60] But the
journalists acquiesced in these limitations as unavoidable or as dictated
by prudence, although their leading spokesman on education, Giuseppe
Sacchi, openly expressed a preference for education under lay control,
and although the journals were always urging the Government forward
to the greatest possible extension of the system. In his vitriolic indictment of Austrian rule in Lombardy in 1847 Cesare Correnti declared
that the educational system had been reduced to a mockery by starva-
tion wages which had thrown the task of instruction into the hands of
retrograde priests, or ignorant, unfit or part-time teachers; by the failure of the Government to enforce attendance; and by the failure of the
Italians to have anything to do with the system.[61] But certainly there

[57] Motion put to the Agronomical and Technological Section of the Lucca
Congress (1843), reported in the *Rivista*, n. s., 1843, I, Pt. 4, note, pp. 156–158.
[58] Ravizza, pp. 14–27, paints an idealized picture of the priest-teacher, but the
assumption that the parish priest would find himself also the village school-
master is probably close to reality. "3000 ecclesiastics," said Ravizza, "scattered throughout the realm direct the schools of the communes." In any case
the problem of school attendance largely devolved on the priests of the country
parishes, as the *Annali* pointed out in one of its frequent discussions of the
question. *Annali*, 1844, LXXIX, 187.
[59] The average annual income of the teachers in the elementary public schools
in 1835–1837 was 404 lire. But "for the greater part of the body of teachers,
especially in the little communes, the honorarium amounts to scarcely 100 lire;
and therefore can be compensation for nothing more than an accessory occupation." Carlo Cattaneo, reviewing Karl Czörnig's, "Prospetto statistico dell'istruzione
elementare in Lombardia nel triennio 1835–37," *Politecnico*, 1839, I, 265. 96 lire
a year was the wages of a kitchen servant in 1836. Ferrante Aporti, *Guida pei
fondatori e direttori delle scuole infantili di carità* (Milan, I. R. Stamperia, 1836),
p. iv.
[60] The law imposed a fine of 50 centesimi a month for non-attendance, but it
was being suspended as late as 1847 in the hope of winning over the people.
Giuseppe Sacchi was growing impatient: "these spontaneous convictions," he
wrote, "diffuse themselves too slowly." *Annali*, 1847, XCIII, 182.
[61] *L'Austria e la Lombardia* (first published 1847, with false title: *Cenni
statistici* di Melchiorre Gioia, Filadelfia, 1840), pp. 34–36; 53.

is nothing in the full discussion of the public school system by Correnti's associates in liberal journalism to prepare our minds for such an attack.[62] Either the journalists were cowardly and dishonest (and Correnti himself had been conspicuously identified with them), or Correnti was carried off his feet by the anger of patriotism.

The liberal journalists praised the public schools, but obviously dearer to their hearts were the schools founded by private initiative— the schools of mutual instruction, the *asili d'infanzia* or pre-schools for the children of the poor, and the scientific and technical courses offered by private institutes for the self-education of the adult public. This marked preference, and not their criticism of the Austrian system, is the striking trait of their discussion of education.

Schools of mutual instruction were part of the program of Confalonieri and the liberals of the *Conciliatore*. He and his friends ambitiously expected that the Lancastrian school would play a great rôle in the life of their country, growing into a universal system that would banish illiteracy[63] and developing a union of Italian minds. A regular exchange of information and letters of encouragement with the secretary of the society that was promoting Lancastrian schools in Tuscany fed their hopes.[64] The "excellent Tuscans," Confalonieri wrote to Capponi in March, 1820, ". . . have taken a step most courteous and best conspiring to the purpose in wishing to inscribe many of themselves in our Association as contributing members. These steps are of the finest example in binding together the Italian family." It was by means of correspondence with Charles Albert on this congenial subject that Confalonieri and his associates entered into their fatal entanglement with the Piedmontese revolutionists of 1821.

From the first the Lancastrian schools encountered clerical opposition and the suspicion of the Austrians.[65] When the liberal tendency of Count Porro's circle became clearly manifest, the Government began to close the schools, announcing that they would be tolerated only until the elementary school system meditated by Austria and forecast in an Imperial decree of 1818 was established. On January 9, 1821, the doors of the last of the Lancastrian schools were peremptorily ordered shut.[66]

---

[62] The one reservation that might be made to this view is the silence of the *Rivista europea* regarding the public school system, in contrast with the generous attention that it bestowed on education.

[63] Confalonieri to Cav. Ferdinando Tartini Salvatici, July 5, 1819, Gallavresi, II, Pt. 1, 130.

[64] See Gallavresi, II, Pt. 1, *passim*.

[65] Confalonieri to Baron Auguste de Staël in 1819, Gallavresi, II, Pt. 1, 108–109.

[66] L'Imp. R. Delegazione Provinciale alla Società istitutrice delle scuole di mutuo insegnamento de Sta. Caterina e di S^t. Agostino, January 9, 1821, Gallavresi, II, Pt. 1, 384.

The principle of mutual instruction continued in vogue in other parts of Italy as part of the program of liberal philanthropy, especially in Tuscany, and eventually died a natural death because of its pedagogical defects.[67] It disappeared from Lombardy because the disasters of 1820–1821 had given it a political taint and made it necessary for the liberals to find a new type of initiative in education as well as in journalism. They found what they wanted in the so-called *asilo d'infanzia* or pre-school for infants.

The *asilo d'infanzia* was first introduced at Cremona in 1829 by a priest, Don Ferrante Aporti, who was Professor of Sacred History and Biblical Interpretation in the Episcopal Seminary, and also principal of the upper elementary public school of the city.[68] The model of Aporti's experiment was the type of school that had been developed by Robert Owen in Scotland—called at that time the "sensibility school"[69]—which had spread to Belgium and France on the continent.[70] The *asilo d'infanzia* was a "pre-school" for children between the ages of two and ten. Aporti's school was primarily intended as a "refuge" (hence the term *asilo*, asylum) for the children of the poor, where they were safeguarded, fed and educated without charge while their parents were at work.

> The instruction consists in the elementary principles of religion and morality; in the prayers customarily used in the liturgy; in reading, writing, and mental arithmetic; in some facts of sacred history; in the Italian denomination of various parts of the body, of objects of clothing and others of domestic use, and of objects of natural history employed in agriculture or the arts; in singing, or the education of the two principal organs of the voice and the ear, keeping in healthful movement the other viscera which contribute to the formation of the voice; and finally in gymnastics appropriate to their tender age, which wisely fulfil the office of recreation after mental occupation, or after [the lunch of] broth or minestra that is given each of them after midday.[71]

From the first Aporti was backed by the provincial inspector of the Austrian school system,[72] and he wisely enlisted the aid and support of the local society. The journalists immediately remarked this social aspect of the new institution with enthusiasm.

---

[67] In 1845 Giuseppe Sacchi characterized it as a misguided attempt to apply military discipline to the education of children. It was found wanting, he said, because of its mechanical and automatic character, but was good for adults, sailors' schools and prison schools. *Rivista*, n. s., 1845, III, Pt. 1, 88.

[68] *Annali*, 1832, XXXII, 99.

[69] Giuseppe Sacchi in the *Ricoglitore italiano e straniero*, 1834, I, 386.

[70] *Annali*, 1830, XXIII, 107.

[71] *Annali*, 1832, XXXII, 98-99.

[72] Nobile D. Giovanni Cavalcabò, *Annali*, 1832, XXXII, 99.

Early in the morning you would see well-to-do citizens [of Cremona]
going each in turn to seek the children of the poor in their wretched
houses, to lead them by the hand to the infant schools and to bring
them home in the evening; in the schools [you would find them]
assisting, governing, caressing [the little ones] as if they were their
own children. . . . From this exchange of generous cordiality on one
side and reverent gratitude on the other, what benefits may accrue to
public morality, what sentiments of mutual affection may arise and
develop, it is not necessary for us to say.[73]

The rich were solicited for financial contributions and provided the
larger part of the means required; but Aporti sought to give his institution a broader foundation. By 1832 he had induced some one hundred
and thirty citizens of every social class to pledge an annual subscription,
and he funded his second school, opened in March 1830, by selling
shares of stock for three lire per annum.[74] Benefit performances were
given by a local company of amateurs, and at New Year's Cremonese
society was induced to substitute a payment of a florin to the school
fund for the customary visit of ceremony to the magistracies.[75]

In the meanwhile, to the delight of the writers of the *Annali,* even the
ladies of Italy, following the example of those of other countries, were
personally taking part in Aporti's enterprise. "All their domestic, their
household life to which they consecrate themselves, must now also
broaden into social life; in this is entrusted to them the sweet burden
of charity." The *asili d'infanzia* at Cremona were developing a social
significance in no restricted sense of the term. "These beneficent influences of the elevated education of well-to-do persons on rough creatures
born in poverty is not the dream of a good man but a solemn fact, attested by experiment, a fact that deserves to be reproduced among us."[76]
In 1834 Giuseppe Sacchi declared: "The holiest, the most respectable
mission that the charity of individuals can exercise is without question
in our times the promotion of the infant schools." Two years later the
Annali referrd to the *asili* as "one of those great Providential means
directed by God to promote in certain epochs the perfection of humanity."

Beginning very simply and informally, by 1836 Aporti had 392 boys
and girls under instruction at Cremona, in two buildings especially
adapted to his purpose.[77] Meanwhile *asili* had begun to spring up elsewhere. Three had appeared in Tuscany. When Cavour returned from

[73] Giuseppe Sacchi, in *Ricoglitore italiano e straniero,* 1834, I, 390.
[74] *Ibid.,* 386; *Annali,* 1832, XXXII, 99–100.
[75] Aporti, *Guida,* p. vi.
[76] G. Sacchi, "Diffusione in Lombardia delle sale d'infanzia," in *Annali,* 1830,
XXIII, 318–321.
[77] Aporti, *Guida,* p. vi.

his tour of England in 1835 he threw himself into the work of founding "infant asylums" in Piedmont.[78] By 1837 there were more than thirty of these schools in Lombardy-Venetia and Tuscany, and others were about to open in Piedmont, Liguria, and the Kingdom of Naples. The institution had rooted itself firmly in Milan. In the capital, as at Cremona, the *asili* had been founded by a priest and society was exerting itself in their behalf. A lottery had been held for their benefit, under the supervision of a committee of important names, headed by that of the same Marchese Giulio Beccaria who had been the leading patron of the ill-fated schools of mutual instruction; ladies and gentlemen were acting as inspectors and even as assistants; physicians, surgeons and druggists were lending their services free; merchants and manufacturers donated the lottery prizes.[79] A literature about the infant schools was appearing.[80] It was evident that they had started a general social movement. The Lombard journals, notably the *Annali*, the *Ricoglitore*, and the *Rivista europea*, followed this movement intently and promoted it vigorously. Although initiated by a priest, developed in an atmosphere of conservative philanthropy, hailed as promising a widespread improvement in social relations, the infant schools of Lombardy would have foundered, like the previous attempt of liberals to educate the poor, without the approval of the Austrian Government. But this was obtained.[81] The Government then sanctioned the diffusion of the institution.[82] Count Hartig, Governor of Lombardy, and the Archduke Ranieri, the Viceroy, visited the Cremona schools in person,[83] and the Government exempted from taxes the lottery held for the benefit of schools of Milan.[84] In 1843 Austria bestowed on Giuseppe Sacchi "the gold medal of civil honor with ribbon" "as the well-deserving promoter of the Institutes of Refuge for Infancy of Milan."[85]

---

[78] "No one contributed a larger share of active intelligence to the undertaking." He was for a long time a member of the committee of management and retired at the instance of the Count de Salmour only because his name was damaging the reputation of the institution with the Government. William de la Rive, *Reminiscences of the Life and Character of Cavour* (tr. from the French by Edward Romilly, London, 1862), pp. 85–86.

[79] *Annali*, 1837, LIII, 89–91; *Ricoglitore*, 1837, Anno IV, Pt. 1, 414.

[80] Aporti published his *Guida* in 1836. In the same year F. S. Fapanni published a *Storia degli asili di carità per l'infanzia in Treviso* (Treviso, Andreola, dicembre 1836), reviewed in the *Ricoglitore, ibid.* This growing literature was regularly reviewed by the *Annali*, the *Ricoglitore*, and the *Rivista europea*.

[81] Decree of August 31, 1830, No. 24778–4751.

[82] Decree of February 1, 1832.

[83] Aporti, *Guida*, pp. ix-x.

[84] Sovereign Resolution of May 30, 1837, reported by G. Sacchi in the *Annali*, 1837, LXIII, 90.

[85] *Rivista*, n. s., 1843, I, Pt. 3, 64, reporting the *Eco di Milano*.

The Church had not approved the new institution in spite of its clerical auspices; and although the Austrian Government seemed complacent, the reactionaries took alarm, and began to sniff a taint of liberalism in the whole movement. In 1837 a priest named Boncompagni published at Lugano a book entitled *Illusioni della pubblica carità,* in which he violently attacked the *asili* as the manifestation of "a plot against the good of society, and those who took part in it as people either saturated with rebellious and so-called liberal principles or else credulous." The institution had "come from the Protestants"; "babies were snatched from the breast of the mother, their sole [true] mistress"; the instruction is inspired by philosophism *à la Voltaire* or by Saintsimonianism: "in short, the *asili* are a plot, a new betrayal, perhaps the worst of all."[86] The skill and energy with which the liberal journalists and the friends of the infant school rallied to its defence shows how deeply it had rooted itself in their purposes. Don Giulio Ratti, senior priest of the parish of San Fedele, immediately published a reply, writing as a member of the commission supervising the *asili d'infanzia* of Milan.[87] He emphasized the clerical supervision of the religious instruction given in the schools, even "in all the little villages, where the parish priest is by law the local school inspector." The liberal journalists made much of the favor in which the schools were held by "our princes and most enlightened citizens," but laid especial stress on the prominent part that the clergy were taking in the movement. The *Rivista europea,* after referring to Boncompagni's attack, gave an edifying picture of the activities of the Milan Commission. "The committee of the *asili* of Milan assembled the contributors on the 23d [of April] in the church of San Fedele to pray for shareholders and donors who had passed to the other world, and on the 24th to nominate a new commission, on which the Reverend Signor Rossi, parish-priest of San Nazzaro, took the place of the senior priest of San Fedele whose term had expired."[88] When the *Rivista* described the coronation of the new Emperor of Austria at Milan, in 1838, it linked the event with "the pious institutions of the

---

[86] This report of Boncompagni's attack is culled from the reply to it entitled: *Brevi risposti del sacerdote Don Giulio Ratti proposto parroco di San Fedele in Milano alle osservazioni pubblicate contro la istruzione popolare e contro gli asili di carità per l'infanzia nell'oposcolo anonimo in data di Lugano tipografia Veladini 1837 col titolo Le illusioni della pubblica carità,* (Milan, Stella, 1838), and from the section entitled *Cronaca,* in the *Rivista europea,* 1838, I, Pt. 2, 246. By 1839 the *Illusioni* was known to have been written by Boncompagni. See *Rivista,* 1839, II, Pt. 3, 176. Professor Codignola erroneously attributes the pamphlet to Monaldo Leopardi, father of the poet. *Educational Yearbook of the International Institute of Columbia University 1929* (New York, 1930), p. 352.

[87] *Brevi risposte,* cited in previous note.

[88] *Rivista,* 1838, I, Pt. 2, 246.

infant asylums and the railways" as "always protected and favored" by his Majesty.[89]

But, in truth, by this time the educational movement that had grown out of Aporti's little schools at Cremona had assumed national proportions and a momentum that would have been very difficult to oppose. In 1839 it was among the many projects fostered by the liberals that found a point of national concentration in the Congresses of Italian Scientists. The *asili* became a regular subject of discussion in the Agronomical and Technological Section of the Congresses, and were henceforth linked with the program of enterprises in which the liberals saw the regeneration of Italy taking place. In 1840 Giuseppe Sacchi declared that "there is not at present a city of Italy which has not already thought or is not thinking of the education of the people through the opening of *asili di carità* for the children of the poor," and proceeded to verify his assertion by calling a roll of the cities in which they were known to exist.[90] Aporti became a national hero. At the Lucca Congress of 1843, he was "received with true enthusiasm by the agrarian section."[91] In 1844 he was called by Charles Albert to direct a normal school of elementary instruction at Turin. He was opposed by Bishop Fransoni, with whom Cavour was later to have such a bitter contest, but his appointment and his public lectures were hailed with enthusiasm by the Lombard journalists as a fresh sign of the spirit of liberalism that was transforming the institutions of Piedmont. The *Rivista europea* declard that Aporti's was a "mind truly Italian, all intent on the intellectual and moral progress of the people, and of that mass of struggling affections of every sort which have need of development, of excitement and restraint and of rules by which they may be directed to noble action and redound to the good of the country."[92]

These are warm and, it would seem, dangerously patriotic words, but by the time they were written there can be no doubt that the *asili* had been inscribed on the banner of liberal nationalism. Massimo d'Azeglio, in *Gli ultimi casi di Romagna* (1846) defined the issue and the position of the schools. "Why be opposed openly or covertly to every attempt to improve the education, the instruction of the people? I know why, let me say it also here: because in these efforts it is thought that there is a vast design of the liberals to change the state. But, let me repeat, do they [the reactionaries at Rome] believe that they run greater risks than Austria? If they confessed this, would it not be the most damag-

[89] *Rivista*, 1838, I, Pt. 3, 509.
[90] *Annali*, 1840, LXIV, 242–244.
[91] *Rivista*, n. s., 1843, I, Pt. 3, 381.
[92] Letter of Gabrio Spinoli to Signor Calvi, *Rivista*, n. s., 1844, II, Pt. 2, 300–303.

ing of all confessions? Is it not perhaps too shameful that while they
make war on Aporti, on his Manual,[93] on his schools, they permit the
censor to pass *The Book of Art,* books on dreams to win the lottery,
The Guessing Cricket, etc., etc.?"[94] The national consecration of the
asili d'infanzia was completed when they received the approval of Pius
IX, who, as if in answer to d'Azeglio's challenge, opened his realm to
the founding of such schools on the same footing as those of the Lombardo-Venetian Kingdom.

Religion and morality, a charity making for self-help, the union of all
classes of society in a philanthropic endeavor: these were the elements
of the movement that supported and disseminated the *asili d'infanzia.*
Although the idea was imported from Scotland, the journals repeatedly
referred to the movement, and to the institution itself, as having a peculiarly Italian character.[95] The feeling seems to have sprung from the
circumstance that the movement for the *asili d'infanzia* was one that
gathered up and harmonized a large number of ideas and impulses that
were then active in Italian life. Support of the infant schools drew men
and women from all classes and all the divisions of Italy into activity
for the public good, under an initiative that came from themselves and
not from the Church or the Government. The schools enjoyed the support of the liberal clergy. Such patronage at once served to exorcise
the alarm of the conservatives and define the position which Italian
liberalism took, opposed to ecclesiasticism but open to the inspiration
and even the guidance of a fraternal Catholicism, a religion of active
charity. There is no reason to question the sincerity of the Italian liberals in this alliance with religion. Perhaps the strongest pledge of
their sincerity was the prevalent feeling that Catholicism itself was profoundly Italian. In the movement for the *asili d'infanzia,* the liberals
had a vision of the whole nation, in a field in which it was safe from
violent interference, uniting to take into its own hands the education of
its children. The feeling with which their hearts welcomed it is reflected
in the fervent words of Giuseppe Sacchi: ". . . to this noble sacrifice
of thought and affection it is well that a country and a people, which
after so many years of peace now feels more than ever reviving in its

[93] d'Azeglio's note: The *"Manuale di educazione ed ammaestramento per le
scuole infantili . . .* was opposed by the Roman Curia because inspired by the
criteria of a Protestant, the Scotsman Robert Owen, head of a Saint Simonian
sect, but really from hostility to sincere and liberal teaching. Furthermore,
Aporti who in 1845 had been called to Turin to teach in the university there
was persecuted by the Archbishop Fransoni who prohibited the clergy from
attending the lectures."
[94] d'Azeglio, *Ultimi casi,* p. 84.
[95] *Ricoglitore italiano e straniero,* 1834, I, 386; *Rivista,* n. s., 1845, III, Pt. 1,
89-90; 1847, V, Pt. 2, 477.

heart the ancient flame of its divine redemption, be incessantly stimulated."[96]

The educational program promoted by the liberal journals was not confined to the *asili d'infanzia*. It embraced science as well as religion and educational philanthropy. The liberals were persuaded that the "progress" of their country required an indoctrination in applied science. Religion and science: these were the poles between which they sought and thought they had found a national, a peculiarly Italian synthesis. To "modernize" instruction was to introduce technical instruction.

One of their objectives was to introduce vocational or technical studies into the existing schools, whether public or private. The gymnasia, the lycées and the private boarding schools and colleges were still dominated by the tradition of classical studies, and this tradition the journalists vigorously attacked. The situation to be reformed is well illustrated by the case of Giovanni Battista Jacini, Junior, gentleman-farmer of Casalbuttano and father of the celebrated Count Stefano Jacini. Wishing to give his sons a secular and technical education he found it necessary to send them abroad, to the famous school of Fellemburg at Hofwyl, Switzerland. But in 1834 the Government compelled him to recall them.[97] Some concessions to the practical were made in the curriculum of the gymnasia, but they seemed insufficient to the journalists. What Romagnosi and his followers wished was a course of studies in harmony with "the clear and irrefragable theorems of the moral and intellectual development of man"—"a course as ordered and as certain as the art of cultivating silkworms. Public instruction which is supported by taxes has as its aim the preparation of men who may usefully serve the public, placing *good taste in literature* as the VARNISH on its work."[98]

Lombardy-Venetia, all Italy indeed, was an agricultural community and the need of practical instruction in agronomy was especially felt. Pleading for this in 1840 a collaborator of the *Rivista europea* pointed out that the class of farm managers sent their sons to the free schools where they were prepared to overcrowd "the ways of industry, the fine arts, and science." "All of our schools lead to university studies; why blame the ignorant fathers if they send their sons into these, when the wise also send theirs there?"[99] Carlo Ravizza represented his "good

[96] "Studi sulla pubblica beneficenza," *Rivista*, n. s., 1845, III, Pt. 2, 37.

[97] Jacini, *Un conservatore*, I, 13. The *Conciliatore* had called attention to the school at Hofwyl. *Conciliatore*, February 4, 1819, No. 45, pp. 177–178; August 8, 1819, No. 98, pp. 395–396.

[98] The words quoted are Romagnosi's in a note to an article describing the public school system of Lombardy-Venetia. *Annali*, 1835, XLIII, 245, note 1.

[99] G. Sega in *Rivista*, 1840, III, Pt. 1, 254.

curate of the Brianza" as discouraging parishioners who wished to send a promising boy off to the gymnasia of the cities *"to study,* that is: to learn the dead languages and to scratch out both his eyes in the thicket of grammar taught at the wrong time." The good curate tried to persuade the proprietor of the local silk mill not to send his lad, Henry, to a college "to have him commence the gymnasial studies." Latin would disgust him. What was the alternative? "In two or three years it will be time enough to send your little boy to Milan, to the home of a good relative who will mother him, and when he has learned the science of commerce, double writing, accounting, agriculture, the more necessary languages, you can bring him back to yourself, and place in his hands this craft of yours," and have him as a prop for your declining years. Behind the attack on the classics was the conception of a new social order, dominated by bourgeois interests, in which even the nobles must equip themselves for a strenuous competition. This is the gist of Count Serristori's argument for the reform of the colleges frequented by young nobles. If the schools were reformed, the reformers "will still have to contend with the stupid insinuations of their parents, who (for the most part) prefer to see their sons dance, play, sing, draw, etc., than to have them versed in letters, philosophy, and physical sciences. And this, alas! is true. Such is the ignorance and frivolity of a great part of the Italian nobility."[100] When a free course in chemistry applied to the "arts" was introduced into one of the lycées of Milan in 1834, Giuseppe Sacchi praised the reform as one answering well to the peculiar needs of the age and of the country, which had, he said, too many poets, doctors, philosophers, and the like, and too few "good artificers, skilled merchants, enlightened entrepreneurs."[101] As the demands of mechanical industry began to be felt more urgently, even the elementary schools did not escape criticism, although their curriculum included the elements of vocational instruction. Like so many other reforms agitated by the journals, the demand for technical education in the schools was given national scope and expression by the Agronomical and Technical Section of the Scientific Congresses. At the Venice meeting in 1847 "was proclaimed the necessity of introducing into the con-

---

[100] L. Serristori, "Considerazioni economico-morali applicate ad alcuni pubblici stabilimenti: collegi e convitti di giovani nobili," *Annali,* 1844, LXXXII, 188–189. The other side of the medal is presented in a picture of "Milan in the Autumn of 1842": The general spirit of education, instruction, and of association which goes on diffusing itself everywhere, true character of the present age, will gradually dissipate from the heads of so many young and well-to-do Milanesi, the frivolous ideas of a rosy and nugatory life, without its being necessary that a new Parini return to flagellate them." G. F. Baruffi in the *Rivista,* n. s., 1843, I, Pt. 1, 365.
[101] *Ricoglitore italiano e straniero,* 1834, I, 393.

servatories for boys and the elementary schools practical instruction in agriculture and the trades."[102]

As early as 1827 the Lombard journalists began to agitate the desirability of establishing special technical schools.[103] Lombardy had had them under the Napoleonic régime, but the Austrian Government did not include them in the system of public instruction projected in 1818. Only the asylums for deaf-mutes, orphans and foundlings, and the reform schools supplied vocational training.[104] In 1831 the languishing Imperial and Royal Institute organized a permanent exhibition of machinery at the Brera in Milan; but this half-measure did not content the *Annali,* which declared that the only radically helpful step would be the founding of free technical schools.[105] The lack of them seemed to the liberal journalists a very grave obstacle to the industrial progress of Italy.[106] As far as Lombardy-Venetia was concerned their hopes were deferred until December 1841 when a technical school founded by the Government was opened in Milan.[107] In 1843 a similar school was opened at Venice. The journals had followed the planning of these schools and their founding was celebrated as an event;[108] but by 1841 a sense of the importance of vocational schools as necessary to equip the Italians for their rightful place in the economic life of the century had developed to such an extent that the two schools set up by Austria seemed inadequate. They were immediately subjected to criticism as not sufficiently practical and as failing to recognize the special need of Italy for agricultural training; only a true Polytechnic Institute modelled on those of Vienna and Paris would satisfy the requirements of Lombardy-Venetia; such schools were not widely enough diffused in Italy at large.[109]

By 1841 the Liberal agitation had progressed so far that it is doubtful whether the journals would have been content with any program of education devised by the Government. Technical education had taken

[102] Report of the Congress, *Rivista,* n. s., 1847, V, Pt. 2, 481.

[103] "We meanwhile flatter ourselves that we shall see adopted also in the Lombardo-Venetian Kingdom the system of schools of arts and crafts, which will rival those of other nations." Romagnosi in the *Annali,* 1827, XII, 152.

[104] This was the situation described by the noted educator L. A. Parravicini as existing in Italy at large as well as in Lombardy-Venetia, as late as 1843. *Annali,* 1843, LXXVI, 90.

[105] *Annali,* 1831, XXVIII, 313–314.

[106] See *Annali,* 1838, LVIII, 191; 1839, LX, 233; *Rivista,* 1838, I, Pt. 3, 524.

[107] *Rivista,* n. s., 1843, I, Pt. 2, 37.

[108] *Annali,* 1838, LVIII, 213; *Rivista,* 1839, II, Pt. 1, 70; *Annali,* 1840, LXIV, 307–314; *Rivista,* 1840, III, Pt. 1, 128–152; *Annali,* 1843, LXXVI, 37–60; 90–91; *Rivista,* n. s., 1843, I, Pt. 2, 34–42.

[109] *Annali,* 1842, LXXIII, 184, note 1; 1843, LXXVI, 90–91; *Rivista,* n. s., 1843, I, Pt. 2, 41–42; 156–158.

e on the program of reforms which they were intent on having
ians carry out on their own initiative and by their own efforts.
technical schooling and the whole matter of giving the public a
scientific indoctrination, the progress made by private initiative, urged
on by the journalists, had indeed been considerable.

In his *asili d'infanzia* Aporti emphasized from the beginning the
acquisition of useful habits and useful knowledge,[110] and the infant
schools immediately suggested a method of giving instruction "in geometry and mechanics applied to the arts and crafts for poor artisans."[111]
Infant schools leading into more advanced instruction of a technical
nature were created by mill-owners for the children of their operatives.[112] Meanwhile a crop of Sunday, holiday and night schools had
sprung up, for the benefit of children employed on the farm or in shop
or factory.[113] At a higher level several schools of applied science had
come into existence in Lombardy and Piedmont.[114] At the same time
some of the private colleges were introducing scientific and practical
courses into their curriculum.[115]

[110] Among other kinds of familiar things the children were taught to name in
Italian "objects of natural history employed in agriculture or the arts." *Annali*,
1832, XXXII, 98.

[111] *Ibid.*, p. 99. In 1838 Baron Corvaia suggested that the lack of technical
schools might be supplied by extending and developing the *asili*. *Annali*, 1838,
LVIII, 192. In 1844 a lawyer of Brescia obtained authorization to set up a
technical school in that city for the instruction of children up to the age of 18
based on the methods of the *asili*. *Rivista*, n. s., 1844, II, Pt. 2, 406–408. In
1847 a plan was on foot in Milan to create a continuation school for the *asili*
of the capital, for children of the working class aged 6 to 9, to prepare them
for industrial life. It was to be formed by the consolidation of three existing
Conservatori della puerizia which had been made possible by the donations of
Enrico Mylius. The *Annali* bespoke the coöperation of manufacturers, and of
the doctors, lady-visitors, priests and others who had assisted with the *asili*.
Annali, 1847, XCIII, 76–80.

[112] For example at the Cini mills at San Marcello, Tuscany, and the mill of
Signor Molino in the Royal Park at Turin, described by Petitti, *Annali*, 1844,
LXXIX, 145–179. Similar schools were connected with factories in Milan.
Annali, 1847, XCIII, 183–184.

[113] *Annali*, 1831, XXX, 96; 1847, XCIII, 183–184; 1833, *Bulletino*, pp. 21–23;
Ricoglitore italiano e straniero, 1834, I, 376. By 1846 there were 8 night schools
in Milan with 21 masters, and 1082 pupils; and in the holiday schools of Milan,
Bergamo, Lodi and Crema more than 6000 pupils of both sexes. *Annali*, 1847,
XCIII, 183–184.

[114] At Milan the schools of Professor Tosoni and Signor Cavenago, and the
Istituto Racheli. *Annali*, 1838, LVIII, 212–213; *Rivista*, 1838, I, Pt. 2, 300–
312; 1841, IV, Pt. 1, 140; n. s., 1843, I, Pt. 2, 42. In Piedmont the Bellini
Institute at Novara and the school supported by the Society for the Advancement
of the Arts, Crafts and Agriculture of Biella. L. A. Parravicini, "Notizie sulle
scuole techniche in Italia," *ibid.*, pp. 34–42.

[115] Ravizza, p. 248.

But for writers stirred by "the debasement and misery of the uncoun-selled multitudes, on whose labors the vivifying ray of science does not shine," and by the loss to Italy of the productive power which their lack of scientific subsidies involved,[116] it was not enough that practical science should be imparted to the next generation. The need was so pressing that the adult population ought to be immediately instructed. A "Polytechnic Athenaeum," with lectures and reading rooms open to the public, "to give life to the study of the sciences, and to promote manufactures," had risen in the center of Confalonieri's vision of a progressive Milan. In the revival of liberal agitation after 1824 there was a general effort to diffuse at once a knowledge of the applications of science. The remarkable crop of journals devoted to useful infor-mation and applied science, and the increasing attention given to these interests by the literary reviews, constituted a considerable addition to the type of literature desired. The translation of books of popular sci-ence from the French was applauded.[117] Books with such titles as *l'Educatore di se stesso*[118] were reviewed with praise. The journal of popular readings for adults which is best represented by Valerio's *Letture di famiglia* did not flourish in Lombardy;[119] but the Lombard journalists were actively interested in this type of publication as a means of diffusing "useful knowledge" among the people, and they kept their readers informed of its progress in the other states of Italy.

The journalists interested themselves further in the compilation of dictionaries and popular encyclopedias which would give Italians terms in which to discuss the new discoveries of "civilization" and a compen-dium of what was known. The *Conciliatore* attacked Vincenzo Monti's work in revising the Dictionary of the Accademia della Crusca as a mis-placed effort when the Italian vocabulary was still lacking in words with which to name the most important facts of modern life.[120] The *Annali* advanced the idea of creating a "New Dictionary," to be financed by a joint-stock company, and edited by a "Philological Industrial Associa-

[116] Carlo Cattaneo, reviewing *Esposizione d'industria e delle belle arti a Torino. —Notizie sulla patria industria di Carlo Ing. Giulio, relator centrale* (Torino, Stamperia reale, 1844), in *Rivista*, n. s., 1845, III, Pt. 1, 608.

[117] For example the *Rivista europea* praised G. Arpesani, C. Porro, and G. Balsamo Crivelli for translating a *Corso elementare di storia naturale* by F. S. Beudant, Milne Edwards and A. Jussieu (Milan, Vallardi, 1846), a work origin-ally emanating from the University of Paris. *Rivista*, n. s., 1847, V, Pt. 1, 255–258.

[118] By Angelo Fava, a collaborator of the *Rivista europea*, published in 1847 (Milan, Turati), in fourteen instalments. *Rivista*, n. s., 1847, V, Pt. 2, 361–366.

[119] The *Cosmorama pittorico* (see above, pp. 191–192) was a magazine that approached this type. The editor announced that "the *Cosmorama* can go into the hands of persons of every age and sex [and] can be good and safe reading for young men, to whom the special care of our century is devoted."

[120] See above, p. 154.

tion," which would contain these useful words. "All Italy is astir with industrialism. . . . The technical language of Europe shows that today we [Italians] abound in words that are useless to associative well-being and that we lack those which are so necessary to name the objects that enrich and embellish life and multiply its comforts." The writer further advocated the compilation of new lexicons which would enable Italians to take advantage of technical works in other languages, "which for lack of the [equivalent Italian] words remain untranslated."[121] In the 'forties popular Italian encyclopedias began to appear. In 1842 Paolo Lampato publishd at Milan an *Enciclopedia popolare*,[122] in weekly instalments running to 12,000 copies, which to the *Rivista europea* seemed to fail of its aim and that of the journalists because it went over the heads of "the people," that is: "the workingmen and servants in the cities, the small proprietors in the country, not to mention the peasants."[123] At the same time Pomba began publishing at Turin his famous *Nuovo Enciclopedia Popolare*.[124] The journalistic criticism of this work and its consequences deserve some attention, as illustrating the deeper purpose and outlook of the liberal journalists.

Francesco Predari, of Milan, writing in the *Rivista europea,* criticized Pomba's effort on the ground that in it "the Italians, presenting themselves to Europe in an encyclopedia composed almost entirely of foreign borrowings, have solemnly produced a document of their incapacity to do what all other nations of Europe now know how to do," namely: to present in their encyclopedias "a thermometer, so to speak, of their civilization and of their knowledge." Pomba immediately took up the gauntlet, and replied that he had made a most diligent effort to attain precisely this desideratum. He had combed the peninsula "from the Alps to Lilybaeum" for contributors, and then had enlisted the Italians living abroad—in vain. "The geographical condition of Italy, its division into little states, municipal rivalries and jealousies, party hatred, the lack of unity in public instruction, the will in those who cannot, and the power in those who will not, which discourages talent and generates laziness, rivalries (incurable plague among us) in the professions and trades, that mutual and assiduous opposition which thwarts the conspiracy of intellectual forces, the lack of a fixed and

[121] Michele Parma in the *Annali*, 1839, LIX, 360, 365–366. The *Eco della borsa* seconded this project of a "Dizionario tecnologico," and urged its readers to consult Parma's article. *Eco*, 1839, III, 2.

[122] *Enciclopedia popolare, o Collezione di letture amene ed utili ad ogni persona.*

[123] *Rivista*, 1842, V, Pt. 2, 239–240. The *Annali* on the other hand reviewed it with approval as a necessary complement to elementary education and as likely to take the wind out of the sails of the demagogue. *Annali*, 1840, LXV, 5–6.

[124] *Nuova enciclopedia popolare . . . opera compilata sulle migliori in tal genere, inglesi, tedesche e francesi ecc.* Reviewed by F. Predari, *Rivista europea,* 1842, V, Pt. 1, 316–342.

common center to accommodate and arrest the national mind, such as exists in London or Paris"—all these things made a representative Italian encyclopedia seem Utopian to Pomba. Faced with such a situation Signor Pomba declared that he had based his encyclopedia on a painstaking comparison of the best in other countries, meanwhile seeking to make it as Italian as possible. Even if he had succeeded in obtaining the full collaboration necessary, he believed that the result would not have satisfied such critics as Predari. The French and the English (on whom, presumably, it was most desirable to make an impression) did not read Italian; besides, "it is undeniable that in the matter of literary and scientific works in some respects we are below the level of many other nations." Confronted with this discouraging situation, Pomba had sought not "to make known to foreigners what is being done in Italy, but to give an account to our country of what is happening abroad in the way of progress, in order to move Italian minds to a praiseworthy emulation."[125]

Pomba's reply was a challenge to the pride of the Italian liberals and to their growing confidence in the revival of Italian civilization. His critic Predari took up the challenge and undertook to show that Pomba was mistaken—with very remarkable consequences. He went to Turin and entered into collaboration with Pomba in securing a staff which would carry out his idea of a truly Italian encyclopedia, and which at the same time accomplished an even more remarkable result in promoting an active coöperation between men of different social classes for a patriotic end. Predari found an invaluable helper in Cesare Balbo, and to his own surprise discovered at Turin, in Balbo's home, the group of liberals who were launching the famous Agrarian Association and shaping the new Piedmont of Cavour and "the great decade."[126] Pomba coöperated valiantly, cancelled the first instalments of his earlier edition, and replaced them *gratis* in the hands of the original subscribers. The new edition was a great success. Three thousand copies were exhausted in less than a year, and a reprint was necessary. In the *Rivista europea* Predari then acknowledged that Pomba had triumphantly met all of his criticisms by creating an encyclopedia derived from the best Italian sources, and praised him for his honesty, courage, and patriotism in taking the risks necessary to accomplish this result.[127]

[125] Risposta di G. Pomba e Compagnia . . . alle critiche del Sig. F. Predari, *Rivista*, 1842, V, Pt. 2, *Appendice*, pp. 1–29.

[126] Predari tells of his experience in *I primi vagità della libertà italiana in Piemonte* (Milan, 1861), pp. 21–22, 43–44, an invaluable source, now unfortunately almost inaccessible.

[127] *Rivista*, n. s., 1844, II, Pt. 2, 197–202. The title of the fresh attempt was: *Nuova enciclopedia popolare, ovvero Dizionario generale di scienza, lettere, arti, storia, geografia, ecc. ecc.* (Turin, Pomba, 1842. Prima edizione, dispense 104. Seconda edizione, 1844, dispense 8).

The popular and instructive literature which the journals reviewed and sought to stimulate included books for children and the young—a literary species just coming into existence in this period.[128] The well-known liberal exile, Bianca Milesi Mojon, translated Maria Edge-worth's *First Lessons*, in several volumes, and A. Lucia Barbauld's *Hymns in Prose for Children* (from the 16th English edition), and herself prepared a *Prime letture pe' fanciulli di tre in quattro anni* (Primer for Children Aged Three to Four).[129] In 1835 Achille Mauri and Carlo Grolli began publishing at Milan a journal for the young, entitled *Il Giovedì*.[130] In 1837 Cesare Cantù brought out his *Letture giovanili*, which for a long time enjoyed an immense popularity, and which were hailed as a pioneer effort of their type.[131] Such literature as this was moral rather than scientific in content, but it was all in the movement to produce reading for the young that would be edifying as well as informative, without being religious. At the same time there was a new outpouring of literature for the teachers of children. Giuseppe Sacchi's regular review of "Works on Popular Education" in the *Rivista europea* shows a steady increase in the proportion of these being published in Italy.[132]

If the liberal journalists favored the writing of books for children in the language of childhood, they were equally intent on evoking a literature in the language of "the people." If the country was to benefit by teaching the poor to read, good books must be put in their hands. In their conception of good books for the people, their basic ideas on education reappear. The reading supplied should contain useful information; and its moral content should be such as to encourage the idea

---

[128] Defendente Sacchi, "Della necessità di scrivere libri per i fanciulli," a review of four books on education published at Milan in 1832–1833, *Annali*, 1833, XXXIV, 17–33.

[129] All of these books were reviewed by the *Ricoglitore italiano e straniero*, 1834, II, 315–316.

[130] Pirotta, Milan. I have seen only Vol. I, Nos. 1–26, November 5, 1835—April 28, 1836. Each number contains a "moral article," with a title such as: "For Young Students," "Love of Religion," etc.; a "historical article"; "biography"; a "moral story," with titles such as: "The Boaster," "Filial Piety," etc.; a "historical tale," with such titles as "Maldonata, or the Grateful Lioness," "George Byron and Robert Peel"; "natural history"; "travels"; and "course of study for young people"; "inventions," for example: "Eyeglasses," "Poetry," "Italian Literature," etc.

[131] The titles of the first three volumes (Milan, Gaspare Truffi e Socii, 1837) were *Il Buon Fanciullo, racconti d'un maestro elementare, Il giovanotto drizzato alla bontà, al sapere, e all'industria*, and *Il galantuomo*. For their history, and strictures by a later contemporary, see Francesco De Sanctis, *La letteratura _ _ _'ana nel secolo XIX* (Napoli, Morano, 1902), Lezione XVI, "Cesare Cantù letteratura popolare," pp. 260–273.

Rivista, n. s., 1845, III, Pt. 1, 78–93; 189–204; 470–493; 1846, IV, Pt. 1, 44; Pt. 2, 671–691.

that "Heaven helps him who helps himself."[133] The reading that must be displaced, as far as the peasants were concerned, is described as consisting of "certain trashy books which were handed down from genera-tion to generation in every family: calendars with prognostications of the seasons and the crops, horoscopes of good and evil fortune, accounts of horrors and works of the evil one, recipes of quack doctors, books of dreams, black arts to determine the lucky number of the lottery, and some others, which, being full of the enterprises of paladins, sometimes heat the heads of little peasants, and make them scornful of their proper condition."[134] Very popular were the almanacs, or *strenne*, circulated at New Year's. The *strenna* ranged in form all the way from the cheap farmer's almanac to the peculiar and often very expensive and elaborate literary confections which the well-to-do presented to each other as a New Year's greeting. The journalists never tired of criticizing the poor almanacs for the quackery and cheap romance which they dispensed to the poor, or satirizing the expensive ones for their elaborate frivolity. In time they perceived the use to which both kinds could be turned as a means of communicating sound and useful information and quickening a patriotic consciousness. A *strenna* for the cultured public which realized the liberal ideal was the *Presagio*, first published in 1835 by a band of young men that included some of the founders of the *Rivista europea*[135]—an enterprise that lasted only two years.[136] The reviews carefully noted encouraging improvements in the almanacs for the people. *Il Nipote di Sesto Caio Bacelli*, published in 1843, was

[133] Spreafico, in his essay on the Brianza, affirmed that this belief was becoming more common among the peasants of the Brianza: astrology, witches and magicians had disappeared, and weather predictions based on phases of the moon and charms of all sorts were disappearing. Spreafico, p. 170. This sounds optimistic but perhaps reflects a tendency.

[134] Ravizza, pp. 146–147. Spreafico was more specific in his account of the books that circulated in the country (he also was writing of the Brianza): "besides Christian doctrine, and some good book received as a prize . . . [they] consist of the *Sette Trombe*, the *Prato Fiorito*, astrological almanacs, the *Avventure di Bertoldo e Bertoldino*, and the *Cabala del Lotto.*"

[135] Cesare Correnti, Cesare and Rinaldo Giulini, Andrea Verga, Pietro Rotondi, Antonio Zoncada, Pietro Molinelli, Giacomo Durini, Attilio Carli, Giulio Spini. Amato Amati, *Carlo Ravizza: studio biografico* (Milano, *Vallardi*, 1896), p. 161. Amati says that the *Presagio* was published in 1836–1837. Actually it appeared in 1835. It was reviewed by "M. S." in the *Ricoglitore italiano e straniero*, 1835, Pt. 1, 147.

[136] It then passed into the hands of a certain "laborious Cremonesi." "This *Strenna* ought to change its title," said Gottardo Calvi in 1839, "inasmuch as its directive purpose and all its collaborators changed after the first two years." *Rivista*, 1839, II, Pt. 1, 135–136. "*Presagio* is a beautiful word and one of good omen, and sounds well when it unites a number of persons who show a common intent and accord. Here there is none, so that no presage can be got out of it." *Rivista*, 1838, I, Pt. 1, 141.

praised as a model: it introduced maxims from Poor Richard, exhortations to use the savings banks, and so forth, under such captions as "Domestic Economy," "Industry," "Education," "Household Medicine," "Agriculture," "History of the Country," and "Morality in Deed" —all in popular form and in rich Tuscan.[137] The liberal and patriotic ideal of the *strenna* was embodied in the famous *Nipote del Vesta-Verde* which Cesare Correnti slipped past the censor and published on January 1, 1848.[138] It contained in popularized form the whole program of the liberal journals of the time—"notions historical and geographical about Italy"; an account of the popular schools and charities; gas illumination at Milan; "progress" typified by the picture of a railroad train and discussed in a colloquy between "The Young Man," "The Old Man," and "Meneghino";[139] an answer to the question "Of what use are the Scientific Congresses to the Poor?"[140] Not content with this encyclopedic or fugitive literature, the Lombard journalists desired to see their ideals of popular literature embodied in "The People's Book," and one of them prepared a report on this subject for the Milan Congress of Scientists in 1844. He proposed an association to prepare the *Libro del Popolo* as a national enterprise endorsed and supported by the Congress. His idea was not carried out, but the proposal is a measure of the interest in the subject among the liberals.[141]

While adequate schools and books were still lacking in Italy, there was another method of reaching the adult public much in favor with the Lombard journalists. This was popular instruction in the form of public lectures, particularly for the purpose of disseminating a knowledge of science and its applications—the method suggested in Confalonieri's idea of an Athenaeum. It first took concrete shape in Milan in the early 'forties with the founding by patriotic individuals of a Civic

[137] G. D. B., "Un esempio di un almanacco utile e popolare," *Rivista*, n. s., 1843, I, Pt. 1, 76-78. Editorial note (p. 88): "This means of instructing the people through almanacs was put in practice some ten years ago in France by a National Society, with the annual publication of the *Almanach de France*, treasure of popular knowledge, which is sold at a very low price, and which was very appropriately given as epigraph that saying of Emile de Girardin: "Quinze millions de Français n'apprennent que par les almanachs, les destins de l'Europe, les lois de leur pays, les progrès des sciences, des arts et de l'industrie."

[138] 30,000 copies were immediately sold. *Rivista*, n. s., 1847, V, Pt. 2, 616. In a letter to Costanza Arconati, November 27, 1847, Antonio Trotti tells how the censor deleted the words "sotto il cessato Regno d'Italia" from the funerary inscription of P. Girolamo. "At the same time that it rejoices in such puerilities it allows the publication of an almanac which contains a summary of the history of Italy for popular consumption, and which has been exhausted in an instant. But they have hastened to forbid a second edition of it." Malvezzi, pp. 202-203.

he comedy incarnation of the Milanese.

Nipote del Vesta-Verde. Strenna popolare per l'anno 1848. Anno I. Prezzo ni 50. Milan, Vallardi (1847).

rico Tazzoli, "Il libro del popolo," *Rivista*, n. s., 1844, II, Pt. 2, 681-690.

Museum, the Mylius Institute, and the Society for the Encouragement of the Arts and Crafts of Milan.[142] At the Museum Professor Jan in 1842 inaugurated a course of lectures on science, sketching its new vistas, and in 1845 young Filippo De Filippi, a collaborator of the *Rivista europea*, taking his place, began giving a two-year course in Mineralogy, Anatomy and Physics, with demonstrations based on the collections of the Museum. The Mylius Institute was founded March 29, 1842 "to enable workingmen to profit by their hours of repose by following public readings in technology and art and by observing appropriate experiments."[143] The journalists followed with enthusiasm the progress of the lecture movement at Milan and in the neighboring state of Piedmont.[144] At Milan it received in 1841 the support of an association which seemed to the liberal journalists to open bright vistas of progress towards the fulfilment of their patriotic hopes. This was the Società d'incoraggiamento per le arti e i mestieri di Milano.[145]

The Society for the Encouragement of the Arts and Crafts in Milan was due to the initiative of an association of businessmen, journalists and representatives of the professions, prominent among whom were Carlo Cattaneo, Enrico Mylius, and Professor Antonio Kramer.[146] The idea of endowing such an institution seems to have grown out of the existence of a fund contributed by the merchants of Milan for the relief of the cholera victims of 1836, and was tactfully associated by the founders with the thought of a continuing expression of "the gratitude of the commerce of Milan to His Majesty, the Emperor and King Ferdinand I, for his visit of coronation to Milan in 1838."[147] The object of the society was to promote industry by the two-fold method of awarding prizes and offering instruction. Now this was precisely the scope of two institutions founded by the Government at the same time: the Istituto Lombardo-Veneto, which the Government had rehabilitated in 1841 with the object of "promoting prosperity" by the award of prizes;[148] and the long-delayed technical schools at Milan and Venice.[149]

[142] The *Museo Civico* was endowed by Giuseppe De Cristoforis and Giorgio Jan. The collections were reorganized in 1844, to improve them for instructional purposes. In 1847 the Civic Museum was, in the opinion of the *Rivista europea*, "one of the finest and most vital glories of Milan." *Rivista*, n. s., 1847, V, Pt. 1, 82.

[143] *Annali*, 1842, LXXII, 286.

[144] See their reports of Aporti's course on method at Turin, and the long report by Petitti on Professor Antonio Scialoja's lectures on political economy in the University of Turin, *Rivista*, n. s., 1846, IV, Pt. 2, 265–310.

[145] For the best account of this organization, see Pugliese, pp. 430–436.

[146] *Rivista*, n. s., 1847, V, Pt. 1, 84.

[147] *Annali*, 1839, LX, 241.

[148] *Giornale dell'istituto Lombardo-Veneto*, 1841, p. 8.

[149] These schools were announced as part of the largess of the Emperor on the occasion of his coronation in Milan in 1838. *Annali*, 1838, LVIII, 326–327.

In this case private initiative was stepping promptly and boldly to the side of the Government to supplement its action.

The Milanese society was modelled on foreign associations for the same purpose which had sprung up in Germany, Austria and France.[150] Its promoters obtained the approval of the Government and the patronage of the Emperor. It began its activities in 1841 and in support of these the Society received an annual subvention from the Chamber of Commerce[151] and an income derived from interest on an invested endowment and from the contributions of members, who at times numbered more than four hundred.[152] The President of the Society was Enrico Mylius, a name honored as that of "a loyal adoptive son," and its Secretary, the patriot publicist Carlo Cattaneo. At first its activity was confined to the offer of medals and subsidies to stimulate a desirable development of local industry.[153] But from the outset it was felt that the Society ought to enter the field of technical education.[154] Experience had shown the inefficacy of prizes, when what those who won them needed was instruction.[155] The Society took its first step as an educational institution in 1842 when the Mylius Institute was placed under its patronage.[156] Professor De Kramer was appointed to give the lectures on this foundation, and out of his course developed a modest "school of industrial chemistry," centering in a laboratory at the headquarters of the Society. The lectures, at first only for students, were thrown open to the public. Crowded halls attested their success.[157] "In the audience, besides physicians, pharmacists, engineers and naturalists, there were many pupils from our lycées, and, what is more important, many workingmen. In this way our people responds to those who would wish, nothing less, to close the elementary schools in order to open congrega-

---

[150] G. Calvi, in an article on the *Società d'incoraggiamento* of Milan, mentions as models the Industrial Institute of Berlin, the Industrial Society of Mühlhausen, the *Société d'encouragement* of Paris, the *Società per l'incoraggiamento dell' industria nell'Austria inferiore e nella Boemia. Rivista*, n. s., 1843, I, Pt. 2, 154. The *Société d'encouragement à l'industrie nationale* was really a scientific academy. Artz, p. 187.

[151] M. C. M., Camera di Commercio, cartella 823.

[152] *Annali*, 1842, LXXII, 281; *Rivista*, n. s., 1843, I, Pt. 2, 156, 158.

[153] G. Calvi, in 1843, announced the object of the Society as two-fold: to improve manufactures and useful arts in every branch, and "to excite a noble emulation among workingmen distinguished for talent, activity, and good behavior." The means were to be (1) premiums in cash and gifts, conferring honor and encouragement; (2) gratuitous subsidies to assist in introducing new methods or machines, and a solution of the industrial problems of the country; and (3) the distribution of medals and testimonials to workmen of blameless conduct or particular ability. *Ibid.*, p. 155.

[154] *Annali*, 1842, LXXII, 286; *Rivista*, n. s., 1843, I, Pt. 2, 158.

[155] *Rivista*, n. s., 1847, V, Pt. 1, 84; 745–746.

[156] *Annali*, 1844, LXXIX, 222.

[157] *Ibid.*

tions of flagellants and mendicants. Now everyone understands that for the poor as for the rich, instruction and work are two conditions of morality."[158]

In 1844 the Society took another step in the field of technical education when it extended its patronage to a course in the art of silk weaving, offered by Angelo Piazza, a master-weaver.[159] Three other courses, too ambitiously called "Schools," sprang up under the protection of the Society, one in "Industrial Physics," one in Geometry, and one in "Applied Mechanics."[160]

The influence of the instruction sponsored by the Society it would be impossible to estimate. It made a great stir in the journals, and the public lectures were crowded, in fact the hall for Professor Kramer's lectures had to be enlarged.[161] One gets the impression that attendance was fashionable, and it kept up as the years wnt on. In 1847 "the technical courses of the *Società d'incoraggiamento* were attended by more than four hundred and fifty listeners."[162] The journalists found encouraging the number of workingmen who used Professor Kramer's laboratory and took the examination in his course. Meanwhile, twenty of Angelo Piazza's auditors in his class on silk-weaving, which comprised from fifty to a hundred "workingmen, masters of shops, sons of small manufacturers and clerks, all obliged to write, to reckon, to solve problems, which are assigned to them every week," had succeeded in passing an excellent public examination.[163]

Such results were assuredly not of revolutionary importance. But the inauguration and the progress of the *Società d'incoraggiamento* seemed to the liberal journalists the incarnation of their hope for the awaken-

[158] *Rivista*, n. s., 1847, V, Pt. 1, 86. Carlo Cattaneo observed that such courses as De Kramer's had their value in making science popular, but that their solid and lasting benefit was to be expected from the eight or ten students who went into the professor's laboratory to conduct experiments. *Politecnico*, 1844, VII, 316–317.

[159] The report on Piazza, made by Gottardo Calvi as chairman of the Technical Committee of the *Cassa d'incoraggiamento*, was published in the *Rivista*, n. s., 1844, II, Pt. 2, 265–275. When Piazza's course had been authorized, both the *Annali* and the *Rivista* published an article by him entitled "Cenno sul setificio," which he had originally read as a paper at the Sixth Congress of Italian Scientists at Milan in 1844. *Annali*, 1844, LXXXII, 173–184; *Rivista*, n. s., 1844, II, Pt. 2, 276–286.

[160] The "School of Industrial Physics" "had no funds of its own and therefore no certain existence." A professor in the Lycée of the Porta Nuova had supplied the lectures, and lacking materials and apparatus for demonstrations had confined himself largely to theory. The other courses had been carried on by Professors Sarti and Jacini and were similarly criticized as too theoretical. *Rivista*, n. s., 1847, V, Pt. 1, 86–88.

[161] *Annali*, 1844, LXXIX, 313.

[162] *Annali*, 1847, XCIII, 196, note 1.

[163] *Annali*, 1847, XCIII, 196; *Rivista*, n. s., 1847, V, Pt. 1, 91.

ing of a genuine and realistic civic consciousness. The instructional activity of the Society awakened bright hopes for the future with respect to scientific and technical education. To the *Rivista europea* the "schools" of the Society formed "the first sketch of a politechnic university."[164] The proposal of the corresponding society at Bergamo to offer courses in metallurgy carried the idea a step further and suggested the need for a territorial distribution of such courses, to avoid wasteful duplications and to supply a well-rounded system of instruction within the realm.[165] At the same time, the success of the *Società d'incoraggiamento* of Milan, and of similar societies, gave birth to the idea that in them was to be found a national instrument which could serve in the cities the same purpose that the agricultural associations were achieving in the country. The idea found expression in the report of the Venice Congress of Scientists published in the *Rivista europea*.[166] The reporter admitted that the suggestion received little discussion at the Congress. But in view of the turn which the development of the agricultural associations, and in particular that of Piedmont, was taking at the time, the statement of the idea throws some light on the larger thought of the moderates, especially on their strong belief in the principle which this particular writer discerned as the basis of both types of association, namely: that of taking life where it was to be found, and attempting to organize only where growth, springing from practical interests, had already taken place.

The combination of public enterprises just reviewed was the program of liberal Italian patriotism in the making. It took shape gradually, emerging from a continuous discussion and a series of practical initiatives extending over a generation, and it came to be supported by the journals with a remarkable unanimity. In fact the grouping of objectives in that program became a kind of *cliché* in current discussions of "progress." To describe a citizen as a liberal patriot in 1835 it was only necessary to say: "He was the first promoter of the *asili d'infanzia*. . . . Where there were men zealous for the common prosperity he was never missing; he was among the subscribers to the national bank, the Silk Bank, the railroads, the excavation of minerals, in short of all the wise ambitions of an era weary of discord and eager for peace and fraternity."[167] "The year 1837!" exclaimed a reviewer in the *Ricoglitore italiano e straniero*, "Let us go back in thought only four or five years. What a difference! What progress! You remember what discussions

---

[164] *Rivista*, n. s., 1847, V, Pt. 1, 88.
[165] *Annali*, 1847, XCIII, 196; *Rivista*, n. s., 1847, V, Pt. 1, 746.
[166] *Rivista*, n. s., 1847, V, Pt. 2, 462–485.
[167] Carlo Cattaneo, "Necrologia di Luigi Azimonti," *Annali*, September, 1835, Supplemento.

were taking place then, and what the fruits of them were. Today? Today the talk is all of railroads, coal, infant schools; today one sees what was never seen before in Italy, spontaneous associations for charitable works, speculative associations dealing in fifties and sixties of millions. Oh, this is progress, both sure and indefeasible, and incalculable in its results." The objectives that took shape and were linked in the journals became the program of the Agronomical and Technological Section of the Congresses of Italian Scientists, and passed over into the writings of the moderate national leaders of 1844–1848, when events at last seemed propitious to the formation of a political party.

CHAPTER VI

FUNDAMENTAL ASSUMPTIONS

BEHIND the program outlined in the last chapter hovers a certain harmony of thought, a certain concord of principles, which if assumed to be present greatly increases the significance of that program in the history of Italy's political regeneration. That these principles, or their implications, were not openly proclaimed, is not surprising. One has always to bear in mind the shadow of the Austrian censor, who, as has become apparent, was actively if unintelligently suspicious, and who would have pounced on any overt reference to such political or semi-political motives as the publicists entertained as a pretext for suppression. Another reason for their reticence is in the very quality of their thought. As M. Julien Luchaire has observed, in his brilliant analysis of Vieusseux's *Antologia* considered as an expression of the Italian liberal program, the editors of that journal did not love too much "anything that does not tend to practical action." They welcomed only what could immediately be "transformed into opinion or will." "This entire absence of the 'metaphysical spirit,' as well as of dilettantism," he further remarks, "is a trait of originality."[1] It will at once be apparent how perfectly this description fits the Lombard journalists.

These writers shunned metaphysics and "great systems," and their reticence, their tone of practicality, has made it easy to assume that in the thought behind the journalism of the twenty years preceding 1848 there was no system at all. It is quite true that to ears accustomed to the tone of modern publicity much of the joy or impatience regarding material progress displayed by the Italian journalists may suggest nothing more significant than the emotions of a chamber of commerce. Is it to be assumed, then, that the *Annali,* in its ninety-five volumes published between 1824 and the Revolution of 1848, was directed merely by an interest in the promotion of bigger and better business for Italy? Or was there, behind all these enterprises in journalism, a statesman-like purpose, a far-seeing patriotism? The difficulty of detecting the "philosophy" of this literature, the failure of the writers to identify themselves with a school of thought or a recognized body of doctrine,

[1] Luchaire, pp. 225–226.

perhaps explains in part why their activity and the history of what it accomplished has received so little attention from historians of the Risorgimento. Did they see whither their efforts were tending? Was there, within the realm of the practical, a goal for the Italian nation towards which they were driving? If there was a "conspiracy in open daylight," when did it begin to be seen as such by the conspirators themselves.[2]

It is evident at once that the Lombard journalists whose work has been reviewed were all animated by a conviction of progress, of a forward movement of European civilization, and that they therefore proceeded from a principle diametrically opposed to the maxim of "govern and change nothing" on which the policy of Austria was based. Civilization in Europe had received a new impulse; it was advancing and changing at an ever-accelerated rate: this is the great fact which the journals proclaimed on every page; and their writers insisted, with increasing urgency, that the Italians could not afford to remain spectators of this movement. It was something inevitable; they could not shut it out. They must adjust themselves to it without delay or suffer a fatal loss.

But "progress" is a vague term; and it becomes necessary to sound the writers of the time and determine, if possible, what it meant to them, and what in their view adjustment to it implied for Italy.

In proclaiming the progress of "the century," the Lombard publicists believed that they were not influenced by a doctrine but announcing an inexorable fact. Giuseppe Pecchio, one of the collaborators of the *Conciliatore* expressed the idea when he wrote: "I laugh at the despotism which wishes to repel liberty while this, in its despite, comes in from every side by means of civilization. . . . If it fetters the liberty of the press, truth enters through the universities. If it persecutes or imprisons a university professor, civilization comes in with foreign commerce. If it adopts the prohibitive system to diminish this inconvenience, the roads, the roads alone, suffice to put minds in contact in a ferment."[3] The same idea came to dominate the mind of Federico Confalonieri and gave him courage when the shadow of the Spielberg was already creeping over his life. He expressed it in a remarkable letter to his discouraged friend Capponi on April 30, 1821:

[2] Typical is Tullo Massarani's characterization of the journalists of Cattaneo's group: they discoursed, he says, of "civil equality, of free trade, of prison systems, of agricultural improvements, of building reforms; they were pioneers, but of a progress pacific and legal; and perhaps only on the captain of that strong band flashed from afar as logically necessary an autonomous constitution." Massarani, *Tenca*, p. 21.

[3] Giuseppe Pecchio, *Osservazioni semi-serie di un esule sull'Inghilterra* (Lugano, G. Ruggia e Comp., 1831), pp. 142–143.

Your depression and despair for the future I do not fully share. The great controversy is not yet decided; on the contrary the great crisis itself which is in preparation shows how much conviction there is even at Laybach, that, in spite of their ephemeral victories, without a great radical crisis their cause would be lost; and the century would drag them by the irresistible moral force with which the young man tells the old man to vacate, and the present takes the place of the past. He that does not row continually against the current is snatched away by it; therefore, if they do not wish to condemn themselves to an eternal travail, it is necessary to find means to render the waters stagnant. To [accomplish] this violation of nature they bend their forces, but the greatest power of which they can dispose is not adequate to the undertaking. But if this immense and arbitrary effort should break down, all thrones might crumble in a day. . . . Inertia alone is barren of combinations; but a clash may always be fertile in events. In a few months, in a few years, we shall see the great cause agitated again, and decided, perhaps in our favor, perhaps against us; never without appeal for us, though perhaps so for our adversaries.[4]

This idea of an irresistible movement operating in their favor was continually present in the writings of the Lombard journalists. The *Rivista europea* declared that anyone could see that life was moving faster, even "without invoking *progress* and *les lumières* (words which have become almost ridiculous from their use by scribblers)."[5] The journalists disassociated themselves from the idealistic "party, [who] with the enthusiasm of souls enamored even to intoxication with the True and Good, dream theories and institutions by which this mortal life would be transformed into a sojourn of heavenly delights,"[6] and professed rather to take their position with reference to "the force of the times which stands over us inexorable."[7] Behind that force they saw a law—a "law of progress" ordained by "Providence," opposed to the human "law of immobility."[8] More often they refer to a law of "nature" or of "the century." "Nature does not permit any people placed in communication with other peoples to remain backward with impunity," cried Gaetano Recchi quoting Romagnosi in the *Annali* in 1843.[9] Again: "there is an immutable norm in nature and in human society, by which the moment one stops advancing, one begins to go

[4] Gallavresi, II, Pt. 1, 420–422.
[5] A. Fava, in *Rivista*, n. s., 1843, I, Pt. 1, 52.
[6] Antonio Guerrieri, "Della società Milanese di patronato pei carcerati e liberati dal carcere," *Rivista*, n. s., 1846, IV, Pt. 1, 586.
[7] Carlo Cattaneo, *Annali*, 1836, XLVIII, 331.
[8] "S—o," "Il movimento amministrativo e statistico del Piemonte nell'anno 1838," *Annali*, 1839, LIX, 256.
[9] "Cenni sul progetto di una lega doganale italiana," *Annali*, 1843, LXXVII, 291.

backwards, the moment one ceases to climb, descent begins, with the risk of a plunge."[10] "To be immovably conservative is not in the laws of nature which wills motion."[11] Progress is "the law of the century which cries to society: 'Forward! forward! or you die.' "[12] Furthermore (and the conception reflected in these words is important) this law was, for these writers, rooted in "the needs of the century, against which there is no force that can prevail."[13] By the end of the epoch the idea had become familiar that the meaning of the term "revolution" must be revised in the light of this conception of progress. "What is revolution?" asked the author of *L'Operaio*—"Almanac of Italy for the Instruction of the People"—in 1851. Who is right? The man who takes off his hat to it, or the man who hides his face from it in horror? Neither, he answered; the true *Revolution* is *Progress,* which is continuous. What is usually called Revolution results from the failure of governments to adapt their institutions to Progress.[14]

Represented as neither a dogma nor merely an aspiration but as a factual necessity, progress was identified in the minds of the Lombard writers with the revolution that was transforming European society in the first half of the nineteenth century. To refer to this as the Industrial Revolution would do an injustice to their conception unless the term is understood in a broad sense. What they saw was a vast movement of economic and intellectual expansion, of which the two great motive forces were free coöperative enterprise and scientific invention. The dominant centers of it were England and, to a lesser degree, France. Its manifestations were to be found in factories, steamships, railroads, gas illumination, iron bridges, scientific agronomy, joint-stock companies, expanding trade, rapid exchanges and economic imperialism; and no less in new scientific and philanthropic institutions and the technical and moral education of the masses. This is the revolution which Confalonieri tried to initiate in Lombardy with his gas-plant, his steamboat and his schools; and that which the band who edited the *Conciliatore* sought to project as the concomitant and background of the revolution

[10] *L'Economista*, August 1847, II, 94.

[11] Report of the Ninth Scientific Congress at Venice, in *Rivista*, n. s., 1847, V, Pt. 2, 474.

[12] Giorgio Barberi, "Lettere sul Piemonte: Lettera prima," *Rivista*, 1840, III, Pt. 2, 305. Cattaneo discussing Vico's theory of historical cycles found it absurd, with progress so manifest. "Our century has gone beyond the humanitarian doctrines of Vico with the two doctrines of progress and variety." Review of Ferrari, *Vico et l'Italie* (Paris, 1839), in *Politecnico*, 1839, II, 274. Stefano Jacini wrote in 1853 that that which distinguished the century was "the consciousness of progress" and man had thereby surprised "the secret of God."

[13] *Rivista*, n. s., 1844, II, Pt. 1, 180.

[14] *L'Operaio*, Secondo anno (Milano, Centenari e Compagnia, 1851).

which they desired to effect in Italian literature. In all its aspects and its bearings on the economic, intellectual and moral life of Italy, it was the theme of the *Annali* and the *Politecnico*; it took a large place in the vision of the *Rivista europea*; and it was the force behind the flood of "useful cognitions" that spread through all the popular literature of the epoch. The diffusion of practical scientific knowledge: it is this, said Giacinto Battaglia in his foreword to the *Indicatore lombardo,* that makes the journals "means of civilization."[15]

What is civilization? Battaglia defined it as "that power of progressive perfection, which is to be found in the human race"; to this "is due the vogue of the journals, as were the press, stenography, steam navigation, in short, all the means of material and intellectual communication among men."[16] The Lombard journalists in their eagerness to draw the Italians into the movement of the age came very near to a glorification of material and mechanical progress as the essence of civilization. They grew lyrical about steamships and railways, "those heroines of the age."[17] "Railroads: in them behold the greatest event of the day; everywhere money and securities fly; who can hope for, who can foresee, all the evil, all the good?"[18]

> We see the learning of nations take the place of that of individuals; we see the enlightened artisan erecting manufacturing establishments on every hand, on every hand the sailor commanding a heavy steamship which carries him into the bosom of the sea, the horse giving place to a swifter force, marvelous tunnels dug under the beds of vast rivers. . . . Modern philosophy does not need Lockes and Kants, but industrious men who will apply the mind to more elevated questions which at all times have been of interest to men. The Cockerills are the great men of our century! these John Cockerills who are opening the great German industrial establishments at Stolberg and Aix-la-Chapelle.[19]

A writer entering a new steam factory at Venice observing with awe the smokestack, the engine, the roar of the machinery, exclaimed that anyone having had the experience would be convinced that "our age lacks neither poetry nor monuments. What can better signify that God has placed man first and most beloved among his creatures, what could signify better that his origins are divine?"[20]

Such dithyrambic outbursts are extreme instances of the enthusiasm for material progress that runs through the liberal journals. But even

[15] *Indicatore lombardo,* 1829, I, 10.
[16] *Ibid.,* p. 15.
[17] *Rivista,* 1838, I, Pt. 2, 251.
[18] *Ibid.,* p. 173.
[19] *Rivista,* 1838, I, Pt. 2, 250–251.
[20] A. Sagredo, in *Annali,* 1842, LXXI, 211–212.

the soberest of the publicists of the time would not have dissented from the conclusion of Petitti, when, in his report of Antonio Scialoja's lectures at Turin, he declared that the economic development of the modern epoch marked a great progress in civilization over preceding ages, in spite of the evils with which modern industrialism had been attended.[21] Nor would they have dissented from the statement of a contributor to the *Annali* in 1839 when he affirmed it to be the philosophy of the age that the pursuit of material interests "is intelligence and morality."[22]

"Intelligence and morality"—the phrase is important; for, as one can see in the program described in the last chapter, the vision of these writers was by no means bounded by the thought of material prosperity. The introduction into Italy of "the new European system"[23] they saw as a means to an end. They urged Italian producers to look abroad and adopt modern habits in their own interest, but their minds were fixed on a horizon of interest that was national. In the new civilization was not only an irresistible force but one that might redeem Italy. This idea gleams through all the discussions of material progress in the *Conciliatore,* the *Annali,* the *Politecnico,* and the *Rivista europea.*

"The publicity of statistics"—that is, a knowledge of the new economic process—wrote "G. P.[ecchio]," reviewing Chaptal's *De l'industrie française* in the *Conciliatore,* "is the most efficacious means of increasing and propagating in the proprietor, in the merchant, in the creditor of the state, instruction, emulation, confidence, a feeling of the national force."[24] "Commercial and industrial progress always brings with it the intellectual and moral progress of the people," Battaglia declared in one of the first numbers of the *Rivista europea.*[25] Italy is backward in such matters, he continued, and then disclosed his vision of more definite "moral advantage" for Italy. "When the journey between the various capitals of the peninsula has become a pastime of a few hours, a pleasure trip, on that day it can be said that the history of Italy's municipal dissensions has become history merely; on that day it will be possible to say that Italy is reborn."[26] The writers of the *Annali* had the same outlook. "Railroads can regenerate Italy, and the princes who rule it can by means of this portentous instrument join in a holy alliance the natural, moral, civic and economic forces scattered through

[21] C. I. Petitti, "Nuovo corso d'economia politica all'Università di Torino," in *Rivista,* n. s., 1846, IV, Pt. 2, 265–310.
[22] "S–o" in *Annali,* 1839, LIX, 256.
[23] Note on the increase of French commerce 1820–1825, *Annali,* 1826, X, 283.
[24] *Conciliatore,* April 11, 1819, No. 64, 257.
[25] "Cenni sulla strada ferrata da Venezia a Milano," *Rivista,* 1838, I, Pt. 1. 151
[26] *Ibid.,* p. 153.

the peninsula, and place anew on the throne that belongs to her the ancient mistress of the nations."[27]

When these words were written, the journalists, visiting the annual Scientific Congresses, could see an Italy—awakened and irrigated by the forces they had invoked—actually coming into existence. "The universities, the hospitals, the institutions of charity, the schools, the factories, all the institutions, all the monuments that do most honor to the modern epoch, . . . are sought out, displayed, admired; and the living Italy, not seen by the collectors of pictures and those who rummage among ancient ruins, is unexpectedly discovered to itself and wonders at itself."[28] In such expressions is to be found precisely the thought of Cavour, by which his economic policy was to be actuated. "We are convinced," he himself wrote in the *Giornale di commercio* of Florence, July 14, 1847, on the occasion of Cobden's visit to Turin, "that in working to lower the barriers that divide us, in working to extend our commercial relations abroad, we are working for the intellectual and moral progress of Italy as well as for its material prosperity."[29] It is the essence of his celebrated maxim that in modern times political economy is "the science of the love of country."

The fundamental assumption of the publicists who wrote in the liberal journals of Lombardy between 1815 and 1848 was that the salvation of Italy was to be found in the economic movement that was revolutionizing Europe and displacing its ancient landmarks. In that movement ran the main current of progress, and the Italians must learn to navigate it. But in spite of occasional lyricism, they did not regard the kind of progress that civilization was making as an unmixed blessing. In short they did not regulate their attitude towards it by the *laissez-faire* economics of the Manchester School and of Jean Baptiste Say. They were horrified by the evils of capitalistic machine production and they believed that in Italy these could be controlled, and in the journals they advocated specific measures to accomplish that result.

In this reaction they displayed an essentially national strain of thought. Italian economists were traditionally liberal but they were anti-abstractionist.[30] They never set up an "economic man" nor accepted the idea of an "atomistic society" harmonized solely by the play of economic

[27] J. Pezzato, reviewing Petitti's *Strade ferrate,* in *Annali,* 1845, LXXXVI, 258.

[28] Report of the Eighth Congress of Italian Scientists at Genoa, in *Rivista,* n. s., 1846, IV, Pt. 2, 505.

[29] Quoted in Ciasca, *Programma,* p. 489.

[30] For an account of the eighteenth-century Italian economists, see Aldo Ferrari, *La preparazione intellettuale del Risorgimento italiano* (Milan, Treves, 1926).

self-interest under the tutelage of a policeman state.[31] Giuseppe Sacchi, in his address on the occasion of Cobden's visit to Milan in 1847, praised Romagnosi as a thinker who repudiated the segregation of economics, treated by his contemporaries as if it began and ended in the calculations of the individual speculator, and who insisted on considering political economy as a part of the science of law. This was the Italian tradition and the liberal journalists remained faithful to it. Eager to invigorate their country with the power of the new industry and science which seemed to be the secret of the might and leadership of England and France, they wished Italy to gain from it what the conditions of Italy required, and to justify a characteristic Italian good sense and humanity by charting the evils and avoiding them.[32] They ended with seeing in the economic, educational and philanthropic institutions that were springing up in Italy in response to the impulses of the revolution a special Italian phase of that revolution.

The aspects of *laissez-faire* industrialism that the journalists felt to be evil and sought to avoid were its tendency to speculation and its exploitation of labor.

Their abhorrence of speculation was rooted in the conservative habits of the Italian business communities. In Lombardy, as we have seen, possession of a piece of land was the dearest ambition even of the merchant, not only as the badge of social respectability but as a requisite to the establishment of his credit. The journalists inveighed against such ultra-conservatism and exerted themselves to stimulate a bolder and more energetic spirit of enterprise and to accustom the community to the idea of mobile forms of wealth.[33] But they were shocked by the speculative spirit and the disastrous crashes that characterized the business history of contemporary England.[34] A fear and abhorrence of speculation ran through all their discussion of Italian railway projects. It was dread of speculation that induced Petitti, though a free-trader by conviction and a warm friend of Cobden, to abandon the principle of *laissez-faire* and advocate government construction and operation of railroads in his famous book on the organization of an Italian railway system.[35]

[31] See *Conciliatore*, August 29, 1819, No. 104, 419–422; Petitti, in *Rivista*, n. s., 1846, IV, Pt. 2, 267–275.

[32] See Dr. Giuseppe Levi, reviewing Theodore Morin, *Essai sur l'organisation du travail et l'avenir des classes laborieuses* (Paris, 1845), in *Rivista*, n. s., 1847, V, Pt. 2, 678.

[33] See above, pp. 203 ff.; also *Annali*, 1824, II, 208; 1825, IV, 176; 1836, XLVIII, 292–293.

[34] For an extreme expression of this dread see the *Album delle notizie del commercio* conducted by G. Sega in the *Rivista europea* in 1840–1842.

[35] Petitti, *Strade ferrate*, pp. 367–394.

The Lombard journalists were even more horrified by the exploitation of labor and the misery and pauperism that English and French machine industry was leaving in its trail.[36] The wretched spectacle shocked a sense of philanthropy which they believed to be preëminently Italian.[37] With some of them the social evils of the factory were an argument for subordinating manufacturers and staking the fate of Italy on scientific agriculture and the opportunities offered by the new commerce of railway and steamship. But all of them believed that the industry of machines and factories must come and Giuseppe Sacchi, whose voice was always in minority dissent from the praise of industrialism that especially characterized the *Annali,* dedicated a carefully documented series of articles to the aim of awakening the public to see that industrialism had already arrived in Lombardy and produced the symptoms of its attendant evils in child labor and inhuman working hours. The journals and the Scientific Congresses devoted themselves to a study of measures to control such evils. The forms of control proposed were consistently philanthropic in character—compulsory education and schools for the poor, savings banks, workingmen's mutual aid societies.[38] The journals did not invoke the intervention of the Austrian Government. The measures they proposed would give the Italian community control of its own social problem, and they insisted that this must be solved on the basis of self-help under the tutelage of an active lay philanthropy.

The liberal journalists proposed to introduce modern progress into Italy by means of specific reforms which have been described in the previous chapter. But they were aware that the new social order required something more fundamental than an equipment of up-to-date institutions and implements; it required certain attitudes, a moral and intellectual re-education of the individual, which was essential to its functioning and also essential to the resurrection of Italy.

What were the elements of the moral code on which this re-education was to be based? Naturally the first was freedom. The journalists recognized freedom—freedom of contract; freedom of trade, even of trade in landed property; freedom of the individual—to be the basis of the new social order which they were ushering into Italy. Hence their emphasis on enterprise, self-reliance and thrift. They manifested no

[36] See, for example, *Annali,* 1826, X, 159; 1829, XX, 131; 1834, XL, 89; 1843, LXXVI, 39–45; *Rivista,* 1842, V, Pt. 2, 185; Pt. 4, 77–101; n. s., 1844, II, Pt. 1, 169; 1846, IV, Pt. 2, 407–425.

[37] See Mittermaier (Italian edition), pp. 150; 158–165.

[38] The proposals that gained general acceptance appear in the reports of the Agronomical and Technological Section of the successive Congresses of Scientists, published in the *Rivista europea.*

enthusiasm for freedom in the abstract. That had been the passion that obsessed a more naïve generation, who had sought Liberty as an end in itself. Applied to politics, liberty had produced the excesses and reactions of the French Revolution. Now they saw it when applied to economic life producing the evils of unbridled industrialism and inordinate commercial greed—the "spirito bancario," the "speculative spirit," which they abhorred. The evils of *laissez-faire* they proposed to temper by common-sense opportunism and by the inculcation of a sense of philanthropy.

Their strong emphasis on philanthropy deserves close attention. It was a universal tendency of the period, but the journalists believed it to be a marked virtue of the Italian character. They praised the philanthropic spirit of Italian factory-owners; they invoked the philanthropy of the well-to-do, the aristocracy and the trading community in support of savings banks, *asili d'infanzia*, technical schools, and workingmen's societies for mutual aid. They engaged in a continual agitation, for instance, to prevent the savings-bank, which immediately attracted the money of comfortable but cautious investors, from becoming a commercial institution and losing its social purpose. But they were equally insistent that thrift and self-help were the object of the new philanthropy, which they sharply distinguished from the old charity of condescension, sentimental and enervating, on which they were seeking to impose an ideal more appropriate to the times and to the needs of Italy. Self-help and philanthropy should go hand in hand in educating the Italian community, uniting it, arousing it to a sense of collective responsibility, at the same time operating to check the excesses of materialism.

It was less to the idea of freedom than to the exercise of it that the journalists sought to educate their countrymen. Naturally individualists, without experience in either economic or political coöperation, the Italians must be taught not only to act but to unite. To this end the journalists never wearied of extolling "the spirit of association" as the essence of successful endeavor in modern life. The association that underlay the sluggish functioning of Italian society had been either forced or conventional. In the era of freedom, Italians must learn the art of voluntary association. Only out of this spirit could the institutions of a new order arise.

Free coöperation the journalists described as "an animating spirit" which "rejuvenates old institutions, creates or meditates new ones, association, that free and predilect child of society, takes its first steps in the blessed fields of charity and science."[39] The field of politics was barred; but the journalists taxed their ingenuity to point out others

[39] *Rivista*, n. s., 1847, V, Pt. 1, 80.

that were free. The form of business organization characteristic of the new industrial capitalism, the limited liability company, offered one—a splendid chance for private initiative and coöperation in organizing insurance companies, steamboat and railroad companies, industrial corporations for the erection of mills and the construction of machinery, companies for gas-lighting and the exploitation of "mineral combustibles." The emphasis laid on the public interest in the arguments for the adoption of this business form, when taken with the whole background of this propaganda, makes it hard to believe that the journalists were motivated solely by the thought of the economic gain to be acquired. There is little doubt that their aim was to establish the habit of spontaneous association and to educate the community to take its business into its own hands with a view to giving Italy its proper place among the nations of Europe. This motive was certainly present when they urged their countrymen to organize themselves for philanthropic endeavors and for the education of the masses through the *asili d'infanzia* and through technical instruction. The curse of Italy was inertia and division. Business and education were ideal schools in which to develop the twice-blessed "spirit of association."

The practical nature of the means by which the development of the habit of association was sought is a key to the spirit of the moderate Italian patriots as opposed to the Mazzinian radicals. The ideal of association was in the air of Western Europe at the beginning of the century; but Mazzini's ecstatic teachings presented an apotheosis of Association, as a stern and beautiful emanation of the *Zeitgeist*, approaching the individual with a moral imperative, while the moderates, without ceasing to hail it as inherent in the spirit of the age, envisaged it as a practical necessity. With joy they saw material interests and the interests of a rejuvenated Italy marching hand in hand, as if to the tune of some fundamental law of nature.

If the moral basis of the new order was free enterprise and association, its intellectual basis was science: the journalists perceived this and exerted themselves to create in their public a frame of mind receptive to science and to its fruit of inventions. This was another of their fundamental objectives. The task was difficult in Italy. Like the new moral discipline it required a re-education of the public, for the Italian mind notwithstanding its brilliant contributions to modern science, was traditionally preoccupied with the glory of literature and art. To offset this addiction the journals assiduously cultivated the social and natural sciences. To characterize their outlook justly it is important to observe that in seeking the cultivation and general diffusion of the natural sciences what they desired was not research, but the application of science to agriculture, industry and commerce. It was modern technology rather than pure science with which they wished to familiarize the thinking public and in which they wished to see the masses trained. Such was the object of the technical schools, the popular lectures, and the scientific literature which they tirelessly advocated. Their limited goal may mark an imperfect comprehension of the ultimate springs of the progress which they desired; it is rather, I believe, an indication of the urgent need they felt that the Italian community should equip itself promptly in order to catch up in the race in which the laurels of modern civilization were to be won. What Italy needed immediately was not the glory of further discoveries but machines and the habit of using them.

A tendency to moralize was one of the traits of the moderate propaganda: this will be immediately apparent to the reader of the foregoing pages. It was a marked trait of all the Italian literature of the period.[40] Advocates of free initiative in the individual, the liberals were yet reluctant to give up the tutelage of morals, the fatherly care, which governments from which they wished to free themselves had felt it their duty to exercise.[41] They exalted the virtue of self-help and they advocated a type of philanthropy that would communicate it to the masses; but they saw clearly the social danger that might arise if the masses were not first indoctrinated with "good principles" of morality.[42] In this predicament the Italian liberals repeatedly invoked the aid of religion. Petitti reported with warm approval that Antonio Scialoja, the economist lecturing at Turin in 1846, was "in accord with the sentence which he attributes to Mably, that prudence, justice, courage are as necessary to us as the fruits of the soil; indeed he appropriately

[40] See Luchaire, ch. VI.

[41] An excellent expression of this moral paternalism is to be found in the Austrian Government's *Piano generale di censura per le provincie lombarde* (Milan, 1841), where the censor is instructed that "Books designed for the general public or for young people, and those of entertainment, are to be treated with all rigor. . . . [In this category are not only subversive books], but also all that do not advantageously influence the heart and the mind, and which tend only to tickle the senses; it is necessary therefore to oppose with firmness the propagation of the harmful reading of romances. Here are not meant those few among them which enlighten the reason and form the heart, but that terrible mass of romances which treat only of love, and which fill the imagination with chimeras." Section 16.

[42] "It has been said that man was born to war with man," remarked the *Rivista europea* quoting Carlo Carcano in favor of infant schools for the poor attended also by the children of the well-to-do, "horrible blasphemy, which unfortunately hints, if not at a law, nevertheless at a fact of every time and place." God wishes to put an end to the inhuman and wasteful war between rich and poor, and there is no better way than to mix them while they are young and impressionable. *Rivista*, 1838, I, Pt. 2, 328.

added to all these virtues religion, which is their perfection and guardian."[43]

What did they mean by religion? It is apparent from the foregoing review of their plans and ideas that their ideal was a lay society completely in charge of its own destinies.[44] Nothing is more striking than the absence of the Church from all this literature. The support of ecclesiastical authority or institutions was never invoked. Until the accession of Piux IX the organized Church took no part in the movement with which this study is concerned, and I have noted only one religious journal circulating in Lombardy between 1815 and 1848.[45] The favorite educational device of the liberal publicists, the *asilo d'infanzia*, was opposed by the higher ecclesiastical authorities and until the advent of Pius IX was excluded from the Papal State, together with modern "progress" and all its works.

Nevertheless a spirit of active piety, of faith in religion, runs through the whole journalistic movement. Confalonieri placed its diffusion in the first rank of the benefits to be sought from the Lancastrian schools ;[46]

[43] *Rivista*, n. s., 1846, IV, Pt. 2, 288. Even De Welz's bourgeois and business-like *Ape delle cognizioni utili* announced in its program that "Morals and religion being two very important parts of social economy, articles regarding them will be admitted." *Ape*, 1833, I, 3–4. "A beneficent morality, pleasant scenes, nature calm and majestic, the errors and the virtues of our fathers, these are the subjects worthy of treatment if glory be the price of utility." *Ricoglitore italiano e straniero*, 1835, I, 47. The *Annali* welcomed the first rural infant school at San Martino in Argine as combining "truly Christian principles and a wise public economy." *Annali*, 1834, XLII, 122. In Ravizza's book the "good curate" of the Brianza declares that "education and religion must be linked, in order to safeguard society against the misuse of knowledge." *Un curato di campagna*, p. 75.

[44] It will suffice to cite the words of Giuseppe Sacchi, educational spokesman of Lombard journalism, in which he is criticizing the Piedmontese school system : "It seems to us that they still confide too much in cloistral corporations for the popular education both of boys and girls. Education is a ministry entirely civil in character, which must not be given as a monopoly to any privileged corporation. The torpid disciplines of the monastery are no longer adapted to the free expansion of Italian thought. The future is in our hands and all social classes have the right themselves freely to direct the instruction of their children." *Annali*, 1848, XCV, 233.

[45] *Il Cattolico: appendice religioso-letteraria alla Gazzetta Ticinese* (Lugano, 1839–1844). In 1830 the proportion of scientific works to the total of books published in Lombardy was the same as that of religious works—one to eight. "These important studies proceed *pari passu* among us," remarked the *Annali*, 1830, XXV, 96.

[46] See his petition to the Government in Gallavresi, II, Pt. 1, 94–96. The emphasis on the religious benefit in Confalonieri's official petition might be construed as strategic, but Giacinto Mompiani wrote him from Brescia August 21, 1820: ". . . until we have instituted instruction in the catechism a vacuum remains in [the schools of Milan], which gives much occasion for slander, and constitutes a defect in that moral and religious instruction which is the principal purpose of our reform." Gallavresi, II, Pt. 1, 317.

the *Annali* and Battaglia's journals hailed its inculcation as one of the chief blessings of the *asili d'infanzia*, and welcomed with joy the coöperation of liberal priests in directing these schools. The *Rivista europea* reported with emotion the spectacle of the Italian scientists at Pisa attending mass before they entered into their deliberations.[47] The spirit of charity, of religious and fraternal benevolence, seemed to the journalists the mark and signature of a peculiarly Italian form that modern civilization was taking in Italy.[48]

The finest expression of this spirit in the literature of the time is the little volume of Carlo Ravizza, friend and disciple of Cattaneo, and collaborator of the *Rivista europea*, *Un curato di campagna*, a "Christian idyl," which he published in 1841.[49] Its subject was the country priest, saintly, enlightened, practical, thoroughly comprehending the needs and blessings of modern life and devoted to the task of educating his peasant flock in the Brianza with regard to them. Ravizza represents him, for example, as seizing the opportunity presented by a hail-storm to expound to his people the benefits of insurance. A sudden storm had pounced on their fields from the heights of the Resegone and laid waste their ripening crops. The peasants, frightened and desolate, assembled in the church to pray while the storm raged. The next day, when the sun began to shine again on the drenched and ruined fields, the good curate gathered them in the piazzetta and explained in simple terms how insurance would spread the loss from such calamities, come to their aid when death struck at the earning power of the family, and provide the means to redeem a son from conscription or set him up in business.[50] In Ravizza's picture of the country priest he became the homely and blessed missionary of a new Italian culture. This beautiful little book breathes a spirit of active pastoral benevolence and love of country; in it religion and modern progress blend in idyllic harmony. Such was the ideal: a religion of active charity, a religion free from dogma; in short, a religion of philanthropy. It is the simple, popular, evangelical Catholicism of Manzoni, whose *I Promessi Sposi* undoubtedly had much

[47] *Rivista*, 1839, II, Pt. 4, 261–262.

[48] Mittermaier observed that charity was a common phenomenon in Europe: "nevertheless we maintain that this shows itself in Italy in a more striking and finer manner than other countries can boast." *Condizioni d'Italia*, p. 150.

[49] "The future," said the *Rivista europea* reporting the Venice Congress of Scientists, "will see poetry and civilization return to the fields. . . . The Christian idyl, so elegantly colored by Carlo Ravizza, is for the present not truly a history even in Italy; but only for Italy can it be a prophecy." *Rivista*, n. s., 1847, V, Pt. 2, 477.

[50] Ravizza, pp. 39–41.

to do with shaping and coloring it in the vision of the Lombard school of journalists.[51]

It was in their religious ideal that the liberal journalists, who represented what may be called the "secular" wing of the still inchoate moderate party, most closely approached the Neo-Guelf wing, who were to dominate the scene with the publication of Gioberti's *Il Primato* (1843) and the advent of Pius IX (1846). The two groups took their departure from premises that were in clear opposition—a fact that is generally overlooked. The Neo-Guelf philosopher Rosmini, who attempted to systematize the pietistic and moralizing tendency in Italian thought and to fortify it against the assumptions of the eighteenth century still persistent in Italy, corresponded with Manzoni regarding the question: "Is economic science likely or not to favor the progress of morality?" and they reached the conclusion that "political economy is the science of materialism,"[52] a position combatted by the liberal journalists on every page of their writings. In his *Primato*, Gioberti, the other great exemplar of Neo-Guelf thought, was entirely preoccupied with ideals and political arrangements. That the Lombard journalists pinned their faith to an entirely different set of forces has been made abundantly clear. To define the two positions it may be said that if the thought of the Neo-Guelf school was polarized by the Liberal Catholic movement of the early nineteenth century, the thought of the Lombard writers was polarized by the secular movement of their age, the movement of industry, commerce and science. But they met in their common belief in a popular active philanthropy in which the secular school saw a social cement with which to avert the class conflict that was developing in the new social order. In his *Speranze d'Italia* Cesare Balbo, who was at once a Neo-Guelf and an honored associate of the Lombard journalists, based the imperative need of reforms on the direction that "Christian civilization" was taking, as well as on the practical necessities of Italian life. Here the blend was complete.[53] But the difference be-

[51] For a full and penetrating discussion of the Manzonian ideal and its influence in Lombardy, see De Sanctis. See also Luchaire, pp. 254–255, where he points out that Manzoni reflected and reinforced a movement in Italian life, a reaction towards pietism that was independent of his influence.

[52] Luchaire, p. 279, who cites Bonola, *Carteggio fra Alessandro Manzoni e Antonio Rosmini* (Milan, 1901), p. 2. Luchaire observes (p. 309) that Leopardi, with entirely different premises, took the same view of social science.

[53] But even so note D'Azeglio's impatience with Balbo's Neo-Guelf leanings: "I am Balbo's friend, God knows; but the one thing in which we are not in accord is that Giobertism of his." Massimo d'Azeglio, *Lettere a sua moglie* (2d. ed., per cura di Giulio Carcano, Milan, 1870), June 5, 1845, p. 151. Giacomo Durando devoted a large part of his *Della nazionalità italiana* to combatting the pernicious tendency of the Neo-Guelfs and staked his hope for Italy on the "Active Rationalists," the group represented by the journalists.

tween the two wings of moderate liberal patriotism, distinct in deri\
tion and in their basic assumptions, is important. It is genera\
neglected, one may suppose, only from ignorance of the force of the
secular element. Between 1846 and 1848 Pius IX, who then seemed to be
both Gioberti's pope and a liberal in the secular sense, though he
refused to identify himself with either party, threw a bridge between
them, and this fact has increased the confusion of historical observers.
But when the myth of Pius IX exploded in April, 1848, the persistent
cleavage was evident and it ran a deep furrow through the subsequent
history of the Risorgimento and of the modern Italian state. The
secular liberals led the march in support of Cavour, who was one of
them, and were ripe for his formula of "a free church in a free state"
as the solution of the Roman question, while the remnant of the Neo-
Guelfs, forsaken even by Gioberti, whose experience had taught him
the importance of economic and social questions, clung to the forlorn
hope of federalism based on a purified temporal power.

In their effort to bring about a moral re-orientation of their countrymen, to get the sails of Italy trimmed to the prevailing winds of modern
life, the liberal publicists encountered a formidable difficulty in the
essentially literary culture and outlook of Italian society. To be sure,
the eighteenth century and its literary academies dominated by Arcadia—
that universal Italian republic of dilettante social scribblers—had been
left well in the rear. Two literary generations had supervened. One
had felt the influence of Encyclopedism, interpreted in *Il Caffè*, by
Verri, Beccaria, and their school, and salted by Parini's satire. A second
had been brought up on Alfieri and Foscolo and their cult of Virtue,
which the Italians were taught to identify passionately with freedom and
the love of country.[54] But if literary fashions changed, the *manie
littéraire* continued to be endemic in Italy.[55] In fact it received a strong
impulse from the example of their adored Alfieri, with his disdain for
anything but literary glory and his spectacular success in achieving it.[56]

But a vigorous element of the next generation, that coming of age
about 1830, while it seems invariably to have memorized Alfieri, nevertheless shared Cavour's clear-headed conviction that political economy
and not the pursuit of literary laurels had now become "the science of
the love of country"; and one of the objects energetically pursued by the
liberal journalists of Lombardy was to bring into ridicule the surviving
literary academies and stimulate a new and more robust literary activity.
The achievement of their object involved not only the production of

[54] See Luchaire, p. 98.
[55] *Ibid.*, pp. 57–65.
[56] *Ibid.*, p. 98.

a literature of information, useful, moral, "scientific" and popular, in the form of journals, books and encyclopedias of "useful knowledge" for the masses. It involved something more delicate and difficult—the evocation of a new literature of art. This was particularly the task of the reviews whose primary aim was literary criticism: the *Conciliatore*, the *Antologia* of Florence, the *Rivista europea*; but in this effort even the *Annali* and Cattaneo's *Politecnico* lent a hand. The assumption which they made in common was that the principle of vitality in literature is its communion with contemporary needs, aspirations and emotions.

This was the doctrine that the *Conciliatore* preached as the advocate of Romanticism, and its young collaborators delighted in taking sarcastic flings at the *Accademia della Crusca*, the outworn national fortress of Classicism and philological pedantry.[57] The later journals, though they abandoned Romanticism as a dead issue, made the same doctrine the burden of their literary criticism.[58] They continued to ridicule the literary frivolity incarnate in the academies but with a fair hope of seeing these turn to more important concerns.

> Once when anyone said academy one meant a meeting of men come together to recite a sonnet or to hear themselves applauded; today instead is meant a society of men of letters, science, or industry, met to join forces in increasing and perfecting the disciplines and the arts. . . . It is no longer only the poet who brings his zither, as they said twenty years ago, or the lute, or harp, as they say today; but the chemist comes to make his experiments with gas or steam; the astronomer and physicist their observations on the heavens and nature; the scholar there investigates the recondite mysteries of antiquity, makes there his observations on the beginnings of language and on the most ancient peoples; the historian and moralist read there a fragment of the work to which they have long consecrated pains and vigils; the statesman brings the fruit of his calculations; the mechanist reveals the powers of his talent and his discovery. For the rest even letters assume there a more august aspect.[59]

[57] See above, pp. 154–155. "Refrain from sending me commentaries on Dante or matrimonial sonnets, books which are fatally coming back into fashion among us. They are now springing up like mushrooms at Brescia and so civilization progresses with the pace of a lobster." Giacinto Mompiani to Federigo Confalonieri, September 24, 1821, Gallavresi, II, Pt. 1, 455.

[58] See especially the masterly critical essays of Carlo Tenca in the *Rivista europea*. An excellent example is his essay on Giambattista Niccolini, *Rivista*, n. s., 1845, III, Pt. 1, 408–432.

[59] Ignazio Cantù, "Delle Accademie italiane viventi," *Annali*, 1841, LXVII, 181–194.

The Academy of the Georgofili at Florence was held up as model.

> Sonnets with and without coda, acrostics, Petrarchian canzoni and such things are banned. Memoirs of agriculture, of economics, of public administration, of mechanics, of public hygiene, etc. are read. This academy, in a word, is celebrated and living, has understood the spirit of the century and the mission of the wise. . . . The Lancastrian schools, the *asili infantili*, the suspension bridges over the Arno, the savings banks, etc. were born of readings given there or were the effect of them; also, I may say the same of the *Guida del educatore* [Raffaele Lambruschini's journal] and of the model farm at Meleto.[60]

It must not be inferred from this that the literature which the critics idealized was purely utilitarian. Industry must be a means to an end, said Giacinto Battaglia, stating the position of the *Rivista europea* in 1842; industry will be desirable or even tolerable only if it makes possible art.[61] When an exuberant collaborator exclaimed ". . . *material improvements* . . . are . . . the copious, perennial and inexhaustible source of civilization, and help the progress and perfection of the human race a hundred times more than all the Esmeraldas, Lelias and Anthonies on earth," Battaglia felt it necessary to demur in a footnote to the effect that "no importance is to be attached to the judgment of those who attribute significance only to what is of purely mechanical or industrial interest," but he agreed with the words of his contributor that "true civilization consists in the just temperament of the social and intellectual development of man."[62] "What the world now asks of poetry is that it assume the character of the century, and transform itself, as Lamartine said, into *ragione cantata* (reason set to music) ; that it become serious, intimate, meditative, social, equally with all other manifestations of human activity":[63] these words are probably the best single statement that could be found of the principle followed in the literary criticism of the journals.

Literature must assume the character of the century and it must be original with the Italians. Only if Italian writers roused themselves to produce a literature of genuine worth and interest to the public could they hope to see Italy freed of a humiliating "inundation of foreign stuff, badly selected and worse translated, which in a short while will become a filthy burden to the public libraries condemned to receive it, and which already is the ruin of the national genius, of good sense, even

---

[60] G. Calvi, "Lo stato attuale della letteratura in Toscana," *Rivista*, 1842, V, Pt. 2, 323.

[61] "L'industria e l'arte: pensieri semiserii," *Rivista*, 1842, V, Pt. 2, 187–188.

[62] *Rivista*, 1840, III, Pt. 3, 347–348, note 1.

[63] *Rivista*, n. s., 1843, I, Pt. 1, 52.

of good morals."[64] Italian literature wanted "lively and fresh aliment." To supply this Cattaneo exhorted the lovers of science "to humble the vanity of a frivolous literature, ranging over against it some of the immense Truth, with which it apparently scorns to nourish itself." "Without the seductive alliance of song," he said, Italian literature "would already seem almost dead and forgotten by those peoples who march with the century and with the century are enterprising and carry weight."[65] There are now three literatures in Europe ahead of ours, he wrote three years later—the English, the French and the German. "The Cyclopean crudity of our scientists and the baroque art of the intarsia-makers of language, who thought it barbarous to lay hand to anything alive, compel the mass of readers to turn to foreign literatures, which either in their native tongue or in a stream of inelegant translations, of re-workings, and of brazen plagiarisms flood the book-trade and usurp the nourishment of native plants."[66]

But pessimism was not the prevailing note of the literary critics. On the contrary, they were moved by pride and hope as they contemplated an awakening in Italian letters, a movement original, vigorous, and patriotic which seemed to promise a return of literary glory to the Italian name. As early as 1830 the *Annali* noted that the proportion of poetical works to the total number of literary works published in Lombardy was one to five; that the ratio of poetry to the total number of books published was one to eleven; while the proportion of philological works to the total was only one to seventeen: this, the editor remarked, was a sufficient answer to foreigners who accused Italy of doing nothing but count on their fingers the works of the dead past.[67] The literary revival was even then seen to have begun in the eighteenth century, with "humble and faithful souls" who "in meditation, in silence and in poverty were preparing themselves," and who yielded to fame such names as Baretti, Genovesi, Galiani, Filangeri, Cuoco, Spedalieri, Gioia, Monti, Beccaria, Verri, Parini, Alfieri. "This universal commotion of Italian geniuses who turned back to the antique cult of wisdom, from love of beauty and the good and not from pride or from idleness and servility, was a a splendid dawn that announced the age of the risorgimento. Letters re-acquired the simple and secure dignity that for a long time seemed almost lost; the sciences shed new and more lively light, to the increase of civilization; the arts flowered anew in the pure taste of antiquity and Canova learned to emulate the immortal works of the Greek chisel." When the spirit of this literature "saw in the future a light of hope that promised days more serene, it sang the religious songs

---

[64] *Rivista*, n. s., 1843, I, Pt. 4, 316.   [66] *Politecnico*, 1841, IV, 5.
[65] *Politecnico*, 1841, IV, 3–4.   [67] *Annali*, 1830, XXV, 96.

of the risorgimento, the elegy of the people, the prophetic lament over its ruin; when on the horizon of humanity only shadows appeared, then it intoned the lugubrious songs of scorn and consecrated itself to the avenging of justice wounded and oppressed."[68] Calvi, reporting the literary news from Tuscany in 1840, could point to Niccolini, Guerrazzi, Guadagnoli, Rosini as having for the past twelve or fifteen years sustained the reputation of Tuscany in Italy and abroad.[69] The correspondent of the *Rivista europea* in Piedmont rejoiced to see literature there returning to current life. "To drawbridges and Toledo blades are succeeding the Scala, the Roman carnival, our manners, our society, our vices, our virtues. Which gladdens our hearts since this fashion tends always more to identify literature with life, to render it more real, to bring the confines of the ideal and the actual closer together."[70] It was a holy thing, amid all the weepings and sobbings by the false lovers of Italy over her past glories, "to show that something is nevertheless being done, has been done, and that much remains to do; that nations are not remade by whimpering childishly but by acting; that in our country some fine names still shine."[71] By the end of the period there were indeed fine names in Italy to inspire faith in the literary vitality of the nation—Manzoni, Grossi, Leopardi, Tommaseo, Guerrazzi, Massimo d'Azeglio, Giusti, Niccolini, and the historians Botta, Colletta, Amari, and Troya—to mention only those of front rank. The quality that limited the value of their work as art, if one excepts Manzoni and Leopardi both of whom achieved a universal position, was their patriotism. But to the Lombard reviewers this was perhaps their highest virtue, the supreme mark of their success in communing with the needs of their time. Thus Battaglia singled out the chief artistic defect of d'Azeglio's *Ettore Fieramosca* as its principal merit, namely that d'Azeglio keeps the reader's attention fastened on the outcome of the hero's challenge to Italy's foes at the expense of every other interest of character or realistic effect. This was justified in Battaglia's view because the subject was such as to appeal to the most delicate emotion of d'Azeglio's public— its *"amour propre nationale"*; and therefore, Battaglia added quite justly, the novel was received with "prodigious favor."[72] In short, the reviewers saw in being what they had stead-

[68] Giulio Carcano, "Della satira in Italia negli ultimi cinquant'anni," *Rivista*, n. s., 1843, I, Pt. 2, 267–281; 363–374.
[69] *Rivista*, 1840, III, Pt. 3, 312.
[70] *Rivista*, 1842, V, Pt. 3, 238.
[71] *Rivista*, n. s., 1847, V, Pt. 2, 366.
[72] G. Battaglia, reviewing d'Azeglio's *Nicolo dei Lapi*, in *Rivista*, 1841, IV, Pt. 3, 252–302. For a penetrating analysis of *Ettore Fieramosca* where the modern critic points out the destructive effect of d'Azeglio's preoccupation with patriotism on the artistic possibilities of his conception, see De Sanctis, pp. 336–340.

fastly sought to evoke, a literature throbbing with the vitality of a new and living Italy.

The harmonies of thought manifested in the more serious journals make it hard to avoid the conclusion that the writers who set the pace in contemporary journalism were guided by a certain unity of principles, what might be called a philosophy, which inspired their ultimate hopes. Furthermore, the evidence to be found in the journals themselves as well as in the lives of the leading journalists leaves little doubt that the ideas by which the group steered its course were largely shaped by a man whom many of them openly acknowledged as master. This was Giandomenico Romagnosi, who, after collaborating with the young editors of the *Conciliatore*, became the intellectual architect of the *Annali*. It would be absurd to maintain that Romagnosi's ideas were the sole inspiration of the Lombard journalists. It is none the less true that his doctrines furnish the key to their intellectual assumptions. To complete an interpretation of the Lombard journalism of our period, and particularly of its longer views ahead, it is important to have the master-ideas of this extraordinary thinker in mind. In his philosophical writings Romagnosi wrapped his thought in such cryptic language and as teacher and publicist fused his thinking so completely with the activities of the day that his rugged figure has been in large part lost to view, although he deserves a place in the Risorgimento and indeed in the history of thought as conspicuous and honored as that of Rosmini or Gioberti.

The teachings of Romagnosi most directly related to the development of a program of action for the Italian liberals center in his doctrine of progress, and his conception of the necessary relationship between social and economic forces and the political evolution of a civilized community.[73]

Romagnosi took over a belief in the progress of civilization from the eighteenth century, more particularly perhaps from Vico.[74] But the eighteenth century deified Reason, and for Romagnosi the mainspring of this progress lay outside the human reason. It was to be found in the nature of the creation, in the force of an historical evolution which is the expression of one of creation's laws. "Man creates nothing," he

---

[73] For the analysis of Romagnosi's thought in the following pages I am chiefly and profoundly indebted to C. Rébora, "G. D. Romagnosi nel pensiero del Risorgimento," *Rivista, d'Italia*, 1911, XIV, Pt. 2, 808–839.

[74] Rébora, p. 830, note 1. Romagnosi's indebtedness to Vico was recognized early. A reviewer in the *Conciliatore*, August 22, 1819, No. 102, 413–414, said: ". . . those who have truly examined the theories of Vico *au fond* are Filangeri, Mario Pagano, Vincenzo Cuoco and G. D. Romagnosi." Carlo Tenca referred to Romagnosi and Ferrari as both illustrators of Vico. *Rivista*, 1840, III, Pt. 3, 467.

said, "but only contemplates what is created, reasons about the creation, acts on the creation."[75] It is the task of philosophy therefore to surprise the world of nations in active motion. "The *'Eppure si muove'* pronounced by Galileo at the beginning of natural philosophy must also be repeated at the beginning of civil philosophy." In this belief Romagnosi followed the idea of Vico that reason and history are inseparable. But he differed from Vico as to the line that the historical process is taking. He did not accept Vico's conclusion that it could be traced in circles. According to Romagnosi's conception, "that which follows can never truly resemble that which precedes." Even "under the veil of destruction," he says, "there acts a progressive reproduction." Society is not like a watch: the wheels themselves change. There is a continuous and unending progress.

What then is the rôle of human intelligence? Romagnosi followed Vico in believing that reason is itself a function of the historical process. It can survey the process and foresee its tendency. Even if historical evolution does not move in cycles its direction is not unpredictable. "Just as, if you know one point of a parabola, you infer the rest, or if you know the causal preparation of a drama, you 'perceive its solution,' " so, he maintained, "a philosophical and historical analysis of civilization could be of value in understanding the present and estimating the probabilities of the future."[76]

But Romagnosi went a step further. Rational thought does not exhaust its potentialities or achieve its end in the rôle of a mere spectator. The human will, guided by the foresight of reason, has the capacity for interaction with the other forces arising from the historical processes of a progressive creation. Man cannot create social institutions as a potter manipulates clay. But he can and indeed he must act on them. Action is not optional with him; it is continually necessary; because, says Romagnosi, "nature does not permit a pause with impunity (between progress and suffering there is no middle course)." Hence his doctrine of "progressive equilibrium." He laid down as the basic formula for the life of a state "the perpetual tendency of all of its parts to an equilibrium of needs (*utilità*) and forces; a conflict excited by the stimuli, tempered by the inertia, perpetuated and dominated by the incessant urges of nature; modified by the condition, retrograde, progressive, or stationary, of individuals and of the whole population, without any cessation of continuity."[77] "Social and political vitality arises precisely from an *antagonism*, mature and regulated, which, he

[75] Rébora, p. 819.
[76] Rébora's paraphrase, p. 819.
[77] Quotation from Cesare Cantù, *Italiani illustri*, p. 537.

says, 'is like the sound of active, robust and prosperous life, and may be likened to the sound of a factory buzzing with labor.' "[78] The process, then, by which society progresses arises from a definite but unstable relation between human needs and the established order. The function of rational thought, which is itself one of those needs and receives its shape and color from them, is to interpret that relationship and to play its part in restoring an equilibrium forever disturbed anew. Its office is to develop the principles of a policy of human action that will reach the destined goal *"col minimo mezzo"*—with a minimum of friction, as we should say, or, more exactly, with a maximum economy of effort and waste. Romagnosi was a determinist in attributing to the changing needs of humanity the force of an inexorable pressure, but he believed that intelligence plays a part in affecting the direction which society takes under this pressure.

The first question to be considered with regard to laws and institutions is their *"opportunità"*—their appropriateness to the historical situation of the moment, to the given "equilibrium." It is vain, as eighteenth century thinking had fondly supposed, to attempt to create them *ex novo*, or to essay "a leap in the air." Laws and institutions will function only if related "to immediate and assignable conditions in the actual necessities of civilization." Thus, to wish "to cause the spirit of a century to retreat is the same as wishing to make the course of a powerful river that is advancing go back." By the same token, maintaining "ordinances that were once useful, but today have become contrary to good sense" is possible only while a "fictitious compression" is exerted.[79] The abstract question, "Which is the best form of government?" seemed even more scholastic and ridiculous to Romagnosi than it had to Montesquieu.

We are thus brought face to face with Romagnosi's teaching as to the relation between forms of government and the free activities of a civilized community. The relation is a necessary one: they are inseparable terms of single law, a law of progressive equilibrium. In this relation is to be found the coefficient of progress. Romagnosi's conception of the nature of the relationship has been summed up in the words: "Necessity is the sole point of contact between law and fact."[80] But

---

[78] Rébora's paraphrase, with quotation from Romagnosi, p. 823.

[79] Rébora, p. 822.

[80] Rébora's summary of Romagnosi's *Genesi del diritto penale, op. cit.,* p. 813. It will be noticed that in this position Romagnosi was with De Maistre and the French thinkers of the Catholic reaction. The following summary of De Maistre's political doctrine might equally describe Romagnosi's: ". . . every constitution that has real validity existed before it was written, and in its explicit form was merely the expression of rights already guaranteed in fact." G. L. Dickinson, *Revolution and Reaction in Modern France* (New York: Brentano's, 1927), p. 70.

that "necessity" is always changing. Romagnosi believed therefore that in the nature of things there could be no peace or life in passivity, and he urged his disciples to a robust political activity. But it was equally clear to him that a free and vigorous civil life must ripen and assert its needs before the forms of free government could emerge or take root.

Such a conclusion was of the profoundest significance for Italians of that generation who desired a free country. For them and for their time the first line of action must be preparatory: its object must be "to root patriotic sentiment in the concrete interests of an active public opinion; for 'the means of making the country loved are precisely the means that render it dear.' " In other words it was necessary to develop vigorous public interests and "a public morality," or as we should say, a social consciousness playing through a set of concrete and vital interests, for without this "liberty itself is a curse."

It must be added that, viewing the progress of Western civilization as the flow of a single stream Romagnosi envisaged Italy as "a function of humanity, or at least of Europe."[81] In the period of his connection with the *Annali* he elaborated and put into practice this side of his thinking, and in his essay *Sull'indole e sui fattori dell'incivilimento con esempio del suo risorgimento in Italia* (1832) he emphasized the necessity that his countrymen should "attach themselves to the simultaneous action of the other parts of Europe, it being impossible to live isolated," entering "into a communion and reciprocal exchange of things and ideas."[82]

The propaganda of civil progress in the journalism of Lombardy would seem a fulfilment of, a direct response, to these teachings of Romagnosi by a group of men who venerated him as master, and repeatedly referred to his teachings as the source of their principles. But from the patriotic point of view the inevitable consequence of such an awakening of civic life as that to which the master pointed is equally important; and it is difficult to believe that this consequence was not apprehended by his disciples. It was that, once "public opinion" as an enlightened expression of concrete needs and interests had been aroused, the "political consolidation" of the nation would come of itself, called into being "by the great voice of the time." Italian unity would come when it was felt to be a necessity, and so, and only so, would it come to abide, because founded on the needs of a self-conscious community. Salvotti, puzzling over Romagnosi's words to Pellico: "I myself hold in my hands the threads of Italian unification," made a shrewd guess in supposing that the old thinker meant the threads of thought by which the pattern of public opinion is woven. His doctrine that there is an inexorable connection between the advance of "civilization" and political

[81] Rébora, p. 825.   [82] Rébora, p. 828.

ends opened to his disciples the prospect of a practicable and fruitful
course of action which an absolutist foreign government could not
successfully oppose. If he was right, it was the only true course. Compared with it the direct action feverishly incited by Mazzini and his
insurrectionists was only a tugging at their own bootstraps. The young
men who followed Romagnosi could think of themselves as in conspiracy
with the overwhelming tendency of the age. In so far as they shared his
views they were inspired by a faith that the stars in their courses were
fighting for Italy.

That Romagnosi exercised a profound and widespread influence on the
Lombard journalists is not only deducible from their writings; it is a
fact attested by their biographies and by their acknowledgments in the
journals themselves. His own participation in the *Conciliatore* and the
Annali has already been described.[83] It has been said, no doubt justly,
that it was "not so much his specific doctrines as the dynamic element
in them"—and, it must be added, in the man himself—that incarnated
itself in the thought of his followers. Even as a thinker Romagnosi was
primarily interested in action. He was not, as Rébora has remarked, a
philosopher who sought to know truth as an end in itself. He loved "to
know with certitude only in order to act with effect."[84] When, an old
man, shackled by espionage and crippled by paralysis, he took in hand
the direction of the *Annali* and turned his mind vigorously to the study
of economics, he showed how ready he always was to live his philosophy.
The personality of the teacher was an embodiment of his doctrines.
"His disciples," says Rébora, "reveal him to us when very old still youth-
fully bounding with vigor and admiring 'all that held of the strong, the
generous, the great'; and the young men . . . understood him, even
under the dead wrappages of the thought. . . ."[85] "In unadorned
chambers on the third floor," wrote one of these "young men" in later
years, "in front of a slow fire and at a table with two tallow candles, the
reverend old man received us with the familiarity of a father and the
authority of a master; and with the good sense of one who has lived
much, tempered the rashness of those who hope everything." "That
activity of his in his old age convinced us that time is elastic, and that
the more one does, the more one can do; and we, when we wrote, had
always to ask ourselves: 'What will the old man say of it?' "[86]

In the light of their devotion to Romagnosi the thought of the
Lombard journalists may be summarized. Progress is continuous and

---

[83] See above, pp. 163–166.
[84] Romagnosi's own phrase, quoted by Rébora, p. 818.
[85] Rébora, p. 832.
[86] Cesare Cantù, *Italiani illustri*, pp. 587 and 589.

inevitable. It develops out of the needs of civilized living; it is the essence of civilization itself. In their time, a time of swift movement, the dominant needs of civilization were expressed in terms of economics and science. The Italians, caught in the onrushing stream, must be awakened to their true interests and re-educated to meet them—disciplined in the spirit of association, in the knowledge of science, in the exercise of social charity. In the acceptance of progress lay the hope of redemption for Italy.

This much they said. The rest they could not say. It was that if the Italian nation collected its forces to advance on the road of progress it was bound to become united and free. This idea was implicit in their philosophy, and it may well be suspected that it was the idea that made their words glow and gave the patriotic publicists steadfastness in their endeavor. It was too soon to speak of political institutions. These must be built up bit by bit as opportunity permitted. First, a national journalism; then steamships, railroads, factories, schools and charities; then national scientific congresses and plans on a national scale for agriculture, technology, prison reform, poor relief; then a national railway net and a customs-league:—with these they had brought into view the necessity for the first step in political union backed by all the force of "the century." The political institutions they desired would inevitably arrive, as they had in France and England; they would come when a genuine community of interests had brought the nation to see in union and freedom not merely a dream but a necessity.

CHAPTER VII

TRANSITION TO A
NATIONAL POLITICAL PROGRAM

O N first thought it would seem that the journalists had taken over
the whole ideology and apparatus of bourgeois liberalism in the form
that it was assuming in France and England. They were against
privilege; they preached enterprise, association, free trade and thrift;
they were moral and conservative; and they favored the education of
the masses as a means of teaching them to be skillful workers and in-
stilling in them virtues of the bourgeoisie, including a dutiful respect
for law and order. If they manifested a strong sentiment of philanthropy, it remained entirely free from any coloration of early philanthropic socialism. The attitude of the nascent directive class in Italy
has been well described as "an active interest of the state on behalf of
the humbler classes, to be manifested however by methods conforming
as closely as possible to individualistic educational precepts, and with a
clear-cut condemnation of anti-economic utopias."[1] As for the aristocracy, they regarded the old-fashioned noble with his privileges and his
leisure as an anachronism, a type happily dwindling, though still far too
common in Italy. Luigi Serristori's affirmation in the *Annali* is typical:
"The nobility is today no longer a class apart in the civil community, a
class recruited only among its own members and whose existence and
preservation is guaranteed by special laws and protected by privileges.
One of the regulative principles of modern civilized society is the
equality of all before the law."[2]

As for constitutionalism, the political corollary of such principles,
open advocacy of it was impossible. But the Italian liberals in Lombardy manifested their sympathy with constitutional parties abroad;[3]

[1] Prato, p. 347.
[2] "Considerazioni economico-morali, applicate ad alcuni pubblici stabilimenti,"
Annali, 1844, LXXXII, 187–193. See also *Conciliatore*, May 27, 1819, No. 77,
312, and *Rivista*, n. s., 1843, I, Pt. 1, 365.
[3] See for example the extended "Notizia storica e bibliografica dei giornali e
delle opere periodiche francesi," *Conciliatore*, May 23, 1819, No. 76, 306–308.
Its comment on the *Censeur* is typical: Its writers "have the merit of having
been the first after the Restoration to dare profess with frankness the principles of
constitutionalism in all their integrity." A reviewer dared to say in the *Rivista
europea* in 1842: "The great deficits of England, France, Holland, Belgium are

and when the opportunity presented itself in 1821 and 1848 put forward as the foundation of their political demands a constitution that gave representation to the bourgeoisie on a footing of equality with the nobles.

It would be natural to infer that Italian liberalism reflected a movement of the middle class to gain control of society. The defect of this thesis is that the liberal program was initiated, expounded and propagated, not by an aspiring and self-conscious bourgeoisie, with strong economic interests to serve, but by landed proprietors and a group of intellectuals many of whose leaders were of the aristocracy.[4] It is quite true that the liberal journalists received support from representatives of the rising commercial and industrial capitalism of Lombardy and Venetia. The sugar refiner Azimonti, intimate of Romagnosi, is a case in point. Michele Battaglia, editor of the *Eco della Borsa*, was secretary of the Chamber of Commerce of Milan. The liberal publicists and leading merchants and manufacturers were associated in such enterprises as the Milan-Venice railway and the *Società d'incoraggiamento*, both projects dear to the heart of Lombard liberalism. The following statement of the silk firm of Marietti and Company in 1826 sounds like a quotation from the *Annali:* "Commerce and the arts are in continual movement; their movement is now more, now less rapid. The merchants who, fixing themselves in the systems of the past, wish to remain immobile, find themselves thrown out of place and sacrifice the country for whose profit they serve. It not being in our power to prevent the movement of things, it is necessary to follow it; if one goes with it, one often succeeds in influencing profitably its direction."[5] The merchants of the Chamber of Commerce of Milan were consistently in favor of free trade on principle as well as for practical reasons.[6] In one of its reports to the Government the Chamber of Commerce of Venice cited the *Annali di statistica* as its authority. But there is no evidence in all this to color the view that the liberal publicists were being pushed by a rising capitalistic class or were prompted to act as its mouthpiece. In fact they were exerting themselves to rouse a timid and lethargic bourgeoisie to a consciousness of its interests. At the same time, as has been made abundantly evident, they viewed with concern the unbridled rapacity of the capitalist under a *laissez-faire* system. "At the present

---

indices to show what must be the state of finances under a different form of constitution, where the expenditures are subject to no rule except the will of the monarch, who does not have to render account to anyone." *Rivista*, 1842, V, Pt. 3, 358–359.

[4] See Massarani, *Tenca*, pp. 15–26.

[5] M. C. M., Camera di Commercio di Milano, cartella 564, November, 1826.

[6] See above, pp. 73–74, 208.

moment industrialism has made itself master of the universe; the factory and the bank have invaded society and have sat down in the place once occupied by gentlemen powerful in arms and possessions and by religious bodies which once represented civic wisdom. Society finds itself in danger of losing head and heart and becoming all belly; and yet this state of materialistic obesity is extolled by blind panegyrists as the ultimate economic perfection of the nations!"[7]

If the thought of the Italian liberals was not determined by a movement actually taking place in Italy, it was undoubtedly influenced by the changes that were occurring in European society at large. The journalists well comprehended and tirelessly emphasized the universal sweep of the economic and social revolution that was spreading from England through the Low Countries, France and Germany, a movement that had as one of its accompaniments the emancipation of the bourgeoisie and their elevation to the governing class. Cavour's view of this movement expresses the attitude towards "the popular tide" which an enlightened aristocrat was bound to take: "Is it a good; is it an evil? I know not; but it is to my way of thinking the inevitable future of mankind."[8] It is only if the European scope of Italian liberalism is taken into consideration that the aim of the journalists can in any sense be construed as an expression of bourgeois class interests in the Marxian sense of that phrase.[9]

In fact from first to last the directive purpose of the Lombard liberals was national and only secondarily economic. Predari said of the Piedmontese Agricultural Association: "Its purpose was to direct the people into great enterprises, thus promoting the union of forces; to accustom them to consider their own interests with enlightened discernment; to render the realm more united . . .; to educate the citizens to publicity and discussion."[10] This description is equally applicable to the work of the Lombard journalists in which Predari also took part. The spring of their intellectual processes was the conception that economic forces could be utilized to effectuate a national program.

Naturally no explicit statement of political objectives, or of antagonism to Austria, is to be found in the discussion of public interests conducted by the journals. The moderates believed it to be important that they should survive and continue in action. Their immediate objective was to incite their countrymen to go as far as they legally could in

[7] G. Sacchi, "Sullo stato dei fanciulli occupati nelle manifatture," *Annali*, 1842, LXXIII, 10.
[8] Letter to the Count de La Rive, in La Rive, *Cavour*, pp. 81–82.
[9] There is an admirably qualified statement of the Italian liberal position and its motives in Prato, pp. 257–258.
[10] Predari, pp. 39–40.

developing an Italy united by vital economic and cultural interests, an Italy which, instead of lamenting its fate or kicking against the pricks, should live vigorously the life that it was permitted to live. This was what d'Azeglio meant when he exhorted his countrymen to "a strenuous resignation." The *Rivista europea* observed that: "The artists and immortal poets whom Italy produced in the sixteenth century were certainly not then more free than they are at present in this country. . . . It is time to put an end to these lamentations over the present epoch; it would be better to try to imitate the illustrious men who were able to struggle victoriously with such adversities of circumstance."[11] What was needed first and foremost in a country divided and dormant was "an entering wedge for the public discussion of fundamental interests,"[12] and this the Lombard journalists created in spite of the censor. Their object was the public discussion of every permissible interest of the community. "From the shock of opinions springs the truth," declared the *Conciliatore*.[13] "The spirit of association has never developed in any country where it was not supported by the most open publicity," cried Cattaneo impatiently in his discussion of a Bank of Discount.[14] The *Rivista europea* "availing itself of the law of a literary republic, is of the opinion that it can declare what it thinks and believes, whether the tyrants are willing or not," wrote its editors with startling boldness in reply to a semi-official critic.[15] "On every side rises a cry which calls every opinion up for discussion, for examination, and meanwhile an invisible chain of understandings and ideas is forming between the genius who creates and the multitude who learn." The sciences, philosophy, history, "lending each day some slight improvement, promise for the future many others that will be great indeed. Sad is the man whose heart does not feel the noble presage."[16]

There are frequent expressions of the conviction that the line between politics and economics in modern life is thin and hard to respect;[17] that there is but a step from common economic interests developed in an atmosphere of full publicity to political reconstruction. "Have you examined well the nexus between morals and economics? between industry and politics? between instruction and liberty?" asked a collaborator of

[11] *Rivista*, 1840, III, Pt. 1, 502, note 1.
[12] The phrase is that with which Prato qualified the work of the Agricutural Association of Piedmont. *Fatti e dottrine*, p. 165.
[13] April 25, 1819, No. 66, 386.
[14] *Annali*, 1838, LVIII, 314.
[15] *Rivista*, 1839, II, Pt. 2, 243.
[16] Giacinto Battaglia, Introduction to the *Indicatore lombardo*, 1829, I, 6–7.
[17] Paraphrase of words used by Sega in his "Cronaca politica e album delle notizie del commercio," when he has to renounce any discussion of the political aspect of current events. *Rivista*, 1841, IV, Pt. 1, 122–123.

the *Ricoglitore*, descanting of the progress in "civilization" that Italy was making; and added (probably to disarm the censor) : "I mean true liberty, which is found only in the exercise of virtue and in emancipation from the true tyrants, vice and prejudice."[18] It is by economic force that society achieves the power to overcome adversity—such was the message of Scialoja to his audience at Turin as reported by Petitti to the readers of the *Rivista europea*. "Society in the Middle Ages was a complex of repellent molecules, because it lacked a force of attraction sufficient to bind them together and construct the *unity* of the state. This *unity*, which is the conquest achieved by modern civilization, could never have been attained without the progress of the economic element." In a moment the economic revolution could become for Italy a political one : this was Petitti's suppressed conclusion. What he said was that the direction of public interest to economic conditions "can be the forerunner of immense advantages to our peninsula, especially in the age of transition in which we find ourselves."[19] "Railroads can regenerate Italy," wrote the reviewer of Petitti's book on railways in the *Annali*, "and the princes who govern it can with this portentous instrument join together in a holy alliance the natural, moral, civic and economic forces scattered through the peninsula, and place once more on the throne that belongs to her the ancient mistress of the world."[20] In view of such doctrines the *Rivista europea* could observe with justice of the Italian journals: "they haven't the flag hoisted, but, for all that, the merchandise they carry is not so lacking in value as one might think."[21]

Political ways and means could not be openly discussed. It is doubtful whether the journalists believed that the time was ripe to consider political measures until after 1843, when the policy of Charles Albert and the action and writings of the Piedmontese moderates began to create an open forum in which they could be discussed. But the reader of the foregoing chapters will be left in no doubt that the journals were permeated with a spirit of independence; that within whatever political framework, they were seeking to create an Italy united, self-respecting and strong. Sometimes their national feeling glimmered through in phrases that seem dangerously explicit; but the moderate liberals were not interested in risky exhibitions of sentiment but rather in creating channels of interest and habit that would give that sentiment cohesion

[18] *Ricoglitore italiano e straniero*, 1837, Anno IV, part 1, 413.

[19] *Rivista*, n. s., 1846, IV, Pt. 2, 285–286, 302.

[20] J. Pezzato, in *Annali*, 1845, LXXXVI, 258. It will be recalled that this was precisely the burden of Cavour's famous review of the same book in the *Revue nouvelle*.

[21] *Rivista*, n. s., 1845, III, Pt. 1, 761.

and force. Italy had long been a poet's dream; now it must become a fact.

The practical ways in which they sought to make it a fact have already been described. Behind this activity lay a profoundly nationalistic conception of Italy and its relation to modern life which is revealed less by what was explicitly said than by the view of their world that the journals disclose. The special point of view of the more important journals has been described, but certain common traits of their outlook deserve closer attention if the relation of the journals to the Risorgimento is fully to be appreciated.

The outlook of the liberal journalism of Lombardy was cosmopolitan, in the sense of reflecting a conviction that Italy must go to the main stream of European civilization for knowledge, cultural reinforcement and power. The first horizon that the journals scanned was that of Europe.

But what was their Europe? In their European perspective Austria and Germany almost dropped out of sight. The reader of these journals learns practically nothing about the culture, the institutions, the laws, the economy of the rest of the Empire of which Lombardy-Venetia was a part.[22] In 1838 the *Annali* published some "statistical notices of Bohemia"—the one descriptive article regarding the transalpine portion of the Austrian Empire with which its readers were furnished.[23] A rare reference to a railroad, the Bank of Vienna, a school, an industrial exposition at Vienna, the meeting of a medical society, a book—generally criticized as slighting Italy;[24] perfunctory notice of the Emperor's coronation at Milan in 1838:[25]—this was all. The Lombard journalists did not oppose the Austrians; they ignored them.

The picture of Germany which the journals yielded was only slightly more illuminating. The editors of the *Rivista europea* declared it to be their practice to "follow closely the march of literature in France, Germany, Russia, Spain, and England";[26] but years passed without a notice of a German book. Those finally noted usually had some direct

[22] It is interesting to note in passing that in the Milanese journals notices of Venetia are no more frequent than those of other Italian states, and much less frequent than those of Piedmont. For them the union with Venice was artificial.

[23] *Annali*, 1838, LVII, 220–225 (numbered by mistake "304[–308]–225" in the original).

[24] *Conciliatore*, No. 113, 455–456; *Annali*, 1840, LXIII, 160–174.

[25] The remark of the chronicler in the *Rivista europea* is curious. The Emperor was assured that he would be received with "the kind of festivities for which the Olona does not envy the Thames." The reviewer immediately proceeded with an extensive account of Victoria's coronation at London. *Rivista*, 1838, I, Pt. 3, 78.

[26] *Rivista*, 1839, II, Pt. 2, 242.

bearing on Italy. One reviewer referred to Germany "as having the reputation for philosophy *par excellence*," but spoke without enthusiasm; on the contrary he wished that the publisher Pomba had undertaken the translation of an English or French instead of a German philosophical compendium for his *Opere utili*.[27] In a review of contemporary German drama, "so little known among us," Gottardo Calvi admitted that he had only secondhand information and described the German stage as characterized by confusion and mediocrity.[28] Curiously enough, the music into which Germany was pouring its genius was entirely ignored. As for German journalism, the reviewers frankly admitted their ignorance. "He who wishes to penetrate the sacred curtain of German journalism, and to judge of that young literature not merely as reflected in French criticism, will employ every effort in vain. If the slender appendix of the Augsburg Gazette did not from time to time reveal a little to us, we should be in the dark as to what is thought and published in Germany."[29] A writer in the *Rivista europea* disclosed the national bias of this vague outlook on things German in an article preparing the public for a forthcoming translation of the Niebelungen Lied when he argued that the Italians were victims of an old Roman prejudice, perpetuated by tradition and literature, in viewing the Germans as isolated barbarians.[30]

It is interesting to note, however, that after the completion of the Zollverein in 1834 descriptive references to Germany in the Lombard journals immediately became more frequent and informing.[31] The Germans had achieved an institution which the Italians could use as a stepping stone to prosperity and union, and the journals began to refer to other German activities—particularly to their railways, their industry, their industrial promotion societies, their rural banks, their model farms —as worthy of emulation.[32] Germany was awakening and moving into

[27] *Rivista*, n. s., 1844, II, Pt. 1, 107. In 1839 the *Rivista europea* published some "Brevi cenni sulla letteratura tedesca nel 1838: I. Filosofia," by Dr. F. De Fiori, who confessed having drawn his information from a brief article in the "Gazzetta letteraria di Berlino." *Rivista*, 1839, II, Pt. 2, 476–484.

[28] "Scrittori drammatici moderni della Germania," *Rivista*, n. s., 1844, II, Pt. 2, 329–355.

[29] *Rivista*, n. s., 1845, III, Pt. 2, 738. In the list of journals provided for the reading club at Codogno, the Augsburg Gazette was the only German periodical. *Annali*, 1845, LXXXIII, 33, note 1. In the famous Reading Cabinet of Vieusseux in 1842 there were 7 German journals out of a total of 140, as compared with 45 French and 18 English. *Rivista*, 1842, V, Pt. 3, 210.

[30] A. Guerrieri, "I Niebelunghi," in *Rivista*, n. s., 1847, V, Pt. 1, 18–51.

[31] See above, pp. 208–209 for the interest with which the development of the Zollverein was followed.

[32] "One sees that Germany follows with alacrity the example, not so much of England and of France, which now begins to lose its lead in railway construction, but rather of the United States of America, whose vast territory is all plowed by

that stream of progress into which the Italian journalists wished to launch their fellow-countrymen.

But Germany sank into insignificance beside England and France. These were the nations that filled the foreign outlook of the journals. From them the shapes and colors and rhythms for their picture of contemporary civilization and progress were drawn; the models of the institutions and attitudes they desired for Italy; the standards of comparison by which they judged the progress that Italy was making. France and England were the "two nations placed at the head of European civilization."[33] The picture of them rendered is complete. From the Lombard journals alone one could make a very fair reconstruction of contemporary French and English history, financial, economic, cultural, and even political.

The Lombard journalists acknowledged the intellectual primacy of France. "The geographical position of France in the civilized world, its means of communication with so many different peoples, the universality of its idiom, its political importance, have rendered it in some degree arbiter and leader of the intellectual movement of Europe":[34]—this is a fair statement of their attitude. The majority of the books which they reviewed were French;[35] they reported in detail the proceedings of the French Academy; they borrowed heavily from the French journals. France, while progressive, presented no such picture of misery as they saw in the state of the English working classes. In France they found "a country that for some years has normally accommodated itself to the good, and which has all the characters of a good social spirit."[36] They

---

communications of this type." *Annali*, 1835, XLV, 277–278. See *ibid. passim* for other detailed accounts of German railway construction. Also *Rivista*, 1838, I, Pt. 2, 172–173; 250–251; 1841, IV, Pt. 1, 143. Serristori included Germany among the nations to whose commerce and industry those of Italy were dwarfs compared with giants. *Annali*, 1845, LXXXV, 14. For the German land banks, see *Annali*, 1835, XLVI, 186–187; 1836; XLIX, 104–106. For model farms, *Rivista*, 1841, IV, Pt. 1, 139–140. The Milan *Società d'incoraggiamento per le arti e i mestieri* was modelled on the Industrial Institute of Berlin, the Industrial Society of Mühlhausen, the *Societé d'encouragement* of Paris and the similar society of Lower Austria and Bohemia. *Rivista*, n. s., 1843, I, Pt. 2, 154.

[33] *Annali*, 1827, XI, 229.

[34] *Rivista*, n. s., 1843, I, Pt. 1, 117.

[35] As was but natural since most of the foreign books read in Lombardy were French. The Chamber of Commerce reported in 1838: "it can be affirmed that barring the books written in the French language, a third of which reach us from Paris and two-thirds from Belgium where they are printed more cheaply, and of which a good number relating to history, travels, the theatre, science, and romances are consumed in Milan . . . , the introduction of German and English books is of no great importance." M. C. M., Camera di commercio, cartella 173, February 26, 1838.

[36] G. Sacchi, "Studi sulla pubblica beneficenza," *Rivista*, n. s., 1846, IV, Pt. 2, 407.

followed with special attention the writings of the French on social problems, though noting that there was a great gap between theory and practice in France in the field of "public beneficence." In short, they felt closer culturally to France than they did to England. French institutions seemed to them to have a special applicability to Italy, "so closely related to France both in manners and in civilization."[37]

England interested them less for its culture than for its economic power. They apparently had little direct contact with English journalism, and English literature, while treated much more amply than German, did not receive full justice.[38] Nor was as close attention given to the operation of the English political system as to that of the French, with the notable exception of British commercial policy.[39] The movement of English opinion in the direction of free trade was followed by the Italian journalists, beginning with Romagnosi in the *Annali*, with the keenest interest and insight; and Richard Cobden was received in Milan, as he was in all the Italian cities that he visited, by an audience that fully understood the background and the significance of his victory.[40] But what fascinated them in the contemplation of England was its colossal energy—"that union of knowledge, of interests, of powers that is to be found at London, at Manchester, at Liverpool."[41] There by means of machinery "supernatural things are executed. Hardly a day passes that some new invention does not appear in London."[42] The England that held their attention was the England rich beyond compare thanks to its "thousand arms of iron and its fire-vomiting jaws";[43] the "illustrious nation that comprises all the miracles of human wisdom and also those of civil power";[44] that "sits at the head of every economic

[37] Dr. Giuseppe Levi, reviewing Theodore Morin, *Essai sur l'organisation du travail, et l'avenir des classes laborieuses* (Paris, 1845), *Rivista*, n. s., 1847, V, Pt. 2, 654.

[38] In the very competently conducted "Rassegna dei giornali," in the *Rivista europea*, English journalism was omitted. In a review of "Di alcune opere recenti pubblicate in Inghilterra," Gottardo Calvi apologized for its incompleteness and attributed it to the thousand difficulties which arise at every step . . . especially at present in regard to English literature, notices of which reach us both delayed and incomplete," *Rivista*, 1838, I, Pt. 2, 518, note 1.

[39] The *Annali* published a series of articles by De Vincke describing the internal administration of Great Britain. *Annali*, 1827, XI, 272–284; 1831, XXVII, 284–312; 1831, XXVIII, 38–62; 194–225. See also "La Camera dei Communi in Inghilterra (relazione di un membro rieletto sette volte)," from the *New Monthly Magazine*, in *Annali*, 1832, XXXII, 36–50.

[40] For his reception in Milan and the address read by Giuseppe Sacchi on that occasion, see the *Rivista*, n. s., 1847, V, Pt. 1, 615–629, and the *Annali*, 1847, XCII, 321–329.

[41] *Annali*, 1824, I, 236.

[42] *Annali di Commercio*, 1816, I, 167.

[43] *Rivista*, 1842, V, Pt. 2, 185.

[44] *Rivista*, n. s., 1846, IV, Pt. 1, 56.

speculation, and holds, one may say, the sceptre of commercial influence."[45] Nothing could avail to resist its power; resistance only increased it. The commerce of France and Germany and the other states of Europe was expanding "precisely because since 1814 everyone seeks to exclude and to imitate with his own means Great Britain."[46] "If other states will adopt the institutions necessary to make industry prosper, they will cease being surprised at the progress which is observable in England and well-being will become the patrimony of all."[47] When Italian gentlemen on the grand tour, from Confalonieri to Cavour, visited England they "renounced in great measure the pleasures of society to occupy [themselves] with the material aspect of the country."[48] England's economic power preoccupied them all.

They were far from viewing all they saw with unqualified admiration. They were repelled by the rapacity of English capitalism, the misery of its industrial workers, and the ruthlessness of its foreign policy. Romagnosi struck a note that continued to reverberate in the journals when he declared that no wise statesman "could propose the English economic state as a model for any civilized country."[49] They found in England "a country truly portentous, where immense wealth is coupled with fatal misery and a public debt of more than twenty millions of francs . . . ; a country where the most liberal, the most reasonable, the most admirable institutions exist along with insulting privileges, greedy monopolies, barbarous laws; . . . where a proverbial egoism shows itself beside the most exquisite charity; . . . where the genius of good is in a constant struggle with the genius of evil."[50] But while they condemned the uses to which the English put their strength; they were awed and fascinated by that prodigious strength, and the nation's enormous fecundity in devices and organizations for increasing its power. "No one would dare to affirm that there do not exist in England capitalists sufficiently daring to supply the necessary funds and engineers skillful enough to overcome the obstacles" to the most seemingly impracticable enterprise.[51] The Italian writers were endlessly inquiring into its sources. First and last their conclusion was that its open secret lay in that "spirit of association" which they so earnestly sought to evoke in Italy. It was the conclusion of the *Annali* in 1825: the editors admon-

[45] Petitti in *Rivista*, n. s., 1846, IV, Pt. 2, 302.
[46] *Annali*, 1826, X, 283.
[47] Editor's note, *Annali*, 1826, VII, 250.
[48] Quoted from a letter of one of them, Visconti d'Aragona to Federico Confalonieri, July 8, 1819, Gallavresi, I, 405.
[49] *Annali*, 1829, XX, 131.
[50] *Rivista*, 1840, III, Pt. 3, 169.
[51] Statement in regard to the project of steam driven vehicles, *Annali*, 1824, II, 165.

ished all good men, especially those possessed of capital, "to be persuaded that it is to their interest to animate the national industry by imitating the English in the spirit of association, sole means that avails to surmount all obstacles."[52] It was likewise the thesis maintained in the *Rivista* at the end of the period, in a passage on England that deserves to be quoted at length. The spirit of association, material and moral, best exemplified in the Anglo-Saxon peoples, said the writer, enables the nation in which it prevails

> to provide for its own needs, employing the capital produced thereby in the greatest enterprises . . . digging canals and mines, draining swamps, reclaiming land, constructing roads and bridges, launching steamships on the water, locomotives on the land, erecting docks, or warehouses . . . , illuminating factories and theatres, houses and cities with gas, manufacturing at low cost pins and steel pens and ships of 1000 horsepower and locomotives weighing 18 tons; issuing insurance against damage by fire, hail, shipwreck and death itself; and more than this, conquering 500,000 square miles of territory, with 100,000 of subjects, as the English Company did in the East Indies.

The Whig Party, a private association, he continued, had in 1828 founded a university, the University of London; the Tory Party in 1829 another, King's College.

> Public benevolence, hospitals, asylums, foundling homes, savings banks and mutual benefit banks, orphan asylums, poor houses, in many regions even the schools, are fruits, blessed fruits [of the] spirit of association. . . . And in England, which is and always will be in this respect the great model country, religious propaganda, the abolition of slavery, the abrogation of the grain laws and free trade were also magnificent consequences of private association.[53]

If the Italians could only develop this power, no object would be beyond their reach!

The exclusion of Austria, the neglect of Germany, and the preoccupation with England and France that characterized the journalism of the Italian liberals is not necessarily to be attributed to deliberate policy. As far as France was concerned, it was grounded in cultural traditions and habits;[54] and it developed naturally out of the fact that France and England had the kind of civilization to which the liberals aspired for Italy. It is not for this reason any less significant. It meant that the Italy struggling to be born was allied by its ideas and aspirations with

[52] *Annali*, 1825, IV, 176.
[53] *Rivista*, n. s., 1847, V, Pt. 1, 156–157.
[54] See Ettore Rota, *L'Austria in Lombardia e la preparazione del movimento democratico-cisalpino*, in *Biblioteca storica del Risorgimento italiano*, (Milan—Rome—Naples) Serie VI, 1911, No. 10.

the Western nations of Europe, and therefore, independently of the suggestions of political expediency, arrayed in spirit and interest against the Central Powers.

If, with the important qualification just noted, the outlook of the free journalism of Lombardy was cosmopolitan or at least European, it was no less decidedly Italian. The journals were Lombard only in the sense that they were directed by Lombards. The editors obtained the fullest possible coöperation from like-minded writers of other parts of the peninsula. In the contents of the journals themselves there was a consistent, unvarying assumption that Italy was a single entity. The journals were addressed to all Italy and their subject was Italy as a whole.[55]

They all declared a national scope, beginning with the shortlived *Annali di Commercio*, in 1816, which proposed to discuss Italian commerce in general, because "Italy, as everyone sees, even if divided into several governments, finds itself bound closely together by reciprocal needs and by infinite relations."[56] The editors of the *Conciliatore* plainly declared that "in desiring the prosperity of the country, and reproving its errors, we never consider a single fraction, but the entire peninsula."[57] The *Annali di statistica*, less given to generalities, left no doubt of its point of view, as for example in complaining immediately that foreign school books interspersed the names of the Italian states with those of other countries in alphabetical order, as "Parma and Piacenza, Portugal" etc., as if they were not parts of a nation.[58] The utilitarian *Ape delle cognizione utili* declared its purpose to be the promotion of industry in all Italy.[59] The *Rivista europea* endeavored to bring Europe to Italy, as its title implied, but it also proposed "particularly to follow every step of the national civilization and to reveal the scientific and literary glories of the common country, not only to foreigners entirely ignorant of our affairs, but also the various provinces of Italy, which know too little of each other's merits and intellectual powers."[60]

Granché! we are sons of the same land, all of us enjoy equally the same sky, speak the same idiom, have the same religion, venerate the

[55] These journals offer a striking corroboration of Luchaire's thesis that after 1815 national sentiment had passed from the lips to the heart. It is true of the journalists as of Manzoni, Giordani, Leopardi, and Niccolini that their thought is characterized by a conviction of the reality of the Italy which they desired and a belief in the inevitability of its redemption. See Luchaire, pp. 137–186.

[56] *Annali di Commercio*, 1816, No. 3, p. 33.

[57] *Conciliatore*, November 19, 1818, No. 23, 92.

[58] *Annali*, 1825, IV, 171.

[59] In the first number it gave a list of the states of Italy in which it had correspondents. It includes all but the Papal State and the Kingdom of the Two Sicilies.

[60] *Rivista*, n. s., 1843, I, Pt. 2, 261.

same glories, and yet some are ignorant of what the others are doing.
. . . It will seem strange at first thought to hear it, but you know well
that morally speaking we are more distant from Turin than from
Vienna; here the literary conditions and activities of Paris are better
known than those of Rome or Tuscany, and comparatively speaking
books reach us more quickly and in greater abundance from London
than from Naples.

These are the words used by a correspondent in applauding the *Rivista*
for systematically undertaking to remedy such ignorance.[61] The professions of purpose are less important than the success which the journals
achieved in producing a coherent picture of Italy—always understood by
them as the new Italy, the Italy that was adopting the ways and attitudes
of modern civilization. The *Conciliatore* achieved a very limited success.
The *Annali* made a more systematic and a far more effective effort,
though if one excepts articles by its non-Lombard contributors, who became fairly numerous, it remained dependent for its notices very largely
on the journals and the proceedings of academies in non-Italian states.[62]
The *Rivista europea*, with its numerous regular correspondents all over
Italy, was the most successful of all. In general the journals furnished a
much better view of the North and Tuscany than of the South. The part of
the Papal domains south of the Apennines yielded little until the advent
of Pius IX; then the notices multiplied. As for Naples, the journalists
made a brave effort to report its progress, of which they gave a surprisingly glowing account, but they complained that it was almost impossible to get the information which they desired.[63]

As in their account of the civilization of Europe the thought of the
Lombard journalists gravitated towards France and England, so in their
account of Italy they manifested an affinity with Piedmont. The picture
of the progress of the neighboring kingdom which they afford is fuller
than that of Venetia—fuller in some respects than that of Lombardy
itself. The Lombard writers noted early the awakening of the Subalpine
kingdom; they saw that it was coming out of its corner to take an active

[61] Gottardo Calvi, "Notizie letterarie della Toscana," *Rivista*, 1840, III, Pt. 3, 311.
[62] In 1827 the editors expressed their gratification that works devoted to statistics were springing up in Italy; they would serve to repair the ignorance of
foreign reviewers, who seemed to think that all Italians were washerwomen and
shine-boys. They besought journalists and academies in all of Italy to send
notices. *Annali*, 1827, XIII, 356–357. The *Annali* began early to run a regular
"Italian statistical bulletin."
[63] For examples of this bright picture of Naples, which may help to explain
the optimism shown by such writers as Torelli and Durando regarding the effective coöperation of Naples in a constitutional league against Austria, see
Ricoglitore italiano e straniero, 1834, II, 157; *Annali*, 1834, XLI, 169–170;
1835, XLIII, 280–291; 1836, XLIX, 233; 1840, LXIII, 182; 1845, LXXXVI,
118; *Rivista*, 1840, III, Pt. 3, 311; 1843, n. s., I, Pt. 1, 131–135.

part in the civilization of Europe and of Italy—even of literary Italy; and they followed its progress with information and sympathy, with friendly criticism, and with increasing enthusiasm. The reader is given the impression that Piedmont and Lombardy are one country except for the political contrast between them, and the Piedmontese side of this contrast the Lombards did not hesitate to underscore, as with Charles Albert's reforms it grew more and more marked.[64] This open door towards Piedmont is one of the most striking traits in the evolution of Lombard journalism before 1848. The activity of the journals in preparing the way for the union of Piedmont and Lombardy needs to be taken much more fully into account as the background of the so-called "Albertist conspiracy" in Milan on the eve of 1848 than it has commonly been.[65] By 1848 the cultural alliance of the two regions was as complete as journalistic publicity could make it.

In affirming that Lombard journalism was Italian in scope one qualification is necessary, which does not however involve an exception. It is that the *Politecnico* reflected the powerful glow of Cattaneo's affection for his own region. While his journal proceeded like the others from the assumption that Italy was a cultural and economic unit, its editorial policy was rooted in the interests of Lombardy. For all the amplitude of its horizon it was primarily occupied with the task of relating life in Lombardy to the economics and science of Europe.

Like the nationalists of other countries the Italian liberals fell in with the tendency to evoke the past and to cultivate historical studies, which had been stimulated in Italy as elsewhere by the Romantic movement.[66] Even the economic journals are scattered with evocations of the

[64] As early as 1828 the *Annali* called attention to an article in the *Gazzetta piemontese* on "Nuovi miglioramenti praticati negli Stati di S. M. il re di Sardegna rispetto alla cognizione morale di quegli abitanti," emphasizing the improvement of prisons and the construction of segregated slaughter-houses, with which Milan was not yet provided. *Annali*, 1828, XVII, 105–112. On the notice of Charles Albert's decree abolishing the corvée in the royal salt-works in Sardinia, they made a remark not too darkly cryptic: "We mention this royal decree because it offers a lucent proof that everything progresses to the advantage of human society." *Annali*, 1836, XLIX, 226. His more noted reforms from 1838 on they followed with increasing enthusiasm.

[65] There is no account of it in Vidal's discussion of this conspiracy in his *Charles-Albert et le Risorgimento italien* although one of the great merits of M. Vidal's work is his alertness to the force of public opinion and particularly of the economic factors in Charles Albert's policy that gained him the coöperation of the Liberals.

[66] The *Conciliatore* sounded the call in its review of Sismondi's *Histoire des républiques italiennes*, exhorting Italians to cultivate "national history, which must form the basis of education" and which "has not too many students." October 18, 1818, No. 14, 54. See Luchaire, pp. 67–72, where he insists that in Italy this tendency was independent of Romanticism though in harmony with it.

"ancient glories of the Italians considered as a mercantile nation,"[67] of the exploits of the Venetians, Florentines and Genoese;[68] of "that adventurous and enterprising living of the Guelfs that produced Enrico Dandolo and Marco Polo and Columbus and Amerigo."[69] The *Rivista europea* ran a section devoted to *Studii di storia patria*, and applauded the publication of the *Monumenti di storia patria* by the *Deputazione di storia patria* of Turin with the financial aid of the king,[70] and the founding of the *Archivio storico italiano* at Florence in 1842 by the indefatigable Vieusseux—the two outstanding events of the time in the progress of organized historiography in Italy. The journals reported fully the resounding controversy over the influence of the Lombard invasion of Italy, which was revived by Manzoni's *Adelchi* and which set the stage for various learned expressions of the sentiment that was rising against the Germans as the dominators of Italy.[71] The Renaissance was shunned; it was Roman antiquity, the age of the communes, and the recent revolutionary epoch, theme of Colletta and Botta, to which the new school of historians as well as the national school of romance and the drama were directing public attention. The publicity which the journalists gave to this renaissance of Italian history reflects their conception that the revival of national history and of social science were two sides of a single movement, as indeed in a nationalistic sense they were.

All this is to say that the Lombard journals were strongly nationalist. Italy was enshrined in their hearts; but the journalists were not content with performing incantations before the shrine. They assumed the task of translating Italy into terms of knowledge and practical interest. This was their first great accomplishment. Even Mazzini never knew the Italy that he proclaimed except in his heart and the more he saw of the actual workaday Italy and its people the less he liked them. The moderate liberals whom he scorned were also idealists, for they evoked an Italy that was only in process of becoming. But they loved it practically, and they achieved a very fair measure of success in giving it body and substance in the minds as well as in the hearts of their readers.

[67] *Annali di commercio*, No. 1, 1816, Introduction.

[68] *Annali*, 1824, I, 285.

[69] *Politecnico*, 1839, I, 390.

[70] "An undeniable boast of the present age for Piedmont will be its having seriously given attention to the study of its own history." The writer, reviewing L. Sauli, *Sulla condizione degli studi nella monarchia di Savoia*, "passing over those who have consecrated their genius to other histories," named Durandi, Tenivalli, Balbo, Vernazzi, Saluzzo, Grassi, Manno, Varese, Serra, Cibrario, Muletti, Gazzera, Provana, Bertolotti, Promis, De Conti, Scacigo della Silva, Martini Pietro. *Rivista*, n. s., 1843, I, Pt. 3, 166.

[71] See, for example, *Rivista*, n. s., 1843, I, Pt. 1, 315–318; 1845, III, Pt. 1, 762.

Partly by means of this accomplishment but also in the very effort they made to accomplish it, they worked their way towards the political redemption of the nation. As Professor Ciasca has pointed out, the political program of 1848, which Cavour ultimately redeemed from the wreckage of the premature revolution of 1848, evolved directly out of the journals. With the publication of Cesare Balbo's *Speranze d'Italia* in 1844, liberal propaganda crossed the line between economics and politics, between the discussion of "progress" and the discussion of the political measures needed to give it way:—the line that Romagnosi had taught the journalists and they in turn had taught their public to regard as thin and artificial. Indeed they had already pressed across that line in their advocacy of a customs-league and a national railway system. It remains to note some of the traits and stages of this gravitation towards politics in the journals of Lombardy.

There was in the first place an evolution in the practical—one might call it the quasi-political—effectiveness of the journals. The *Conciliatore* in spite of its idealization of a vigorously progressive Italy never wholly emerged from the literary cloud-bank and came to grips with the concrete realities of modern life. The *Annali* plunged straight into these realities and sought in statistics "a weapon less worn and blunted than historical lamentations and poetical anathemas." Then Cattaneo, apparently because he was impatient with the tendency of the *Annali* to scatter its fire, endeavored by means of the *Politecnico* to concentrate and deepen a public knowledge of the bearings of science and the economic revolution on the interests of Lombardy and Italy. Finally the *Rivista europea*, with its national battery of correspondents, with a staff that embraced the best minds of the new profession of journalism that had been developing for twenty years—heir to the *Conciliatore* and the *Antologia* ot Florence, as well as to the *Annali* and the *Politecnico*—achieved a synthesis of the whole new economic, scientific, and cultural life of Italy and spoke, criticized, and exhorted in the name of the nation with a weight of authority that none of the others had achieved. Meanwhile the *Annali* had been visibly gaining in the depth and thoroughness of its discussion of national problems.

In the very process of constructing these journals a step had been taken towards organizing the political forces of Italy. A class of publicists had been trained who were conscious of the influence and dignity of their profession. In close relations with both the aristocracy and the leaders of the business community they became an intimate and well-knit group not only in Lombardy but in Italy at large. Confalonieri and his friends of the *Conciliatore* corresponded with Capponi and his friends at Florence, and the expiring *Conciliatore* literally passed its torch to the *Antologia*.[72] The *Annali* carried on this intimate exchange of news and opinions.[73] The *Politecnico* stemmed directly from the *Annali*, and the *Rivista europea* drew its staff from both and affiliated itself closely with the journals of Tuscany, with the rising and vigorous journalism of Piedmont, and as far as possible with the journals of the rest of Italy. Through these affiliations, through correspondence, and finally through an exchange of visits, which received an immense impetus from the annual meetings of the Congress of Italian Scientists in the various capitals of the peninsula, a directive class in the field of national opinion was organized, found its leaders, and consolidated its views. One of the important offices that the liberal journals performed was to familiarize the whole Italian public with the names, the writings and the opinions of its future political leaders. Among these were Cesare Correnti, Carlo Cattaneo; Cosimo Ridolfi, Gino Capponi, F. D. Guerrazzi, and Giuseppe Montanelli; Nicolò Tommaseo and Daniele Manin; Massimo d'Azeglio, Cesare Balbo, Vincenzo Gioberti, Lorenzo Valerio, and Camillo Cavour.[74] Most of these names were brought before the readers of the journals frequently and conspicuously. Of those on the list only Ridolfi wrote for the *Conciliatore*: in its time contacts with leaders outside of Lombardy were dependent on chance social relations. The wide and frequent correspondence that grew up in the 'thirties and 'forties is a measure of what the journals had accomplished in organizing a public opinion.

The Scientific Congresses, which began to meet in 1839, were the natural crown and fruition of this journalism and of the associations

[72] For the correspondence between the Milanese and Florentine groups, see Gallavresi, II, Pt. 1, *passim*, and Cesare Cantù, *Il Conciliatore e i Carbonari*, particularly pp. 48 and 109. Confalonieri would seem virtually to have dictated the plan that Capponi imposed on the *Antologia* at first, against the judgment of Vieusseux. See his letter to Capponi, November 15, 1820, Gallavresi, II, Pt. 1, 360–362, and Vieusseux's letter to Confalonieri, May 18, 1821, *ibid.*, pp. 432–433.

[73] "The readers of our *Annali* will have been able to perceive on several occasions with what a sense of reverence and affection we have cited and reproduced the masterly articles appearing in the highly meritorious *Antologia* of Florence, which has been published for eleven years by G. P. Vieusseux, name dear to those who cultivate good studies." The editorial note proceeded to approve Vieusseux's intention to publish more statistics of progress: "We should desire then that there might be a public exchange between our *Annali* and the *Antologia*, alternately producing in the two journals those results of fact which may make better known the united and living picture of Italian activity in every sort of economic and civil improvement." *Annali*, 1832, XXXI, 89–91. (It will be noticed that this cordial salutation was extended just before the *Antologia* was suppressed.)

[74] Cavour appeared in the *Annali* as the author of an article entitled: "Della strada di ferro da Ciamberi al lago di Bourget e della navigazione a vapore su quel lago e sul Rodano," *Annali*, 1840, LXIII, 103–107.

and ideas that it promoted.[75] The Lombard journals hailed and adopted the institution with unbounded enthusiasm. Representing the first meeting at Pisa as a love-feast of Italian pride and fraternity, the reporter of the *Annali* attributed its success to Leopold II, a "prince not imitable . . . I am wrong. There is another prince who will imitate him. . . . Charles Albert of Savoy, of Piedmont, of Sardinia! Oh! I shall no longer despair. Victory! Victory! The good is possible. Progress comes on iron rails. Write in adamant the year 1839, the first to the fifteenth of October, Leopold, Charles Albert, Pisa, Turin."[76] The *Rivista europea* showed equal excitement in describing that "cohort of illustrious men, of scholars come together from every part of the fair land where the *sì* is heard, to confer, to become reciprocally acquainted, to coöperate fraternally in the splendor and progress of science, in the glory of the common country."[77] The journalists themselves took part in the meetings and nourished their journals with the results of the deliberations.[78] On the committees they worked with the men whom they had acclaimed from afar as the natural leaders of a progressive Italy. They saw the whole program of reforms that they had advocated endorsed and given a nation-wide diffusion by the Agronomical and Technological Section, which was especially dear to them.[79] When the prestige of the Congresses was threatened by ridicule, they came to the rescue and met the criticisms vigorously on the ground of the national utility of the institution. Were the Congresses not truly scientific in spirit, like those of other countries? The journals answered that what Italy needed was not pure science but technology and applied economics and strong institutions for their diffusion, and they pointed to the achievements of the Agronomical and Technological Section as sufficient justification for

---

[75] The *Annali* in April, 1831, reproduced an article by Mayer from the *Antologia* advocating conventions of scientists and seconded the proposal. In 1833 it published a letter from a correspondent who had attended a congress of scientists at Cambridge, England: "to me," he wrote, "it was like a restorative to find myself in a place where man can without hindrance fraternize with his kind in the love of science and the human race." *Annali,* 1833, Bulletino, pp. 378–379.

[76] *Annali,* 1839, LXII, 289.

[77] *Rivista,* 1839, II, Pt. 4, 261.

[78] Thus the *Rivista* in 1844 began to run a special rubric "Congresso scientifico italiano," which in volume II for that year comprised fourteen articles and two circulars drawn from the Milan Congress.

[79] Thus the cause of the *asili d'infanzia* was entrusted to a permanent commission, which "was to make a special report every year, and the documents which are sent to the commission will be made public in the journals of the peninsula. So amid loyal debates the cause of the good will grow ever stronger and will become in time a common cause." *Rivista,* n. s., 1845, III, Pt. 1, 204, note 2.

the annual meetings.[80] Were the meetings frivolous, assuming the aspect of festive manifestations of the local pride of the cities that entertained them? The journalists replied: "the institution is good." The meetings perform a mission "which we would call social . . . and for this exciting and vital influence we believe the Congresses to be one of the forms of spiritual régime which will bind the present to the distant future. . . ." "Instead of shutting science into a privileged park, it leads it from land to land, an authoritative visitor, a sharp admonisher, a guest rejoicing and fêted."[81] "The institution is good"—good for a national purpose: practical, in diffusing modern institutions and habits of thought through the peninsula; moral, in effecting an annual fraternization of Italian minds. Reporting the Genoa Congress, the correspondent of the *Rivista europea* wrote:

> To us who live almost on the northern edge of the peninsula, who have read much about trans-Apennine Italy in books, have heard it much talked about in the heart and imagination, some foreign countries were better known than the most beautiful and glorious parts of our own. . . . But now, to the pilgrim Congresses, not only the galleries and museums are open, nor is one offered only the companionship of the mercenary and the abject; but the entire citizenry, ordinarily shy of new and easy friendships, puts itself forward to meet the desires and inquiries of its guests, and puts on exhibition those loyal virtues, that frank vigor of words and thought, which for a long time had disappeared from large assemblies, and which is found only among old and tried friends.[82]

The true value of the Congresses was to be sought in "an auspicious impetus to public life and to a civilization not only of phrases and forms, . . . but to a civilization so much more important and rare, alone

---

[80] *Rivista*, n. s., 1843, I, Pt. 2, 345–364 and 376–382; 1844, II, Pt. 2, 372–383. In Italy the Congresses, "which in England and in Germany lived a modest life, almost unnoticed amid the tumultuous activity of politics and industry" had assumed a peculiar form, and it seemed that the institution "instead of closing itself within a severely defined circle, austere and accessible only to the few, sought to diffuse in the multitudes a love and respect for studies, to bring into contact good minds, to reaffirm the concord of scholars, to give a benediction to the best institutions." *Rivista*, n. s., 1845, III, Pt. 2, 464–465. These words are quoted from a defense of the Congress at Naples in 1845 which seems to have been inordinately festive. For a more confident review of achievements see the report of the Genoa Congress in 1846, *Rivista*, n. s., 1846, IV, Pt. 2, 497–545, and of the Ninth Congress at Venice in 1847, *Rivista*, 1847, V, Pt. 2, 462–485.

[81] From the report of the Naples Congress in *Rivista*, n. s., III, Pt. 2, 466–468. For an admirable statement of this aspect of the Congress, see A. Hortis, *Le riunioni degli scienziati italiani prima delle guerre d'indipendenza* (Città di Castello, 1922), p. 20.

[82] *Rivista*, n. s., 1846, IV, Pt. 2, 504–505.

entitled to the name, a civilization of opinions and of minds—the patient, respectful research of the true and the good, the chief foundation of virtuous moderation."[83] The liberal journals made the Congresses theirs because they were an extension and reinforcement of their own program for the rebirth of Italy.

The program of the liberal journalists, matured and consolidated by discussion, was launched into the field of open political agitation with the publication of Balbo's *Speranze d'Italia* in 1844. Gioberti had cautiously opened the field in the previous year with his *Primato morale e civile degli Italiani*. Balbo brought in the whole range of practical questions that the journalists had been agitating. Without the preparation which they had effected Balbo's book would have been marching orders with no army ready to execute them—a fact which historians of the Risorgimento persistently overlook. Cesare Balbo and his father before him had been marked figures in the Lombard journals and he was himself to become a journalist as editor of Predari's *Antologia italiana* and then, with Cavour, of the *Risorgimento*.[84] Balbo's book carried their ideas into the political arena: their conception of civilization, tinged somewhat by his own Neo-Guelf propensities; their idea of "progress"; their sense of the urgent need for action if Italy was to derive a profit from that progress; their faith in a free-trading customs-union and a national railways system as steps immediately necessary to the conquest of a place in the contemporary revolution of Europe. The debt became reciprocal; from the *Speranze d'Italia* the journalists all over Italy drew weapons in the discussion of public questions during the critical years from 1844 to 1848.

Petitti, with his book on railroads,[85] and Massimo d'Azeglio, with his

[83] Report of the Venice Congress of 1847, in *Rivista*, n. s., 1847, V, Pt. 2, 463.
[84] "Who Count Prospero Balbo is there is no need to tell Italy," the *Annali* declared in 1831, reviewing his *Opere varie* (Turin, 1830). *Annali*, 1831, XXVII, 80. In the same year reviewing Cesare Balbo's *Storia d'Italia*, the *Annali* eulogized him as "nephew [sic] of the celebrated Count Prospero Balbo," a richly endowed young man, and "a historian truly national," ranking him with Machiavelli, Guicciardini, Davanzati, Davila and Sarpi. *Annali*, 1832, XXXI, 225–230. Cesare Balbo was a contributor to the *Rivista europea*, and tha' journal reviewing his *Meditazioni storiche* in 1843 remarked that "Italy already counts Balbo . . . among her chief writer-thinkers." If this, as he said, was his last work, he could enjoy the comfort in his old age of "the gratitude which he deserves from the country for his works, of the glory with which his name is accompanied from one end of Italy to the other, of the imperishable fame which will survive him." *Rivista*, n. s., 1843, I, Pt. 3, 44. It will be remembered that it was in Balbo's home that Predari found the elect company of Piedmontese liberals who gave him such lively hopes for the speedy redemption of Italy. Predari, pp. 43–44.
[85] *Delle strade ferrate italiane e del migliore ordinamento di esse* (Capolago, 1845).

famous tract *Degli ultimi casi di Romagna* (1846), continued the discussion which Balbo had begun. Petitti followed up the journalists in pushing to the point of detailed application the ideal of a national railway system, which Balbo had only touched.[86] D'Azeglio's tract was a *pièce d'occasion*, and naturally contained no sweeping statement of program; but the author advanced on ground that the liberal journals had consolidated. Public opinion was now "the true dominating power of the world, of princes as of peoples,"[87] and d'Azeglio's whole case was based on the assumption that public opinion had in Italy become an effective and reliable force. When he called on the people to forsake conspiracy and put their faith in "strenuous resignation," he clearly meant by this strenuous resignation the kind of activity which the journals had successfully stimulated—an endeavor prosecuted "with civil courage" to obtain from our governments improvements, institutions, and temperate liberties."[88] When he turned on the Pope and demanded that the Papal Government meet this aspiration half way, the institutions he specified were railroads and schools, which d'Azeglio, like the journalists, represented as public interests that could not now be suppressed.

> Commerce (everyone is aware of it and we have already made reference to the fact) has already resumed, and is about to resume still more, the ancient road through which Pisa, Amalfi, Venice, Genoa, Florence came to such wealth and power and through which Italy became the emporium of Europe and the most civilized of the Christian nations. If at that epoch (certainly not distant) when commerce, passing through the Isthmus of Suez, will once more and solely throw its stream from the Mediterranean into the Red Sea and the Indian Ocean, if then, I say, Italy is traversed through its whole length by a railroad, it is evident what immense profits it will derive. . . . If the government of Rome persists in rendering that road impossible, if it wills it to be interrupted and therefore useless, what universal anathema will it not bring down on all Italy? What jests, what contempt, from all Europe, from civilization, from universal opinion! . . . This conspiracy in open daylight, with its own name written on the brow of everyone, is the only kind useful, the only kind worthy of us and of the favor of opinion, and in this manner of conspiracy I also declare

[86] The *Annali*, prevented by the censorship from speaking of Balbo's *Speranze*, published a letter from Petitti to Balbo apprising him of the fact that the King of Naples had authorized the construction of a line to Barletta, to be prolonged through Brindisi to Otranto, tending thus "to effectuate the projects of which you spoke *first*, in your book which I have cited, repeated afterwards in mine." *Annali*, 1846, LXXXVIII, 96.

[87] d'Azeglio, *Degli ultimi casi* (ed. De Rubris), p. 8.

[88] *Ibid.*, p. 90.

myself a conspirator in the view of all; in this manner I also incite
every good Italian to conspire.[89]

The "conspiracy" in behalf of all the interests of which it was permissible to speak openly went forward with redoubled intensity after
1845, with the reviews of Petitti's book, including the famous one by
Cavour in the *Revue nouvelle* of May, 1846, and with the aliment
secretly derived from Balbo's and d'Azeglio's writings.[90] Then in 1847
d'Azeglio spoke again. He drafted a "Proposed Program" of reforms which seemed to him at the moment politically negotiable.[91] The
tract is a dress rehearsal of the reforms and principles which the
journals, with "strenuous resignation," had been weaving out of the
interests of Italy since the days of the *Conciliatore*. The motives of the
moderates, said d'Azeglio, do not grow out of abstract principles but
represent "those progressive improvements which are required by the
necessity of the times."[92] He quoted the phrase from a speech by Peel;
he might have quoted Romagnosi. The "necessity" had arisen in which
Romagnosi saw the "point of contact between fact and law." Political
organizations, d'Azeglio affirmed, cannot be just, "and therefore useful,
and hence enduring, when solely the fruit of the will of men. We
believe that instead they are just and useful and durable when they are
the consequence of that social condition to which they are applied, and
of whose practices they are the necessary expression."[93] In short, events
had now reached the point where the independence of Italy was being
called for by "the great voice of the times." In 1847 d'Azeglio still
insisted that the great need prompting Italy to independence was
"moral," but behind this lay a concrete buttress of material interests
which could not be ignored with impunity either by Austria or by the
princes of Italy. Therefore, he declared, it behooved the princes to grant
at once representative institutions; a reform of the military system, including the establishment of civic guards; a reform of the legal codes,
which would banish from the law all traces of monopoly and special

[89] *Ibid.*, p. 93.

[90] Their program can be traced not only in the journals but in the petitions
for reform presented by the local governments of the Romagna and Lombardy.
Ciasca, *Programma*, pp. 534 ff.

[91] Full title: *Proposta di un programma per l'opinione nazionale italiana*
(Rome, July 1847). I have used the ed. De Rubris, *Scritti e discorsi politici*, I
(Florence, 1930).

[92] *Proposta*, p. 230.

[93] *Ibid.*, p. 253. How close at heart d'Azeglio was to the Romagnosian conception appears in a letter to his wife that he wrote on January 4, 1849: "To
reduce the thing to a formula, I say that every social state has a political state
which is its necessary consequence. This truth the princes have not seen for
thirty years. We shall see how many years it will be before the peoples see it."
Lettere a sua moglie, p. 339.

privilege; the liberation of the press; railways; the abolition of internal tariffs and a uniform system of money, weights and measures, which would stimulate commerce; a uniform copyright, which would encourage literature; reform of the universities in the interest of a uniform program of higher studies, and measures to make education general among the lower classes; and with all this, a strict adherence to legality on the part of the princes as well as the people.

The principle of loyal coöperation between the people and the Italian princes is a plank of the moderate liberal platform that needs no emphasis, since it is the one traditionally emphasized to the neglect of all the rest. The coöperation of the princes was important, not only because they had legality and force on their side, not only because it was a guarantee of moderation, but for a strategic reason as well. The princes were the natural leaders of the aristocracy, and it was impossible to hope for the whole-hearted coöperation of this revered and powerful class without them. When the princes began to move, the program of the liberals at once passed to the field of the politically possible. The first to move was Leopold of Tuscany, when he extended his patronage to the Congress of Italian Scientists in 1839. Then, with Balbo's book, the Albertist movement got under way; and finally, with the accession of Pius IX in 1846 came the emotional landslide precipitated by construing his mild reforms in the light of Gioberti's book and of the fires kindled around him by liberal and radical agitators. In all this agitation the journalists of Lombardy were prevented from taking an active part. But it is a neglected fact of the greatest importance that long before 1844 they had been preparing their public to think of Charles Albert as a liberal and progressive prince, whose policy betrayed a sympathy with their aims. Very early they began to report the steps that he was taking on the path of "progress." The earliest which they noted were the measures he took in the interest of a greater freedom of trade, reported to the *Annali* by Giacomo Giovanetti, the economist, who was the chief instigator of them.[94] All the moves that betrayed the "secret" of Charles Albert were reported with increasing detail and enthusiasm: the statistical survey of the realm in 1837-38, in which Cavour took part; the new civil code promulgated January 1, 1838; the patronage extended by

[94] Giovanetti first reported the new forest regulations promulgated by Charles Albert in terms of highest praise as liberating the trade in wood. *Annali*, 1833, Bulletino, pp. 498–502. Then came the decrees liberating the export of raw silk from Piedmont. *Annali*, 1835, XLIV, 136; 268–271; 1836, XLVIII, 89–90. The silk industry was now free thanks to the efforts of Giovanetti, the good counsel of some ministers, and among these the illustrious Signor Cavaliere Balbo, and to the "great heart of Charles Albert." "Blessed also be the decree liberating the grain trade." *Annali*, 1839, LX, 357–361.

the king to the *Deputazione di storia patria* in 1838; his decision to create a model farm at his own expense; his railroad project designed to open Genoa to the traffic of Northern Europe and to challenge Austria by a branch to the Lombard frontier; his patronage of the *asili d'infanzia* signalized by the appointment of Aporti himself to lecture on method in the University of Turin in 1844, and his encouragement of economic studies by the appointment of Antonio Scialoja to give a course in the same university—a lectureship suppressed in 1821 as having a subversive tendency.[95] In 1847 the *Annali* openly acclaimed Charles Albert's judicial reforms and the new press law as manifesting a "wise determination to forward the public business of the state as the lights of our century demand."[96] We know now that they were not mistaken regarding the mind of Charles Albert. He alone among the rulers of Italy had grasped the idea that the forces of modern life—technology, the railroad, freer trade, public opinion—could be used as instruments of policy in working towards the independence of his kingdom and the extension of its frontiers which was his fundamental and tragic aim.[97]

How early did the liberal journalists perceive the political goals towards which their agitation of the public interests of Italy was tending? It is impossible to answer. It is doubtful if the answer to such a question is of much more than curious interest to the historian. The detection of foresight or insight is important to the biographer; the historian is less concerned with conscious aims than with all that contributed to prepare the way for the subsequent result whether consciously directed towards it or not. Perhaps the journalists "builded better than they knew." Their thinking was essentially evolutionary. It was inspired by the maxim of *opportunità* which their greatest thinker had taught them. In this it resembled the mental action of Cavour, the great executor of their principles. Much must be allowed for the difference which the censorship made between their ideas and their public utterances; how much, can be partially measured by the

[95] For Charles Albert's statistical survey, see *Annali*, 1839, LIX, 258; 1840, LXIV, 315; *Rivista*, 1840, III, Pt. 2, 345–360; for the Civil Code, *Annali*, 1837, LIII, 282–291; for the *Monumenti di storia patria, Rivista*, 1838, I, Pt. 2, 168; Pt. 3, 194; for the model farm established by the King, *ibid.*, Pt. 4, 252; for his railroad projects, *Annali*, 1840, LXVI, 126–129; 1841, LXVII, 356–369; LXX, 232–239; 1844, LXXXI, 118–120; for Aporti's lectures, *ibid.*, pp. 348–351; for Scialoja's lectures, reported by Petitti in a magisterial review, *Rivista*, n. s., 1846, IV, Pt. 2, 265–310.

[96] *Annali*, 1847, XCIV, 191–195.

[97] For a summary reflecting the important recent studies of Charles Albert by Piedmontese historians, see Vidal. Since the publication of Vidal's volume the important studies of Rodolico and Salata have appeared.

professions and the position of the Lombard journalists, and of the journals themselves, as soon as that veil was torn away. Cesare Correnti, perhaps at the very desk at which he had been writing temperate articles on economics and philosophy for the *Annali* and the *Rivista europea*, penned in 1847 his scathing indictment of Austrian rule in Lombardy, in which he declared that "the Austrian government in every circumstance is our enemy by nature, our enemy by election, our enemy by necessity."[98] In March, 1848, the *Annali* appeared under the revolutionary device: "ITALIA LIBERA! EVVIVA PIO NONO," and Lampato, called to take part in the Provisional Government, left the journal to Giuseppe Sacchi, entrusting him with "the task of writing the report of our glorious days, which will serve as an historical document to the subscribers and readers of this periodical, which can rightly glory in having had its part in the marvelous result, with the liberal doctrines that were continually scattered through its pages, as far at least as it could escape the shadow of the censorship of tyranny from which we are forever liberated."[99] The *Rivista europea* went further: it celebrated its liberation by reviewing Mazzini's *L'Italia del popolo* and reprinting in full the great radical's *Manifesto* from that journal, signed by Mazzini and by a list of names which include those of Carlo Tenca and Emilio Visconti Venosta.[100] With all due allowance for the fact that these professions were made and these positions taken in the superheated atmosphere of a revolution, they were a logical outcome of the course which the journals had been taking.

In any event it is clear that in the inner circle of publicists who ventilated the public interests of Italy between 1815 and 1848 there was a common idea that even when coöperating with Austria they were working towards ends that were beyond the reach of Austrian policy, and also a common conviction that they were in conspiracy with the course of events, with the march of "the century"; in other words, that they had found a method of action which compelled even the national adversary to coöperate with them, in so far as that power was alert to its material interests. This was their "conspiracy in open daylight." They were right in their strategy: witness the confused and helpless opposition of Austria, whose rulers suspected but never fully comprehended their power. Metternich, with his germ theory of revolution, his persistent

---

[98] *L'Austria e la Lombardia*, p. viii. The *Annali* reviewed the second edition of the tract ("*Italia*," 1847) with full endorsement as "a most conscientious history of fierce and greedy Austrian administration in Lombardy." *Annali*, 1848, XCVI, 4–5.

[99] "Avviso del Compilatore degli *Annali di Statistica*," "Milano li 10 Aprile e 1° ᵈⁱⁿendenza italiana," *Annali*, 1848, XCV, opposite p. 230.

      ι, n. s., 1847, V, Pt. 2, 753–759.

obsession that it grew solely out of a Jacobinical conspiracy which could be isolated and destroyed if the governments would only act in concert, proved incapable of meeting them on their own ground.

It may also be said that the liberal journalists saw at least a partial fulfilment of their hopes. By 1848, largely through their efforts, an Italian public opinion had been formed that could never again be governed successfully by the principles and methods of the *ancien régime*, less because the material interests of the Italian community had been revolutionized than because the public had been indoctrinated with a new conception of those interests. This conception had contributed to the consolidation of a cultural alliance of the rising Italy with France and England against the Austrian Empire, and had nourished in the Italian mind a new kind of self-respect and independence of spirit. The liberals were to be defeated and humiliated in 1848–1849. But the wisdom that they acquired from that experience was of a political character. They needed no further education regarding their economic and cultural position, or indeed even with regard to the fundamental lines of a correct political strategy, to prepare them to follow Cavour to the achievement of their ideal.

BIBLIOGRAPHICAL NOTE

The full bibliographical data for the published works on which I have drawn will be found in the footnote in which the first reference to each of them occurs. This can be located through the index, where abbreviated titles of all the works consulted appear in italics.

The bulk of the primary material used divides into manuscripts and journals. The largest collection of manuscripts explored was the archives of the Chamber of Commerce of Milan (*Archivio della Camera di Commercio*) and of the City Auditing Department (*Ragioneria municipale*), deposited in the Museo Civico of Milan in the Castello Sforzesco (referred to in the notes as M.C.M.). No less important were the letters and papers of Carlo Cattaneo in the *Fondo Cattaneo,* which is in the custody of the Museo del Risorgimento of Milan (referred to in the notes as M.R.M.), also located in the Castello Sforzesco. I found many pamphlets and valuable fugitive writings in the great Bertarelli Collection in the same Museum, a catalogue of which is in print.[1] I also drew on the secret acts of the Austrian Government in Lombardy-Venetia (classified under *Regno Lombardo Veneto, Presidenza, Atti segreti*) and the records of the Censor's office (*I. R. Uffizio di Censura*) in the unpublished official documents of the Lombardo-Venetian Kingdom, deposited in the R. Archivio di Stato in the Palazzo Senato, Milan (referred to in the notes as A. S. M.).

Many of the journals used are in the Biblioteca Nazionale Braidense in the Palazzo Brera, Milan, and in the Biblioteca Nazionale Vittorio Emanuele, Rome. The journals are a printed source which has hitherto been barely skimmed or entirely neglected by students of Italian civilization. Many of the most important are now accessible to American students in the Sterling Memorial Library of Yale University and in the Widener Library of Harvard. The Widener Library, since acquiring the unique Risorgimento collection of H. Nelson Gay, contains the richest single body of printed material for the study of modern Italian history in existence.

[1] *Inventario della raccolta donata da A. Bertarelli al Comune di Milano* (Bergamo, Istituto italiano d'arti grafiche, 1915–1921).

INDEX

Absenteeism, 15, 22, 27, 28, 29
Academies, 153, 174, 189, 251–53, 274
Accademia dei Georgofili, 204, 209n., 253
Accademia della Crusca, 154, 225, 252
Acerbi, Giuseppe, 72n., 151
Agnelli, A., "Il fattore economico nella formazione dell'unità italiana," 2n.,
—, "Il materialismo storico. . .", 3n.
Agrarian Association, of Piedmont, 48, 204, 227, 234, 264, 265n.
Agriculture: area under cultivation, 41–42; capitalistic, 28–29, 30, 32, 49; day-labor in, 12, 25, 30–31, 55; discussion of, 158n., 166, 172n., 178, 203–4, 230, 261; farm buildings, 10, 23–25, 45–46, 51, 136; farms, size of, 10, 11–12, 12n., 13–14, 15, 19, 21–22, 22n., 48–49, 50–51; implements, 11, 22–23, 47, 91; improvements and progress, 16, 18, 19, 22–23, 26–27, 30, Part I, Chap. I, *passim*, 153, 156; product, increase of, 16, 36–38, 40ff., 42–45; reclamation, 40–42, 50–51, 53; science applied to, 16, 27, 29, 35, 45, 47–48, 171, 204; supervision (operational), 13–14, 15–16, 23–25, 27–29, 31–32, 45–46, 50. *See also* Absenteeism
"Albertist conspiracy," 275, 284–85. *See* Charles Albert
Album, 171n.
Alfieri, Vittorio, 251, 254
Almanacco Bresciano, 65n.
Almanacco del Regno Lombardo-Veneto, 65n., 69n.
Almanacco provinciale (Bergamo), 66n.
Almanacs (*strenne*), 229–30, 239
Amari, Michele, 255
Amati, Amato, *Carlo Ravizza,* 229n.
America, as market for silk, 38
Annali di commercio, 157, 158, 174, 205, 208n., 273
Annali di fisica, chimica, e scienze affini, 158n.
Annali di medicina e chirurgia, 158n.
Annali di tecnologia, 158n., 171
Annali universali di agricoltura, 158n.
Annali universali di statistica, 40–41,

47, 150, 151n., 158 and n., 160–71, 181n., 182–83, 191, 192, 205, 226–37, 241–42, 254, 256, 263, 274, 277–78, 286; circulation of, 170–71
Antologia (of Florence), 174, 186, 236, 252, 272 and n.
Antologia Italiana (of Turin), 281
Ape delle cognizioni utili, 172–73, 176, 191, 273; circulation of, 173
Ape italiana, **176-77**
Aporti, Don Ferrante, 34, 188, 215–20, 224, 231n., 285
—, *Guida,* 213n., 216n., 217n.
—, *Manuale di educazione,* 220
Archivio della Camera di Commercio di Milano, 288
Archivio storico italiano, 276
Aristocracy, *see* Nobility
Artisans, 38, 98, 224, 232–33
Artists, 68n. *See also* Fine Arts
Artz, *France under the Bourbon Restoration,* 39n., 59n.
Asili d'infanzia, 117, 197, 214–20, 224, 235, 245, 246, 248, 253, 279n., 285
A.S.M., Archivio di Stato di Milano, 20n. *et passim,* 288
Athenaeum, of Brescia, 125n.; of Milan, 52, 201–2, 225, 230
Augsburg Gazette, 268
Austria, 37, 53, 148–49, 194–97, 209, 212n., 219, 237, 283, 285, 286–87; commerce with, 56–57, 58–59, 60, 66, 72, 125; commercial policy of, 74–78, 80, 125; outlook of journals on, 177, 194–97, 267
Austrian Government, 35, 61–63, 64–65, 73–79, 90–91, 109–10, 113–14, 117, 118, 122, 125, 127, 138, 150–51, 155, 156, 163–64, 175, 184, 192–96, 201–3, 204, 212–14, 217–19, 223–24, 231–32, 244, 247n., 286
Austrian, Lloyd, 75, 78
Avvenire, L', 175
Azeglio, Massimo, marchese d', 1, 147, 148, 149, 188, 189, 219–20, 250n., 255, 278, 283–84
—, *Ettore fieramosca,* 255

289